I0274329

Enigmatic Ink

Contact: enigmaticinkpress@yahoo.ca

First Paperback Edition 2011
Published Simultaneously in Canada and the US
Book Design: Michael J. Seidlinger

Enigmatic Ink, London, Canada
www.enigmaticink.com

ISBN: 978-1-926617-14-5

# Azimute: Critical Essays on Deleuze and Guattari

*

Enigmatic Ink: London, Canada

# Contents

# Foreword

by Robert Lort

Azimute.org began in 2000 as a website based in Australia for publishing critical theory, philosophy, reviews, translations and experimental fiction directly related or influenced by Gilles Deleuze and Felix Guattari. Back in 2000 the main English based web resources for Deleuze and Guattari were Charles Stivale's extensive website and several very active Email lists, there was no dedicated website for publishing Deleuze/Guattari theory in the English language.[1] Ten years ago the development of a website dedicated to Deleuze and Guattari looked like it would fill a gap in the cultural networks. The Azimute site sustained 10 years, existing outside of University structures, run on a shoe-string and attracting and nurturing a small but radically engaged group of writers, philosophers and Deleuze/Guattarian enthusiasts.

The word 'Azimute' has a French origin however it is not commonly used. Azimuté is an adjective meaning crazy or nuts, but it is also used in expressions such as "tous azimuts," meaning something is everywhere, all over the place, all out or wide ranging. The term has never appeared amongst the creative lingoism employed by Deleuze and Guattari, but I nevertheless sensed a certain rhizomatic, schizoanalytical and multiplical character in the word.

The Azimute project was an experiment in itself, actively inviting readers to rhizomatically engage in multiple and diverse realms. Radical thought and ideas analyzed from a Deleuze and Guattarian perspective were sought after. A long list of the cutting edge was suggested: "Anti-globalisation, Dada, Bataille, Duchamp, electronic art, Throbbing Gristle, Artaud, the Situationists, Stockhausen, Kathy Acker, Stelarc, Lautremont, Kafka, Godard, E-poetry, Beuys, Foucault, Burroughs, Bacon, Nietzsche, Body Art, Tarkovsky, Herzog, Cage, queer theory, hacktivism, Butoh, L'Art brut, Svankmajer, Guyotat, Hakim Bey, Xenakis, Jake Chapman, Negri's Empire... and whatever you care to introduce to us."[2]

The azimute.org site carried with it a sort of manifesto:

> "We are interested in publishing both academic and non-academic texts, and endeavor to provide a place for texts with a radical, activist and experimental focus.
>
> Azimute wishes to fill the gap in the difficulty of getting published texts which are thematically or stylistically outside academic arenas, popular interest or existing political/artistic paradigms.
>
> Azimute is also interested in developing collaborations and sharing ideas on what this project should be, so please let us know your ideas.
>
> The success of this project depends on readers and writers to contribute texts, ideas, make suggestions and provide material. That means you! Let's make things happen!"[3]

Ten years ago Email lists were the best way to connect with readers, issue announcements and to invite submissions - very slowly the site began to grow. However, soon after this time net culture quickly began to transform. Email lists soon became clogged with spam and were being taken over by the blogosphere. The long diatribes more conducive to in-depth and detailed analysis, long acceptable in Email, were taken over by the short snippets of blog culture.[4] The increasing commercialisation of the web was of cause followed by the MySpace frenzy and subsequently by the Facebook era. Many Deleuze fan sites have been established within MySpace and Facebook, but have never developed into a dedicated community nor, to my knowledge, facilitated the kinds of activity and open discussions that occurred on Email lists. Many of these communities have since moved back underneath the academic banner. The Azimute site did not progress into the MySpace or Facebook realm for a number of reasons.[5] With the changes set afoot on the net Azimute struggled to keep pace and evolve.[6] The loosely formatted, multiple, criss-crossing subject realms of those old clunky Email lists had been reterritorialized onto the single channel of the blogged self.

One of the purposes of Azimute was to exist outside of formal academic structures, the website was never affiliated with any university or institutional organization. The intention and motivation of the site was to break free from these types of overarching structures to provide a context where radical, creative or activist texts could be published, which don't necessarily conform with strict and rigorous academic protocols – a place where one can *enfourcher son dada* (carry out one's 'pet' project). No formal academic peer review process or editing was carried out on texts. Almost all of the contributors have, in some way, come from within academic institutions.

Deleuze, like Foucault was only too aware of the position and role of the intellectual in society, specifically in relation to the establishment of knowledge and truth and the systems of power that it enforced and bolstered. "The intellectual's role is no longer to place himself "somewhat ahead and to the side" in order to express the stifled truth of the collectivity; rather it is to struggle against the forms of power that transform him into its object and instrument in the sphere of "knowledge," "truth," "consciousness," and "discourse"."[7] This Deleuzian ethos was central to the spirit and ideas of the Azimute site. In a *Letter To A Harsh Critic* Deleuze wrote, "Who's to say I can't talk about medicine unless I'm a doctor, if I talk about it like a dog? What's to stop me talking about drugs without being an addict, if I talk about them like a little bird? And why shouldn't I invent some way, however fantastic and contrived, of talking about something, without someone having to ask whether I'm qualified to talk like that?"[8]

The literary work and career of William Burroughs was influential in forming Deleuze's concepts of the Body Without Organs and the Control Society. In "November 28, 1947: How Do You Make Yourself A Body Without Organs?" Deleuze quotes from Burroughs' *Naked Lunch*, "No organ is constant as regards either function or position,...sex organs sprout anywhere,...rectums open, defecate and close,... the entire organism changes color and consistency in split-second adjustments."[9] Burroughs' key literary innovation was the invention of the cut-up made with Brion Gysin which came to the fore in the novels that followed after *Naked*

*Lunch.*[10] One of the few writers to apply the concept of the cut-up was the avant-punk writer Kathy Acker. An outsider in many ways, Acker became familiar with the post-structuralist ideas of Foucault, Deleuze and Guattari, through the art and underground milieus of New York. "I became very interested in the model of schizophrenia. I wanted to explore the use of the word I, that's the only thing I wanted to do. So I placed very direct autobiographical, just diary material, right next to fake diary material. I tried to figure out who I wasn't . . . I was experimenting about identity in terms of language."[11] The cut-up and it's development and use in the writings of Kathy Acker are analyzed in Edward Robinson's "From Cut-Up to Cut and Paste, Plagiarism and Adaptation: Kathy Acker's Evolution of Burroughs and Gysin's Cut-Up Technique". A Japanese writer who has pushed Burroughs' cut-up technique to the extreme is Kenji Siratori. A short literary work and an interview of sorts, is included here. Kenji Siratori came to renown through the publication of *Blood Electric* - opening at a random place, ":soul/gram inoculates neural jack of the desire-mechanism of the suck=blood chromosome where it was input in the junk area of the artificial sun where it congested to her vital=serum>With the DNA=channel of the vital sheet metal hydromania spasm internal::hyper-links to the bio=less=consciousness of the suck=blood chromosome that exploded the wild phantasy of the acid dog"[12] His writing exemplifies a delirious, plugged-in state of a writing-machine, continually mutating it's DNA in a hybrid flux of information overload and junk thirsty desiring-machines. Moving from cut-ups to sampling, Kenji Siratori has since become increasingly focused on noise music, amassing a tirade of CD releases.

Three texts are included by K. Osmosis, "The Fluid Materialism of Deleuze and Bergson," "Kristeva and the Politics of Abjection" and a third on Deleuze and the artist Francis Bacon. Deleuze's fondness for the works of Francis Bacon extended to even having several paintings by the artist hanging in his apartment.[13] The enigmatic K. Osmosis, named after Guattari's *Chaosmosis* may very well exemplify what Deleuze and Guattari have in mind when they speak of a full Body Without Organs. Diagnosed with Asperger's Syndrome, K. Osmosis is a political activist, 'Archive Rat' and 'autodidact' in the fields of art, philosophy and multi-media. His incredibly varied career has included work in various 'meat industries':

Parasitology, Sexual Health, Defence and Refugee Processing. His political affiliations are equally rhizomatic; the Trotskyist Fourth International (POSADIST), various anarcho-communist sects, and environmental activism: he is currently General Secretary of the Gordon Childe Cliff Hangers Collective (Marxist-Leninist). In 2007 he joined the reformed industrial band <S.P.K> for the DVD release of *Despair*.[14]

Véronique Rat-Morris proposed a French language text on the difficulties and intricacies of translating the work of the Austrian playwright Werner Schwab. The text, drawing notably on Deleuze's concept of Minor Literature, the writings of Kafka and Antonin Artaud and the music-theatre work of Einstürzende Neubauten was eventually published on the site in French, German and English.[15] The English language version is included here. Kane X Faucher is a researcher into transcendental empiricism, digital pathologies, cryptoanalysis, social networks and cybernetics to name but a few. He has published several books of fiction, travelogues and experimental poetry.[16] His contributions to this volume include the polemical, "The Pataphysics of Shit: Toward an Abjecta Membra" which, aside from the work of Deleuze and Guattari cites Georges Bataille, Antonin Artaud and artist Piero Manzoni's famous can of shit from 1961. Kane X Faucher's other contributions include an analysis of capitalism and economics, notably written prior to the financial crisis, which engages in depth with Toni Negri's *Empire*. "Capital sets up false contradictions everywhere, Self-Other, Center-Periphery, Developed-Underdeveloped, Modernized-Primitive, etc. the Odyssean movement of capital discovers itself in all that it is not, as an absolute exteriority, absorbs and levels all affirmative differences in the social by rearticulating the Other as lack, and then repatriates itself within the center. Through a process of negative determinations, the reactive character of capital as a carcinogenic nihilism subverts the active forces of social production beyond its limit and absorbs everything within the immanent sphere of complete determination."

Deleuze's music interests are well known - Pierre Boulez, John Cage, Edgar Varese... Since Deleuze's voice was first sampled on Heldon's *Electronique Guerilla* album of 1974 his music and philosophical concepts have influenced a whole new generation of experimental and noise musicians.[17] The pioneering Industrial acts Einstürzende Neubauten and Zoviet France, renowned for both their dissonant and musique concrete influences, are analyzed here in their connections with Derrida, Artaud and Nietzsche. It was by chance that I came across the music of Georgian composer Giya Kancheli performed by a local ensemble. In every way, far from the avant-garde, Giya Kancheli is more frequently parceled up with the tintinnaulation of Arvo Pärt. The exemplary *Exil* release features eerie and absolutely harrowing compositions based on the poems of Paul Celan. Dylan Trigg has written two texts on Giya Kancheli here drawing on themes of absence, nostalgia and mourning.

Deleuze was an avid film fanatic which his two texts on cinema, *The Movement-Image* and *The Time-Image* substantiate.[18] Included in this text, is Barbara M. Kennedy's *Constituting Bodies: Constituting Life: from subjectivity to affect and the "becoming-woman" of the cinematic.* In Barbara's larger work, *Deleuze and Cinema: The Aesthetics of Sensation,* she analyses Deleuze's challenge to cinepsychoanalysis by moving from a textual representation of cinema to one actively experienced as a bodily-assemblage.[19] Barbara's response to an online review seems most apt where she describes the development of her relationship to the Deleuzian film books as a 'dance with a stranger'. In her critical response she writes,"the book articulates an aleatory performance of Deleuzian *spirit*... My *dance with a stranger* was clearly an unprecedented (and obviously contentious) move in transdisciplinarity, crossing the borderlands and mestiza of critical theory and creative writing -- such a monstrous and anomolous coupling of which Deleuze, I am sure, would have approved."[20]

The extent to which Azimute achieved its goals remains difficult to answer. As an experiment the website has certainly touched and supported those on the outer fringes, those arguably closer to effecting a more radical and creative engagement of Deleuze and Guattari's ethos and concepts. Like those, "who, without ever having read a word of Nietzsche, [are] more Nietzschean... than any academic, Nietzschean scholar," these writers have challenged the solidification and recourse to academic 'schooling' of Deleuze and Guattari.[21] It is with great appreciation that sufficient interest has developed into allowing the content of the Azimute site to be published and the contributions bought to new readers and greater renown. I would like to thank all the writers and supporters over the years and a special thanks to Enigmatic Ink for supporting and validating this project.

---

**Notes**

1. Today the principal online sites are the French Chimeres site http://www.revue-chimeres.fr founded by Deleuze and Guattari, Richard Pinhas' http://webdeleuze.com and http://rhizomes.net. Charles Stivale's website is located at http://www.langlab.wayne.edu/CStivale/D-G/index.html. The deleuze-guattari mailing list was once hosted on http://lists.village.virginia.edu
2. From the original 'about' page.
3. From the original 'about' page.
4. Blog comments are commonly limited to 4096 characters and Facebook posts are limited to 1000 characters.
5. I was unable to envision a transformation of Azimute into the MySpace or Facebook structure. With the exception of the discussion groups set-up in the subscriber only Einsturzende Neubauten site at http://www.neubauten.org which I was a member of, I had not seen an effective model of what could be done. All of the web page development for the Azimute site was done in raw HTML, without the use of web page development software and carried out entirely in Linux. Beyond making simple webpages, I didn't have the more advanced programming skills required to develop a fully fledged discussion and networking site.
6. The very nature of the publishing model is radically altered on the net. For example, part of the requirements of having an ISBN is to publish periodic 'Volumes,' which runs counter to the very immediacy of the internet. I would upload new texts as soon as possible, usually in a day or two, and subsequently add the texts to a specific 'Volume' at a later date.
7. Foucault in conversation with Deleuze, "Intellectuals and Power" in Michel Foucault *Language, Counter-Memory, Practice. Selected Essays and Interviews* New York, Cornell University Press, 1977, p. 207.

8. Gilles Deleuze, "Letter To A Harsh Critic" (published elsewhere as "I Have Nothing To Admit") in *Negotiations 1972 – 1990,* New York, Columbia University Press, 1995 p. 11 It is also of note that Guattari himself studied pharmacy but never obtained any degrees, neither in psychiatry nor philosophy.
9. William Burroughs *Naked Lunch,* Hammersmith London, Paladin, 1992, p. 22 or New York, Grove Press, 1966, p. 8, quoted by Gilles Deleuze and Felix Guattari, *A Thousand Plateaus Capitalism and Schizophrenia,* Minneapolis, University of Minnesota Press, p.153
10. The invention of the cut-up and it's lineage from the Dada games of Tristian Tzara is explained in "The Cut-Up Method of Brion Gysin" in William Burroughs and Brion Gysin *The Third Mind,* New York, Viking Press, 1978 or V.Vale *RE/Search William Burroughs, Throbbing Gristle, Brion Gysin,* Issue #4/5, San Francisco, 1982, p. 35
11. Kathy Acker interviewed by Sylvere Lotringer in *Hannibal Lecter: My Father,* New York, Semiotext(e), 1991, p.7
12. Kenji Siratori *Blood Electric* Creation Books, 2002, p. 94
13. Deleuze analyzes the work of Francis Bacon in *Francis Bacon: The Logic Of Sensation* Minnesota, University of Minnesota Press, 2005.
14. Guattari's *Chaosmosis* is published by both The Power Institute of Fine Arts and by The Indiana University Press, 1995. For further details on K. Osmosis visit http://spk.id.au.
15. For Gilles Deleuze and Felix Guattari's concept of Minor Literature see *Kafka, Towards a Minor Literature,* Minneapolis, University of Minnesota Press, 1986.
16. For more information on Kane X Faucher see http://kanexfaucher.weebly.com
17. See for example "In Memoriam Gilles Deleuze" on the Mille Plateaux label (a label named after Deleuze), "Folds and Rhizomes" and "Double Articulation" on the Sub Rosa label and the music of Richard Pinhas.
18. Gilles Deleuze *Cinema 1 The Movement-Image,* London, Continuum, 1986 and Gilles Deleuze *Cinema 2 The Time-Image,* London, Continuum, 1989
19. Barbara M. Kennedy *Deleuze and Cinema: The Aesthetics of Sensation,* Edinburgh, Edinburgh University Press, 2000.
20. Barbara M. Kennedy "Fugitive Spaces -- Between the Critical and the Creative A Reply to Amy Herzog" in *Film Philosophy,*

*Deleuze Special Issue,* Vol. 5 No. 41, November 2001 http://www.film-philosophy.com/vol5-2001/n41kennedy
21. Rolando Perez *On An(archy) And Schizoanalysis,* New York, Autonomedia,1990, p. 66

# Rhizomedia as an Oversold Ideal?: From Rhizomes to the Book

Kane X. Faucher

There is no shortage of techno-optimists who will declare, more from hope than demonstrable arguments, the Internet is aligned harmoniously with the Deleuzo-Guattarian concept of the rhizome, that Internet activity somehow honours what appears the utopian fulfillment of the six cardinal principles of the rhizome.

Deleuze and Guattari's specific usage of nomad, bodies without organs, and rhizomes does tend toward misprision, especially among those who would hastily rally these terms in direct application to contemporary media studies. Richard Barbrook's "Holy Fools" does raise a few of these issues, but is largely marred by a reactionary polemic that can be accused of resorting to the same dogmatic mode of discourse he accuses the "ultra-left" of employing. We do not dispute that there have been some hasty applications of Deleuze and Guattari terminology, nor do we disagree with Barbrook's pointed assertion that an understanding of the Internet (his example) through a boiled down version of rhizomatics errs on the side of simplification. Indeed, to speak of a "rhizomedia" at all is more than merely ideologically positioning a few plucked themes from *A Thousand Plateaus* as some form of extreme autonomous relativism. We may preserve some of these themes such as non-hierarchical networks, but these need to be appropriately developed in light of real circumstances that will not conflate utopian ideals with actual media practices. Fidelity to the Deleuzo-Guattarian texts necessitates a careful revisitation of their plethora of interconnected concepts. If, as Paul Patton says in *Deleuze and the Political, a* political program is much more nuanced than what critics of Deleuze and Guattari brusquely dismiss as anarchic State-bashing or an implicit endorsement of fascism, then it may also be true that some media theorists and critics err in the haste and enthusiasm by which they hasten to apply Deleuze and Guattari's conceptual array.

Deleuze and Guattari describe three lines: molar, molecular, and lines of flight. These are not definitional islets, but any of these lines can occur or become within any of the others. Molarity is the totalizing line, the organized structure that is most likely arborescent in nature. The molecular line is a fracture within the molar which announces the possibility of a rupture or line of flight that takes off in a kind of tangential vector to become *something else*. Declaring that the internet as a whole is a bundle of flight lines is perhaps too romantic and unrealistic. In fact, the internet possesses all three variants of the line. Some sites are totalizing in nature, and their content as well. Whereas other sites, like creative blogs or post-media sources of alternative news, are representative of the molecular type. Internet lines of flight are much more difficult to locate, but can include essentially content-less "junk sites" that are merely long lists obtained from a web-trawling bot. These junk sites, when there is no announced criteria for the population of these lists (such as being named "a site where t-shirts are mentioned") lack any overt organizational principles, and may even lack the basic sequence of alphabetization. Their apparent purpose is to redirect traffic, a site of capture. There is even in this line of flight an aspect of molarity.

For those who would maintain that collaborative blogs are lines of flight may be too simplistic. Collaborative writing is not new, and the only novelty is perhaps in the global reach for possible participants and the same reach for dissemination of text. Some of these collaborative blogs may also have a hierarchy that is either preformed or a necessary effect of circumstances. Of the former type, the blog may be maintained and edited by the blog owner whose discretion may allow or disallow certain participants or content. Of the latter type, more active bloggers may take social prominence upon the blog and be accorded more decision-making power in the direction of the blog's content.

What becomes more of an escape, more of a line of flight is the indirect effects of digitization of literature - especially that literature which is produced solely for digital consumption. The numerical and catalogue hierarchy of ISBNs may be succumbing to increasing irrelevance in the face of digital literature. Digital literature may also be evading the usual classificatory process of the librarian, and instead focusing on keywords - if any are furnished at all. There is an inherent molarity to this as well since the placement of the text in a search engine's rankings is based on a pre-set search algorithm. Some search engines, as a function of obtaining revenue, will place sponsored links above non-sponsored links. The search algorithms themselves are based on a calculation of quantity and quality - that is, a higher quantity of sites that link to a specific site or mention a particular term, and the quality of those links as being judged as "relevant". This prevents someone from creating a site that merely mentions the word "hidalgo" a thousand times with no other content from being bumped up in the search rankings. However, this, too, is a simplification of the search algorithm process.

In order for media to be truly rhizomatic, or "rhizomedia", it must conform to the definition of the rhizome. What must be discerned is if media must be rhizomatic in either form or content, or if it must be both.

Azimute has been able, in its decade-long operation, to resist the overt and covert molarization of the Internet. We are now poised to obtain our miscellaneous information (encouraging this format of miscellanea) via the "big three" oligopolists of digital global information: Google, Yahoo, and MSN. Information acquisition is now molarized by corporate profit motive, and the virtual domain becomes simply the metastatic expansion of rampant capitalism with all its spectacles and its encouragement of a parlous cultural narcissism first identified by Christopher Lasch, and later followed up by J.R. Slosar's scorching indictment in *The Culture of Excess*. And, if we are feeling even more pessimistic, we could include the likes of Guy Debord to import the idea of the spectacle (or, if you prefer the more advanced arc of Gramsci and Marcuse rather than Adorno and Lukacs, Baudrillard's concept of the simulacrum and the death of production). The Internet is a vast area of waste-production and redundancy which, although redundancy plays a vital role in Claude Shannon's theory of communication to ensure the transmission of information, also gets muddled when we consider the social realm of that communication. There are enough echo chambers in the comment pits and in the endless serial repetitions and repostings on blogs to suggest that far too many Internet users are acquiring zero to little information: it becomes a unary device for self-confirmation. Boredom and banality have not increased because of the Internet - but the endless diarizing of ourselves in a continuing upward arc of nearly pathological narcissist behaviour has only made it more visible. If there was one potent and telling image I would apply from history to visually describe the false transcendence of contemporary digital life, it would be Albrecht Durer's *Melancolia*: surrounded by all the gadgets and gewgaws of our decanted techno-progress, we are left in the most ersatz position of befuddled malaise, disappointment, acute alienation, anxiety, and listlessness. There is only this eternal present, and autonomous capitalism with its goal of simply growth by a series of crises has successfully transformed us into directionless surplus-aggression machines. This is hardly the celebratory moment Deleuze and Guattari would have hoped for us.

What we have been presented with instead by dominant online media is the appearance of a rhizome. Is there free connectivity? Yes, in a very promiscuous way. Is there heterogeneity? Perhaps if we consider the miscellanea of the web as a chief product of its social text heterogeneous, but not so much if we consider the amount of polarization toward dogmatic extremes in religion and politics. Does the Internet provide us with asignifying rupture? Perhaps, but it also reinforces the signifying apparatus of fixed signs and preset forms (one has only to bump up against the constraints of places like Facebook and Twitter with fill-in-the-molar-blanks). Does the web present us with a new cartography? Some will argue, adopting what is meant by ergodic reading coined by Espen J. Aarseth, that we are indeed tracing new paths and maps, but will we walk them or continue to gravitate to the more well worn digital trails to congregate at the sites most popular? Multiplicity may have also been co-opted by the interference and noise of capitalism where quantitative increases are what stand in for the qualitative differentiation of content and use. The illusions of choice seem to convey difference, but they are just variations within the regime of capital. Some of us retreat from this domain out of numerophrenia gravis: a fear of numbers.

Is there hope? Zones of difference like Azimute stand as islands not opposed to capital, but indifferent to it. In S/Z Roland Barthes tells us that the ideal text is composed of networks that "are many and interact, without any one of them being able to surpass the rest; this text is a galaxy of signifiers, not a structure of signifieds; it has no beginning; it is reversible; we gain access to it by several entrances, none of which can be authoritatively declared to be the main one; the codes it mobilizes extend as far as the eye can reach, they are indeterminable" - Barthes effectively predicts the pluralization of textuality. J. David Bolter in *Writing Space* adds: "what is unnatural in print becomes natural in the electronic medium and will soon no longer need saying at all, because it can be shown." These are all very nice and optimistic statements that speak to a possibly inherent pliability of the Internet and virtual text. The structuralist and poststructuralist view of the open text errs slightly on the side of idealization. For although it capably demonstrates the positive potentials of open text for producing new forms of narrative, discourse, and multi-referencing systems the book is far too limited to provide, some digital text we find on the Internet attempts to mimic and conform to the conventional aesthetic of books, or mimics the ingrained method of sequential, linear reading we are familiar with in terms of our education in literacy. But, if continuing demand for pithy, bold, and context-less information continues, we might find that we less read and more engage in the *Augenblick* derivative of reading.

***Azimute in print?***

So, what began online goes offline, into a book, and yet despite the rushed migration from print to online media, we may still not understand what a book really is.

What is the contemporary state of the papered world - and by papered world we mean that it is in consultation *with* paper and the derivative modes of existence *from* paper that has set the perhaps now anachronistic conditions of the world's function. When once, not too long ago, the heavy reliance on paper, along that historical paper trail of paper itself, books were considered of some higher degree of value as concrete object. This has inarguably changed. The book dissolved down into the pithier journal dissolved down even further into the newspaper or brochure or postcard. We have for centuries depended on our papered world, for upon which the pressure stroke of heavy pens have signed charters, treaties, property transfers, the body of law enshrouded in a paper domain. Codified en corps, this body of laws and documentation made entirely out of paper.

Between the sheets we may be able to follow that historical trail of the technical advancements of inscription.

Digital publishing - but is it inscription? All inscription is a form of writing, and so it may be of some significance to treat digital publishing, digital writing as a new mode of inscription despite perhaps our more literal and concrete prejudices that inscription is something that involves a carving or the pressing of some implement against a surface. Indeed, the finger is such an implement even as it taps away at keys for words to appear on a screen (the inscribed surface). This surface does not bear a permanent inscription as would pen perform on a piece of paper. The dance of the pen upon the surface is replaced by a new kind of concerted ballet of fingers somewhat magically transcribing through the right concatenation of motions transferred through a keypad the right internal programming codes to produce the desired letters to appear on the screened surface - like playing a synthesizer. The difficulty in uniting this type of inscription with that of its predecessor would be the fact that in "traditional" writing we can actually see the implements and the direct result with very little mediation: the written word, the pen tip in motion, the ink tube that fuels it, the hand of the author who pushes the pen. With anything digital, it is the finger's touch that prompts a series of internal and invisible commands that translates pressing one specific region to mean a visual output of, say, the letter F. This is our new (techno)mysticism.

It is difficult to discuss digital works like e-books, blogs, electronic journals, etc when we still may not even know what a book *is*. What is a book? Would it be any more revealing to follow the history of documentation, from hieroglyphs to scrolls to codices to what we now know today to be the model or figure of the book? It is important to realize that what we may be so complicit to call a book on the tendency of general linguistic consensus effaces a more robust and open-ended definition of books themselves. Does a cover and a binding assure that what we are holding is a book? A book is indeed a bounded item, for it contains a finite number of pages. The only book that is infinite - beyond our interpretations of the contents which can be infinite - belongs in the realm of literary magical realism. In Jorge Luis Borges' short story, the Book of Sand, his fictional self trades for a mysterious book that, whenever he opens it, the pages are always different - in fact, they are infinite. By the end, the madness of possessing something infinite prompts him to abandon it in the public library.

What is a book? The open history of this term will not yield up an answer to that object which is intended to be a totality given it has a definitive beginning and end (even if it will continue, like a serial or volume of collected works). We ought to consider the unacknowledged natural inspiration for the common form of the book, bequeathed to us by the physical sciences. Geologists have been able to name a collection of mica or shale as "books", doubtless taking their cue to name them as such from their resemblance to books. Shale, for instance, is a collection of sediments under the high pressure of the weight upon them as the sediment levels increase. When we open a book of shale, the story of previous existence is inscribed therein. We may see fossils which, like words in relation to the objects they refer to, are not the animals themselves, but their representation - the replacement of organic tissue by minerals like pyrite and calcite.

Interestingly enough, much of the same metaphors associated with books, reading, and writing have been applied to virtual or digital texts. We can open a book, and we can open a webpage. We can bookmark webpages - the very notion of calling an electronic site a webpage draws from the hereditary lineage of book production and consumption. Although, some physical aspects specific to physical books do not necessarily hold as easily: there are no real "covers" or "spines". A webpage, however, does not necessarily follow the regular serial order of pagination that physical books do. It makes sense to number something that moves in a single direction, but a webpage with its radiating links, its rhizomal networks, cannot be numbered as such. A webpage that would be have the incipit of some original text could be considered a "ground zero" of that particular text - deviations or citations thereof being at a degree of remove and not necessarily a page 2 - there was no page 1 to begin with. What has existed in many webpages has been the "title page" that announces the content, allowing it to be classified according to a general taxonomy. And, like library databases of contents, "keywords" identify the core terms of the page so that it may be referenced and found by others, the difference being that these keywords are embedded within the coding of the webpage, for use by search engine algorithms.

Not knowing exactly what a book is, since the very notion of the book is itself a question, we may think to perform a biopsy of the book as though particulars of anatomy will ferry us toward a holistic understanding. There is in this an autopsia - the beatific vision - in revealing the inner contents of the book piece by piece, this beatification paradoxically merged with the forensic "laying bare" of objective science, both sacralizing and desacralizing the book itself. There is in this the tension of death, the death of the book as we know it, the death of all books if supplanted (or supplemented) by digital publishing. What of this death? This death has happened many times before, and we've only to turn to history to read how technical improvements upon the act of inscription and collection of contents into a portable document have essentially brought about the "death" of what came before. From the papyrus to the volumen to the hand-lettered codex to the democratization of texts via the Gutenberg press of circa 1450 - right up until now: the internet. It is far too common and well known an observation that each technical improvement works along the trajectory of democratizing text, as though technical advancement is synonymous with broadening social inclusion.

So here we are. Robert Lort opened up what could be called a rhizomal space and we, the eternal nomads of thought and creativity, found ourselves populating this zone. I was asked by a colleague if I still stood by the articles I had submitted to Azimute so many years ago, and I would have to say that I stand by the very idea of them, perhaps the nostalgia I feel in being in a "place" and "time" where so many just had to "be there" to understand. Are they works of juvenilia? Maybe. It is not for me to say or to pretend they never happened. That all these essays have migrated from the site suggests their freezing in time, in a rare opposite move from online to print. It is a kind of death knell for Azimute online, bracketed in its own historical singularity from before the 9/11 birthing pains of the new millennium and the death of Osama bin Laden (an event that, although will temporarily satisfy many people's conception of just retribution, in the long term may never be enough). RIP Azimute online, 2000 - 2010.

# Azimute - Main Essays

# From the Keller <S.P.K.> The Fluid Materialism of Deleuze and Bergson

by K.Osmosis

Gilles Deleuze resurrects the neglected, marginalised and unconventional names of philosophy - such as the philosopher Henri Bergson - in order to reanimate some of the concepts and problems produced. Ultimately, they point in different ways to a cardinal point: the irreducible materiality of life or 'being' suspended in an endless process of variation or 'becoming'. 'Being is becoming' is a guiding principle in Deleuze's work. For Deleuze: "The life of philosophers conforms to the ordinary laws of succession; but their proper names coexist and shine as luminous points that take us through the components of a concept once more or as the cardinal points of a stratum or layer that continually come back to us, like dead stars whose light is brighter than ever".

Deleuze's 'practical vitalism' points to Bergson's *Creative Evolution* (1911), where the fluid structure of the *élan vital* is described as a form of materiality in process of becoming, which eludes intellectual analysis and can only be comprehended through empathy and intuition; it is an expression of the pre-individual, of the flux and indeterminacy of life, where the constraints of identity are yet to be applied. As Bergson points out, the intellect tends to spatialise, to immobilise the flux of life. In this way, the perception of being is reduced and impoverished. Accordingly, Deleuze adopts a mode of thought and a style of exposition subtle enough to penetrate the flow of life: "Your writing has to be liquid or gaseous simply because normal perception and opinion are solid, geometric".

Deleuze adopts Bergson's model of perception which conceives the world as 'flowing-matter'. This involves a constant process of transformation, and a metaphysics in which the light of consciousness is already *in* things themselves, where 'movement-image' and 'flowing matter', 'pure spiritualism' (philosophical idealism) and 'radical materialism', converge. A world 'without eyes', without an 'ego' or 'self' – free from that defensive 'cortical layer' separating the 'inside' from the 'outside', the perceiving 'subject' from the perceived 'object'. "In other words, the eye is in things, in luminous images in themselves". Deleuze's Bergsonism therefore considers consciousness as immanent to matter. A monistic, fluid materialism that provides us with 'a world without a subject':

> My eye, my brain, are images, parts of my body. How could my brain contain images since it is one image among others? External images act on me, transmit movement to me, and I return movement: how could images be in my consciousness, since I am myself image, that is, movement? And can I even, at this level, speak of 'ego', of eye, of brain and of body? Only for simple convenience; for nothing can yet be identified in this way. It is rather a gaseous state. Me, my body, are rather a set of molecules and atoms which are constantly renewed. It is a state of matter too hot for one to be able to distinguish solid bodies in it. It is a world of universal variation, of universal undulation, universal rippling: there are neither axes, nor centre, nor left, nor right, nor high nor low.

Deleuze's delirious world-view questions an established hierarchy privileging the primacy of disembodied mind or intellect over the 'base' physicality of the sensate, corporeal body. It amounts to a full frontal attack upon a traditional dualism responsible for the polarisation or split between the flesh and the spirit, the carnal and the divine, masters and slaves; and that division of the sexes in which men are associated with the divine qualities of spirit and transcendence while women are associated with an inferior and degraded material realm encompassing the body, flesh, carnality, nature, and the earth.

The fluid materialism of Deleuze's Bergsonism emerges as the direct and immediate continuation of, and as the legitimate successor to, the ancient Greek philosophers of the Ionian school, who assert that the principle of all things is in matter alone; for it is that out of which all things are and from which they come into being, and into which, at the last, they pass away. This they say is the element and principle of all things.

Thus the philosopher Thales singles out water as the primary, material substance from which all else is derived and to which it returns. Many have questioned as to why Thales takes water as the primary stuff of nature, the essential reality of all other phenomena. The philosopher Aristotle writes that Thales observed that every living thing contains moisture. Plants contain moisture, all foodstuffs contain moisture, whereas rocks are dry and cadavers very soon desiccate. Thales sees the essential part played by water in nourishing life so that the hot element can come from it, since what is alive has heat. Water is also the essence of seeds. His favourite phrase is: "Water is the most beautiful thing in the world". Thales also chooses the moist element because of his special studies of climatic conditions: water assumes such different forms as ice, liquid, and vapour, and to the ancient Greeks the phenomena of evaporation, mist, wind, animal breath, the germination of plants and the origins of life are all intermingled and identified.

Aristotle also suggests that Thales might have been carrying forward the primacy that Greek and Egyptian mythology accorded water, for he had spent time in arid zones such as Egypt and Mesopotamia, where water-cults were widespread, owing to the fact that agriculture and the very survival of the population depended upon the flooding of the rivers. The Egyptians worshipped the river Nile as a God. Thales also holds that everything has a soul and is therefore "full of gods". This hearkens back to the animistic phase of religion, the knowledge that the body has of its essential union with nature, that sense of awe, wonderment and reverence towards nature as the outward, physical manifestation of a purpose that is essentially spiritual, springing forth from depths unseen. It is a picture of an enchanted world where every tree and river has its local indwelling spirit, god or goddess. Thales considers water to be the soul of the world, the universal essence of life: "A divine power is present in the element of water by which it is endowed with *movement.*"

"Everything is in a flux, everything changes" observes the ancient Greek philosopher Heraclitus. For nothing remains what, where and as it was: everything is and also is not, for everything is constantly changing, constantly coming into being and passing away. "All things are flowing" and change is universal, "for nothing ever is, everything is becoming". This is a world where concrete sensuous 'living' opposites merge into one another. According to Heraclitus, "Souls are vaporised from what is wet. To souls, it is death to become water; to water, it is death to become earth. From earth comes water, and from water, soul. Fire lives the death of earth, and air lives the death of fire; water lives the death of air, earth - that of water."

The impermanence and mutability of all things is expressed by Heraclitus in his famous aphorism: "It is not possible to step twice in to the same river; for fresh waters are ever flowing in upon you: we are, and are not."

A radical follower of Heraclitus, the philosopher Cratylus, argues against Heraclitus that it is impossible to step into the same river even once, seeing that, while we are stepping into the river, it is changing, is becoming another river. The extant being is, so to speak, dissolved in the very process of becoming. Thus every existing state of things inevitably breaks up, and every developed form is in fluid movement.

For example, picture an eternally flowing stream of molecules in motion, joining one with another, and forming certain *combinations,* 'things', 'objects'. Such combinations are distinguished by the greater or lesser degree of there stability, existing for a more or less prolonged period of time, and then passing away, to be replaced by others.

In like manner, every organic being is at each moment the same and not the same; at each moment it is assimilating matter drawn from without, and excreting other matter; at each moment the cells of the body are dying and new ones are being formed; in a longer or shorter period of time the matter of the body is completely renewed and is replaced by other molecules of matter, so that every organic being is always itself, and yet something other than itself.

This celebration of the fundamental fluidity and sacredness of nature, with its concomitant hostility towards a disenchanted, cold hearted rationalism, cruelly ignorant of a vital and sacred organic reality, is beautifully and poetically evoked in Ovid's *Metamorphosis:*

> As for Cyane, she lamented the rape of the goddess, and the contempt shown for her fountain's rights, nursing silently in her heart a wound that none could heal; until, entirely wasted away with weeping, she dissolved into those waters of which she had lately been the powerful spirit. Her limbs could be seen melting away, her bones growing flexible her nails losing their firmness. The slenderest parts of her body dissolved first of all, her dark hair, her fingers, her legs and feet. It needed but a little change to transform her slight limbs into chill waters; after that her shoulders, her back, her sides, her breast disappeared, fading away into insubstantial streams, till at last, instead of living blood, water flowed through her softened veins, and nothing remained for anyone to grasp.

Everything *becomes* but nothing *is*. Like the Lethe and Mnemosyne rivers, the streams of forgetfulness and memory, substance, matter, is in a perpetual state of motion and change. The material 'objects' of the physical world exist for a moment of time only as temporary combinations amidst the perpetual flux of Becoming. However, for however long as these combinations remain the same, we tend to judge and define them as fixed, rigid objects of investigation, given once and for all in accordance with the formula of traditional logic: 'Either yes or no'. Thus a thing either exists or does not exist; and cannot at the same time be itself or something else. Natural objects and processes are therefore perceived in rigid isolation, isolated from their general context; they are examined not in their motion, but in a state of immobility; not in their life, but in their death. This mechanistic point of view is one-sided, restricted and abstract: individual things are perceived outside of their relationships, in a state of rest devoid of motion, where, in the presence of their existence, their coming into being and passing away is ignored. We cease to see the wood for the trees.

Inevitably, however, in proportion as things change to the extent to which they cease to exist as they did formerly, and to the extent that we observe the movements, transitions, connections, rather than the *things* that move, change and are connected, we must apply a very different kind of logic: the logic of contradiction; we say "Yes and no, they exist and they do not exist". Things are now perceived in their *fluidity*: in other words, in their connection, their interlacement, their movement, their appearance and disappearance. Everything is and also is not, for everything is *in flux*, is constantly changing, constantly coming into being and passing away.

This, while supplying a positive understanding of the existing state of things, at the same time enables us to recognise that that state of things will inevitably break up. Accordingly we are led to regard the things of the natural world, and their concepts in the human brain, not as distinct, unchangeable, rigid objects, given once and for all, but instead as transient, in fluid movement, in their appearance and disappearance, in the perpetual flow of their life.

Furthermore, we find upon closer examination that the two poles of any apparent division or dichotomy, like subject and object, mind and body, self and other, male and female, are inseparable, and interpenetrate; they are two different aspects of a single entity, living, mobile, perpetually changing themselves into one another; an interdependence or unity of opposites, known in logic under the name of *principium coincidentiae oppositorium* (the principle of the coincidence of opposites). This unity of opposites is something more, however, than a mere juxtaposition of opposing factors, but is, in the opinion of one philosopher, "the root of all movement and life, and it is only insofar as it contains a Contradiction that anything moves and has impulse and activity".

We know that structurally the physical world exhibits a fluctuating and dynamic equilibrium of opposing forces in all its forms, down to the minutest combination of electrical particles. The very life processes of the human body itself depend upon the interconnection of opposing processes: the anabolic building-up processes and the katabolic, breaking down processes. And the body's simplest movement involves an interconnected opposition of flexor and tensor muscles. In like manner, we find that cause and effect are conceptions which only hold good in their application to the individual case as such; but as soon as we consider the individual case in its general connection with the universe as a whole, they merge; they dissolve in the process of universal action and reaction in which causes and effects are constantly changing places, so that what is effect here and now will be cause there and then, in a world where all things are linked and tangled a thousandfold and every deed gives birth to countless others.

Ancient Greek philosophers such as Thales, Anaximander, Anaximenes and Heraclitus promote a 'fluid' and poetic mode of thought, a reverential approach to the substances of the natural world. An outlook where concrete, sensuous, 'living' 'opposites' are interchangeable, permitting the continuous 'flow' or transmutation of one element into another. Nature is experienced as a living, all-embracing and magical entity. For these philosophers, matter consists of four primal elements: earth, air, water, and fire. Water is opposed to fire but allied to earth, while air is opposed to earth but allied to fire. By arranging these elements in pairs, four primary qualities evolve: namely heat (fire and water), dryness (fire and earth), cold (earth and water), and moisture (water and air). A conception later extended to the human body, which is held to be composed of four fluids or 'humours': blood, phlegm, yellow bile (or choler) and black bile (or melancholy), characteristic of the four human 'temperaments': choleric (warm and dry, quick and strong), sanguine (warm and moist, quick and weak), phlegmatic (cold and moist, slow and weak), and melancholic (cold and dry, slow and strong). This is a world-view that establishes an intimate and physical connection between the microcosm of the human body, consisting of 70% water, and the macrocosm of the natural environment.

The ancient Greek physician Hippocrates, known as "the father of medicine", investigates the link between disease and environment in accordance with the theory that an imbalance in the four humours, or bodily fluids, is responsible for disease. The voluminous writings of Hippocrates, totalling up to sixty or so texts, amount to a palimpsest or Corpus of works extensively elaborated upon by succeeding generations of physicians. Two texts, *On Regimen* and *On the Nature of Man*, portray the human body as eternally flowing in a condition of perpetual flux: health is a matter of keeping the body within specific boundaries in order to ensure a proper balance or equilibrium. Imbalance produces illness if it results in an undue concentration of fluids in any particular zone of the body. What are being kept in balance are bodily fluids or *chymoi*. Though naturally present in the body, two fluids - bile and phlegm - are particularly associated with illness, flowing immoderately from the body of the sick patient. Thus excessive phlegm produces winter colds, surplus bile produces summer diarrhoea and vomiting, and mania results from bile boiling in the brain.

Blood is regarded by Hippocrates as essential to life, yet even blood can exceed its natural bounds, and is periodically expelled from the body in menstruation and nose-bleeds. Such natural evacuation of excess blood suggested the need to maintain a balanced bodily equilibrium of this life-giving fluid through the practice of blood-letting, a therapeutic device devised by the Hippocratics, systemised by the physician Galen, and serving for centuries as a cure for a host of maladies.

In his text *On the Nature of Man*, Hippocrates describes black bile as an important, though predominantly harmful, humour. Visible in vomit and excreta, it contributes to the dark colour of dried blood. Observing clotted blood, Hippocrates asserts that the darkest part corresponds to black bile, the serum above the clot to yellow bile, while the light matter at the top is phlegm. Hippocrates correlates these four bodily fluids or 'humours' - blood, yellow bile, black bile and phlegm - to the four primary climatic qualities: hot, dry, cold and wet; to the four seasons; to the four ages of human development (infancy, youth, adulthood and old age); to the four elements (air, fire, earth and water); and to the four human 'temperaments' (sanguine, choleric, melancholic and phlegmatic). The four fluids or 'humours' of the human body are the organising principles employed by Hippocrates and his disciples to situate the body into a coherent, symmetrical grid, a system of binary oppositions guaranteeing secure boundaries, physical health, and the established hierarchical order of society. For example, Hippocrates affirms the 'natural' superiority of men over women to the binary distinction between wetness and dryness:

> The female flourishes more in an environment of water, from things cold and wet and soft. The male flourishes more in an environment of fire, from dry, hot foods and mode of life.

According to Hippocrates, the male body is characterised by a condition of dry stability never attained by the female physique, which remains cold and wet all its life. Due to her innate wetness, Hippocrates considers women at greater risk than men to liquefying incursions upon the integrity of their bodies and minds, especially those of love and emotion, regarded as particularly endangering forms of wetness. Of special danger and concern is what he considers the intrinsically liquefying emotions associated with female *eros*, which threaten to soften, loosen, melt and dissolve physiological and psychological boundaries men pride themselves on being able to resist.

The medical treatises of Hippocrates are coloured by the subservient role of women in ancient Greek patriarchal society. However, research conducted by generations of historians, anthropologists, philosophers and archaeologists; for example, Lewis Morgan, Johann Bachofen, Friedrich Engels, Elizabeth Gould Davis, Mary Daly, and Marija Gimbutas, reveal, before the onset of patriarchy, women had enjoyed an especially revered status. The evidence for women's pre-eminent role in ancient Greek matriarchal societies is recorded in historical accounts of ancient religious rites involving acts of symbolic death and rebirth linked with baptism in the waters of the Styx. The waters of this underworld river, across which all souls had to pass after death, were believed to possess the fecundity and sacred powers associated with the cyclic flow of menstrual blood. The place where the river was thought to originate was commemorated by a shrine at the city of Clitor, or Kleitoris, sacred to Gaia, the Mother of the Earth.

The philosopher Luce Irigaray argues that the historically dominant 'masculine' culture of the West idealises formal structural qualities above everything else. According to Irigaray, this sterile formalism in turn seeks and imposes unity, stability, consistency and completion, everywhere. Thus everything incongruous, jarring, asymmetrical, random and unfinished become terms of criticism, instead of praise. The emphasis on unity and stability of form sees the production of fixed and final meanings as the supreme goal of both philosophical reflection and scientific investigation. The idea that anything may have a dynamically changing or polymorphous identity, or have contradiction as its very essence or animating principle, is defined as monstrous and abominable in a phallomorphic culture that can tolerate only the homogeneous, the defined, knowable, consistent, and contained.

Irigaray therefore affirms alternative 'female' values subversive of that traditional emphasis upon unity and consistency of meaning and identity. According to Irigaray, "'She' is indefinitely other than 'herself'": there is no longer an insistence upon a strict dividing line between the 'self', and what is outside of it (the other). The armour of an alienating identity, the fortress-like exclusion of the isolated 'ego' or 'monad', is identified with the tension, paranoia and self-obsession of traditional masculine, bourgeois society and philosophy. The alternative is described by Irigaray thus: "'she' goes off in all directions in which 'he' is unable to discern the coherence of any meaning. Contradictory words seem a little crazy to the either/or logic of reason, and are completely inaudible to those who listen with ready-made grids and a code prepared in advance". This rejection of a mechanistic, either/or logic culminates in the philosopher Julia Kristeva's assertion: "To believe that one 'is a woman' is almost as absurd and obscurantist as to believe that one 'is a man'". Thus it is not the sexual difference between subjects that is important, as the sexual differentiation within each subject: an androgyny celebrated by Kristeva in the following terms: "She was a man; she was a woman.......It was a most bewildering and whirligig state to be in".

Irigaray claims that the traditional disquiet about that which is fluid is based upon an obsessive fear of anything that might disrupt the apparent solidity of things, entities, and objects; anything that threatens traditional notions of the self-identical, the one, the unified, the solid. Within a phallomorphic culture female sexuality is regarded as an uncontainable flow (associated with the menstrual flow); it is regarded as a threat to secure boundaries, attesting to the body's permeability, its vulnerable dependence on an outside, and to the precarious division between the body's inside and its outside. Bodily fluids flow, seep, and infiltrate; their control is a matter of perpetual uncertainty to the established order: "What she emits is flowing, fluctuating. *Blurring*. Fluid - like that other, inside/outside of philosophical discourse - is, by nature, unstable. It overflows the 'subject', who attempts to congeal, freeze and paralyse the flow, subordinating it to geometrism". For Irigaray:

> Fluids surge and move, and a metaphysics that thinks being as fluid would tend to privilege the living, moving, pulsing over the inert matter of the Cartesian world-view. The triumph of a mechanistic rationality equates with transformation of fluid to solid. Solid mechanics and rationality have maintained a relationship of very long standing, one against which fluids have never stopped arguing.

The school of thought established by the Swiss physician and alchemist Philippus Aureolus Paracelsus (1493-1541) perceives the world as a vast chemical laboratory. An internal fire located deep within the earth provides the explanation for the existence of mountain springs and streams, understood as distilled by the earth's central fire from vast subterranean water reservoirs. Heat from the earth's central fire vaporises this water, causing it to rise and erupt through cracks in the earth's surface; the result is the "distilled" mountain spring. Through a complicated process of distillation and fermentation, mountains act as vast chemical alembics responsible for the origin of hot and cold mineral springs and pure mountain streams.

Nature, the striving to probe it and to know it, is for the English philosopher and statesman Sir Francis Bacon (1561-1626) an unquestionable law. In his view, matter "seems to attract man's whole entity by winning smiles". According to Bacon, scientific truth is impossible "without dissecting and anatomising the world most diligently". In his treatise, *Novum Organum,* Bacon describes nature as female, who has to be "vexed" and thus "forced to yield her secrets". As the historian Carolyn Merchant points out:

> Much of the imagery he used in delineating his new scientific objectives and methods derives from the courtroom, and, because it treats nature as a female to be tortured through mechanical inventions, strongly suggests the interrogations of the witch trials and the mechanical devices used to torture witches.....Bacon stated that the method by which nature's secrets might be discovered

> corresponded to investigating the secrets of witchcraft by inquisition.

For Bacon, science exists as a means towards power and domination, and the progress of science and technological innovation is assessed against its capacity to subdue and control the natural environment; 'binding her into service', 'constraining' and moulding her:

> For you have to follow and as it were hound nature in her wanderings, and you will be able when you like to lead and drive her afterward to the same place again...... For like as a man's disposition is never well known or proved till he be crossed, nor Proteus ever changed shapes till he was straitened and held fast, so nature exhibits herself more clearly under the trials and vexations of art (mechanical devices) than when left to herself.

The English philosopher Thomas Hobbes (1588-1679), the systematiser of Bacon's scientific method, continues Bacon's quest; and it is precisely with Hobbes that knowledge "based upon the senses loses its poetic blossom, it passes into the abstract experience of the geometrician. Physical motion is sacrificed to mechanical or mathematical motion....Materialism takes to misanthropy".

This results in an impoverishment and mortification of the senses, to the disenchantment of nature, and its reduction to geometrical and mechanical laws. In like manner, humanity is also impoverished, is also regarded as a mechanism, and is imprisoned by the same laws. It is a world-view actively promoted by the French philosopher Rene Descartes (1596-1650). A major physicist, mathematician, and one of the creators of analytical geometry and modern algebra, Descartes conceptualises the body of nature as a mechanical device and the physical bodies of human beings themselves as soulless and lifeless corporeal mechanisms directed by a 'soul' which alone is endowed with intelligence and will. The Cartesian world-view tears asunder and fragments the organic unity of living beings by establishing the centrality of the individualised and atomised 'ego' or 'subject', the metaphysical opposition of the thinking being to nature expressed by Descartes in his famous dictum: *Cogito, ergo sum* - "(I) think, therefore (I) am".

Descartes then proceeds to radically differentiate mind ('thinking substance', *res cogitans*) from matter ('extended substance', *res extensa*). Through detached visualisation, the disembodied rational intellect apprehends "clearly and distinctly" the natural world of extended, material substance. The mind of the rational (male) subject is proclaimed as the incorporeal and transcendent "lord and possessor" of corporeal nature, which is perceived as a mechanical device, infinitely divisible into discrete units; the cries and writhing of animals beneath the vivisectionist's scalpel regarded as insensate, mechanical reflexes. The physical world of nature is treated as lifeless stuff to be quantified and manipulated in accordance with the rules of mathematics, geometry, and mechanics:

> Lonely and lifeless nature lay prone, fettered with an iron chain, strict measure and the arid number prevailed. As into dust and winds, into dark words the immeasurable flower of life disintegrated.

According to Descartes, the totality of nature can be reduced to extended bodies differentiated by magnitude, configuration, situation and motion; that is to say, the world can be reduced to a system of measurements and mechanical laws. Like automatons, the movements of human beings are viewed as the effects of mechanical laws that describe the actions within the human body of the bony levers set into motion by the processes of muscular expansion and contraction. Descartes duly compares the internal workings of the human body to the novel mechanical artefacts produced by the developing science of hydraulic engineering:

> One may very well liken the nerves of the animal machine I have described to the pipes of the machines of those fountains; its muscles and its tendons to the other different engines and springs that serve to move them; and its animal spirits, of which the heart is the source and the ventricles of

> the brain the reservoirs, to the water that moves these engines. Moreover, respiration and other similar functions which are usual and natural in the animal machine and which depend on the flow of the spirits are like the movements of a clock or of a mill, which the ordinary flow of water can make continuous.

Henri Bergson, a leading French philosopher at the beginning of the Twentieth Century, argues that life flows, and that any attempt to cut this flow into segments kills it. Reality, according to Bergson, is fluid, a fluidity that a mechanistic mind-set attempts to grasp within a set of rigid, frozen concepts. Mechanism for Bergson is merely the external, objectified form of an inner creative activity, a vital impetus (*élan vital);* and we sense the flow of this creative life force through a primary inner experience called *intuition.*

In place of the dominance in our thinking of an *"esprit de geometrie"* mode of life, Bergson affirms the*"esprit de finesse"*. This involves distinguishing between the geometrical time that occurs in the theories of an overly analytical, mechanistic scientific world-view, and the real time that we directly experience in our consciousness introspectively, culminating in a fuller awareness and a deeper understanding of reality as in a perpetual state of flux, a fluid *duree* of Becoming, of which genuine understanding can only be had by a very different way of knowing - through *intuition,* involving empathy, feeling and participation. Thus it is possible to comprehend reality's fundamental fluidity, on the wing, as it were, instead of freezing it, as is customarily done, into fixed, ready-made categories:

> There is one reality, at least, which we all seize from within, by intuition and not by simple analysis. It is our own personality in its flowing through time. Our intelligence can place itself within this mobile reality, and adopt its ceaselessly changing direction; in short, can grasp by means of that *intellectual sympathy* which we call intuition. This is extremely difficult. The mind has to do violence to itself, has to reverse the direction of the operation by which it habitually

> thinks. But in this way it will attain to fluid concepts, capable of following reality in all is sinuosities and of adopting the very movement of the inward life of things.

Bergson condemns the mechanistic and geometrical notion of time as lifelessly abstract and mathematical; it is measured by clocks, scales and yardsticks. Time is represented spatially, and is broken up into homogeneous units (years, hours, and minutes). This mechanistic and mathematical notion of time neither flows nor acts. It exists passively. Most of Western humanity's practical life in society is dominated by this conception, resulting in a loss of spontaneity, and the rigidification of human responses to the stereotyped and mechanical actions of automata. This overly abstract, intellectualistic and mathematical approach to reality is at home only when dealing with what is static, fixed, and immobile. The mind turns its back on the fundamental fluidity of existence and solidifies everything it touches. Such an intellect freezes, fixes, and coagulates movement into a homogeneous series of static concepts, arbitrarily making abstract cuts into life's continuum. It invents "things" - an artificial world of hard facts: the domain of the solid, dead, and inert.

Bergson perceives this tendency as expressing a technocracy's tragically misguided attempt to assert power over nature through industry and the mechanical automatism of the machine. And Bergson repeatedly takes the large, impersonal business concern and the subdivided, Taylorised tasks of factory machine production to illustrate the life-denying economic rationalism he is determined to criticise and devalue. For Bergson the abstract, degrading and alienated life experience of the factory hand and office worker of today, compared with the concrete, symbolic and humanly fulfilling activities of the artisan and craft worker of a pre-industrial age, corresponds to the disappearance of the qualitative, individual characteristics of work, and the transformation of time from the concrete duration of creative activity into a process subject to mechanical laws.

Consequently time loses its qualitative, changing, fluid character; it freezes into a rigid, exactly delimited, quantifiable continuum, filled with quantitatively measurable "things" (which are the mechanically objectified "performance" and "productions" of the worker, wholly detached from their total human personality); in short, time is transformed into abstract, exactly measurable, physical space. The personality of the worker can do no more than look on and suffer helplessly as merely a rationalised and mechanically fragmented object of labour power, an isolated particle fed into an alien system. The increasing mechanical disintegration of the process of production into specialised sub-components also destroys those bonds that had once bound individuals into a community in the days when work was still 'whole' and 'organic'. Articulating it philosophically, Bergson points out that a qualitative 'whole' consists of several quantitative 'parts': a 'part' is that of which many make a 'whole'; therefore, the part is less than the whole - and the whole is always greater than the sum of its individual parts. Tragically, the mechanical rigidification of industry reduces and fragments workers into isolated, abstract atoms whose labour activity no longer brings them together directly and organically; instead, they are overtaken exclusively and to an ever increasing degree by the abstract laws of a mechanism that imprisons them.

Nostalgia for an organic and integrated community in comparison with the moral impoverishment and 'transcendental homelessness' of the modern world colours the cultural critic Walter Benjamin's most cogent essays. In 'The Storyteller', for instance, Benjamin compares printing and the dispersal of feeling in modern urban society - what Benjamin describes as a growing inability to exchange experiences - with the exemplary and authentic, highly personal and entertaining forms of verbal art, which the modern world of industry and mass media are in the process of destroying. Benjamin describes the yarns, the oral narratives woven by the storyteller as a type of craft, "an artisan form of communication, as it were. It does not seek to convey the pure essence of the thing, like information or a report. It sinks the thing into the life of the storyteller, in order to bring it out again. Thus traces of the storyteller cling to the story the way the handprints of the potter cling to the clay vessel."

Life, for Henri Bergson, is like a flowing torrent of creative activity, a ceaseless flow of energy, an *élan vital*. Matter, the condensed state of free activity, represents the cessation, the 'objectification' of the creative action. Life's creative *élan* is ceaselessly solidified into finite, material 'things' or 'objects'; calcified or crystalline deposits which are, in time, dissolved and reabsorbed back into the stream of life, into its creative flow. Bergson compares this process, and life itself, to a shell, bursting into fragments which are again shells. A view Bergson reiterates and extends into a veritable cosmology:

> Let us imagine a vessel full of boiling water heated at a high pressure, and here and there in its sides a crack appears through which a jet of steam escapes. The steam thrown into the air is nearly all condensed into little drops that fall, and this condensation and this fall represent simply the loss of something, an interruption, a deficit. But a small part of the jet of steam persists, uncondensed, for some seconds; it is making an effort to raise the drops which are falling; it succeeds at most in retarding their fall. So, from an immense reservoir of life, jets gush out unceasingly, of which each, falling, is a world. The evolution of living species within this world represents what subsists of the primitive direction of the original jet, and of an impulsion which continues itself in a direction the inverse of materiality.

It would appear, therefore, that for Bergson the manifestations of Life (the *élan vital*) exist in perpetual conflict with "matter", in any sense of that term in which it means something dead, inert, lifeless - in short, the utter opposite of Life.

How, then, does Bergson derive matter from Life? By the device, which is as old as Heraclitus, of balancing the upward movement of life by a downward movement. For every upward push there is a downward fall, for every tension of movement, a torpor or slackening of effort, for every creative urge, the relaxation and listlessness of fatigue. So, again, an action which, when first performed, was fresh and original, a new achievement in doing or thinking, becomes, by repetition, a habit. Plasticity yields to rigidity, variation to uniformity, effort to inertia.

Thus, we get matter - the burden against which Life is constantly struggling, yet at the same time the very life-process itself. For Bergson, evolution is not from matter to life, but from life to matter. Matter is derivative from life, a deposit or sediment (as it were) of the cosmic flux or *Élan*, produced by its slackening and receding from its own creations.

This is another aspect of Bergson's philosophy: like a river flowing through an alluvial plain, we continue to follow the course which, aeons ago, the water once carved out - only, with the passage of the years, the original irregularities of the channel become exaggerated, the course more and more elaborately curved, the rate of movement slower and slower. The river does not change: it only becomes more and more characteristically itself. The sedimentation and accumulated weight of these past external objectifications of the human spirit express an endlessly flowing creativity concretised into 'things' that infuse and enrich our lives through the birth, internalisation and historical transmission of the outward forms of 'culture', as the stream of time moves on, inexorably.

"Life is a continuous stream proceeding through sequences of generations". And what are human individuals? They are the bearers of this process. Is life more than the *totality* of its bearers? Yes and No. Life flows "as these individuals". But individuals are not continuous. Life is continuous, yet it "dams up" in individuals, or more generally as individuated forms. All forms, social and cultural, represent the same sort of crystallization and even rigidification of life. The forms (including individuals) first appear as the "subjects" of life, but they turn out to be instruments that are themselves transcended by the flow of life.

The ideological encounter of Gilles Deleuze with Henri Bergson results in a salutary dismantling of identity, amounting to a 'disenfranchisement of the subject'. "To be conscious of real duration is to lose a sense of one's individuality in the world". A liberation of the self amounting to the experience of "a succession of heterogeneous states melting into one another and flowing in an indivisible process" allowing the subject to become "identical with being in itself".

Similarly, the European colonist Bernard O'Reilly, in his autobiography *Cullenbenbong,* describes the language of Australia's Blue Mountains Kanimbla people, an ancient people whose culture expresses a direct, participatory experience of plants, animals, and elements - the sounds of insects, the speech of birds, the tastes in the winds, the flux of sounds and smells - in terms that seem to reproduce the breakdown of the split between the self and the world of sensory particulars, thus questioning the traditional dominion of European reason over a natural world construed as a passive and mechanical set of 'objects':

> The language of the blacks was not made for white man's tongue and that is why it sounds like blasphemy to hear him try to pronounce an Aboriginal word. Black man's words should never nave been put on paper for their is nothing in our alphabet as we understand its sounds which would make the written word any nearer to the original than a feeble parody. It is with regret then and some shame that the name Cullenbenbong must be written here; how cold and lifeless it looks in white man's type, yet to hear it pronounced by the Kanimbla was to hear majestic thunder re-echoing amongst the granite mountains of their hunting grounds. A strange thing this language of nature; a haunting echoing softness might give way to unbelievable drama and there were dread words which made your spine creep even though you didn't know their meaning. If you listened to the Aborigines speaking together you didn't hear a mumble of foreign words, you heard the sighing of trees, the voice of birds, the sounds of storm and flood and wind, the rolling of rocks on a landslide; you heard stark fear and infinite sadness.

# Transcendental and Immanent Capital: An Economics of an Oncological Order

by Kane X Faucher

There is an inhering irony to Adam Smith's "invisible hand", how greedy self-interest for profit lends itself to the alleged collective good of material and economic exchange, the profit matrix of production-consumption-excretion of a model of capitalist economics that is patterned on a vertical transcendence, or what Hegel had called "civil society."

A second emergent irony arises when the drive to accumulate capital, brought to its absolute limit would render the value of the totality of capital as zero, and so it is only the *relation* of capital exchange that has real value.

As the mode of capital's expression has been changed due to the disintegration and redistribution of its power among the plenum, so too has its character of transcendent verticality changed into that of an immanent horizon where all capital functions on a plane of immanence without striations, smoothing out what we now know to be a global economy. Our proposed method of analysis will be to give a cursory analysis of this exchange from transcendent verticality to immanent horizontality, to utilize the condition of cancer as a suitable metaphor to be mapped unto this new immanent mode of capital, and to consecutively propose an alternative to the falsely immanent character of capital and economic exchange. We do not claim here to give a full exposition of this rather complex transition from one mode to its successor, from the imperial to the global, but rather assume a certain complicity with this historical phenomena to assist in our giving full breadth to a newly minted theory of immanent economics that does not rely on the metastasis of the capital-economic order.

**Kane X. Faucher**

## *The Caesar-Christ Paradigm: The Rupture of the Transcendent Order*

Although the historical transition between imperial Rome and Christian Rome entailed a dissolution or rearticulation of the imperial, the transcendence of the western order was not made immanent in the east, but rather replaced by a new transcendent order.

In the time of the Caesars, the emperor was an Emanation, or the Great Chain of Capital. In the time of the sovereign, all capital emanated from one singular despotic "origin" that disseminated its power like a web over subjects, in a model of verticality where the sovereign extends the credit and guarantee of capital to subjects who receive it as a kind of symbolic debt insofar as the use of this capital is in recognition of a kind of gift that in turn recognizes the sovereign who guarantees its value. And although this capital was guaranteed by the face of the individual emblazoned upon the obverse of a coin, the character of the indexical that provided this guarantee was little more than a role. That is, the symbolic order of Caligula was finite and would be succeeded by Claudius, and then Nero, and so forth. But what remained was the static transcendentalism of the vertical model of the order-institution of the emperor-or Godhead of despotic capital. The fiat character of monetary currency still had its origin in the guarantor, the emperor, and participation by subjects guaranteed the legitimacy of the sovereign as guarantor of all economic exchanges.

However, when Christ said "render unto Caesar what is Caesar's", this was a direct assault against the value of the sovereign as guarantor of economic exchange. Of course, in the short term, very few former participants in the Caesarian economy shared the view that the value of the emperor's guarantee of currency was illegitimate, and should be brought to bear on that which was more immanent. The result of this insurgency by Christ and his close associates failed in the short term: he was placed on the rood as a common insurgent. Despite this rather brusque death sentence, Christ's challenge against the transcendent verity of the empire had created something of an anxiety or a zone of rupture in the monolith of the imperial sovereign's image, exposing a crack wherein rushed a trickle of doubt. This doubt would intensify after Christ's crucifixion, and would signal the end of the transcendent signifying order of the emperor and the beginning of a nascent immanent order. However, Christ did not propose an immanent alternative, but rather re-assigned the transcendent origin to a "higher power" above that of Caesar: God. This displacement of origin and center to another transcendent order would not prove too difficult an obstacle for sovereignty to overcome, for as the emperors of Byzantium had done, they integrated the new transcendent order into their own, making themselves the conduit of this order by way of a genealogical succession; "God's ambassador on earth." Although the sovereign was not the absolute transcendental origin, he was the next best thing, and the only material representative of this power. It was by the command of God that the sovereign ruled and guaranteed economic exchange, as an extended legitimacy of his power. The relevance of this paradigm is necessary as an illustration of our more contemporary discussion of immanent capital as merely an exchange of transcendent orders, that in fact the *immanent character of capital at its very base is nothing more than a newly reconstituted plane of transcendence.* This is to say that the only change that has occurred is capital's method of deployment when its more theoretical underpinnings remain that of the transcendent.

The Urdoxa of transcendent capital has moved from material exchange to the virtualization of the number or the numeralization of the virtual as capital itself has been transformed from the transcendent to the immanent mode. The character of a transcendent capital order has lost its head. The crisis of modernity was the scene of the loss of origin. That is, the sovereign that stood in the place of the guarantor of all hard currency has been a monolith since dismantled, reproduced in portions, and eventually distributed along a series of chains and networks in the domains of labour and finance. And even a central governing body (governmentality replacing sovereignty or the monarchic) or financial organization does not operate alone, but rather functions in concert with a larger machinic apparatus of intermediaries put in place and instaurated by the demands and the promise of capital's limit. The interests of the "center" now overlap with that of the "periphery", and so the partitions of static sovereignty have all been dissolved or leveled, and any imposed organizational partition succumbs to frame leakage as the machinic and onco-ontological character of capital seeps and appropriates new milieus. What Deleuze identifies as the "transcendence of the despotic signifier...its consecutive decomposition into minimal elements within a field of immanence uncovered by the withdrawl of the despot"(AO 240) is manifest in the continued dissolution of primitive accumulation among more traditional nation-based economies on the periphery of an ever-englobing capitalist regime.

### *The Virtualization or Demonetization of the Monetary Order*

One of the allegedly clear signs of a global monetary system and how capital demonstrates its immanent character is the rise of the Internet as mediation and mediatization of money. As a communicative global nexus, it has served as a tool for the freer flow of capital across borders. Capital is literally "screened" or mediated through the Internet, creating a system of double-fiat: the fiat of currency itself now filtered through the fiat of the numerical order as bits of transferred data streaming across fiber optic lines. Money is now "virtual" in the sense that its code can be transferred without recourse to its materiality. In fact, it is perhaps possible to live without ever setting hands upon any hard currency whatsoever. This new "soft" currency portrays the very virtualization and numeralization of the monetary order, but before any claim of immanence can be assigned to this mode of exchange, it should be reminded that it is still anchored to real, hard currency. Deleuze defines capital as "the deterritorialization of wealth through monetary abstraction."[1] Capital's tendency is toward concretization: "the abstraction has not ceased to be what it is, but it no longer appears in the simple quantity as a variable relation between independent terms."[2] Capital absorbs this function and assigns the quality of terms and the quantity of their relations. Capital "operates on the plane of *immanence,* through relays and networks of relationships of domination, without reliance on a transcendent center of power."[3] Following from this, the "general equivalence of money brings all elements together in quantifiable, commensurable relations, and then the immanent laws or equations of capital determine their deployment and relation according to the particular constants that are substituted for the variables of the equations."[4] And so "money represents a potential break-deduction in a flow of consumption" and "a break-detachment and a rearticulation of economic chains directed toward the adaptation of flows of production to the disjunctions of capital."[5] One of the chief principles of a mutational capitalism is its ability to appropriate production, for in fact "capitalism doesn't begin, the capitalist machine is not assembled until capital directly appropriates production, and until financial capital and merchant capital are no longer anything but specific functions corresponding to a division of labour in the capitalist mode of production in general."[6] By appropriating all production within its immanent encasement, "capital becomes the full body, the new socius or the quasi-cause that appropriates all the productive forces."[7] Capitalism is reactive, limiting what active forces can do through a process of subversion and co-opting of the codes and flows of economic exchange outside its own domain.

An example of how the virtualization of the monetary order, or the "demonetization of the monetary" is the relay system of debt and credit: "bank credit effects a demonetization or dematerialization of money, and is based on the circulation of drafts instead of the circulation of money...[T]he dualism of these two forms of money, payment and financing-the two aspects of banking practice."[8] Append to this dualism the added technical feature of the "Internetization" of money, and one may trace the continued immanent fluidity of the mode capitalism takes in its dissolution of partitions. But what is circulated as debt and credit is in fact not "real" money at all; what begins as "virtual" money gains interest, adding to the dematerialization of the monetary.
This aspect is one of the many central principles of capital's field of immanence: "Capitalism defines a field of immanence and never ceases to fully occupy this field. But this deterritorialized field finds itself determined by an axiomatic."[9] This axiomatic is "a set of equations and relationships that determines and combines variables and coefficients immediately and equally across various terrains without reference to prior and fixed definitions or terms."[10] As a reiteration of Deleuze's understanding of capitalism, Hardt and Negri state that capital

"tends toward a smooth space defined by uncoded flows, flexibility, continual modulation, and tendential equalization."[11] Capital is the new sovereignty insofar as its immanence is little more than a transcendent order. This is echoed in Hardt and Negri: "As national monetary structures tend to lose any characteristics of sovereignty, we can see emerging through them the shadows of a new unilateral monetary reterritorialization that is concentrated at the political and financial centers of Empire, the global cities...[I]t is a monetary construction based purely on the political necessities of Empire. Money is the imperial arbiter [and] this arbiter has neither a determinate location nor a transcendent status."[12]

If capital's tendency is to condense and concentrate wealth in as few bodies as possible, the virtualization of money is an attempt to recode the flow to force capital into an illusory state of equilibrium, and this can only happen if all capital is actualized. But what is actualized is not the currency as either "hard" or "soft", but rather its relations of exchange. All capital exchange is actualized and made transparent: its relations across borders has allowed it to manifest itself everywhere. What makes capital an immanence of actualization rather than a true virtual immanence is its analogous relation with the properties of cancer.

### *Capitalism is Cancer*

John McMurtry's claim that a voracious money market capital places social equity in a state of perilous instability is perhaps more true when considering the theoretical nuances of virtual capital as immanent.[13] The system of attraction and repulsion between forms of stability between the axiomatic of virtual capital and the social matrix provides for a transmission of stabilizing and destabilizing features. That is, virtual capital is stabilized into an equilibrium at the expense of social equity. This equilibrium concerns only the interests of capital itself, and has no parallel effect on the social; in fact the relationship is inversely proportional just as the relationship between cancer and a healthy cell: at the rate of cancer's own benefit and growth, the health of the cell itself declines in proportion to this. As we factor this carcinogenic quality on a broader scale, concerning capital-cancer's effect on a more global model of many cells or nations, we witness the proliferation of capital-cancer as it dissolves all partitions: "The general equalization or smoothing of social space, however, in both the withering of civil society and the decline of national boundaries, does not indicate that social inequalities and segmentations have disappeared. On the contrary, they have in many respects become more severe."[14] This is to say that capital reorganizes or rearticulates the social according to its own interest and image.[15]

This stabilization of virtual capital is completely indifferent to the social matrix and its stability from the start, and so the myopic capitalist strategy is to secure the equilibrium of capital with perhaps the adjacent hope that the social matrix will be benefited as an effect. But a collective good requires a more direct approach rather than to take the more neoconservative view that invigoration of business through finance capital (which thereby results in cuts to social programs) will all somehow "work out" to the advantage of the mores.

"Social breakdown under the strains of blind money-profit maximization was for a time resisted by newly accountable government bodies", but despite "this development of a social immune system...a relatively sudden mutation of social orders has recently emerged."[16] McMurtry continues to enumerate the bleak consequences of capitalist mutation and how this directly impacts the fragility of the social network. But perhaps what is more pertinent to our discourse, beyond the shocking forecast McMurtry presents, is his deployment of cancer as a metaphor for the late stage of capital, a metaphor we have here retained for its theoretical fecundity in analyzing and assessing the transition from transcendent mode of capital to an immanent mode. In sum, the uncontrolled and unregulated proliferation and reproduction of the capital agent that adiaphoristically negatively affects the host social body without assisting the host body in its regular social functions encompasses the very beginning of a severe dualism between the preservation of the social and the maintenance of the axiomatic of capital. Following this, carcinogenic capital appropriates "nutriments" from the host body for its own wild, metastasizing growth.[17] McMurtry indicates that cancer-capital operates "under the radar" of the social immune system that in itself is not equipped with a sufficient signal-response system to detect the carcinogenic agent, and so cannot respond and defend against what is otherwise an invasion of the social by a co-opting power of capital. Rather, the signal-response system is already under the power of capital in terms of a media communications system that is chiefly operated by a handful of conglomerates whose interests are very particularly capitalistic. Moreover, cancer-capital has the ability to extend itself and invade healthy cells on the periphery of its operation, which is to say that it has free movement throughout the global economy precisely because it imposes the image of this global economy upon those milieus that are still relatively self-sufficient or articulating their employment of capital in ways that are still nation-based. Once the image of the global is grafted upon the periphery, the partitions that once stood for the division of nations in the time of sovereignty are dissolved, and cancer-capital has free ingress to infect those areas. And, finally, the end result, says McMurtry, is the death of the host. Cancer-capital does not respond to the nutritive demands of the host itself, but rather parasitically draws upon necessary resources that would better benefit the host (such as clean air, labour capacity, oil, etc.). It is in this way that cancer-capital is indifferent to the social body qua its aims.

The question remains to be posed as to why the social body has not yet collapsed. Certainly, McMurtry gives suitable examples of the beginning of the decline, showing that the immanent mode of capital is the imminent end of the social. However, we would here append that the process of decline-however inevitable it may be-is delayed or deferred by the very special function of capital to reproduce itself as image, and to deploy this image as a temporary form of sustenance to the social body. The body is artificially sustained by the images and representations capital (re)produces in each of its nodes. There is always a sense of deferment of the death of the social as new crises force a condensation of capital into a given acute problem field, but the response is always somehow re-articulated in the interest of capital and the solution to a very acute crisis is generally a short-term solution that only serves to strengthen capital itself and exacerbate the social body in the long term. As in any logic of consumption, if no contingency plans are made to either consume more prudently the resources that sustain the social body, or to locate renewable forms of resources through alternatives, then the solutions cancer-capital employs to extremely acute crises is not sustainable. Moreover, cancer-capital's response to acute crises in the social are never altruistic, but always aims toward the artificial sustainability of the body only for as long as capital itself can continue its process of subsisting off the body and increasing its immanent code of dominance. But the end result is the same: if a parasitism is not indefinitely sustainable, then the body enervates and eventually expires.-The social cannot subsist off images or immediate short-term solutions forever. In fact, the situation for the social body is dire and perhaps even terminal: "the capitalist cancer increasingly diverts effective demand for use-value product on to its own growth and self-multiplication."[18] The significant problem facing the social body is that "the host body's immune system does not effectively recognize or respond to the cancer's challenge and advance."[19]

One alternative to the lack of signal and response would be to utilize the media as a signal transmitter to the social body so that the latter can adequately respond to the threat. This solution is, however, idealistic and unfeasible on the grounds that the "capitalist organized media and information systems select for dissemination only messages that do not contradict the capitalist organization of social bodies."(McM8) Add to this the character of capitalist organized media to foment fear: "the fundamental content of the information that the enormous communication corporations present is fear. The constant fear of poverty and anxiety over the future are the keys to creating a struggle among the imperial proletariat. Fear is the ultimate guarantee of the new segmentations."[20]

McMurtry's solution is a seemingly simple one, but a solution fraught with almost insurmountable difficulties: "the social immune system must recognize the disease agent before it can effectively respond to its invasion. Only when this recognition is clear can an effective defense be mounted."[21] (McM9). But in order for this solution to be realized, it would appear that this depends on the social body reclaiming what is now capitalist organized media. An insurgent movement of this order would require a great deal of organization and planning, but the first requirement of this solution is to disseminate knowledge of the threat. McMurtry's solution sets itself up for failure in the sense that the only way that the social body can be made aware of the cancerous threat of capital's effects is to disseminate information of this threat, but the means through which this can be achieved, i.e., capitalist organized media, is itself working in league with the capitalist ethos. This does not doom McMurtry's solution to unfeasibility per se if it can somehow be possible to co-opt the capitalist organized media to disseminate information contrary to its own aims. On these grounds we can concur, but it may be more fecund at this stage to append an added prerequisite that a major theoretical shift must occur that will either push capital to its absolute limit (the creative-destructive active nihilism of Nietzsche) and then to reorganize capitalism in a new articulation of virtual immanence. For this to be done, capital needs to be counter-actualized.

Exploring the link between capitalism and cancer in more thorough terms, the mutating property of capital as the tendency to reproduce itself "has no end, it has no exterior limit it could reach or even approximate. The tendency's limit is internal, and it is continually going beyond it, but by displacing this limit-that is, by reconstituting it, by rediscovering it as an internal limit to be surpassed again by means of a displacement."[22] Contrary to the traditional transcendent model, there is no center to be found, no origin: capital is a constant displacement of center and origin. "If capitalism is the exterior limit of all societies, this is because capitalism for its part has no exterior limit, but only an interior limit that is capital itself and that it does not encounter, but reproduces by way of displacing it."[23] The notion of center is not entirely abandoned, for capital relies on producing the *image* of a center in order to justify its actions on a *periphery* that it moves toward. It is in this sense that a "veritable 'development of underdevelopment' on the periphery ensures a rise in the rate of surplus value, in the form of an increasing exploitation of the peripheral proletariat in relation to that of the center."[24]-Or, how capital appropriates production according to its own axiomatic. Again, a clear case of how reactive forces limit what active forces can do. Moreover, "capitalist deterritorialization is developing from the center to the periphery, the decoding of flows on the periphery develops by means of a 'disarticulation' that ensures the ruin of traditional sectors."[25] This is enough to lend support to an argument that states that capital's *in articulo vita* is the *in articulo mortis* of the social.

Deleuze goes on to state "the ever widening circle of capitalism is completed, while reproducing its immanent limits on an even larger scale, only if the surplus value is not merely produced or extorted, but absorbed or realized."[26] What Deleuze does not explicitly signify here is the very Hegelian character of capital. Capital proceeds dialectically through monocentering circles, resolving false binaries in the totality of capital itself. Capital sets up false contradictions everywhere, Self-Other, Center-Periphery, Developed-Underdeveloped, Modernized-Primitive, etc. the Odyssean movement of capital discovers itself in all that it is not, as an absolute exteriority, absorbs and levels all affirmative differences in the social by rearticulating the Other as lack, and then repatriates itself within the center. Through a process of negative determinations, the reactive character of capital as a carcinogenic nihilism subverts the active forces of social production beyond its limit and absorbs everything within the immanent sphere of complete determination. "Capitalism's supreme goal, which is to produce lack in the large aggregates, to introduce lack where there is always too much, by effecting the absorption of overabundant resources."[27] Integration of the social productive forces within the carcinogenic system of capital's immanent totality is how capital sustains its own metastasizing growth. "The co-opting power of capitalism...its axiomatic is not more flexible, but wider and more englobing. In such a system no one escapes participation in the activity of antiproduction that drives the entire productive system."[28] If the parallel between the Hegelian and capitalist systems is retained with any degree of seriousness, we must be made aware of all the caveats that come with disputing the former. That is, to directly confront either Hegel or capital is to be led back and reabsorbed by Hegelianism or capitalism. Both Hegel and capital, by virtue of their systems, cannot be confronted directly without resorting to the very dialectical method that would thereby ensure their verity. Foucault's statement that at the end of history awaits Hegel is perhaps equally applicable to capital. An alternative needs to be devised that does not utilize a negative dialectics of opposition.

Our own cancer-capital analogy extends beyond McMurtry's fine exposition insofar as it summarizes the composite viewpoints of McMurtry and Deleuzians such as Hardt, and neo-marxists such as Negri. Moreover, the actual scientific terms employed grant us a new trajectory of thinking capital as oncological. We do not claim to exhaust the possibilities and linkages here, but rather enumerate a brief itemized list:[29]

1. Self-sufficiency in growth signals = capital less relies on external agency for reproduction of itself as surplus value. Virtual money. Nodes rather than Modes of production.

2. Insensitivity to anti-growth signals = attempts to curb free flow of capital through imposed signals such as stagflation and slumpflation fail to recode the flow of capital which, by its immanence, is a becoming. Market cannot respond to redirection.

3. Evading apoptosis = unstoppable production of capital. Surplus value not curbed by systems of power that usually operate by checks and balances. The value less determined by a central organizing body, but by the force or affinity of relation globally.

4. Limitless replicative potential = as capital appropriates production as reproduction and representation ad infinitum, capital reproduces its image without limit-or at least until the body expires.

5. Sustained angiogenesis = re-production of image. After appropriating everything in its dual logic of consumption-production, it can reproduce all it needs from itself with very little direct nutritive sources.

6. Tissue invasion and metastasis = Capital consumes and appropriates new milieus, bodies, nations, etc. Infects "healthy cells" and appropriates modes of production for its own genesis-transmutes these into NODES of re-production through constant de- and reterritorialization.

In sum, Capital tends toward the dysgenesis of its host.

### *Some Finer Points and Implications of Capitalism as Oncological*

Not only is the content of labour, the content of the social (the one who wields both quantifiable wealth and labour capacity) merely arbitrary and adjacent figures to the regime of virtual capital, but the content of capital itself (the constituent components of wealth involved in exchange) are now equally merely figural representations. And so, on both sides, the wielder and the wielded of wealth are little more than variables in a larger tangential function toward the englobing metastasis of capital as it proceeds to deterritorialize older regimes of "primitive" codes in a flow from a "center" to the "periphery." Individuals locked up in the game of capital's expansion are nothing more than statistical variables, and slight deviations from a more encompassing function set toward the appropriation and consumption of new milieus. Once this is effected, capital can turn on itself and appropriate its own inner limits, reproducing for itself images. Personified capital and "capitalized" personhood: their mutual arbitrariness is not to be taken to mean that there can be a seamless substitution between the two, but that both person and capital as individuations are hollowed out and put into play as vehicles of a meta-capital axiomatic. As capital submerged into the false virtual, becoming actualized and no longer revealing its theoretical "origin", it brought along in this descent the wielder of capital who must-in order to participate-be actualized...that is, to divest the self and mint a new Self that is both the actualization of capital-as-personified-in-the-Self-as-image. This new image is of "virtual" capital.

Movement of capital creates excess. This excess is not lost but reabsorbed as image, completing the circle of production-consumption. It is no longer the case, contra Bataille, that an excess maximal investment of energy is squandered in some glorious dissolution, but that capital has a relay uptake system that allows it to reabsorb excess and reproduce this excess as image rather than to be mere exudation. The excess forms the constituent components for the manufacture of the

virtual image. Although much of Bataille's reading of general economy can now be considered outdated and inapplicable to the current situation of capital, what we may retain are the components of the analysis which have indicated the problems facing capital that have since been overcome in its continuation of an immanent mode. Of course, many of the problems Bataille raises have only been temporarily abated by capital's transition to immanence, but these problems will once again return to haunt capital at the point when it has reached its absolute limit.
Firstly, Bataille understands the problem of capital spatially rather than temporally. The more immanent quality of capital is its ability to inscribe itself upon the temporal order as a perpetual displacement and becoming-other. As Bataille quite "spatially" notes, "it is the size of the terrestrial space that limits overall growth."[30](B AC 29). Bataille assumes a synchrony between capital and labour, production and consumption. But, as we have noted above, capital and the social do not operate synchronically, but rather that capital is diachronic. The diachrony of capital is what grants it the power to itself remain immanent *and* to reorganize or segment the social. Moreover, in conceiving of the problem of capital in terms of time, Deleuze is able to illustrate that the terrestrial limit is not a true limit, for capital can always reterritorialize itself according to inner limit. Even in consideration of a somewhat mundane example, we can see how this is the case: commercial advertising is always devising new strategies to reterritorialize upon its own terrain. That is, billboards can be erected *between* billboards, people can be paid to have ads painted on their back windshields, some Internet services come with a flurry of pop-ups (and with the advent of pop-up blocker software, the reterritorialization of the Internet space took the form of "pop-unders" that the software could not block-yet another instance of the unstoppable seepage of advertising and capital), and so forth, all examples of how a spatial zone can constantly be reterritorialized according to internal limits. The compounding of advertising within an already advertisement-glutted zone is but a very minor example of a larger phenomenon.

Secondly, Bataille points out that "if there is no outlet anywhere, nothing bursts; but the pressure is there."[31] Once again, Bataille is operating under an overly spatialized understanding of capital. However, he is correct to invoke the notion of pressure insofar as capital does respond to zones where its pressures are not felt, where there is a vacuum. These vacuums allow capital to rush in and deterritorialize these spaces, to infect them. In order for capital to be able to continue in its process of reproducing its own image, it must constantly appropriate production from its "periphery", and so when the pressure-quotient of production to appropriate is low in its own domain, it must locate new sources beyond its boundaries to be included in its totality. But supposing "there is no longer any growth possible, what is to be done with the seething energy that remains?"[32] We must here concede to Bataille on this point, for Deleuze's claim that capital could indefinitely reproduce itself seems counter-intuitive. There needs to be some maximum point of saturation, a point when the social bodies in a global network have been segmented to their extreme and there is no more production to appropriate. However, even Deleuze holds the view that this saturation point is possible, and that the closure of capital's growth is a result of capital going to its limit and succumbing to its own logic of consumption. That is, in a different way than Bataille's claim that capital or Reason can attain its limit and expire, Deleuze will claim that capital's reproduction of images will eventually plunge it into the depths. That is, capital will desire its own demise at the very point that it has assimilated and leveled out all differences. These differences, or appropriations of production will create a toxic mixture within the very constitution of capital which will result in a point of rupture, thus beginning the process of counter-actualization. In terms of pressure, Bataille explains "a pressure everywhere equal to itself would result in a state of rest, in a general substitution of heat loss for reproduction. But real pressure has different results: It puts unequal organisms in competition with one another."[33] But what is truly unequal is the relation between capital and the social. The pressure capital exerts upon the social in order to reproduce image and create surplus value will result in the complete absorption of the social. When this occurs, capital will have nothing left to appropriate, and will, once again, desire its own demise. Capital thrives on the inequality it creates in the social, but its tendency is toward a complete appropriation and equilibrium state. However, if it achieves this objective of complete equilibrium, it will begin to rupture from within.

Bataille makes an interesting point that "possible growth is reduced to a compensation for the destructions that are brought about."[34] And in fact, capital justifies its own extension of itself into new milieus by deterritorializing these milieus, thereby destroying nation-economies and traditional forms of capital exchange, but it does so precisely through subversion and not an outright destruction. In fact the actual destruction has yet to occur, and can only come about if capital goes to its absolute limit when it completes its own nihilistic project. But this form of destruction, this nihilism, is complete insofar as it will have nothing left to appropriate or exploit, and so will perform this destruction upon itself. Bataille further warns that growth "is by nature a transitory state. It cannot continue indefinitely."[35] And although this is correct, it should be noted that the growth of capital can only cease once it has successfully appropriated all production.

In terms of giving and the gift, capital can "give" nothing more than itself, its own "zero point" of equilibrium. Capital, already defined and non-delineated as immanent, has a value of nil, whereas that which it seeks to consume, appropriate, and transmute outside of it (modes into nodes) has a value of +1. If capital is motivated by what it yet does not have, would it not have a value of -1 in order to fulfill itself as a utopic harmony of 0? This would only be the case if the image were subtracted from capital's auto-production, which is to say that this is impossible. It is already in itself full, and the image it produces is the credit it extends beyond its limit to which the only restitution possible to repay the debt is for the older regimes to open its border to capital's invasive metastasis. A value of +/- 1 is contingent upon there being striations or partitions. But this level of organization of capital is defunct; socially it is not that labour determines capital, but vice versa in such a way that the immanence of capital smoothes out all striations as a one-all. Its ubiquity is guaranteed by its axiomatic, but this axiomatic is the source of a veiled new form of transcendence, with the chief difference being that no sovereign-subject governs over the horizon-just the image of a center and an origin.

## *The Onco-ontology of Actualization and Counter-actualization*[36]

Deleuze muses "perhaps the flows [of capital] are not yet deterritorialized enough"[37] which is to say that nihilism is not yet complete. Capitalism as cancer is nihilistic, but it needs to succumb to its own logic of consumption and be brought to a critical point of rupture. "The capitalist State completes the becoming-concrete so fully that, in another sense, it alone represents a veritable rupture with this becoming, a break with it."[38] This is the first stage of capital's counter-actualization.

A useful heuristic tool for explaining counter-actualization is by recourse to oncology. Cancer is a metastasis of cells, a wild and unchecked growth that eventually consumes and destroys the host. Apoptosis is the process by which cells are limited and destroyed before metastasis can take place. Apoptosis is, simply put, planned obsolescence, or pre-programmed cell death. Taken in another way, metastasis is the becoming-active of forces in the descent to the virtual, and apoptosis is the becoming-reactive of forces in actualization. However, as we will demonstrate, the roles of metastasis and apoptosis switch in the inverted image of capital; that is, metastasis serves the aims of actualization toward the constitution of universals just as counter-actualization itself has a mode of apoptosis that resists the static and inverted image of capital.. The "cancer" of actualization is deleterious while for counter-actualization it is a beneficial destruction that opens the way for a logic of production rather than consumption.

Actualization operates by what we call a *logic of consumption*. That is, the aim of capital's actualization is to appropriate all production and encase it into universal categories for capital. It is the desire to actualize, a will-to-actualize that motors this process. This form of desire posits objects as idealizations and moves toward their idealizations in the depths. However, what it is truly chasing is nothing more than a projected inverted image of the real, and once the "object" of desire is achieved, this is followed by a malaise, a fatigue or exhaustion brought upon by a feeling of lack and dissatisfaction. By universalizing objects under categories, this falsely exhausts the content of objects and denies the many ways in which the object can be expressed. Madness results from this dissatisfaction (a mid-life crisis is an example) and there are two possible responses: resignation (passive nihilism and the desire to fade away) and insurgency (active nihilism). The metastasis of this logic of consumption is precisely the metastasis of universals in capitalism under which all of life is depreciated; it is also the metastasis of consumption itself as it can do nothing more than appropriate and consume. This logic of consumption eventually succumbs to its own logic, consuming and eventually negating itself-an Uroboros. This logic is seen in common profusion within the social, especially in terms of habit and comfort and the vain belief that particular objects will bring about the completion and validity of the Self. That is, when it becomes a moral Good to achieve a state of peaceful equilibrium, to obtain those objects that are invested by capital with the belief of their ability to provide this equilibrium, to structure a life under the grand ought of desirable things to facilitate the comfort and reinforce the habit of a "promised" life, this is when life is depreciated and reduced to the value of nil. The person who has projected this transcendental Good and follows the strictures of the ought out of a desire to attain this transcendentally harmonious Good through whatever means (the attainment of property, material acquisitions, the Christian demand of being fruitful and multiplying as the ethical duty to validate oneself through the transcendental category of Family, etc.) realizes perhaps in the depths of Self a certain dissatisfaction at the point when these features of the allegedly "successful" life are acquired. It is then that the Self succumbs to a kind of existential crisis where it reflects upon the meaning of having structured life in such a way, and realizes soon thereafter that these objects-for-desire, these large and baggy moral oughts, do not access the true character of the real. Moreover, the prudence by which such a Self lives, the way in which it seeks to rig outcomes and deny chance through several means as to exclude or barricade a life from the fortuitousness of contingent events takes the form of so many insurance policies and financial investment strategies to protect the Self from losing all it has acquired. And, indeed, what is the underlying logic of a suburb but a place where one can take a family *away* from the heterogeneity of the city and to live in a utopic homogeneous setting where all homes resemble one another and there is a common majoritarian value that unites the inhabitants? Or, consider the logic of consumption in action in social interaction wherein we most commonly congregate together in social settings to consume products and services, be it meeting over coffee or taking in a movie. The mania for consumption operates as an almost unconscious force, yet it still is linked to a transcendental moral ought: I shop therefore I am.

The apoptotic function of the logic of consumption is reactivity: to assimilate sameness from the different, to expel true difference through a series of determinations, and to deny chance. By excluding true difference through subsumption under universal categories (limiting what active forces can do), the process of actualization equilibrates the world according to a static, banal, and predictable image that denies or attempts to blockade chance. The Uroboros is the mascot of actualization, for its principle is to assimilate its other or shadow by devouring its own tail. The Uroboros engages in an act of killing itself and being reborn, but it is the rebirth of the same. Just as in the stage of negative nihilism, man denies life by creating a supersensible world and a God, he then murders God and takes his place, thereby performing an act of sameness: the creation of a transcendental plane. The Uroboros is the time of capitalism, and the scene of its devouring and recreation of self is the privileged present. The circle is infinite, but the variety of infinite that is only circuitous movement. Apoptosis assimilates the resemblance the past and future have with the present while denying or annihilating from itself the differences. Apoptosis in capitalism banishes differences while metastasis is merely the genesis of sameness.

The characteristic functions of metastasis and apoptosis in counter-actualization operate on a *logic of production*. What metastasizes is the fracturing of the once unified 'I' into an infinite bifurcation into true differences of nature. The apoptosis function of counter-actualization takes place when it expels the last vestiges of the negative in the act of transmutation or active negation. A logic of production is a creative and generative activity, for it is the desire to produce infinite and divergent variations across a plane of immanence. It is the affirmative act that leads to joy. No longer under the tyranny of the universal, difference is free to be different in the affirmative sense, no longer assimilated as an other. This production is an excretion, but the excretion of the negative. It is the moment when the plane of transcendence succumbs to the rupture and empties its heavy bowels in an act of necessary purgation.

Counter-actualization is an apoptosis insofar as the pre-programmed death of the organi(ci)sm is the result of actualization going to its limit and expiring, going mad and negating the metastasis of transcendental images that do nothing more than cause despair. Counter-actualization becomes a counter-memory (the act of forgetting universals) and a counter-desire (as desire negatively defined in terms of lack). Counter-actualization is a metastasis insofar as it engenders a logic of production where the active forces of difference freely express their difference without the apoptotic function of actualization as a becoming active of forces. It is the present that is emptied and infinitely split by the play of forces of the past and future. It is this character of the virtual and the immanent that can truly be called thus, whereas capitalism is only the *image* of the virtual and the *image* of immanence.

### *Concluding Remarks*

Derrida's question, What is Economy? resonates for us: "economy no doubt includes the values of law (*nomos*) and of home (*oikos*, home, property, family, the hearth, the fire indoors). *Nomos* does not only signify the law in general, but also the law of distribution (*nemein*), the law of partition (*moira*), the given or assigned part, participation."[39] A little further on in the passage, he states that as soon as there is law, "there is partition: as soon as there is *nomy*, there is economy."[40] But can there be an eco-*a*nomy? Is not the immanently smooth space of capital as such an eco-anomaly? If so, then (immanent) capital can have no return (unless to itself as a veiled process) and no surplus, i.e., it is pure absorption and re-production. Nothing *returns* to cancer-capital but its own image reflected at the very absolute limit of the cellular partition *and* as a projected image beyond the cellular-national partitions. The parergon of national economies outside of capital's exuberant metastasizing reach become little more than a leaky frame through which capital can gain hold as a sort of seepage. The projection of its image (as lack) facilitates its flow where it can then pool and recommence its metastasis until the entire globe is made to resonate with its imposed global-capital equilibrium. The figure of eco-anomaly is particularly pertinent to the continuing function of capital as a carcinogen, for it depends on reproducing its own anomalous image in rank repetition of an illusory center or origin that does not truly exist. That is, capital acts *as though* it appeals to a principle dictated by a center that organizes and regulates actions on the periphery, but this center is little more than a collective fiction of a capitalist laity. And it is precisely this absent throne of the "centre" or "origin" which furnishes economy-belief and creates a new (albeit illusory) transcendent order. It is this constantly destabilized center that capital constantly recreates as an image. If anything jeopardizes the claim that capital is *actually* immanent, it would be its creation of a transcendent image at the very summit of its image-reproduction. Capital functions *as though* it were immanent, and *as though* the transcendent center was there in full.

Capital functions as a "superconductor" of its own furiously reproduced image. However, the mass reproduction of images in capitalism is hypertelic, and so its function far exceeds, and is a deviation from, the social body and its functional aims. Just as now capital determines labour, capital no longer serves the social; the social is organized within capital in a false virtual milieu without any structure. A hypertrophy of capital follows along on its own exuberant course while the social field continues to atrophy in their new "segmentations."

To counter-actualize capital would be to push capital's seemingly innate principle of metastasis and consumption to its limit, bringing it to the critical mass of rupture. Its tendency will already inevitably bring it to this point, but the scene of creation immediately following this conflagration of capital's image will most definitely require the skills and creative adeptness of a people to come.

---

Notes

1. Gilles Deleuze. *Anti-Oedipus: Capitalism and Schizophrenia.* Trans. Robert Hurley, Mark Seem, and Helen R. Lane (Minneapolis: University of Minnesota Press, 1983) 225.

2. Ibid. 227.
3. Michael Hardt and Antonio Negri. *Empire* (Cambridge: Harvard University Press, 2000) 326.
4. Ibid. 327.
5. Gilles Deleuze. *Anti-Oedipus* 228-9.
6. Ibid. 226.
7. Ibid. 227.
8. Ibid. 229.
9. Ibid. 250.
10.Hardt and Negri. *Empire* 326-7.
11.Ibid. 327.
12. Ibid. 346
13. John McMurtry. "The Cancer Stage of Capitalism: Our social immune system is being overwhelmed by growing out-of-control money market cancer" dl October 18, 2003...http://www.flora.org/library/mai/cancer.html originally published in the CCPA Monitor, July/August 1996.
14. Ibid. 336.
15.This results in what Hardt and Negri will call "the society of control" as a shift from the disciplinary society. In an immanent network such as capital, there are no masters or disciplinarians, but rather the social body is made to regulate itself without a transcendent figure to dictate law. Deleuze also speaks of the social as being reorganized as a collective of slaves who regulate their own slavery. Although this issue is of considerable merit, we cannot permit ourselves the luxury of exploring it further here.
16. McMurtry. "The Cancer Stage of Capitalism" 2.
17.This enumeration is abstracted from McMurtry, "The Cancer Stage of Capitalism" 5.
18. Ibid. 7.
19. Ibid. 8.
20. Hardt and Negri *Empire* 339.
21. McMurtry 9.
22. Deleuze *Anti-Oedipus* 230.
23. Ibid. 230-1.
24. Ibid. 231.
25. Ibid. 232.
26. Ibid. 234.
27. Ibid. 235.
28. Ibid. 236.

29. Abstracted from Douglas Hanohan and Robert A. Weinberg, "The Hallmarks of Cancer" *Cell* v. 100 57-70, Jan. 7th 2000
30. Georges Bataille. *The Accursed Share v. 1.* Trans. Robert Hurley (New York: Zone Books, 1991) 29.
31. Ibid. 30.
32. Ibid. 31.
33. Ibid. 33.
34. Ibid. 33.
35. Ibid. 45.
36. Counter-actualization is a concept introduced and well defined by Gilles Deleuze. See Deleuze, *Logic of Sense, Difference and Repetition,* and an analogue of how this functions in chapter five of *Nietzsche and Philosophy.*
37. Gilles Deleuze *Anti-Oedipus* 239.
38. Ibid. 252.
39. Jacques Derrida. *Given Time:1. Counterfeit Money*. Trans. Peggy Kamuf (Chicago: University of Chicago Press, 1992) 6.
40. Ibid. 6.

# Translating Werner Schwab Translation Hypotheses

by Véronique Rat-Morris

**Abstract:** Werner Schwab is said to be an untranslatable author. However, the subversive plays of the Austrian playwright are regularly and successfully staged throughout all Europe. Werner Schwab invites translators to transgress along with him the restrictions and borders which are not so much those of translation or correct language as those of our own relation to language, of the strangeness in our own language.

Werner Schwab died on the night of December 31, 1993, at the peak of a career as a writer and playwright which had been as short as it was fulgurating. His plays, inherited not only from the so called *popular* and *absurd* theatres, but also from Antonin Artaud's "theatre of cruelty" ("*théâtre de la cruauté*"), literally caused the European stages to be drenched in blood - challenging even the best directors, interpreters as well as musicians. Let us turn to another challenge: that of translation. Although reputed as tough, these plays provide translators with an opportunity to reconsider their activity, and above all to reconsider the adage accusing them of being traitors. These plays are an invitation to call into question the position of the accuser: this invisible *one*, this censor acting with impunity within the very bosom of the language.

### *Traduttore, tradittore*

*There are many ways to destroy a book. You may throw it up in the air with full swing, let a page-turning machine lacerate it slowly, saw it into pieces, shove it by bundles into an enormous shredder - or adapt it.* [2]

"I believe that it is impossible to translate Schwab"[3], said Marc Günther to Mike Sens, in 1995. Marc Günther, as the artistic director of the Schauspielhaus in Graz, had just staged the "Cover-Drama"[4] *Troiluswahn und Cressidatheater*[5]. Mike Sens had just translated into French, in collaboration with Michael Bugdahn, *Die Präsidentinnen*[6] and *Übergewicht, unwichtig:*

*Unform*[7], which were the first plays of Werner Schwab to be staged in French[8].

Isolated from its context, this assertion seems to condemn any attempt to perform the works of the Austrian playwright before a non German-speaking public. Indeed, although Marc Günther adds immediately afterwards: "one can perhaps rewrite it, by acting as a poet"[9], the prospect of a translation is burdened by his first denial and the distinction between the translator's gesture and the poet's inaugural gesture is affirmed. Yet the director says he himself had to resort to "a literal *translation*, of a double length, from Schwab's German into standard German"[10] in order to allow his actors to *interpret* the play. This double *translation* and the proceeding *interpretation* are forms of the work's "survival"[11] which are surprisingly not called into question.

Moreover, while paradoxically affirming that "the sense is bursting out at once", Marc Günther insists on the idea that "we first have to understand this universe to be able to interpret it", that a "good knowledge" of Werner Schwab's work is "objectively essential" in order to understand exactly "what is under the text", that it is finally necessary to "bring back" the poem "to the imagination of the author". The director all the same assumes that French speakers proceed in the same way with Paul Verlaine's poems, which could not be "explained spontaneously"[12]. The vocabulary used ends up convincing me that this reflection belongs to a negative ontology of translation- and more generally of the poetic work - since it is all about *bringing back* the text into the claws of a correct language (responsible for its *standardization* and *clarification*) after it has been entrusted to a smuggler in order to be *translated*, or more generally *transmitted*.

*Apprehended* through the negative ontology mentioned above, the text entrusted to the smuggler (translator, interpreter) is thus suspected of *treason*: what won't we discover, dissimulated "under the text"? However, as skillful as those who try to *decipher* Werner Schwab's text might be, they will not find any message hidden there- no more than in the modern notation of the scores of the Polish composer Krzysztof Penderecki, which were held back at customs during the time of the iron curtain. For good reason! As the Belgian director Michel Dezoteux puts it, for Werner Schwab, the characters themselves "are made of linguistic material"[13]. We should thus not expect to find any tracks leading us to some "underworld" ("*arrière-monde*") still to be discovered, nor any tangible *signified* beyond the *signifier*. Such administrators of the language will never understand that the message designates itself - and designates them too - since its contents are the very language in which it is being expressed, or-as Walter Benjamin puts it - since this message "does not communicate anything but communication" ("*vermittelt nichts als die Mitteilung*").

In spite of his *correct* approach towards Werner Schwab's work, Marc Günther reveals, at the beginning of the same article, one of the *dialectical knots* which will help us translate Werner Schwab:

> *Graz is a singular city.* [...], *settled at the south-eastern edge of the German linguistic territory.* [...] *Styria has a very strong anti-Viennese tendency. This region is very exclusive* [...]. *This concept of exclusion is accentuated by a deeply implanted fascistic tradition, which comes from the time when Styria was being used as a so to speak protective forest on the linguistic border of the German empire, to which it belonged* [...].[14]

This cultural and linguistic isolation, this conviction of being the last rampart against barbarians (those who do not speak German, obviously) is not proper to Werner Schwab's birth region only, since it also reminds us, among others, of Franz Kafka's German - speaking Prague. On this singular and urban linguistic island - an impoverished ground encircled by a rural Czech-speaking population - a "paper German" had developed[15], an uprooted German, unable to reproduce the richness of expression of a local dialect. Werner Schwab's own German (the "*Hochschwab*"), like Franz Kafka's ("a most personal *Hochdeutsch*": "*ein allpersönlichstes* Höchdeutsch"), is a minor language - or rather it constitutes, within a language which is itself a minor language (the Grazer German is a minor language in relation to the Viennese German, and further more in relation to the German *Hochdeutsch,* like Franz Kafka's Prager German), a "minor use"[16] of it.

The fact that the first director staging the works of Werner Schwab in French was a Belgian is probably not due to chance only. Michel Dezoteux, being sensitive to this *dialectical knot*, reminds us that "to Belgians, French is an acquired language, even if they are French-speaking by birth. [They] do not have a "satisfied" relation to the language"[17]. The borders that the translators are invited to transgress along with Werner Schwab are not so much the illusory and fantasized borders between languages, as those borders which we are erecting from the innermost bosom of our language.

Michael Bugdahn, who, together with Mike Sens, translated for Michel Dezoteux Werner Schwab's texts, was also sensitive to this particularity of the playwright's language:

> *Translating is like sailing between two worlds. All those who discovered Werner Schwab's world confirm that its principal characteristic is the language which is spoken there. As strange as it is fascinating, it is in fact the very material which this universe is made of.*[18]

However, Michael Bugdahn seems to remain a prisoner of the dichotomy established by the myth of the border, since, some lines later, he wonders: "up to what point can we deform the *target* language (French in this case) to remain faithful to Schwab?"[19] In other words: can we submit French language to the same violence as that to which Werner Schwab submits German language (which is why he is threatened to be "brought back" to a "standard" language-and behavior)?[20] The real question would be to know if it might even turn out differently, since the language is the very material which has to be carved.

Michael Bugdahn appreciates the fact that "German, especially written German, is perfectly fitted for very complex syntactic structures", and that, in German, there is "the choice between four different verbs to express the concept 'should' "[21]. He seems to regret thereby the lesser plasticity of the French language. He goes even as far as accusing himself, a translator, of "linguistic massacre" ("*massacre linguistique*")! But are we to let go and assume a substance which would be specific to each language? Shouldn't we rather consider, as Michel Dezoteux suggests, that the translator obeys a very strong self-censorship requirement?

> *[...] we, French-speaking people, have a cultural relation to our language, an abstract relation. This language evolves very little, is somehow stiff, authorizes few agglomerates of words and sounds and accepts accents unwillingly. It is somehow as if there was only one way to speak French.*[22]

The fact that French was standardized much earlier in the history than German may certainly explains this phenomenon, but does not imply the need for subjecting oneself to this self-censorship requirement.

### *A walk into the woods...*

*Radical translation begins at home.*[23]

Let us now consider the following assumption: the difficulties the translator runs into when *working* Werner Schwab's texts are not so much due to *trans*lation itself as to the "systemic position" that these texts are likely to occupy within a complex semiotic and/or cultural structure. These difficulties are not so much due to the "*trans*position" from a system into another as to the "*com*position"[24]. The translation, or more generally the transmission of a text is not only a matter of passive *reception,* as constrained as it might be; violence, if violence there is, is not the mere doing of some other: a new work is created, which also goes through a "poietic" moment[25] within its own system. This moment even precedes the moment at which the work does exist as a work. Thus, the translator should not wear away, should not surrender to the prime author the responsibility for poetic action, should not take refuge into the "ancillary"[26] function of a mere *porte-parole* (spokesman) or "lieu-tenant"[27]: "new language: new life: new suffering", proclaims Werner Schwab's Faust[28].

It is proper to question our own concept of translation. Jean Molino, while reminding us that "a work is a complex reality which constitutes a whole social fact"[29], invites us to leave behind - first of all - the logocentrist point of view. The anthropological approach, in particular, such as presented by Lieven Tack and based on Jean Gagnepain's "theory of mediation" ("*théorie de la médiation*"), is likely to bring essential elements to our reflection[30]. Indeed, according to this theory, which is thus close to W.V.O. Quine's theory of indetermination of translation, any communication is translation, is *appropriation,* which means reaffirmation of identity to oneself and difference to others: thus, "we are always only tracking down our own language"[31], to project our own categories. Werner Schwab's Faust himself encourages us to proceed in this way: "to no message from outside is then the key stolen any more / the desire will burn in its own foreign language / and the self-foreignness will be my own foreign own"[32]. It is thus indeed necessary for us to reconsider the concepts according to which we think the translation:

> *The stakes of the problem [...] consist [...] in [...] turning from a bipolar definition (translation = transgression of border) to a definition articulating the translation with what constantly condemns us to establish it. This means a reversal from a dualistic understanding of things to a dialectical vision.*[33]

The lexical field of the *passage*, of the *border*, which we already pointed out, belongs clearly to the first definition. Conceiving the translation as a "real, substantial and positive exchange of *something*" (this, even if *there is only language*!), while supposing a double equivalence of the signifying and the signified, amounts to denying the difference which forces us to operate the aforementioned translation, thus undermining on the one hand its very necessity (if there is no difference, why should we translate?) and establishing in addition the idea that, to a "source" text, would correspond a single *valid* translation into a "target"[34] language - from which comes the threat of the impossibility of translation and the generally widespread myth of its defect.

Let us now turn again to Werner Schwab's native Styria, this "linguistic protection forest", and dare, along with the Dutch director Theu Boermans, to penetrate it on the tracks of the playwright: "I can imagine that Schwab crossed the forest while speaking to himself, like that, and thus developed a specific language"[35]. It is thus well *in* the border itself that the language is created. The "composition" of a complex cultural identity, which is at the origin of every poietic gesture, being the interpretation of a work on the stage or its writing, constitutes the dialectical knot to which we referred in our first part. The "systemic position" of Michel Dezoteux, who creates in a "learned" language or the position of Werner Schwab, who writes in a "minor" language, invite us to consider dialectically the positioning of the translator in the forest of his own language, and this before any "transposition".

Thus, any univocal attempt to clarify and/or standardize the text, be it the "translation" in "standard German" realized by Marc Günther or an unspecified form of a "beautiful infidel"[36], amounts to "reinforcing ethnolinguistic borders", to confine ourselves into the edge of the woods, from where we could have no glimpse of either the variety of species, nor directions indicated through the woods by Werner Schwab's broken branches, or "*Holzwege*"[37].

***Breaking language to touch life, is like making or remaking theatre***[38]

To the question "what can Schwab bring to the French-speaking theatre?", Michel Dezoteux answers without hesitating: "returning its body to it" - which means putting an end to any dichotomy, in order to give back to language the ability to move freely inside itself. Not only Werner Schwab's characters "are made of linguistic matter", but the staging itself is carried out "inside the writing"[39], with a staging allowing the author to completely escape the codified theatrical language as denounced by Antonin Artaud.

It should however be specified that the methods recommended by Artaud in his theory of the "theatre of cruelty" are more drastic still than those practiced by Werner Schwab. Indeed, in the play *The Cenci*, the only concrete example that the poet left for us to consider, the staging reaches beyond language, which is reduced to the bare minimum, as much in the stage direction as in the semiotic register of the characters, which readily leave behind the linguistic field for the somatic field, evicting even the meaning. For Werner Schwab, on the contrary, the signifier evicts the signified and invades all space: thus, in Faust's "Walpurgis little night party" ("*Walpurgisnachtsfestchen*"), the stage directions are written to such a degree that they take precedence over any theatrical action.

If the means used by Antonin Artaud and Werner Schwab differ clearly, one thing draws them closer: both, in their manner, while tackling the "worm-eaten structures" of language and language in general, offer a possibility of "survival" to the work they are absorbed in - be it the very theatre, its interpretation on stage, its adaptation as "Cover-Drama", or even its musical interpretation.

Thus, to Schwab's *interpretation* of the "*Beamtensprache*" corresponds, in order to accompany the performances of the play *Faust: My Breastbone: My Helmet* (*Faust:: Mein Brustkorb: Mein Helm*[40]), Einstürzende Neubauten's interpretation of a music which means to be "bureaucratic":

> *We wanted to play a bureaucratic music, a music which consists only of tables and books. A wood music, a library music. Book-drums, hollowed-out books, knocking signals, folios. Tables, manipulated tables, various tables set with ropes or cables, tables sawn to pieces, kalimba-tables, the pushing along of tables. Book machines, page-turning-machines, a motorized book-hi-hat, a whole orchestrion composed of various book-machines (what is actually meant by library* [Bibliothek], *as an analogy to the discotheque). Faust-machines, Faust-machinettes (books lacerating machines)... and a shredding-machine.*[41]

F.M. Einheit, a member of the band, declares concerning the work: "I do not believe it to be useful to make music to illustrate the action on stage"[42]. Moreover, he reproaches directors with this intention to illustrate the writing of the playwright: "the language is sufficient to itself. We need to banish all theatrical effects, reflection on theatre also, because what we need is only language, and not much more"[43].

### *Conclusion*

To translate Werner Schwab, we will have to stand resolutely in a position of *com*position and, like the author, in our turn to "transform the language [...] into a battle field"[44], to read "aloud", to mix sounds and noises, signifier and signified. Thus we will be able "to enter into the rhythm", as the director of the Schauspielhaus in Vienna, Hans Gratzer[45], advises us to, and to avoid the temptation of transcription of isolated motifs, which would overshadow the integrity of the speech, as well as that of clarification and standardization of the text, which would prevent the translation - as a new text-to find (if not to engrave) its place into the French-speaking linguistic and cultural sphere.

---

Bibliographie

Artaud (Antonin), *Le Théâtre et son double*, followed by *Le Théâtre de Séraphin*, Paris: Gallimard, coll. Idées, 1964.

Baudelaire (Charles), *Tableaux parisiens*, translated by Benjamin (Walter), Weisbach: Heidelberg, 1923.

Benjamin (Walter), "Die Aufgabe des Übersetzers", forword to

Berman (Antoine), *L'Épreuve de l'étranger*, Paris: Gallimard, 1984.

Deleuze (Gilles) & Guattari (Félix), "Qu'est-ce qu'une littérature mineure?", in Deleuze (Gilles) & Guattari (Félix), *Kafka. Pour une littérature mineure*, Paris: Minuit, 1975.

Derrida (Jacques), *Le toucher. Jean-Luc Nancy*, Paris: Galilée, 2000.

Die Einstürzende Neubauten, *Faustmusik*, Musik für "Faust:: Mein Brustkorb: Mein Helm" von Werner Schwab, Mute, 1996.

Fuchs (Gerhard) & Pechmann (Paul), ed., *Werner Schwab*, Graz: Droschl, Dossier, Band 16, 2000.

Gagnepain (Jean), *Du vouloir dire. Traité d'épistémologie des sciences humaines*, vol. I & II, Paris/Bruxelles: Deboeck, 1993.

Heidegger (Martin), *Holzwege*, Frankfurt a. M.: Klostermann, 1963.

Hulst (Lieven d'), Herman (Jan) & Tack (Lieven), "Les *Pierrot lunaire* d'Albert Giraud, O. E. Hartleben et Arnold Schönberg : pour une analyse des transferts interculturels et intersémiotiques", in *Neophilologus*, LXXXIII, 3, 1999, pp. 333-347.

Krause (Günter), ed., *Literalität und Körperlichkeit / Littéralité et corporalité*, Tübingen: Stauffenburg, 1997.

Ladmiral (Jean-René), *Traduire : théorèmes pour la traduction*, Paris: Gallimard, 1994.

Molino (Jean), "Fondement symbolique de l'expérience esthétique et analyse comparée : musique, poésie, peinture", in *Analyse musicale*, 3rd quarter 1986.

Quine (W. V. O.), "Ontological relativity", in *The Journal of Philosophy*, LXV, 7, April 4, 1968, p. 46.

**Véronique Rat-Morris**


Rat-Morris (Véronique), directed by Werner Wögerbauer, *Pierrot lunaire. Giraud - Hartleben - Schönberg. Éléments d'analyse d'un transfert interculturel et intersémiotique,* master's thesis in Germanistic - Language, Culture and Civilization, Université de Nantes, 2001.

Schwab (Werner), *Dramen III [Troiluswahn und Cressidatheater; Faust:: Mein Brustkorb: Mein Helm; Pornogeographie; Eskalation ordinär; Anticlima$_x$],* Graz: Droschl, 1994. French translations: Schwab (Werner), *La Ravissante ronde, d'après La Ronde du ravissant Monsieur Arthur Schnitzler; Enfin mort enfin plus de souffle; Anticlima$_x$,* translated by Sens (Mike)& Bugdahn (Michael), Paris: L'Arche, 2000 ; Schwab (Werner), *Escalade ordinaire; Extermination du peuple, translated by Sens (Mike) & Bugdahn (Michael), Paris: L'Arche, 1998.*

*Schwab (Werner), Fäkaliendramen [Die Präsidentinnen; Übergewicht, unwichtig: Unform; Volksvernichtung; Mein Hundemund*], Graz: Droschl, 1991. French translations: Schwab (Werner), *Les Présidentes,* translated by Sens (Mike) & Bugdahn (Michael), in *Alternatives théâtrales,* n° 49, 1995, pp. 51-65 ; Schwab (Werner), Les Présidentes ; *Excédent de poids, insignifiant, amorphe,* translated by Sens (Mike) & Bugdahn (Michael), Paris : L'Arche, 1997. English translations : Schwab (Werner), *An Anthology of Plays [First Ladies; OVERWEIGHT unimportant: MISSHAPE ; The Round of Pleasure after The Round Dance from the Pen of the Pleasant Mr. Arthur Schnitzler],* translated by Michael Mitchell, Riverside: Ariadne, 2000.

Sens (Mike), ed., in collaboration with Bugdahn (Michael) & Stern (Danièle), "Werner Schwab", dossier, followed by the full text of Schwab (Werner), *Les Présidentes,* translated by Sens (Mike) & Bugdahn (Michael), in *Alternatives théâtrales,* 49, 1995, pp. 2-65.

Tack (Lieven), "Pour une construction théorique de la traduction (De l'appropriation du dire, du relativisme anthropologique et du référent traductionnel)", in Guibert (Clément de), ed., *Médiations culturelles. Actes du 5e Colloque d'Anthropologie Clinique* (suite et fin), special issue of *Tétralogiques,* 14, January 2002.

Notes

1. "Es gibt viele Möglichkeiten, ein Buch zu zerstören. Man kann es in hohem Bogen durch die Luft werfen, von einer kleinen Umblättermaschine langsam zerfetzen lassen, mit einer Säge zerteilen, Packenweise in einen riesigen Shredder stecken- oder es nachdichten." (Wille (Franz), "Goethe tot, Operation gelungen", in *Frankfurter Allgemeine Zeitung,* 1.11.1994, quoted in Fuchs (Gerhard) & Pechmann (Paul), 2000, p. 227).
2. "Je crois qu'il est impossible de traduire Schwab." Quoted in Sens (Mike), "L'Autriche n'est pas seulement le pays de Mozart...", interview with Marc Günther, in Sens (Mike), 1995, p. 12. Quotations in the next two paragraphs are excerpt from this article.
3. Werner Schwab calls "Cover-Drama" his three plays adapted from classics: *Troiluswahn und Cressidatheater,* a revival of *Troilus and Cressida* by William Shakespeare; *Faust: Mein Brustkorb:: Mein Helm,* a remake of Johann Wolfgang Goethe's *Faust* and *Der reizende Reigen nach dem Reigen des reizenden Herrn Arthur Schnitzler,* after Arthur Schnitzler's *Reigen.*
4. "Troïlus's madness and Cressida's theatre". This play does not seem to have been translated into English yet. See Schwab (Werner), *Troiluswahn und Cressidatheater,* in Schwab (Werner), 1994, pp. 7-74. It was first staged at the Schauspielhaus in Graz, Austria, on March 25, 1995.
5. *First Ladies,* in Schwab (Werner), 2000. Also translated as *The Presidents* or *Holy Mothers.* See Schwab (Werner), *Die Präsidentinnen,* in Schwab (Werner), 1991, pp. 9-58.
6. *OVERWEIGHT unimportant: MISSHAPE,* in Schwab (Werner), 2000. See also Schwab (Werner), *Übergewicht, unwichtig: Unform,* in Schwab (Werner), 1991, pp. 59-120.
7. Both plays, along with extracts from *Volksvernichtung* (translated into French by Henri Christophe), were first staged by Michel Dezoteux on February 6,1995, at the Théâtre Varia in Bruxelles.
8. "Peut-être peut-on le réécrire, en faisant œuvre de poète."
9. "[...], une traduction littérale, d'une double longueur, de l'allemand de Schwab en allemand standard."
10. The term of "survival" is used as an echo to Walter Benjamin's "*Nachleben*" (cf. Benjamin (Walter), 1923).

11. "[...], le sens jaillit aussitôt."; "Il faut d'abord comprendre cet univers avant de pouvoir l'interpréter. "; "Objectivement, une bonne connaissance de son œuvre est indispensable."; "[...], on comprend [...], ce qui se trouve sous le texte."; "[...], on ne peut pas non plus expliquer spontanément le sens d'un poème de Verlaine sans le ramener à l'imaginaire de l'auteur."
12. "Chez lui, les personnages sont faits de matière linguistique, [...]."Quoted in Sens (Mike), "Si je te coupe la carotide, t'es mort...", interview with Michel Dezoteux, in Sens (Mike), 1995, p. 48. Michel Dezoteux actually quotes a declaration from Werner Schwab himself : "These are not characters, but semantic fragments." ("*Das sind keine Personen, sondern semantische Broken.*"), quoted in Schödel (Helmut), "Geisterfahrer", in *Die Zeit*, Hamburg, 31.1.1992, quoted in Landa (Jutta), "Schwabrede = Redekörper", in Fuchs (Gerhard) & Pechmann (Paul), 2000, p. 40). Moreover, Werner Schwab introduces almost systematically the "language" ("*Sprache*") along with the characters at the beginning of his plays.
13. "Graz est une ville singulière. [...] qui se trouve à la bordure sud-est du territoire linguistique allemand. [...] La Styrie a une tendance anti-viennoise très forte. Cette région est très fermée [...]. Cette notion d'exclusion est accentuée par une tradition fasciste profondément enracinée, qui vient du temps où la Styrie servait pour ainsi dire de forêt de protection à la frontière linguistique de l'empire allemand, auquel elle appartenait, [...]." Cf. Sens (Mike), 1995, p. 11. F. M. Einheit, one of the members of Einstürzende Neubauten, also draws our attention to the following point concerning Werner Schwab: "His language was very built up. To understand it, you have to consider his relation to Austria, in particular his youth in Graz, a small conservative and Catholic city. He analyzed the German spoken by the civil servants (*Beamtendeutsch*) in this area and ended up finding his own style." Quoted in Sens (Mike), "Il faut développer l'insolence", interview with F. M. Einheit, in Sens (Mike), 1995, p. 16.
14. This expression invented by Gilles Deleuze and Félix Guattari stands for the absurd emanation of the bureaucratic language in use among the German-speaking civil servants: "the German population [... ] speaks a language cut off from the masses, like a "paper language" or an artificial language" ("la

population allemande [...] parle une langue coupée des masses, comme un "langage de papier" ou d'artifice"). Cf. Deleuze (Gilles) & Guattari (Félix), 1975.

15. Again we borrow this vocabulary from Gilles Deleuze and Félix Guattari (cf. Deleuze (Gilles) & Guattari (Félix), 1975). The concept of "minority" is associated by these authors with "deterritorialization". Werner Schwab thus chooses to free himself from his daily language-which is alienated by isolation and particularization-by singularizing it in the extreme. This will allow the author-scout to venture into foreign linguistic territory.
16. "Pour les Belges, le français est une langue apprise, même s'ils sont francophones d'origine. On n'a pas un rapport "satisfait" à la langue."
17. "Traduire, c'est naviguer entre deux mondes. Tous ceux qui ont découvert celui de Werner Schwab vous confirmeront que sa principale particularité est la langue qu'on y parle. Aussi étrange que fascinante, elle est la matière même dont cet univers est fait." Cf. Bugdahn (Michael), "Le continent Schwab", in Sens (Mike), 1995, p. 27.
18. "Jusqu'où peut-on aller dans la déformation de la langue d'arrivée (en l'occurrence le français) pour rester fidèle à Schwab?"
19. In a remarkable manner, the same pejorative approach of Werner Schwab's use of language is to be found, coupled with the phantasm of a "secret code" giving access to a signified hidden "under the text", by Jutta Landa: "Schwab's linguistic operations constitute deliberated infringements of grammatical syntactic and lexical nature, which let proliferate the language in an unhealthy way, like a tumor. The result is a coded language, which is, in particular when reading, not easily decipherable." ("Bei den Sprachoperationen Schwabs handelt es sich um gezielte Verstöße grammatischer, syntaktischer und lexi[k]alischer [!] Natur, die die Sprache ungesund wuchern lassen wie eine Tumor. Das Ergebnis ist eine kodierte Sprache, die vor allem beim Lesen mühsam dechiffriert werden muß.") Quoted in Krause (Günter), "'Wir sind in die Welt gevögelt und können nicht fliegen'. Sprache als theatralischer Körper bei Werner Schwab", in Krause (Günter), 1997.).

20. "[...] l'allemand, surtout l'allemand écrit, se prête parfaitement à des structures syntaxiques très complexes."; "[...] en allemand, on a le choix entre quatre verbes différents pour rendre la notion de 'devoir'."
21. "[...] nous, les francophones, avons un rapport culturel à notre langue, de l'ordre de l'abstraction. C'est une langue qui évolue très peu, qui est un peu figée, qui autorise peu les agglomérats de sons et de mots, qui accepte mal les accents. C'est un peu comme s'il n'y avait qu'une seule façon de parler le français." Op. cit., p. 48. We feel here the influence of Antonin Artaud, although Antonin Artaud does not tackle the "satisfied" entrenchment into French language in particular but the *cultivated* language in general: "the fixing of theatre in a language: written words, music, lights, noises, points to its loss in the near future, the choice of a language proving the taste we have for the fluency of this language; and the drying-out of the language arises from its limitation" ("et la fixation du théâtre dans un langage : paroles écrites, musique, lumières, bruits, indique à bref délai sa perte, le choix d'un langage prouvant le goût que l'on a pour les facilités de ce langage ; et le dessèchement du langage accompagne sa limitation"). Cf. Artaud (Antonin), "Le Théâtre et la culture", forword to Artaud (Antonin), 1964, pp. 18-19.
22. Quine (W. V. O.), 1968, p. 46.
23. Cf. Hulst (Lieven d'), Herman (Jan) & Tack (Lieven), 1999, pp. 333-347. These three authors invite us to be particularly sensitive to the complexity of the "*co(n)*text of emergence" of a work, which implies a true *com*position, which is infinitely more delicate than a mere *trans*fer.
24. The Greek term ποίησις used by Jean Molino, means creation, composition and more generally, of course, poetic activity (cf. Molino (Jean), 1986).
25. Antoine Berman uses this out-of-date adjective refering to the relations maintained to servants, or more exactly to maidservants (Latin *ancilla*), to illustrate, probably not without humour, our relation to translation (cf. Berman (Antoine), 1984). It is remarkable that the vocabulary of illicit love serves so readily to define translation: think only of the classical "*belles infidèles*" (beautiful infidels)!
26. As Derrida points it out, the "lieu-tenant" is actually the one who takes the place of another. Cf. Derrida (Jacques), 2000.

27. "neue Zunge: neues Leben: neues Leiden" (Schwab (Werner), 1994, p. 89).
28. "Une œuvre est une réalité complexe qui constitue un fait social total."
29. "The model invites us to think negatively, within the theoretical construction of translation, the mirage of a full, substantial communication, identical or "equivalent" to itself, in order to substitute to it a complex modeling the dialectics between differentiation and constituted identity, which determines on both sides the relation to translation." ("Le modèle invite à dépositiver, dans la construction théorique de la traduction, le mirage d'une communication pleine, substantielle, identique ou "équivalente" à elle-même, pour y substituer une modélisation complexe de la dialectique entre différenciation et constitution identitaire, qui détermine de part et d'autre la relation traductive.") Cf. Tack (Lieven), 2002. The "theory of mediation" is exposed in Gagnepain (Jean), 1993.
30. "[...] nous ne faisons [...] que retrouver toujours notre propre langue." Lieven Tack also quotes Laugier : "Translation remains internal, immanent to our language. It is a language game within the language which we learned, and there is no more exile out of the conceptual design than there is an angelic point of view." ("La traduction demeure interne, immanente à notre langue. Elle est un jeu de langage à l'intérieur de la langue que nous avons apprise, et il n'y a pas plus d'exil hors du schème conceptuel qu'il n'existe de point de vue angélique.").
31. "keiner Meldung von außen wird der Schlüssel dann entwendet mehr / die Lust wird kochen in der eignen fremden Sprache / und die Eigenfremdheit wird mein eignes fremdes Eigen sein" (Schwab (Werner), 1994, p. 88).
32. "L'enjeu de la problématique ne consiste pas à choisir pour une option plutôt que pour l'autre, pour la traduction comme équivalence plutôt que comme transformation, mais de passer d'une définition bipolaire (traduction = transgression de frontière) à une définition articulant la traduction à ce qui nous condamne constamment à l'instaurer. Renversement donc d'une conception dualiste des choses à une vision dialectique." Cf Tack (Lieven), 2002.

33. These terms are those of Jean-René Ladmiral (cf. Ladmiral (Jean-René), 1994).
34. "[...] je peux m'imaginer que Schwab traversait la forêt en se parlant à lui-même, comme ça, et qu'il a développé ainsi un langage spécifique."Quoted in Sens (Mike), "Un théâtre qui veut sortir du théâtre", interview with Theu Boermans, in Sens (Mike), 1995, p. 29. One also finds the image of the *forest* in the mouth of Werner Schwab's Faust: "und die verirren sich jetzt rücksichtlos geschichterlich in einem imaginären Wald" ("and they now go regardless historishly astray in an imaginary forest", Schwab (Werner), 1994, p. 78).
35. The name given to traditional French translations, which are very elegant, in conformity with the taste (and morals) of the time, but very "fickle" in their relationship to the original. One of most famous is that of the *Thousand and One Nights* by Antoine Galland, published in 1704.
36. Cf. Heidegger (Martin), 1963. Jean Gagnepain's understanding of language also evokes the metaphor of the "language's forest": like we may consider that the generic concept of forest is empty (there is nothing but a more or less dense concentration of varied species), Jean Gagnepain indicates that "language does not exist, there exist only more or less important sets of divergences and convergences", like clusters ("la langue n'existe pas, il n'existe que des ensembles plus ou moins importants de divergences et de convergences"). Quoted in Tack (Lieven), 2002.
37. Artaud (Antonin), 1964, p. 19.
38."à l'intérieur de l'écriture". Quoted in Sens (Mike), "Schwab à Vienne", interview with Hans Gratzer and Helmut Schödel, in Sens (Mike), 1995, p. 13. Helmut Schödel is the speaker quoted here.
39. "Faust: My Breastbone: My Helmet"-this play does not seem to have been translated into English yet.
40. "Wir wollten eine bürokratische Musik spielen, eine Musik die nur aus Tischen und Büchern besteht. Eine hölzerne Musik, Bibliotheksmusik. Büchertrommeln, ausgehöhlte Bücher, Klopfzeichen, Folianten. Tische, manipulierte Tische, verschiedene mit Saiten oder Drähten bespannte Tische, ausgesägte Tische, Kalimbatische, das Rücken von Tischen. Buchmaschinen, Umblättermaschinen, eine motorisierte Bücher-Hi-Hat, ein ganzes aus verschiedenen Buchmaschinen

zusammengesetztes Orchestrion (was eigentlich, analog zur Diskothek, eine Bibliothek bedeutet). Faustmaschinen, Faustmaschinchen (Bücherzerreiss-maschinen)... und eine Shredderanlage." (Die Einstürzende Neubauten, 1996). The play was created on October 29, 1994, at the Hans Otto Theater in Potsdam, Germany.

41. "Je ne crois pas qu'il soit utile de faire de la musique pour illustrer l'action sur scène." Quoted in Sens (Mike), "Il faut développer l'insolence", interview with F. M. Einheit, in Sens (Mike), 1995, p. 15.
42. "[...] la langue se suffit à elle-même. Il faut bannir toutes les astuces théâtrales, la réflexion sur le théâtre aussi, car ce qu'il fat, c'est uniquement la langue, et pas beaucoup plus."
43. "[...] transforme la langue [...] en champ de bataille." Kleijn (Tom), "Je chie donc je suis. La langue de Werner Schwab", in Sens (Mike), 1995, p. 25.
44. "entrer dans le rythme". Sens (Mike), 1995, p. 13.

# The Prisoners Cannot See The Walls

by Robert Lort

The post-capitalist regime operates indirectly rather than directly, subjectively as opposed to objectively and internally rather than externally. The system functions at the internal level of desire, in order to generate desire for repression, and consequential complicity and concurrence to the system.

Because the post-capitalist system is established in conflict and opposed to the regimes of communism, despotism and royalism the systems of control must also differ. The authority must, above all be desired by its subjects. Totalitarian and despotic control, with its mechanism of direct and objective control are what are opposed even by the capitalist. Because post-capitalism superseded and opposes these previous regimes, the capitalist control machine must therefore differentiate itself, and find a new mechanism, a new part, more devious, discreet, elusive and more hidden than even simple mind/information control, and of course just as effective. Indirect and subjective control is, for post-capitalism far more effective. Overall this is what the system is continually heading towards, despite the present need to still regularly retract into its old moulds.

It is seen that one of the principle mechanisms of capitalism operates by alienating and thus neutralising the dissenters, by continually unifying and channelling collective desire onto non-diversified forms of consumption and engagement. This means continually modifying and homogenising the subjects desire towards collective centres, thus excluding the marginal and dissenting. This is an effect which is fundamental to profit motive; saturation and monopolisation of the non-diversified; the model, the sign, mainstream TV. The ill-conforming is always adjusted by a counter saturation wave of the non-diversified.

"There is no wall, therefore I am no prisoner". The regime operates so much more smoothly when "the prisoners cannot see the walls". It is all together so much more effective, the masses then foolishly perceive themselves as free. When the prison walls become the subjects very own, they also become invisible to them. Indeed the system is always manufacturing a certain facade of freedom, mediated most of all through advertising, but because the prisoners of society cannot see the "walls", they conclude they are not imprisoned, and it is through exactly this deception that the system operates. Their best form of control is indirect, since most will not even suspect they're being controlled. We become prisoners of debt, prisoners of our image, prisoners of our desires, and not prisoners of chains. Noam Chomsky has so effectively demonstrated the censorship operating in the American media and doubtless others. But what Chomsky shows is that media censorship in America operates not objectively and directly, but is instead abstract and unseeable. The censorship that he describes operates not by censorship laws, its operation is instead invisible and indirect. And maintains the fallacy of "there are no censorship laws, so there is no censorship". The capitalist censorship machine is markedly different to and supersedes the old state-communist censorship machine.

The post-capitalist mechanisms of discipline, regulation and control operate by methods of discretion and by means of internalization and subjectification; rather than those of indiscretion and externalisation, with all their public spectacles of corporeal beatings and perpetual torture. The wounds inflicted have instead become invisible. Internalization instead makes use of the bodies potential utility. The collective mass of non-workers, vagabonds, thieves, madmen, prostitutes, and so forth all pose a threat to the security and stability of the system as a whole. As demonstrated by Michel Foucault in *Discipline and Punish*, from as early as the seventeenth century onwards outsiders were increasingly assimilated and absorbed into the expanding systems of capitalism, thus neutralising their inherent collective threat. With the impossibility of correcting every deviation by punishment, the solution increasingly became one of no longer subjecting the outsider to perpetual and unending floggings and beatings, but to progressively incorporate such individuals into the expanding socius, not only appropriating their utility, but ensuring that any outside continually diminished to a controllable level. Not only was this nourishing the systems urgent need for consumers and maximising consumptive demand, but it enabled the system to absorb every possible individual, every possible micro-uprising. The importance here is for the system to directly control the number of outsiders. What is apparent is that it is still necessary for the system to maintain a small number of outsiders to alone justify the regimes of discipline and control. Hence the prison system must just as much produce criminality as it must mitigate it, in order to perpetuate its cycle of authority. The unemployed could similarly be compared to the position of prisoners. The state that just as much produces unemployment as it eradicates it, (providing the quantity of unemployed are contained and regulated) it continues to maintain a job market that is favourable to capitalism; ie where there are no pressures to provide higher wages or improved working conditions in order to attract applicants. Similarly the psychoanalyst must just as much produce madness as cure it, in order to prolong the fee paying relationship between the patient and the psychoanalyst.

The system always operates by widening its margins and consuming the unregulated into its universal and totalising regime of economics and profiteering. This widening of the margins, is paradoxically both progressive and regressive or in Deleuzian/Guattarian terms "what they deterritorialize with one hand, they reterritorialize with the other"[1]. The deterritorializations are progressive since elements such as 60's rock, punk, heterosexual and homosexual liberation and unconventional or radical art, feminism, literature and film making have been progressively accepted, incorporated and made available to the masses. But attached to these movements has been an associated reterritorialization such that the above elements are subjugated onto the regimes universal and totalising surface of economics and profiteering. Thus experimental film makers must conform to profit motive and compete against the massive promotional, screening and advertising resources of Hollywood, sexuality consequently becomes grossly commodified, stereotyped and homogenised, punk becomes the model instead of the anti-model, the anti-logo becomes a logo itself.

How to interpret Deleuze/Guattari's terminology, what is deterritorialization? One can say that deterritorialization is a movement of increasing abstraction, it is any movement, engagement or line that is disorganising, disassembling and disarranging. Deterritorialization is a degrounding, a flight transformation, a manoeuvre that has as its result indistinct, blurred and scattered forms. Deterritorialization is always unforming, it is always dismantling the origins and heading out on a line of flight, towards the outside. It is any action which dislodges a territory, and places it amongst new connections, and configurations. And on the other hand, its opposite, reterritorialization is a movement of decreasing abstraction. Reterritorialization always fixes, regulates movement and sequences time. Reterritorialization is always associated with movements of hierarchization, organisation and centralisation. Lines or actions of reterritorialization are always invariant and always rigidifying.

These two kinds of movements become the new vectors of political analysis. We should always consider these two movements (reterritorialization and deterritorialization) and their many reciprocal characteristics; reterritorialization reduces towards the singular, while its opposite proliferates into multiplicities; reterritorialization erects blockages to flows, while the other gushes and augments the flows; reterritorialization assembles majoritarian thought, the other assembles minoritarian thought. Movements of deterritorialization will always be considered preferable, in the revolutionary sense, to those movements that reterritorialize, recoagulate and totalise the distributions. You will have assuredly noticed the multiple senses that exist for these two terms. The words themselves effect their own high degree of deterritorialization, as they encompass not only a multitude of forms and meanings, but also a significant degree of abstraction. They are difficult terms to capture, elusive because they are always disappearing off the page? And still this is exactly their nature. They are deterritorialized, the terms themselves are always avoiding being reduced and determined. But in any case we still don't know how they work and what they act on.

Deleuze's analysis of economic flows reveals instead the fluidity of economic exchange rather than its concreteness. We see that flows of monetary exchange exist on a plane significantly removed from material or objective values. Thus the flows (money, commodities, property, labour) become deterritorialized with their dispersal as interest, insurance, stocks, exchange rates, shares, taxation, inflation and advertising.

The larger the amount the greater is its deterritorializing tendencies. We are already quite familiar with deterritorializing commodities, and the extent that a brand name deterritorializes the value of a pair of joggers into something far greater than its use value. (This is what Jean Baudrillard has called the forming of sign value, and its effect of dematerialising the commodity. The commodities use value becomes subordinated to abstract determinations made up of signs and images). The effect of technologies and automation deterritorialize the capitalist system and relinquish the systems absolute dependence on workers, but this deterritorialization is always subsequently reterritorialized, by ensuring the reabsorption of the workers into expanding fields of anti-production (bureaucracy, education, advertising, sales, police and state militarism), which maintain, absorb and regulate the systems modes of overabundance and overload, and always act to repress the subjects desire by focusing it towards activities that enable profits. Labour power becomes deterritorialized through a need to continually extend its value beyond simple subsistence and maintenance of workers needs, it adjoins a requirement to continually saturate the mechanisms of consumption and the circulation of wealth. Too ask for its augmentation is to ask for exactly what the systems demands. The entire legal and justice system is deterritorialized by a flow of money that underlies its every minute. Foreign debt is calculated in real time as it spirals into unfathomable (infinite) immensity, exchange rates exist in states of incessant fluctuation, tariffs and subsidies threaten to send global economic exchange in directions that tend more and more towards absurdity and towards seemingly infeasible directions. The frequent calls for economic rationalism are then not at all surprising. This is the inherent irony of capitalism, merged in its two tendances or its two hands; on one hand an incessant tendency towards abstraction and deterritorialization, and on the other hand the development of universal abstracts, the dollar equivalent being one of the most dominant, that act to then recentre and reterritorialize all the flows - performing a reduction and contraction of all the flows back onto the universal abstract. Economic exchange then is not about circulation, but about a tendency towards spinning off into dizziness, that is continually reterritorialized. This irony is also to our advantage, it offers the opportunity to accelerate the mechanisms of capitalism into their own collapse, to accelerate deterritorializing mechanisms.

The mechanisms of deterritorialization are directed towards depositionings of three main forms: signifiance (grammaticality and the regime of signs), subjectivity (the self, memory and consciousness), and organs (the body and face). The deterritorialization of signifiance makes language flow in the sense described by Antonin Artaud, it engenders the shattering of that territory belonging to grammar. The cut up techniques and the junky-slang used in novels by William Burroughs do just as similar. They form a language of discord, that stutters and shouts out, that wails, whispers and laughs. It is children who lose their scribbling-machines (paints, crayons, feltpens) to the reterritorializations that come from dictionaries and the rules of grammar. And still, we are not objecting to "words" per se. What is required is to make words function like scribbles, to make them disappear/fly off of the page if they so desire. To deterritorialize words out of fixed definitions, to form fluxes and continuums of meaning. To form traces and intensities which stretch language to its limits, engendering a final collapse of grammar and structurizations. With the deterritorialization of subjectivity the territories of the self are dividuated (as contrasted with individuated), the schizo is produced, shattering any fixed territorial conception of identity. The deterritorialization of the body entails the dislocating of the senses, organs and desires, as we will see it produces the Body without Organs.

Let's consider another of the falsehoods, "Sexuality is no longer forbidden, therefore there is no sexual repression", initially postulated in the theory of Michel Foucault. While sexuality may dominate magazine literature, the internet and the video library, has this meant its liberation? We can see that sexuality has certainly been transformed and displaced from its previous mould(s). What can be said is that sexuality has attained a relative liberation, fused with an accompanying commodification, but it is a condition whereby, this progressiveness has however still been accompanied by a simultaneous regression. The solution however is not to return; ie to decommodify sexuality, and to similarly re-aesthetize the libidinal divergences of the sixties. The solution is to give to sexuality a degree of deterritorialization greater than the degree attached to the commodity. For sexuality to surpass the rudimentary thresholds established by the capitalist system of commodification. The important consequence is that the commodity will no longer be capable of reterritorializing sexuality, of re-confining its movement, by finding a unitarizing model with which to entrap it all again. The critical component of this deterritorializing sexuality is it's aspect of multiplicity. It eschews any re-containment into aesthetics and commodities, which are so dependent on establishing singular ideals and models.

Sexual liberation was fine so long as it was accompanied by a simultaneous reterritorialization onto the fetishized product. So long as it produced a marketing scheme of advertising which attracted everyone and enabled profits previously denied and unattainable to the system. As long as any shift still maintained the channelling of desires within a well bounded grid of capitalist consumption; it was safe so long as the escapes were always absorbed and pulled back onto a specularized ideal and model. The whole shift withdrew itself form one territory and replanted itself into another. All the scattered pieces seemed to be so quickly re-absorbed and reterritorialized into the discourse of cosmetics, health, fashion, dieting and advertising industries.

By enabling the channelling and orienting of sexuality into alignment with capital and therefore inside the systems accepted thresholds and bounds, the system continues to maintain control over its productions and effects. The system will continually fend off any escapes by individuals outside these boundaries, but because the system is continually forced to maintain the number of outsiders to a controllable minimum, it arises that the boundaries inevitably have to be widened, to reintegrate and subordinate the outsiders into the systematic regime. Ideally for the authorities, every individuals sexuality must be contained and absorbed within these bounds and no activity or engagement must lie outside the reach of capital, any such flow or activity outside the limits, jeopardises the stability of the system as a whole. The underlying motive becomes, always and fundamentally that of profit, every individuals sexuality must enable profits, and must effect a certain utility, the production of heterosexual consumption. The radical are continually reabsorbed into the regimes of subjugation through each widening of the bounds. The entire system breeds by producing a sexual alienation, that exists both culturally, and in juxtaposition to the fetishized ideal.

Capitalist processes of subjectification and signifiance, and the conditionings relating to the organism all act in a territorialization of sexuality, each thoroughly intertwined in the other. Analysis should always avoid simple reductions to one or two of the three, the problem still remains triplicate. I would suggest that one can certainly envision a situation of processes of social subjectification and signifiance funnelling and mutating the desires relating to the organism, so that the outcome produced a sexuality almost entirely engendered and determined in alignment with capitalist objectives. But if we resolve to redetermine and reconfine sexuality around new equilibriums, then we risk reestablishing new centres which still eschew activating and freeing the vast multiplicities. In consequence we will still be territorializing and trammelling desire. Whenever we oppose a desirable against an undesirable, a correct against an incorrect, we will be blocking and regulating the multiplicities. We will have been heading in the wrong direction, we will have bypassed engaging with the multiplicities, and returned to movements of reterritorialization which seek to reduce, contract and unitarize the multiplical flows of libidinal desire. The multiplical (or molecular) sexuality will always be found in the other direction, that is a pluralist decentring direction. The direction of deterritorialization is a taste for continuous expansion and augmentation of new and unformed segments. A taste for multiplicity and the proliferation of attachments, of enabling new forms rather than truncating and regularising forms. It is the activation and development of sexual alterity (otherness), modes of becoming and new modes of sexual engagement. The result produces and engages with a planar expanse, a multiplicity. What previously fettered our movements and engagements (subjectification, signifiance, organismal desire), may still coexist within this multiplicity, but the point is that they will no longer totalise it. Attempts to crush these constructed desires will only lead to a death instinct. All that is needed to do is to overstep the limits of the capitalist sexuality, to encounter an unbounded space. But above all we must not relocate the limits, we must not reintroduce mechanisms which block and disallow flows. Deterritorialization will always carry us off in the direction of addition and never that of subtraction. Movements of divergence, rather than contracting and reducing, are lines of flight, actions which append further connections, always multiplying, proliferating, expanding and assembling.

The image as it functions in society and in its many forms as commodity, as cinema, and as advertisement, must also be looked at in terms of processes of deterritorialization and reterritorialization. What is the effect of these deterritorializing images? They are deterritorialized in the sense that they are displaced from collective and real actualities, but also and simultaneously reterritorialized in the sense that the images effect a reconfiguring and reformatting of the body into a mask of specularized, commodified and fetishized signs. But from where we are at, it is not the images displacement from cultural reality that is at fault, what is really at fault is its resistance to multiplicity. The superiority contained in a perfected and unblemished image, crumbles the moment we no longer use a single code of evaluation. The problem is never the images unreality and artificiality, the fault exists entirely in its singularity, whereby it enforces an exclusive and limiting code that establishes a single ideal and all pervasive model onto which everything is forced to conform, and is likewise subordinated to. The image should not be forcibly reduced back onto so called realism and social reality. We will not ask that it be truncated and reterritorialized onto a constrained reflection of reality, and materialism. In truth, we are already too sick of the real! We might ask, since when did real and unreal exist, just as we might ask, since when did conscious and subconscious exist? For we refuse to conceive these forms as ontologically disparate, as pre-existing true and false dichotomies. The unreal is real, and conscious is subconscious. The answer is that the image simply isn't deterritorialized enough! That is, to the extent that it might develop an immense plurality of desires, that override the reterritorializations that occur either from movements onto the collective real, or from movements onto a singular commodified aesthetic.

Capitalism no longer makes use of any despotic figure-head. Every individual is subjected to and absorbed into the systems totalising regime, without exception. The proletariat is as much "capitalist", as any so called capitalist is proletariat.

There can be no great division between those who are oppressed and those who are the oppressors, everyone is repressed and everyone is repressing.

Power is no longer installed in large concentrated aggregates separated from those who are controlled, but is instead increasing installed in micro-aggregates, installed and embodied within the very individuals that are controlled. This is why even those most exploited in our society have wholeheartedly embraced and desired their greater immersion in it. Hitler, mainstream TV and police, are all things that even the most exploited have desired and sought to maintain. The question is; how could this desire for our own repression have come about? This repression of desire is it's oedipalization, it arises from the micro-powers, which operate, in Michel Foucault's words, "not by law but by normalization, not by punishment but by control, methods that are employed on all levels and in forms that go beyond the state and its apparatus"[2].

A concept used by Deleuze and Guattari stems from Franz Kafka's description of the execution-machine which appears In *The Penal Colony*. From this description of an apparatus which cruelly and somewhat eccentrically executes its victim by inscribing, a tattooed text onto the victim's body, Deleuze and Guattari develop a metaphor which interprets the bodies corporeality as a surface which is inscribed and written on with various texts and signifiers as a form of social control and conditioning of the subject. The apparatus described by Kafka, accentuates the way the socius's signs and codes penetrate, and insert themselves into the body, manipulating its surface, into a skin-mask, a writing surface for representing signs, advertisements, uniforms, alliances. This process of inscription is interpreted as a form of internalization, a process of moulding and transforming the desire of the subject into compliance with the objectives of authority. The oedipalization of the subject, involves the development within the subject of those desires that form the subject productive to authority, and at the same time the trammelling and blocking of those desires that move in counter directions to the authority. Oedipalization is a process which brings about a territorialization of the individuals subjectivity; the offshoots and flows of divergent subjectivities, are continually truncated, cut off and blocked, to render an undifferentiated subjectivity; a subjectivity of reactive-desire and one-dimensionality. Throughout childhood the process of inscription is intensified such that the body is continuously inscribed, by selectively amplifying and stimulating those flows and engagements that enable the subject as useful for labour and brutally suppressing and crushing those flows and engagements that are not amendable, pliable or conductive to the needs of the authority. The subjects desire and knowledge is continually shaped through the various social constructs: the school, the factory, the army, the church, the family, the prison, the psychiatric institution and the television. The body struggles against the successive inscriptions and powers of the social authority, but after the process has been prolonged, to the extent that the body has become wholly internalised and oedipalized, the subjects psychic repression and reactive desires then come back around to actually reinforce the systems control machines, such that the subject actively participates in oppressing others and themselves. Desire has then been entirely constructed and modelled in total alignment to the needs of the system. The subjects submissiveness then eagerly accepts fascistic and priestly desires, desires to repress and to be repressed, self enforcing the absurd regimes of family, punishment, judgement and bourgeoisie aesthetics of decency and decorum.

Oedipus is the omnipresent limit, delimiting the segregations and binarisms (true/false, debit/credit, father/mother, real/unreal, normal/abnormal, equitable/unequitable, and so forth), that define the bounds of the socius and its centres, and the disavowed departures and divergences from those centres. It is the limit that immures the flows of desire, confining them to fixed centres of subjectivity, always acting to restrict the complete release onto unbounded multiplicities of engagement and being. Oedipus is the universal limit, that wards off the absolute unfettered deterritorialization. "Oedipus is universal... it is universal because it is the displacement of the limit that haunts all societies, the displaced represented that disfigures what all societies dread absolutely as their most profound negative; namely the decoded flows of desire"[3]. Oedipus is then blocking and contaminating desire within all societies. In their work it is important to understand that their use of the word "Oedipus" here is thoroughly in opposition to psychoanalytical interpretations, for them Oedipus is instead the loci of imperialism and power; nor is this an ontologically fixed position, the oedipal limit is not an absolute limit but a displaced limit. Oedipus is the limit that says, "Careful go no further", and it is true that this limit is mobile in comparing different societies and even different historical periods, but the principal remains that it always appears. One might imagine it as a stone circular wall delimiting a forbidden externality, an outer-territory of the unadjusted forms. This wall would then have different shapes for different societies, certain territories would be encouraged in some societies and in others those same territories might be discouraged. Capitalism itself operates by continually warding off the surpassing of this limit, it is always warding off the schizophrenic break, that absolute level of deterritorialization that would smash the wall and open the whole system into vertigo. It is also apparent that capitalism maintains itself by continually altering the shape of this wall, pushing out the limits here, to appropriate new forms and modes and maybe contracting the limits elsewhere, but the confining limits always remain so long as the socius's stability and existence remains.

The universalism of Oedipus does not foreclose the possibility of eschewing it, but any attempt at deoedipalization must not simply succeed in giving rise to new enclosing hierarchizations and new recenterings of power. Deoedipalization is not an undertaking that leads us to uncovering and restoring a latent instinct or primal desire, that is repressed and concealed by modern civilisation. We will not escape Oedipus by returning to pre-internalised and pre-socialised forms of being. "It is not a question of "returning" to the presignifying and presubjective semiotics of primitive peoples"[4]. Any attempt at this only leads us astray. That there are just as many power centres in primitive societies, as there are in modern societies, continually ensures that any return to primitive and so called instinctual desires will only eventuate in shortcomings. Statist forms and power existed long before any military, industrial, or technological revolution, their engendering was certainly not made possible through the advent of these machines. In feminist terms, the domination of women has never been exempted from the codes of repression in any epoch. Overall the conclusion that Deleuze and Guattari reach is that the state has quite simply always existed, found everywhere, even in the most distant reaches of humanity. Primitive societies already manifest the fundamental components of statism; family, religion, militarism, sex binarism, social hierarchies, these are all evident. What remains to be seen is if these disparate power centres coagulate, by locking up together, to form a single axis as in our current manifestation of capitalism. The catalysis for this coagulation of power is of course universalism, whether it be the dollar sign, the totalisation of knowledge, or whatever. The dollar sign reduces all possible values to integrals of the one same economic value. The totalisation of knowledge retracts discourse and therefore alternative forms of knowing and becoming, onto universal truths. This is why multiplicity is inherently opposed to power, because it is always against the aggregating and centring of power.

All revolutionary engagements, to be effective, must confront the full expanse of the crisis, and emerge on paths of deoedipalization. It is the schizo that provides the revolutionary momentum, the non-oedipal desire. "So who is mad; the primitive, the schizophrenic, the capitalist, the child or the old priest?" The schizo roars again with giddy laughter. The converses of the schizo are only too recognisable, they are always saying, "you should think like I, you should make love like I, you should look like I". Quite simply they say "I" too much. The schizo brings forth the most differentiated flows of desire, flows that do not have an "against", that do not become astringed into binarisms of "for" and "against". The schizo body is a planar surface, it is unconfined space, emerging between all the centres and heading out on a line of flight that smashes apart Oedipus. "The schizophrenic deliberately seeks out the very limit of capitalism; he is its inherent tendency brought to fulfilment, its surplus product, its proletariat, and its exterminating angel"[5]. Already, "society is schizophrenizing at the level of its infrastructure, its mode of production, its most precise capitalist economic circuits"[6]. This is also precisely capitalisms imminent collapse, its out bursting of flows of untrammelled deterritorialization, the complete effusion of unconscious desire.

### *The Asylum Machine*

The human machine; a mad parade, a stupefied farce of belief and truth. On every street corner, in every shopping mall, the floating dead reside. The omnipresent phenomena of manequinised flesh; bodies ossified, rigid and ineffectual; their desires plugged up, their orifices blocked, their flows chocked into asphyxiation. Their language remaining codified, regulated and linearised; gross lesions traversing the corporeal surface of every body. The ubiquity of cadaverous bodies, on every freeway, on every mainstream channel; corpses collapsing against walls, estranged objects sunken and moribund. Humanities delight in scarified and tortured flesh, in ritual and the maintenance of absurd mores. The unending expanse of defunct and demented corpses; a silent scream from a mute body exploring its traumatised anonymity; the debilitated paranoiac asserting another truth; to further tyrannise, crush and strangulate desire. The despotic consciousness, ego trapped and insensate is unceasingly manufactured into its complicity to the universal and infinite asylum.

Everywhere it is the one same asylum, the disciplinary asylum exists not only in the psychiatric ward or the prison system, but equally in the factory, the school and the home. Screws over inmates, the teacher over the pupil, the parent over the child, one might even rearrange it as unit A over unit B, and say that the difference (the power of unit B subtracted from the power of unit A) is always the same. In this sense the screw is to the inmate, exactly what the father is to the child.

In the home, the child is immured by the parents "you are my child", the wife is immured by the husband "you are my wife". Here the omnipresent mechanism of subjectification dominates. Trouble arises when the child does not act as a "child", as when it becomes a little monster, or when the wife does not act as a "wife", as when she has a drunken affair with a neighbour. When one smashes Oedipus, one does not only smash the father to the child component, one also smashes the screw to the inmate and the component of boss to the subordinate; the schizo smashes a great deal, because the schizo gets to the very bottom, at the fundamental causes. The schizo smashes the very mentality that erects walls. Whether these walls delimit nations, races, political identities or sexualities. The schizo hits at the very motivations and mentalities that produce these walls. If a repressive power mechanism is collapsed, but the original motivations and mentalities, the collective reasonings and desires that erected it remain, then the same orders and mechanisms will continually return their ugly heads.

If only the material elements of a repressing society are altered, then the pre-existing psychic repressions in that society, will simply reinstate the prior social repressions. Revolutions are inherently revolutions of desire, at the very construction of rationality.

---

Notes

1. Gilles Deleuze and Felix Guattari, *Anti-Oedipus Capitalism and Schizophrenia,* Minneapolis, University of Minnesota Press, 1983, p. 257
2. Michel Foucault, *The History of sexuality Vol 1, An Introduction,,* New York, Vintage Books, 1980, p. 89
3. Gilles Deleuze and Felix Guattari, *Anti-Oedipus Capitalism and Schizophrenia,* p. 177
4. Gilles Deleuze and Felix Guattari, *A Thousand Plateaus Capitalism and Schizophrenia,* Minneapolis, University of Minnesota Press, 1987, p. 188
5. Gilles Deleuze and Felix Guattari, *Anti-Oedipus Capitalism and Schizophrenia,* p. 35
6. ibid, p. 361

# The Pataphysics of Shit: Toward A *Membra Abjecta*

by Kane X. Faucher

"Shit in one hand and wish in the other, and see which one is heavier."
-US Marine proverb

One of the many preoccupations of both contemporary art and theory has been an engagement with the notion of the abject, and how this functions as a conceptual practice in both milieus. However, what is lacking, especially in the domain of the scatological, is a more metaphysical fundament by which such practices can best ground themselves. It is for this reason that I would propose that the way to theorizing the abject, and the scatological in particular, is by recourse to the metaphysical "scaffolding" inaugurated by the pataphysics of Alfred Jarry and with particular reference to subsequent artistic practices that reflect how the scatological manifests itself in both theory and practice. The scope of this project will attempt to unite, in brushstroke terms, Jarry's pataphysics as a metaphysics of inversion/contradiction with the conceptual motivation of such "scat" artists as Piero Manzoni et al. In this way, I hope to illustrate how certain robust theoretical considerations have allowed artists such as Manzoni to address the relationship between excreta, class, utility, value, and production. Following this, I hope to ground a prolegomena to a more comprehensive and global view of a theory of abjection in both art and contemporary theory.

Our first consideration ought to be this: How does "fecal art" and shit in general relate to pataphysics? How can one construct a pataphysics of shit? In the "scategories" of metaphysics, wherein the *specie* appear as anomalous excesses deposited there by the exceptionality of emergences, and the *forma* is merely an intestinal tube pushing forth what is sought to be shaped, pataphysics shares a borderline with "scat art". It is not on the order of mere equivalences, of pre-set categories under which the products of the abject may be held under nominal subjugation. Rather, it is a pure *anomie* that characterizes the curious affair of abject differences. A chiasm produces them as a means of unfolding the contents of Being to show its internal anti-structure: a "bag of shit" (which must be said to lack any distinguishable structure since it would, in Aristotelian parlance, qualify as a confused and mixed composite). It is by the very virtue of the schismatic curve of the abject that Being exhibits itself by a perspective of differential *anomie*. However, the path to viewing Being this way cannot be the result of a clinical *autopsia*, or beatific vision wherein all is revealed like a Borgesian Aleph, but a way of amplifying the oblique slice, an abjective synthesis, the churning out of Spirit's true product: an accursed and enduring negativity that cannot be subsumed under the clarity of the Concept since the process (also its product) is composed of "mixed matters". Shit is a reconstitution of matter that resists much possible direct commodification given its taboo signification.

To better understand the last century's preoccupation with excreta, one must turn to two sources that will form a complementary reflection: the reaction against modern art as far as this can be traced from the works of Piero Manzoni up through Wim Delvoye, and the pataphysics of Alfred Jarry that has declared through its inversions and hyperboles that technology represents the end of metaphysics. At the core of both is a commitment to the question of negativity. Whereas metaphysics found its ideal expression in the Hegelian system of an *Aufhebung* that attempted to articulate the synthetic process and goal of all history, much of the subsequent engagement with metaphysics has been in confronting the ugly remainders and the incommensurability between the "big questions" of World, God, History, etc., and the reality of a lived practice that cannot be adequately explained by recourse to such categories. The first strike against metaphysics occurs with Nietzsche's denouncements on one hand, and the positivist movement concerned with empirically verifiable facticity on the other. The same Hegelian claims, despite emendations by subsequent followers of Hegel, could no longer satisfy the conditions of experience given the rise of industrialized production and the ways in which technology called into question the role of humans to their "natural environment". Attempts of another stripe which serviced the reprise of phenomenology to ground a presuppositionless science that would spare certain features of metaphysics from the crisis it was experiencing would not prove to redeem it either given that its reliance on the *noein-logos* incommensurability was the very recipe of its own ruin and unfeasibility, and so the incorporation of the psychological sciences and the inclusion of the question of perception and technology would prove to be little more than a hasty graft.

Emerging from the crisis surrounding metaphysics would be an unlikely French author by the name of Alfred Jarry who declared, as Heidegger would later reiterate in more couched terms, that the rise in technology signalled the death of metaphysics: "it is the culmination of metaphysics in technology that makes possible the overcoming of metaphysics, that is, pataphysics."(Deleuze CC 93). In pataphysics, there is no confusion between Being and beings as one would find in the muddiness of metaphysical speculation; rather, Being is subsumed under a technological sign that both reveals and veils it, demonstrating its existence whilst simultaneously negating it. This curious operation of affirmation-negation exists at the heart of the pataphysical "absolute": all that is negated is affirmed through hyperbolic excess. "Pataphysics represents a supplement to metaphysics, accenting it, then replacing it, in order to create a philosophic alternative to rationalism" (Bök 3). It is important to note that pataphysics is *not* an empiricism since it pushes scientificity to its extreme, and even empiricism itself is still a ratiocentric enterprise (a critique raised initially by Hegel in the *Logic* and echoed again in Heidegger's *Time & Being*). In this way, ratiocentric discourse gives way to a kind of hyperbolic ratiocination. It is only through a rigorous system of bringing the contradiction of every term to its limit that the term itself can be elaborated, operating like a Hegelian dialectic powered by a jet engine. Such effects of a pronounced and hyperbolic negation are rearticulated in the Bataillean project of pushing toward the absolute dissolution of all knowledge through a perpetual enterprise of negations with an infinite remainder. Such a method is not isolated to Jarry alone. As an illustration, the writer, Guido Ceronetti, utilizes a similar pataphysical method in order to achieve access to other meanings that would otherwise be blocked, and this is done by problematizing a meaning with ambiguity in order to reveal another.

Abjection is a form of exception, and "pataphysics valorizes the exception to each rule in order to subvert the procrustean constraints of science."(Bök 5). Bök rightly points out that the pataphysical "method" of subversion is not to reduce science by becoming its mere opposite, but to radicalize it to its extreme. However, this is just the first principle of pataphysics. It is Jarry's engagement with shit, in essence to write it as a kind of *fecalligraphy*, where the byproducts of the pataphysical method are best exemplified.

Isolated from a system of generalizing categories, apart from a generic production-consumption bifold, shit is its own *shitself* and shit-for-itself, and in that way oscillates within its own synthetic potentiality. Because it stands in its own logical relation, it is indeed *shitself.* Shit can only produce and repeat itself, thereby making it tautological, self-referential, what could also be called a bad infinite "reissue", all this despite the hermeneutic instinct that would construct an etiology making reference to the single author of a particular instantiation of shit by which an intention could be revealed. Shit reveals itself at the very limit as that which is to be forgotten in oblivion (*lethe*), but a revelation that signals its own taboo nature, a negativity that prompts its being disposed of and buried from all perception. What is marked to be forgotten must be effectively managed to *be forgotten,* which entails some form of waste management system (a good account of the chronology of waste management systems can be found in Dominique Laporte's *History of Shit*). In all, that which is to be forgotten installs by necessity an entire system of disposal whose necessity is conjured up by the need to *forget* what is considered taboo. But still its semiotic "scent" lingers. The *phainomenon* cannot be covered since it is in this covering (*lethe* in the Heideggerian rather than Platonic sense) that is also itself a revealing (*aletheia*). Shit is orphaned production in much the same way writing is (cf. Derrida, *Dissemination,* 146). If shit is an orphan product, what does it speak on behalf of? The absence of the producer him or herself. It is the "testament" or "writing" of a body expelling its own waste. If it is orphaned, it is only so because the generative author may refuse to take account for it. And so, this strange orphan of ontology is left hidden behind a bush or floating conspicuously in the absence of its author.

Alleged "enlightened man" (closer to *Dasein* than *Das Mann*) keeps his distance from his fecal production. S/he makes of it an opposition (production of the anus as being non-utilitarian as opposed to the productions of the mind, corporeal antipodes. In Platonic terms, feces is the poorest copy of Man (himself already being a copy of the Form, "Man"), and so shit is simulacra (copy of a copy). This makes shit reside outside the Form-Copy relationship. There is the danger of losing soul in flatulence, says Plato, which informs his prohibition against the eating of beans. Even Artaud, in one of his letters from Rodez, calls every event issuing from the anus as being attended by a kind of terror, a potential risking up of soul. Reason attempts to suture up the gaping chasm that widens and accompanies a non-utilitarian production, but such a carapace is little more than an amalgam of judgement and fear. If human beings can be said to have an innate function as makers, even the organs responsible for excretion can be colonosculpteurs. Shit can indeed be a "making" and a "happening", indicative of a kind of cultural production.

Deriving the positive from the hitherto (or prevailing) negative in shit, to recognize the useful role in the non-utilitarian nature of it, is the attitude of the kynical philosopher who does not blanch with nausea or disgust at the prospect of constructing an entirely new philosophy of nature from the taboo of refuse (Sloterdijk 151). In this way, *Hygiea* reassesses shit beyond the duality of the to-be-hidden and the safely-revealed (in Heideggerean parlance, beyond the clearing that covers another possibility, the full view of the toilet as instrument of banishing excrement from sight). To shit - or at least to admit openly to doing so - is healthy: as soon as the biological necessity of it is laid bare and unmoored from the port of negative value, a psychological health - akin to a revelation or (bio-)catharsis that unburdens toward acceptance - is attained which opens up a new epistemological relation between thought and shit.

But the old attitudes remain; the revelation does not extend universally, and so there is still the potential for tension and shock value between those who embrace and those who deny the abject that is excrement. Piero Manzoni ties shit to production and wealth as a form of artistic expression, thereby redeeming shit from its label of non-utility and negativity (or, perhaps, consigning production and wealth to the domain of the fundamentally useless in a Bataillean manner where negativity is infinite), Tied to the ego of the artist, Manzoni's canned refuse owns up to the relation that even the artist shits, a case of "I shit, ergo I am." All production, even that of the biological body, is made useful and so therefore, following the prevailing Platonic law, has *value* and is therefore *good.* In this way, the pataphysical *jeu d'esprit* is felt as the contrary is raised to the highest level: excreta is offensive, therefore bad, but it can be a useful production, so therefore good. What is denied is salvaged by an affirmation through pataphysical contradiction, and the gateway to such an inversion is the artist's satirical comedy that critiques the very nature of class and assigned value.

In Jarry's *Ubu Cocu,* eating and shitting are not merely fortuitous; both actions, one of nourishment and the other of excretion, are situated at the site of the body as a reminder of the human connection to the "lower classes", but as a function that unites all classes universally. This "democratization" is not so much a critique of effete bourgeois elitism, but more of an inversion of the transcendent values under which classes are generally derived and evaluated. Notions such as class cease to have conceptual hold in favour of an abject unity. To say that it is the abject hijacks notions of a moral ought acting as a categorical absolute or that the ontological unity of beings is underwritten by some transcendent force that is both useful and good.

One of Jarry's neologisms, *Merdre*: "is a defiant child-like projectile hurled at the disdained order of the adult world. Ubu deifies excrement, singing hymns to his *merdre*-pump"[Pompe Rouget] (Stillman 47). "Jarry, like the alchemists he admired, transmuted matter, making even of feces an extraordinary symbol of the union of opposites."(Stillman 47) - keep in mind that the pataphysical method requires that opposition becomes the equivalence between terms, so gold = feces. Indeed this highlights exactly what Manzoni did when he indexed the price of his canned feces to the price of gold on the day of sale. This sets up an order of oppositional equivalences that reveal the meaning of both terms through an ambiguation of their orders. Jarry's puns *merdre* and *phynance* indicate the relation of oppositional equivalence so marked by pataphysics... Shit is pumped (effectively "mined for" from the ground), gold is eaten, and so the completion of the sequence is that one is nourished on finance in order to produce feces, extracting the lowest symbolic value from something belonging to the highest - a pataphysical reversal, an inverse magic goose that will lay the opposite of golden eggs. This inversion of value (where shit stands for the highest symbolic value and gold the lowest) is an inversion of economics insofar as it is generally the process that something of higher symbolic value is produced from something lower in order to derive profit. Manzoni is seemingly well aware of this inversion, but in the case of his canned shit, the shit-gold relation stands in pataphysical equivalence (product-price) as they are synthesized (with some irony) into a higher symbolic order: that of *art.* Manzoni effectively constructs a triadic synthesis where art's existence is predicated by a relationship between the highest and lowest symbolic orders.

Sheissein: is not the portmanteau here, *Sheisse* and *Sein,* not necessarily a coquettish cleverness, but rather demonstrative of two heterogeneous series entering into complementary relation, a paradoxical duality of shit and being that resolves itself pataphysically from opposition to equivalence? As Artaud writes, "shit to the spirit" (spiritu cloaca taken down a Cartesian detour to give expression to the opposition of Mind as Being versus Being as fecality). The duality to shit and to speak reflects the same relation as shit (as proper noun and not verb action) is to Being.

> Ubu is also called the Chancellor of the Excreta in addition to Master of Phynance. It is in this play as well that we learn of the true function of the "pschittapump," which is just another word for a flush toilet. Ubu is accompanied by such characters as Crapentake, Achras, and Scytotomille. The last is a cobbler who sells shoes called "Turd-Crunchers" that come in special varieties: "still-steaming, horsedung, the oldest coproliths, sullen cowpats, the innocent meconium of a breast-fed baby, something special for policeman's droppings, and a pair for the stools of middle-aged men."(30)" Elizabeth K. Menon. "Potty Talk in Parisian Plays:

**Kane X. Faucher**

> Henry Somm's La Berline de l'Emigre and Alfred Jarry's *Ubu Roi*. *Art Journal* vol. 52, no. 3, (Fall, 1993), pp. 59-64.

But the point is lost if we do not realize that both *shit* and *Being,* combined in their unity as *Sheissein* is univocal. It is expressed by a proposition of sense rather than relates to the genera of Aristotle, rather than the idea of an analogy which requires (in categorical systems from Aristotle to Hegel) judgement, and so therefore is shoaled within the domain of representation. Sheissein is not an affiliate of the fourfold root of identity, but can be perceived as such if one chooses - by analogous judgement - to subsume it according to the ligature of representational thinking. But that is to resort to a view of differentiation as negative and on the order of lack rather than to consider difference in the affirmative. Shit *exists* and *has being,* and would therefore be subject to ontological explanation. However, being and existence are different, and it is credited to Heidegger that this difference has been explicated given that the ambiguity of the "to be" indicates that there are many ways of being. Shit's definition could be theoretically expanded to include all things that are waste products, but if we reject both a genesis and telos to all Being and beings (entities), as Nietzsche has done through his notion of the innocence of becoming, then there is no way of distinguishing what is "waste" since ontologically nothing has a final purpose. It is the role of epistemology to take the reins and assign to the many suitors that would be named "beings" to be judged as such, and this takes place as a form of categorical thinking that both distributes and hierarchicalizes (cf. Deleuze, *Difference and Repetition* 33). If, for example, we take Artaud's injunction against judgement seriously, we gain a different picture. For Jarry, shit itself is not a non-entity or something that is deficient and lacking; rather, it is judgement itself that is the waste product, which gives particular colour to the moment when Ubu sentences his conscience to the chamberpot. That is, Jarry rejects the hitherto metaphysical unity of categories as a means of explaining Being - and this includes shit which plays a primary role in his pataphysical enterprise.

Shit isn't frivolous - it is taboo (Bataille), thaumaturgical/magical (Jarry), and a zone of commodifying anti-commodity rhetoric where an *aneconomic* universe produces and is explained by economic rules (Manzoni). The closest we may find in the history of philosophy to approximate both univocity and the mystical that Jarry puts forth would be in John Duns Scotus who says that Being is univocal for finite entities as well as the infinite mode of God. Jarry raises shit to this mystical level of the infinite, the very univocity of the infinite which expresses and is expressed by all finite beings. None too heretically, therefore, Jarry makes a relation that God is shit. In Manzoni's case, shit's property is to demonstrate through its contradictory nature that the economy is aneconomical since it can be subverted by a fundamentally arbitrary inversion of values. Both Jarry and Manzoni arrive at their curious demonstration through such a pataphysical assault, and it is the only means by which the real, so coveted and necessary for any ontological explanation of *what is* can come to pass: "Subjective invention is the only means of discovering objective reality" (Manzoni, "For the Discovery of a Zone of Images" 17). In Jarry's case, shit "reveals" God (Ubu) through the hyperbole of the *als ob* of his pataphysical method, or exemplified as the negation and concealing which reveals in the works of Guido Ceronetti. But shit also represents an emancipation of play in the face of gravid reasoning, as can be noted in the function of the chorus in the "Chanson Polonaise" in Jarry's *Ubu Roi* with the refrains of "pee pee pee", "ca ca ca", and "poo poo poo". (51). The host of characters including Papa and Mama Turd, Coccyx, and Pile are types that hold the banner of a different sort of revolution that attempts to reclaim the body. The "potty humour" of this play is intentional as a means of fulfilling the conceptual aims of pataphysics. The reversal of nobility as being excreta. The body is the battleground as it was in the works of Nietzsche who declaimed the Platonico-Christian tradition for vilifying the body as unclean and anti-truth.

*Canned Manzoni*

The process of pataphysical inversion or undersigning the real is a common thread that unites much of Manzoni's work. Be it his inverted monument that declares the entire earth as his work of art (thereby reversing the chronological relation between earth and Manzoni by means of reassigning "authorship" - already revealed to be a bankrupt term), the containment of his own breath in balloons, or arguably his most famous work of ninety cans of the artist's shit indexed to the price of gold on their day of sale, Manzoni operates through these methods of reversal and inversion in order to demonstrate the arbitrary nature (and failure) of categorical ontological relations. Shit, for example, is a "sign", but it subverts semiotic relationships since the "seme" in this case is the irreconcilable abject - irreconcilable since it would generally have the economic value of null.

What is particularly interesting about Manzoni's "Ninety Cans" is the choice of container itself. The canister (following the French idea of using jars) was invented in 1810 by Peter Durand in England and was considered a vogue item among the more affluent due to the labour-intensive procedures required for their manufacture that priced "cans" beyond the reach of most. One of the benefits it presented was that food could be properly preserved through the process of canning which uses heat to kill microorganisms that would otherwise contaminate food. It would not be until the First World War that a powerful demand in transportable foods that would not spoil under difficult conditions, as well as vast improvements in the mechanization of the canning process, would introduce canned goods to the working class. The quality of foods declined with overproduction and the need to supply troops (a good example would be Britain's "Bully Beef", a low quality brine-cured brisket which offered high calories in low quantities). With said higher production values and lower yield quality of products, canned goods lost their particular social cachet, becoming a fare more symbolic of the lower-middle and working class. With the rise of supermarkets cans became prominent stock and representative of mass production in the food industry.

The very idea of "canning" possesses its own particular negative connotation. Something "canned" (as decanted from a reaction against industrial over-production) is generally of lower quality, mass-produced, and synthetic. In television situation comedies, we speak of "canned laughter" as a recording played at particular moments when the viewing audience is cued to laugh. This idea of a disembodied laughter that laughs *in the place of and for the viewer*, as invented by Charles R. Douglass in the 1950s for such shows as *Jack Benny* and *I love Lucy*, presents us with a paradox, says Zizek. It is not so much that another human being is laughing in our place, but that a machine has been designated to fill this role, much akin to the use of prayer wheels (cf. Slavoj Zizek, "Will You Laugh for Me, Please?" in 16Beaver, 07.22.03, dl August 11, 2007). This mechanical substitution is a boon for those too tired or too short on expressive emotion, although Zizek's quick comparison to "primitive" function may be suspended under question for a more concerted analysis. It is perhaps more fecund to make the relationship one on the order of transgression, where shit is transgression and laughter a response to transgression. That there is a machine that emulates a response is itself, then, on the same order as shit: it is a transgression of what we customarily would expect, i.e., that laughter is a felt response, and machines are incapable of experiencing feeling of any kind. The laughter is reproduced, perhaps not too dissimilar to shit being a reproduction if not a representation of Being.

Manzoni's sealing of his own fecal matter in cans has been commonly viewed as a critique of mass production (Wim Delvoye has taken this a step further in his own work where a machine actually manufactures its own shit and replicates the processes of digestion). In the same way, Manzoni is also wryly critiquing the role of the artist in an era of mechanical reproduction. Shit in itself has no apparent market value, but that its authorship is tied to a renowned artist increases its capital significantly. However, the true conceptual stroke is in his insistence upon assigning its value by indexing it to the price of gold, historically symbolic as being of the highest trade value. It is an echo of Jarry's pataphysical method: to unite the two terms of shit and gold in order that one negates the other and reveals a "higher" truth.

### *Risky Communication*

The communication that takes place in our relation to shit is indexed on a conceptual parity between "civilized" moral cleanliness and physical cleanliness. Judaism, Christianity, and Islamic texts contain several directions for the maintenance or acquiring of physical cleanliness as being the road to spiritual cleanliness. St, Paul's epistles are rife with prescriptions on bodily management, and even the Koran gives advice to the devotee to clean themselves with sand if no water is available.

However parceled out, these faiths have strict proscriptions on the governance of the body and its relation to waste. Religion has merely institutionalized an already established social practice of waste management. As Bataille writes, "I have already posited that the abhorrence of animal needs, together with the repugnance for death and dead persons, on the one hand, and the experience of work, on the other, marked the 'transition from animal to man'. Man is the animal that negates nature: he negates it through labour." (Bataille AC II/III 61). Already, in this formulation, to eject is not considered a viable form of labour. Labour, construed as a production of value, is restricted to those efforts that will have useful ends. We find this in the story of Onan who was punished by God for "wasting his seed" since the purpose of sexual release is for procreation only. Labour's value is thus constrained to that which is useful and good, the latter governed by the former in most cases.

That other, banished form of labour that squanders its excess without return is considered the "dark" side of production: "The place for filth is in the dark... The same horror banishes the sexual function and excretion to the same darkness." (Ibid., 62). This may be the reprise of the naturalist tradition in French 19th century literature where there is a merger of filth and flesh, reacting against what Huysmans' character Durtal calls romanticism's cadre of "booby-idealists and sex-starved maids." (J. K. Huysmans, *La Bas* 8). And, as Bataille continues, "We take our children out of the muck, then we do our very best to wipe out the traces of that origin. We busy ourselves in terrifying them as soon as they are old enough to take part (little by little) in our disgust for excrement."(Bataille AC II/III 63). Just as in terms of menses, shit would also qualify thusly: "We are inclined to believe that this discharge is *impure* because the organ from which it issues is thought to be so." (Bataille AC II/III 64). Here we can read *organ* as *origin*. According to Bataille, an education or inculcation in the rhetoric of disgust begins early, and it is hinged on being apostate to whatever is perceived as the "natural order" in stark relief to being "civilized" - but the very notion of being human entails this irreconcilability between our corporeal nature and the vaunted ideals of purity. In essence, our communication with origin is pernicious and undergoes considerable revision in terms of moral progress. It is in this way that we are called upon to separate ourselves from the uncouth and unclean, the "animal state".

Shit is a participatory process in a system of general economy; it is error to isolate it from other productions, processes, and functions. For Bataille, the force which undergirds wealth of any kind is energy as such. There is always an excess to that energetic production, and this must be utilized, even if it is by squander (and the better for it, Bataille might add). *To exude* as *waste* is the keystone to the Bataillean aspect of what it means to be "sovereign". In order to punctuate his point about the necessity to squander excess and surplus, Bataille states that the relative peace between the rise of the Industrial Revolution and the First World War was broken by a need to squander the fruits of efficient overproduction (a rather broad if not slightly morally disconnected view), and that *war* was the only means by which such waste could be effectively managed (cf. AC I, 24-5). Now, if waste is risk, and risk is communication, then we have an altogether new conception of "waste management" as the very means by which we mediate our "waste products" as "cultural expressions", perhaps of the highest order, at least in terms of its urgency so as better to offset any kind of "repressive build-up": "if there is no outlet anywhere, nothing bursts; but the pressure is there." (AC I 30).Here, the growth principle that Bataille advocates as being the base root of excess as the very possibility of existence is shared as a metaphysical principle by Nietzsche's will to power and sociologically by Elias Canetti's study of the open versus closed crowd. What is frequently misunderstood is that such growth is not indexed to finite individuals as particular instantiations: it is the principle of metastatic growth *in general* that persists, not the particularity of a person or a crowd that is limited in its finite conditions of space or capacity to be affected. Nietzsche says as much in reference to the idea of "types" insofar as the mask wears us for a time, and it is the ethical selection of the will to power that "affirms and selects" that the type returns. And, as much as perpetual growth, against the possibility of a cosmic homeostasis, would be rendered a "bad infinite" to Hegelian reasoning, it is the very principle of perpetuation, a kind of Spinozist *conatus,* however construed, that desires to persist in its being as contrary to any importuning of inertia.

It is a conventional commonplace wisdom in financial investing that only risk can be managed as the collective flow of the market rides the wave of internal forces that determine its constitution. And, if Bataille names all communication as risk, then it follows that all our communicative acts (be them speaking, laughing, or even excreting if we allow to extend the definition of such an act as a potential form of communicative expression as Manzoni has done) are risk factors that we manage. To manage has its etymological root as being "to handle" or "control" (*maneggiare* in Italian), and so to manage the risk that shit presents nearly means that we must handle it.

***Shit Today***

Since Manzoni, there have been several notable artists who have made use of feces and other bodily ejecta in their artistic practice. Chris Ofili of the Young British Artists movement is one notable example who used elephant dung in his depiction of the Virgin Mary at the Sensation Exhibit. The Sensation exhibit (1997), made possible by Charles Saatchi's private collection, helped popularize and catapult many of the YBAs into the public sphere with their use of shock sensationalism and the use of abject materials. This vogue for shock-art (with its derivation from post-Dada influences) had a limited shelf life, and the controversies surrounding much of the group's work has since diminished, thereby perhaps making the Sensation Exhibit both a consolidation of their conceptual aims as well as their last testament toward being canonized in the institutionalization of art. Echoes of the YBA shock-works can be seen in the works of Jubal Brown (*Mondrian Piece* and his *Harbour at le Favre* - both pieces which Brown spewed coloured vomit at, staging a "happening" in reaction against the staleness of high Modern Art which quickly earned him a ban from New York's MoMA). The reaction of disgust against modern art by means of shock and abject obscenity already had a firm precedent in the Vienna Aktionist group of the 1960s. In an ever-expanding list of "abject" artistry, we could also include the post-industrial "hyperdelic" musical work of Genesis P –Orridge or Marc Quinn's *Self* made from eight pints of his own blood.

Most recently, Huang Yong Ping's work has incorporated the fecal into cultural production, and it has its precedent historically established prior to Manzoni: "Packing the artist's feces into glittering cans (Manzoni) to answer the question 'What is art?' [is] exactly the same as Chan masters using 'a dried feces stick' (Master Yunmen) or 'three pounds of flax' (Master Dongshan) as the answer to the question 'What is Buddha?' (Huang Yong Ping "Xiamen Dada - Postmodern?" 1986). Huang Yong Ping's conceptual practice indexes itself to the notion of residues, the "missing authorship". And, indeed, shit is a form similar to that of writing where the author is absent, but in this case the "work" is not necessarily signed since there is nothing visually distinct about feces that tie it to any author in particular. But when utilized to answer the unanswerable, such as broad stroke questions on art as such, God, or Being, there is in this type of response enfolded both the impossibility of answering such questions as well as having their answer lodged within the domain of the unspeakable. What is unspeakable perhaps may be written, and in this case the means is the intestinal pen. As a speech act, shitting shares a domain with vomit insofar as both lack the same linguistic meaning structures that are inherent in the written or spoken word. And yet it speaks since it is an event that has its own logical cohesion and meaning-value. Be it to encounter feces in an unlikely place or among paleontologists who study the fossilized coprae of dinosaurs for clues to their diet.

### *Cloaca Automata*

Extending the stock *arte rigeur* metaphor of machinic production and its relation to excreta, artist Wim Delvoye has been able to knock out the human being's necessity entirely from the equation of fecal production. In his famed "Cloaca", Delvoye has succeeded in constructing a machine that shits while only being fed the inputs of foodstuffs and electricity. Each machine in the procession is a reductive imitation of human organs required to produce feces. All the functions and byproducts are faithfully reproduced: the gurgling of the guts, farting, the unmistakable smell, and the final product itself whose consistency and even shape is shockingly near-identical to the "real thing." But rather than associating the value of production at the site of the artist, as in Manzoni's case, the value is attributed to the technology that is capable of mimicking life. This techno-mimesis privileges the very iconographic theme of celebratory simulacra.

As if taking a page from Jarry, Delvoye's unifying or blurring the distinction between the clean and unclean, the useful from the useless, is manifest in his newest practice of establishing a Church of Cloaca. Ironically using corporate icons (the merger of Ford and Coca Cola logos in the Cloaca logo, not to mention the fortuitous anagrammatic feature that one cannot spell Coca Cola without the same collection of letters) as the imprimatur of a machine devoted to producing the useless, Delvoye's conceptual gains bear the mark of the pataphysical enterprise. Religion and big business are marshaled to the aid of useless production, and it is perhaps a dispelling of the belief that either institutions produce the useful at all. Nowhere is the split between the clean and unclean being blurred or pataphysically inverted than in his "Scatalogue" where he uses the iconic "Mr. Clean" as the Cloaca mascot. The ironic switch here being that that which is generally associated with the removal of filth also stands as the vanguard of filth itself. Perhaps to compound the irony a touch further, the notions that associate machinic production as clean and representative of an ordered clockwork universe that manufactures perfect and sterile products are troubled insofar as here we have a machine that mimics the heterogeneous, imperfect and unclean productions of the animal body.

What remains for Delvoye is to successfully produce a purely unified input/output machine where all nutritive inputs occur from the same orifice as that which produces all varieties of ejecta. This could be achieved through a channel system of tubes that manufacture *in corpus* each of the requisite effluvia.

---

Sources:

Artaud, Antonin.
Bataille, Georges. *The Accursed Share v. I*
Bataille, Georges. *The Accursed Share v.II-III.*
Bök, Christian. *'Pataphysics: The Poetics of an Imaginary Science.* Northwestern UP, Illinois: 2002.
Deleuze, Gilles. *Essays Critical and Clinical.*
Delvoye, Wim. *Cloaca.*
Huysmans, J.K. *La Bas.*

Manzoni, Piero. *Paintings* Trans. Caroline Tisdall and Angelo Bozzola. Tate Gallery, London: 1974.

Stillman, Linda Klieger. *Alfred Jarry*. Twayne Publishers, Boston: 1983.

Zizek, Slavoj. "Will You Laugh for Me, Please?" in 16Beaver, 07.22.03, dl August 11, 200

# From The Keller <S.P.K.> *Polylogue:* Julia Kristeva & The Politics of Abjection

by K.Osmosis

The linguist, philosopher and psychoanalyst Julia Kristeva, in her essay "Motherhood According to Giovanni Bellini", explores the Renaissance painter Giovanni Bellini's pictorial representation of motherhood. Kristeva's essay commences with a fascinating description of the cellular transformations that provide the very foundations of the biological processes of gestation driving the 'biosocial history 'of the maternal project. A project and a 'history' Kristeva describes as a 'process without a subject', where the very meaning of concepts like 'subject' and 'identity' are brought into question:

> Cells accumulating, dividing, fusing, splitting, multiplying and proliferating without any *identity* (biological or socio-symbolical); volumes grow, tissues stretch, and body fluids change rhythm, speeding up or slowing down. Master-Mother of instinctual drive. Material compulsion, spasm of a memory belonging to the species, the same continuity differentiating itself that either binds together or splits apart to perpetuate itself, with no other significance than the eternal return of the life-death biological cycle.

Julia Kristeva describes Giovanni Bellini as both a 'subject-in-process', producing himself through the production of his art, and as the product of a particular time and place, namely, the city of Venice at the dawn of the Renaissance. A culture organically connected with the iconography of Byzantine depictions of the Virgin Mary as an image "accomplished in its truth-likeness within the luminous serenity of the unrepresentable through a predominance of a luminous density of colour, and chromatic differences beyond and despite corporeal representation." Images that combine the historical remnants of a matriarchal oriental paganism with Christian mysticism, alloyed with an incipient Renaissance humanism presented in accordance with the iconographic traditions of Byzantine culture. For Kristeva, Bellini's brushwork preserves "the traces of a marginal experience, through and across which a maternal body might recognise its own, otherwise inexpressible in our culture".

Marginal, inexpressible, heterogeneous experiences; an endless flow of bodily pulsions gathered up in the *chora* (from the Greek word meaning an enclosed space, womb or 'nurse'), which Plato in his *Timaeus* describes as "an invisible and formless being which receives all things and in some mysterious way partakes of the intelligible, and is most incomprehensible." Kristeva appropriates and redefines Plato's concept and concludes that the *chora* designates a site of undifferentiated being: the shared bodily space of mother and child; and the child's sensation of continuity or fusion with the maternal body, experienced as an infinite space.

In what Kristeva terms the 'semiotic', the newly-born child possesses no sense of itself as an identity separate from its mother; it therefore perceives no distinction between 'self' and 'other'. Devoid of language, its existence is regulated by a rhythmic flow of bodily desires, pulsations and instinctual drives - impulses mobile, fluid and heterogeneous. A space where opposites (subject and object, male and female, inside and outside, attraction and repulsion, life and death) merge together into a contradictory unity: archaic and potentially disruptive desires curtailed only through the arbitrary imposition of paternal law and the 'symbolic order' of language.

For Kristeva, the maternal function subverts the traditional notion of a fixed division between active subject and passive object. Instead, pregnancy transforms the woman-as-subject into the passive object or effect of a series of uncontrollable bodily processes. The biological processes of gestation places women at the point where 'nature' intersects with 'culture', as a sort of 'inside-out' mediator between the internal and the external, such that the relationship between them is explained by their reciprocal connection, their unity; a unity of the opposition of the maternal body to itself which leads to a division of its unity and to a splitting of its flesh. A position where the mother exists as a mere cipher or *"filter"* whose role is to fulfil the 'biosocial program' of reproducing the species; where, "to imagine that there is *someone* in that filter - such is the source of religious mystifications, the font that nourishes them." The childbearing woman is immersed in the corporeality of the maternal function, the subject of "physiological operations and instinctual drives dividing and multiplying her".

As a process the woman is subjected to, the experience of gestation and birth leads to a disintegration of the mother's self-image and symbolic identity and a confusion and subsequent reorganisation of the boundaries between Self and Other. This results in the mother internalising the Self/Other split, producing a self-division accompanied by feelings of alienation and estrangement towards the foetus developing within her womb, which is experienced as an 'abject' 'other' inhabiting her body, akin to an invasive foreign organism or internal parasite:

> Within the body, growing as a graft, indomitable, there is an other. And no one is present, within that simultaneously dual and alien space, to signify what is going on. 'It happens but I'm not there'.

An internal self-contradiction finally resolved in the birth of the child and the establishment of a maternal unity between mother and child. A unity Kristeva pictures as an "auto-erotic circle": an imaginary fusion of mother and child enclosed within a protective 'shell' (or "enceinte"), where distinctions between self and other, subject and object, are dissolved: "Narcissus like, touching without eyes, sight dissolving in muscles, hair, deep, smooth, peaceful colours". This imagined unity is, however, a complex unity of opposites, a heterogeneous and ambivalent conglomeration of experiences involving mixed emotions associated with the processes of differentiation and separation; feelings of love and hate, pain and pleasure, desire and fear, fulfilment and loss:

> Frozen placenta, live limb of a skeleton, monstrous graft of life on myself, a living death. Life....death....undecidable....My removed marrow, which nevertheless acts as a graft, which wounds

> but increases me. Paradox: deprivation and benefit of childbirth. But calm finally hovers over pain, over the terror of this dried branch that comes back to life, cut off wounded, deprived of its sparkling bark.

Giovanni Bellini's painting *Madonna and Child* (1455-1460), represents for Kristeva the theme of the separation of mother and child. The painting is a "witness to a maternal appropriation of the child." Against the backdrop of the Flemish countryside, the child is portrayed as enfolded in a symbiotic embrace that appears to prohibit any separation; where the mother and child appear as "branches of the same trunk, skin against skin, flesh against flesh". The child is painted with an expression of intense fear and anxiety as it struggles to free itself from the suffocating grip of its possessive mother, prompting Kristeva to pose the question: "could it be that, in relationship to the child, the mother experiences the symbiotic clinging syndrome?" For Kristeva, Bellini's portrayal of this complex and ambivalent relationship between mother and child resurrects "an archaic memory of maternal seduction, a recollection of the hand whose precocious, already sexual caresses are more threatening than comforting".

Bellini's painting *Madonna and Child* (1487), signals for Kristeva a further development along this theme. Alongside a painterly change in bodily stance and facial expression, there is a marked transition from the pictorial representation of the "possessive mother" towards a representation of the "hostile mother." The hostility, however, is expressed by the child, who, "eluding the hands of the henceforth weary mother, he grabs her by the neck as if to strangle her – the guilty mother."

These themes connect with Kristeva's exploration of Melanie Klein's psychoanalytical theories concerning the aggressive drives and body-destruction phantasies of children. Thus the developing child acquires an image of itself as an integrated 'whole', and not simply as a mess of conflicting sensations and fragmented body parts, through a traumatic and never fully completed process in which 'good' objects and pleasurable sensations are incorporated into the body ('introjected'), while objects and sensations perceived as 'bad' are expelled ('projected') out into the external world. This precipitates a process that includes aggressive phantasies involving the child's murder, dismemberment and consumption of the maternal body. These phantasies, when projected by the infant onto the figure of the mother, generate in the mind of the infant traumatic experiences of imminent bodily disintegration: the image of a hostile mother conceived as a terrifying figure intent on eviscerating, devouring and destroying it.

There is an interesting link between these psychoanalytical theories of bodily fragmentation and disintegration and historically archaic beliefs concerning the deformed and the monstrous. According to the ancient Greek natural philosopher and physician Empedocles, the evolution of "whole-natured forms" was preceded by a lengthy period when the earth was peopled by hybrids and mutants, "dream shapes" consisting of "separate parts which were disjointed". Empedocles describes this earlier world and its variety of polymorphously perverse forms and monstrous combinations with a certain horrified fascination:

> Many foreheads without necks sprang up on the earth, arms wandered naked, separated from shoulders, and eyes wandered alone, needing brows..........and creatures made partly with male bodies and partly with female bodies, equipped with shadowy limbs.

In paintings such as *Virgin and Child with St. Anne*(1500-1510), and *Mona Lisa* (1503), the artist Leonardo Da Vinci represents for Kristeva the identification of femininity with motherhood and the ideal of the Virgin, where the female body is divested of its material aspects and is transmuted through the development of a progressively formalised set of artistic conventions and practices into the spiritualised and reified figure of the 'phallic mother'. The maternal (phallic body) is represented as inviolate, distinct and whole, symbolising an established order that maintains secure and impervious boundaries separating and distinguishing the inside from the outside, the proper from the improper, order from chaos, and the spiritually aesthetic or beautiful from what is deemed abject and material.

For Kristeva, this fantasy of the phallic mother consists of an idealisation that shields us from the threat of non-being, and the experience of nothingness and the collapse of identity: "If, on the contrary, the mother was not phallic, then every speaker (or 'subject') would be lead to conceive of its Being in relation to some void, a nothingness asymmetrically opposed to this Being, a permanent threat against, first, its mastery, and ultimately, its stability". Kristeva concludes that the artist Leonardo Da Vinci is a dutiful "servant of the maternal phallus"; his paintings are expressive of "the eye and hand of a child, underage to be sure, but of one who is the universal and complex-ridden centre confronting that other function, which carries the appropriation of objects to its limit: *science* ".

Kristeva challenges the Cartesian notion of the isolated, self-contained human being or 'ego', unmixed with others. She replaces it by the awareness that we exist as members one of another, as a system of surfaces that briefly intersect around a centre or constellation that dissolves, forming parts of a 'self' conceived as a 'subject-in-process' (or better still, as an open-ended 'work-in-progress'); a 'subject' both constant and fluid, immersed in a continuous process of formation and exchange, summation and integration.

This compares with Antonin Artaud's rigorous interrogation of the fragmented but transforming body - in art, literature and performance – combining chance and necessity, disintegration and reconstitution. Artaud's body-in movement – "this dislocated assemblage, this fragment of decayed geology" - attacking stasis in favour of transcendence and regeneration, in conjunction with an apocalyptic will to obliterate society; reconstituting the embodied self through a process of creative destruction.

The body painfully contorted, steeped in desire, combining, through vocal movements and screams, violent and erotic anatomical manipulations. Artaud enacts in his gestural performances experiences of fragmentation, delirium and desire. Representation is debunked in favour of a visceral, bodily immediacy – Artaud's 'Theatre of Cruelty', where the body comes before the word, and before the world:

> Who am I?
> Where do I come from?

I am Antonin Artaud and I say this
As I know how to say this
Immediately
You will see my present body
Burst into fragments
And remake itself
Under ten thousand notorious aspects
A new body
Where you will
Never forget me.

Artaud's is the voice of the shipwrecked survivor raging against the world (and self). A stance informed by the poet Rainer Maria Rilke, who compares the artist to "a dancer whose movements are broken by the constraints of his cell. That which finds no expression in his steps and the limited swing of his arms, comes in exhaustion from his lips, or else he has to scratch the unlived lines of his body into the walls with his wounded fingers."

The notion of a dual or a divided universe, consisting of carefully demarcated distinctions and fixed oppositions, is an idea forcefully propounded and meticulously elaborated upon in the cosmology of the philosopher Plato, as outlined in his *Timaeus,* which defines the primal dualism that underlies reality, and its subsequent division into two realms: an invisible, eternal realm of pure thought; and a visible, mutable realm of bodily sensations connected with the corporeal substance of nature. The invisible realm of thought is considered by Plato as primal and original. In the beginning there existed along side it the unshaped matrix of physical being – the ineffable space and receptacle of the *chora,* conceptualised as "an invisible and formless being"

In-between these two realms resides Plato's 'Demiurgus', who creates by 'making'. This is a metaphor for cosmogenesis taken from the activities of the artisan, who shapes things from dead stuff, as opposed to the reproductive processes of begetting and gestating. This concept of the cosmos as 'made' and not 'begotten' later emerges in Christian theology as the primary means of distinguishing between the generation of the divine in the Trinity, and God's creation of the world. The Platonic Demiurgos first shapes this space into the primal elements of fire, air, water, and earth, and then shapes these into the spherical body of the cosmos.

Plato conceptualises this sphere as a kind of living entity, without an inside or an outside, perfectly self-contained: "Nor would there have been use of organs by which it might receive its food or get rid of what it had already digested, since there was nothing that went from it or came into it". A universe, therefore, where organs of ingestion, digestion and excretion are unnecessary, for there is nothing else in existence, no 'other' to incorporate or excrete, nothing outside itself it could eat even if it desired to eat, in fact, nothing it could desire even if it desired. A perfectly self-sufficient universe complete unto itself: "By design it was created thus, its own waste providing its own food, and all that it did and suffered taking place in and by itself".

Plato's idea of the universe as some kind of living entity, is a theme explored in the nature philosophy of Baron Friedrich von Hardenberg (pen name, Novalis), a leading poet and novelist of European Romanticism, who contends that when we look at what is generally regarded as inert matter we fall into the error that it has no consciousness at all. But it may well be that its consciousness is so fragmented and diffused that we can only understand it through rational systems of statistical organisation which the study of science as hitherto revealed as the so-called 'laws' of nature. This means that in the human knowledge of nature, nature perceives itself; and that the subject-object (male/female) relationship to nature is in fact nature's relationship to itself. Where, to quote Novalis, "the organs of thought are the sexual organs of nature, the world's genitals". A conception of nature that the inveterate anti-Platonist Friedrich Nietzsche reacts to with disgust and revulsion: "The modern scientific pendant to a belief in God is the belief in the universe as organism: such belief makes me want to throw up".

Novalis continues: for him the process of self-knowledge is a natural and universal drive towards expansion and fulfilment, where the urge to know is identical with the urge to appropriate and ingest, where differences and distinctions are abolished, and the 'other' becomes the same as 'oneself': "How can a human being have a sensibility for something if he does not have the germ of it in himself? What I am to understand must develop organically within me; and what I seem to learn is but nourishment - something to incite the organism. Thus learning is quite similar to eating".

For Novalis, "Life, or the essence of spirit, consists in the engendering bearing and rearing of one's like. The human being engages in a happy marriage with itself, an act of self-embrace". A state where the traditional antithesis between subject and object falls away, and the knower and the known become one. Like the myth of the youth Narcissus, hopelessly in love and unwilling to separate himself from the beauty of his face reflected in a pool of water, his body gradually fading away, to be replaced by a flower: a *jouissance* involving a blissful acceptance of life's transience, a willing immersion into the chaos of unformed matter into one all-encompassing unity. Leading to a pantheism like that of the heretic and philosopher Baruch Spinoza, who rejects the philosophical dualism and the principles of transcendence and sublimation of the established Christian order in favour of a God who is the immanent cause of all existence, where everything is considered alive and all things in the world are one, and what's in all things is God.

A mystical and pantheistic view of Nature, amounting to an "oceanic feeling of oneness with the universe", which, according to Freud, consists in the restoration or recollection (*anamnesis*) of an archaic, infantile state of limitless ('primary') narcissism; a condition articulated poetically by the philosopher Gaston Bachelard, who describes the world as "an immense Narcissus in the act of thinking about himself". All this amounts to the philosophical possibility of a metaphysical pantheism where the birth of humanity on the planet Earth is the means employed by the Universe in order to perceive itself; in the human species it creates the mirror (*speculum*) of its own reflections.

In accordance with Kristeva's re-mix of themes and stanzas sampled from the Romanticism of Novalis, 'love', or the desire that is expressed in song, in the disposition to rhythm and intonation, "makes individualities communicable and comprehensible;" makes nonsense abound with sense: makes (one) laugh. For Kristeva, "The amorous and artistic experiences are the only ways of preserving our psychic space as a 'living system'" 'opening' up the individual's psyche to the point where the outside world of the other is no longer perceived as a threat but instead becomes a stimulus to adaptation, change and self-transformation, revealing the participating 'subject' as "a work in progress capable of auto-organisation on condition of maintaining a kind of link with the other. I have called this the amorous state".

To rediscover the intonations, the lyrical patterns, repetitions and rhythms preceding the subject's establishment within the paternal (symbolic) order of language, is to discover the voiced breath that fastens us to an undifferentiated mother, a semiotic motility, a playful polyvalence, released and restructured in the poetry of art. The discovery-in-utterance is also at the same time an act of losing, of distancing, of separating oneself from what has been discovered; it is an act of unknowing, a dissolution back into an active potential. The potentiality of the fragmented unity of the symbolic revitalised by energies borrowed from the prehistoric and archaic realms of the semiotic; a disruptive negativity involving a dialectical tension between dispersal and unity, rupture and completion, producing a 'fluid subjectivity'. This is a 'subjectivity' of 'difference' where continuity is achieved through an ongoing process of transformation.

Accordingly, it is not the possession of a fixed 'truth' so much as the realisation of the 'known' so that it becomes the 'given', thereby not arresting reflection, but renewing and stimulating it. Novalis compares it to the ignition of a flame, a leaping outside oneself in desire and ecstasy: "The act of leaping outside oneself is everywhere the supreme act - the primal point - the genesis of life. Thus the flame is nothing other than such an act. Philosophy arises whenever the one philosophizing philosophizes himself, that is, simultaneously consumes (determines, necessitates) and renews again (does not determine, liberates). The history of this process is philosophy".

Plato's notion of the *chora* is re-conceptualised by Kristeva to describe the fusion and continuity of the infant with the maternal body, experienced as an infinite space of undifferentiated being: an ineffable, mystical state of fusion with the maternal body along the lines of a 'primary narcissism', where subject and object, self and other merge into a single entity. For Kristeva this archaic experience of union with the mother's body, and the shared bodily ('semiotic') space/time of the original mother/child dyad, underlies the socio-symbolic order, furnishing the foundations, or the primeval archetype, for all our future, adult desires (which are forever unfulfilled). A space where irruptions of polymorphously perverse sexuality, and experiences of the uncanny and the mystical, possess the capacity to resist, threaten, subvert and potentially undermine the socio-symbolic order of the unified 'subject', language, representation, and the established system of existing social relations.

For Kristeva, reactionary efforts to prevent the disruption and destabilisation of the socially determined and 'ideological' belief that we exist as stable, rigid 'subjects' with fixed identities, organised within a static social order, consist in denying and excluding as unclean and disgusting anything that reminds us of our (material) corporeal natures. This dual process of denial (repression) and exclusion (projection) is, however, only ever partially successful. The pre-signifying traces of the *chora:* the maternal, corporeal desires that underlie the socio-symbolic order of signification, are forever irrupting as emotional affects, permanently threatening to destabilise the finite unity and autonomous, fixed and singular identity of the 'ego' or 'subject'.

The whole affair revolves around the establishment of a series of demarcations and dichotomies between an "inside-outside", a "me-not me", and a "'not-yet me' with an 'object'". A theme initially explored by the Kleinian school of psychoanalysis:

> Owing to these mechanisms (of introjection and projection) the infant's object can be defined as what is inside or outside his own body, but even while outside, it is still part of himself, since 'outside' results from being ejected, 'spat out': thus the body boundaries are blurred. This might also be put the other way round: because the object outside the body is 'spat out', and still relates to the infant's body, there is no sharp distinction between his body and what is outside.

This brings into question the whole Cartesian 'inside' and 'outside' dichotomy. The cohesion and unity of the 'subject' or 'ego' is based upon its ability to distinguish itself from those objects that lie outside it. The ego's relationship to the outside world is explained by psychoanalysis through the processes of 'projection' and 'introjection'; processes that create the distinction between the internality of the 'ego', or 'subject', and the 'externality' of 'objects' residing in the world 'outside'. For both introjection and projection are mutually interdependent, one upon the other, both inside and outside each other at the same time; thus the inside is also on the outside, while the outside is both inside and outside too. The ego wants to 'introject', to bring 'inside', only that part of the external world with which it can identify. However, this very identification of the subject with these external objects puts the absolute externality of these objects in doubt. The question therefore arises: is it a part of the outside world that the subject wishes to introject, or is it merely a part of the subject itself; a part, moreover, which has to be 'projected' and externalised into the world 'outside' before it can be introjected 'inside'? This is a question (and a potential antagonism) first expressed in the language of the "oldest" instinctual drives - the oral - through the contrast between incorporation (eating) and expulsion.

Accordingly the 'ego' introjects and incorporates into itself everything that is 'good', and ejects from itself everything that is 'bad'. The boundary between subject (ego) and object (external world) is, however, somewhat paradoxical: the 'outside' is forged and maintained at the heart of the 'inside', and is kept 'outside' by the very living organism from which it is supposed to be separated. The ego's boundaries resemble a form similar to that of the mouth. Like the mouth (which is also a point of incorporation or 'taking in'), the ego's 'boundary' is not just a system of surfaces that divides inside from outside; it is also and equally a meeting of surfaces, a permeable interface, amounting to a blurring of boundaries.

The mouth is both a place of entry and exit, one of the body's orifices that connects inside with outside, forming a vulnerable corporeal boundary or threshold that can easily be trespassed. The mouth can eat, kiss, suck, emit sounds, and produce language. In addition, cultures and religions elaborate complex taboos concerning food designated as 'unclean', setting the boundaries between what may or may not be legitimately consumed. Thus for Kristeva, "food is the oral object (the abject) that sets up archaic relationships between the human being and its other, its mother who wields a power as vital as it is fierce".

This reveals a complex borderline between Self and Other, initially permeable, like the embryo in the womb, and, after birth, as the infant sustained by milk from its mother's breasts. However, in the process of accepting the gift of milk, we confront the realisation that we exist as the separate objects of our mother's desire. Thus the infant's refusal to separate is expressed as physical nausea. The sensation of nausea not only exposes the complex relationship of sameness and difference between our mothers and ourselves, but also reveals the threat posed by the maternal space as the final collapse of the divide between subject and object; the loss of identity and of an integrated sense of 'self ' which the contained body represents; and a slippage between opposites, suggesting an indivisibility of erotic attraction and repulsion which are held apart within the conventional binary division of sexual difference.

Like a hermaphrodite who combines the two sexes in one body (in accordance with Artaud's study of the dimorphic sexuality of the third-century Roman Emperor Heliogabalus), a potential bisexuality of desires in which male and female cannot be fully separated. For Kristeva, "To believe that one 'is a woman' is almost as absurd and obscurantist as to believe that one 'is a man'". It is not the sexual difference between subjects that is important, as much as the sexual differentiation within each subject. The bisexual constitution of the child, the presence of masculinity and femininity within the same body, informs her view. Thus the anorexic's refusal to eat can be explained as a desperate attempt to maintain the boundaries that separate; boundaries simultaneously denying and reminding us of our mortality and the materiality that necessitates our decay. The attempt of an irrevocably divided subject to become united with itself; where the wholeness and integrity of the human body and of the unitary 'subject' is equated with holiness, and connected to the being and goodness of God - the Ideal: "To be holy is to be whole, to be one; holiness is unity, integrity, perfection of the individual. Dietary rules and prohibitions merely develop the metaphor of holiness".

Eating dissolves the boundaries separating the self from the world, a process described by the philosopher Georg Wilhelm Friedrich Hegel, in his meditation on the mystery of the Eucharist: "Yet the love made objective, this subjective element becomes a *thing*, and only reverts once more to its nature, becoming subjective again in eating". Hegel describes his philosophy as "a circle returning upon itself, the end being wound into the beginning, a circle of circles" culminating in "the crowning glory of a spiritual world", the Absolute Idea, where spirit is reality and reality is spiritual. For Hegel the identification of the object with itself can be thought of as a unity of the opposition of the object to itself up to and including identity, which leads to a splitting of its unity.

This dialectical notion of the self-motion of the object takes the form of an impulse, a vital tension, or, to borrow a term used by the medieval mystic Jakob Bohme, a 'qual' of matter. 'Qual' meaning an internalised pain or torture, an agony issuing from within; a quality Bohme considers as intrinsic to all material substance, which drives to action of some kind; an activating principle, arising from, and promoting in its turn, the self-movement and spontaneous development of a thing, in contradistinction to the development or movement of a thing derived from a pain or pressure inflicted from without. This dialectical notion of the self-motion of the object includes an identity of the object with itself such that the object is and is not, at one and the same time, and in one and the same relation, in one and the same state, which leads ultimately, by virtue of the internal dynamic of its 'qual' or agony, to its transformation into another object. The contradictoriness of this self-transformation of the self-moving object is logically overcome by admitting of the possibility of relating the self-moving object with itself as with 'its other', which appears as the identity of equal quantities, but of opposite sign.

For Julia Kristeva, an androgyny or bisexuality seen as the traversing or transgression of boundaries, where the 'subject' no longer experiences sexual difference in 'essentialist' terms as a fixed opposition between 'man' and 'woman', but as a liberating process of sexual differentiation amounting to a perpetual alternation and confusion of 'subject-positions', eluding the totalising grasp, or the *Aufhebung* of the philosopher Hegel, which expresses his desire for a final resolution or synthesis of the opposed terms; where spirit unites with nature and indeed becomes its master, because nature turns out to belong to spirit, to be nothing other than spirit, where, as Hegel writes, "nature is the bride which spirit marries". A reunion of opposites essentially identical, just like the marriage of Adam and Eve.

By rejecting the invasion of the body by external matter, and avoiding the consumption of food as an external 'pollutant', the anorexic - like a true philosophical Idealist! - aspires to escape from the confused, mutable and brutish world of materiality towards a stabilised unity of identity, the Good and the Perfect, the Absolute Idea or Universal Subject, which is God: disembodied thought thinking itself. For the anorexic, therefore, "The ultimate self-abjective wish becomes the desire to completely eliminate 'flesh', to become 'pure'."

As an alternative to the transcendental ego of the Hegelian spirit, Kristeva opts for a disordered and lyrical 'subject-in-process'; a subversion of the "convenient lie" of the symbolic order: that sequence of time and life of the classical narrative, with its "extreme precision, its orderly and military progress"; for, "there is always deep below it a rushing stream of broken dreams, nursery rhymes, street cries, half-finished sentences and sights". A dislocation of historical syntax such that history is experienced not as a narrative progression and sequential unfolding of a story-line or 'plot', in accordance with notions of 'historical development' and inevitable 'progression' towards some climactic conclusion or final synthesis, but is instead pictured as *"rhythmic"*, and even cyclic: somatic drives that disrupt, oppose and threaten meaning and social order. Thus the cyclical rhythm of the culturally defined biological phenomenon of menstruation subtly interrupts conventional depictions of linear temporality as an infinite line of progress (the metaphor of the line to describe our experience of time) with a renewed recognition of the cyclical and the monumental; a recognition of the interrelations that circulate between future, present and past.

These instinctual, biological drives destabilise the fixity and allocated 'subject-positions' of the speaking 'I' or unitary 'ego', resulting in a more primitive and dynamic aggregation of pleasurable and erotic bodily sensations. A process of perpetual negation involving continual irruptions of powerful semiotic pulsations and desires, with the potential to break up the inertia and calcified rigidities (character armour) of routine behaviour patterns and the sclerotic deposits (clichés) of language habits, thus presenting a threat to such fixed signs of the symbolic order as paternal authority, the state, the family, private property, and propriety.

Antonin Artaud structures his account of the Roman Emperor Heliogabalus' life around the breaking of borders and the expulsion of fluids, notably blood and sperm: "Around the corpse of Heliogabalus – dead without a tomb, and cut apart by his police in the latrines of his own palace – there is an intense circulation (and symbolic communication) of blood and excrement, while around his cradle, there is an intense circulation of sperm." Artaud declares: "I am Heliogabalus, the mad Roman Emperor", whose anarchic reign expresses the poetry of sexuality and a cruelty that exceeds all boundaries:

> Poetry is the grinding of a multiplicity which throws out flames. And poetry, which brings back order, first of all resuscitates disorder, disorder with inflamed appearances; it makes appearances collide and brings them back to a unique point: fire, gesture, blood, scream.

The polymorphously perverse desires and pulsating drives of the semiotic body are revealed in rhythmic flows, intonations, repetitions, and psychotic babble. A poetic text where rupture and discontinuity predominate, and fragmentation replaces cohesion. A condition that resolves itself into an 'impossible dialectic': a transgression and dissolution of boundaries; a hybridity and an androgyny, simultaneously enacting socially prohibited impulses while demanding their 'symbolic' repression, containment, ordered articulation and enunciation, in the organised form of a speaking 'subject'. A process culminating in the necessary curtailment and organised 'symbolic' articulation, codification and recuperation of an ambivalent and provisional 'unity' of opposed desires: "(appropriation / rejection, orality / anality, love / hate, life / death)". A condition described by Kristeva in the following terms: "She was a man; she was a woman.......It was a most bewildering and whirligig state to be in".

The 'abject' is a term employed by Kristeva to refer to a class of unspeakable phenomena that are excluded from our sense of social order, phenomena that "disturbs identities, systems, orders. Something that doesn't respect limits, positions, rules. The in-between, the ambiguous, the mixed". The 'abject' also includes whatever reminds us of our material natures, threatening to disrupt the notion of ourselves as individual subjects, with secure borders and an unchanging essence or inner 'core' of identity, unified and in command of our identities and our environment. Abjection is a complex mixture of yearning and condemnation, the proper and the improper, order and chaos, preserving "what existed in the archaism of pre-objectal relationships, in the immemorial violence with which the body becomes separated from another body in order to be".

Human beings therefore repress that which reminds them of their corporeality by categorising it as unclean and disgusting. This attempt at exclusion can only ever be partially successful. At moments when we are forced to recognise this, the reaction is one of extreme repulsion - what Kristeva calls an 'act of abjection'. Dirt, disorder and formlessness pose a threat to the body and its boundaries, in the form of a vital distinction between the inside of the body and its outside, the self from the space of the other. In other words, the fixing of limits and boundaries is bound up with the construction of the individual subject as a unified self, with a central 'core' of identity unique to each individual. Conceptualised as wanton materiality, the female body is perceived as a potential threat to this order, lacking containment and issuing filth and corruption from permeable boundaries, porous surfaces and indefinite outlines:

> Any structure of ideas is vulnerable at its margins. We should expect the orifices of the body to symbolise its especially vulnerable points. Matter issuing from them is marginal stuff of the most obvious kind. Spittle, blood, milk, urine, faeces or tears by simply issuing forth have traversed the boundary of the body.

In addition, Kristeva describes the abject as possessing the qualities of Otherness, and the ambivalence of horror and desire. The abject is a polluting agent, defined against the boundaries it threatens. Excluded as unclean and improper from the logical and social order of the 'symbolic', its psychic structure can be traced back, according to Kristeva, to a primary narcissism ; a narcissism laden with an hostility without limits, where the instincts of life and death merge together into a "violence of mourning for an 'object' that has always already been lost".

The lost object is the mother, and the unfulfilled desire for her is laden with unacceptable wishes of forbidden (polymorphously perverse) pleasures and drives (love/hate, life/death) that need to be sublimated. Like a taboo it is born out of primal repression which designates and excludes the mother's body as the non-object (or 'abject-object') of desire. According to Kristeva, this primal repression, which is pre-verbal (unspeakable), is displaced through a process of denial onto another object, a metaphor, through signification, symbolisation and sublimation (including fetishism and phobia). Thus the psychic and social mechanisms of displacing the abject are a transformation of the impossible object into a fantasy of desire, where the unspeakable is uttered through rhythm and song and the sublimation of artistic production.

According to Kristeva, "the existence of psychoanalysis reveals the permanence, the ineluctability of crisis" of "The speaking being (who) is a wounded being, with its discourse dumb from the disorder of love, and the 'death drive' (Freud) coextensive with humanity". In *Beyond the Pleasure Principle,* Sigmund Freud describes the death drive as "the most universal endeavour of all living substance - namely to return to the quiescence of the inorganic world". Like a river winding its way back to the sea, life is but a series of "complicated *detours*" or "circuitous paths to death". Freud's illustrations of this drive include the "momentary extinction" of orgasm, and a story of origins derived from "the poet-philosopher" Plato: "the hypothesis that living substance at the time of its coming to life was torn apart into small particles, which have ever since endeavoured to reunite through the sexual instincts".

The speculations of Freud on the nature of living substance at the time of its coming into being, bears a resemblance to the theories of the biochemist Lynn Margulis on the origin of nucleated cells. According to Margulis, for millions of years before cells with nuclei appeared, living prokaryotes (cells without nuclei) dominated the Earth. Margulis contends that nucleated cells originated when non-nucleated bacteria devoured one another. Some of the bacteria that were eaten were not digested or destroyed, but somehow managed to survive and adapt to live inside their host predator cells as symbiotic organelles: little organs. Cells within cells utterly interdependent (endosymbiotic), forming stable, compound organisms - new wholes far greater than the sum of their parts. These compound organisms gradually evolved into fully fledged eukaryotes - living cells that possess a central nucleus suspended in cytoplasm: the whole wrapped in a cell wall, like the yolk of an egg surrounded by a protein sac, safely enveloped within a protective shell (an 'enceinte'). For Margulis, multicellular organisms, such as our-selves, are coordinated collective composites or colonies of cells, and each individual cell is likewise a composite of cooperating micro-organisms.

Margulis' theories intersect with Freud's own speculations about the history of living substance, with the added twist that for Freud this substance was originally a unity that has somehow been torn apart and is forever striving towards regaining this long lost unity in the form of an ever more complex "combination of the particles into which living substance is dispersed". Freud marvels at the seemingly insurmountable difficulties encountered by these early unicellular organisms - "splintered fragments of living substance" - in their first attempts at reuniting as multicellular entities, and the necessity "which compelled them to form a protective cortical layer.......by an environment charged with dangerous stimuli". For Freud it would appear that the colonies of cells that make up the multicellular organism collectively constitute a defence mechanism against a hostile external environment.

Then there is Freud's equation of life and death, the animate and the inanimate: "the hypothesis of a death instinct, the task of which is to lead organic life back into the inanimate state". Perhaps this final state of entropic dissolution and restful oblivion is a return to the unity originally lost. Freud's answer to the question of life's purpose and direction appears endlessly circular, a ceaseless ebb and flow - "But here, I think, the moment has come for breaking off".

For Artaud 'cruelty' encapsulates the tight rapport between life and death:

> Above all, cruelty is lucid; it is a kind of rigid direction, submission to necessity. No cruelty without consciousness, without a kind of applied

> consciousness. It is consciousness which gives to the exercise of every action in life its colour of blood, its cruel touch, since it must be understood that to live is always through the death of someone else.

The process "which makes mammiferous larvae into human children, *masculine* or *feminine subjects*" begins with the body of the newly-born infant, which is a seething mass of excitations, impulses and instinctual drives; a disorganised bundle of parts and sensations (the body 'in bits and pieces'), completely lacking in any sense of itself as a coherent, unified entity. Freud terms this the 'primary narcissistic' or 'polymorphously perverse' stage of infantile development: a stage with no sense of 'self', centring or organisation, where the desiring sensations ('libido') are diffused throughout the entire body, internally and upon the skin's surface. This amounts to a strange blend of self-sufficiency on the one hand, mobility and dispersion on the other.

Gradually the infant begins to view itself as a coherent, unified being, distinct from its mother and its environment. This awareness of the difference between the self and the rest of the world is the foundation upon which the infant begins to acquire language. Language provides the infant with the means for articulating reality, realising its struggle for reintegration as a coherent subject. For Kristeva, however, both the infant's and adult's idealised representation of themselves as autonomous, whole beings is an illusion. The 'self' or 'ego' is 'in reality' fragmented and disjointed; and the sense of completeness, wholeness, and oneness characteristic of the imaginary, ideal self which we identify with and seek, exists as an unattainable fiction.

For Kristeva, cultural production is implicated in this ideological process of constituting – *'interpellating'* – human beings as coherent Subjects in conformity with the controlling ego of traditional Western philosophy (a view enunciated by the philosopher Rene Descartes, who declares: '(I) think therefore (I) am'). The fractured, multifaceted, fragmentary and contradictory nature of the self is denied, and anything that threatens the illusory integrity of the ego and its borders is ruthlessly excluded as 'abject'. The classic realist text or painting plays its part in constituting the subject by inscribing the viewer or reader within the work itself, providing a place for the viewer or reader to occupy if 'he' or 'she' is to enter this ideal fiction of an integrated subject, basking in the illusion of possessing secure boundaries and a stable, fixed 'subject-position' (and sense of 'self').

Indeed, Kristeva has coined the concept of *intertextuality* to describe the use of poetic language that "pluralizes, pulverizes" and "musicalizes" all static socio-symbolic order – from the bourgeois state and family to the naturalist text and the punctual, unitary subject. In place of one voice (the 'internal monologue'), a multitude of voices (an 'external polylogue'). Thus, in place of a subjectivity conceived as expressing itself from some 'inner space', there is an explosion or hollowing out of the subject, and its mutation into a 'surface' where a dynamic mix of languages intersect. Writing that shifts from one topic to another, challenging and transgressing limits and boundaries in an operation that transforms verbal energy, its discontinuities and mobile contradictions, into a polyphonic musicality. This involves a limitless "perspective of citations, fragments, of voices from other texts, other codes....silent quotations, without inverted commas, with no precise source.....an exploitation of the plurality of language, through processes of echoing, re-calling". According to Kristeva, "What is implied is that language, and thus sociability, are defined by boundaries admitting of upheaval, dissolution and transformation."

A practice described by the writer Helene Cixous: "I was eating the texts, I was sucking, licking, kissing them, I am the innumerable child of their multitudes." An intertextuality involving techniques of layering, over-lapping, intercutting and collage, akin to the poetry of T.S. Eliot, staunchly criticised by Conrad Aiken for having created " 'a literature of literature', a kind of parasitic growth on literature, a sort of mistletoe." Ultimately, "It is not so much that the author produces his text, as that the text 'produces itself' through the author".

If the classic realist text provides the reader with the illusion of stable boundaries and a fixed subjectivity and identity, for Kristeva the 'revolutionary' ('avant-garde') art of the late nineteenth and twentieth centuries exploits the semiotic dimension of the signifying process. Mallarme, Nerval, Joyce, Celine and Artaud (to name but a few) subvert the existing configuration of the symbolic order and the rational defences of conventional social meaning through 'revolutionary' forms of writing. The presence of abrupt shifts, breaks and the apparent lack of logical, 'authorial' construction or intentionality, facilitates the release of the semiotic rhythms of the body and the unconscious, producing a 'subject in process': "every individual is a conglomeration of social influences, tied in a small knot", derived from the tension, dialectical contradiction and provisional synthesis between the symbolic (ordered/social) and the semiotic (instinctual/somatic) realms. The resulting 'subject' exists as an anomalous reverberation of the semiotic within the symbolic; a reverberation that combines unity, separation and fragmentation ("the fractured I – the dissolved self"). Thus for Kristeva:

> Artaud interrogates the established institutions in order to have done with language and the unity of consciousness. He sets up this tug of war with possibility, where on the one hand there is the possibility of speaking to people who come to hear him or of writing books, and on the other hand there is the experience of non-sense, for example in the texts composed of glossololalia which mean nothing and are totally explosive, which are no longer language but pure drive. So it is this kind of balancing act that he is trying to sustain with regard to values – whilst exposing himself in an immense rage against others and himself – that I was examining and was attempting to go along with.

The notion of the infant's body as fragmented and fluid (the body 'in bits and pieces') corresponds to the psychoanalyst Jacques Lacan's 'pre-mirror' stage. For Lacan, the newly-born infant is not yet a complete human being: physiologically the nervous system is not yet fully formed, and socially language is still to be acquired. The infant is unable to differentiate itself from its mother or its surrounding environment. A condition described by Freud as resolving itself through a process whereby the child's disorganised desiring sensations gradually coalesce and become focussed onto the mouth as the first in a developmental succession of organs of pleasure ('erogenous zones'). For it is through the mouth that the child makes contact with the principle object of desire - the mother's breast.

To the newly-born infant, the outer world with its infinite stimuli is chaotic, a chaos from which the sensations from its own body are a part. Ego and outer world, self and other, are experienced as a unity. All that is pleasurable belongs to an expanded ego, "which absorbs into identity with itself the sources of its pleasure, its world, its mother". With time, this changes. Sensations belonging to the outer world are recognised as internal to the body, while parts of the outer world which are pleasurable, such as the maternal nipple, are recognised as belonging to the world outside. In this way, a unified ego gradually crystallises from the primordial chaos of internal and external perceptions, and establishes boundaries separating itself from an outside reality. The ego thus becomes "a shrunken vestige of a far more extensive (oceanic) feeling - a feeling which embraced the universe and expressed an inseparable connection of the ego with the external world".

Freud's pre-Oedipal stage of the self-absorbed, narcissistic infant, shares with Lacan's notion of the 'pre-mirror' stage a common understanding of the similarity between the infant's and the schizophrenic adult's manner of experiencing the world. Both describe the experience of a harmony without any boundary between ego ('self' or 'subject') and an outer world of 'external' 'objects'.

The onset of Jacques Lacan's 'mirror stage' marks the illusory and complex development of a separate ego formed as part of a narcissistic relationship between self and other, and the division of an androgynous whole into two symmetrical male and female images; torn halves that gaze longingly at each other across an abyss of difference that both joins and separates. Lacan uses the term 'imaginary' to denote the way in which the subject is seduced by this image of otherness (initially the mirror reflection of the body) taking this image as a representation of the 'self'. In the mirror stage, the human being attempts to coordinate an amalgam of sensory and motor reflexes and responses via the establishment of a fixed and rigid 'Ideal-I', consisting of an imaginary, ideal image with which he or she will never coincide, and an 'I' that can never be realised. This ideal domain of the self-contained ego belongs to the symbolic order of language, of the Name-of-the-Father, of castration and the unconscious (an internalised authority Lacan describes as the 'ideal incubus').

Lacan contends that at the heart of the ego lies a complete void: "The ego is constructed like an onion; one could peel it, and discover the successive identifications which have constituted it". An inexhaustible search comparable to the endless labour of 'laying bare', 'extracting' and 'refining', involved in the process of revealing that elusive 'rational kernel' concealed somewhere beneath the superimposed skins - "of a certain crust which is more or less thick (think of a fruit, an onion, or even an artichoke)" - constituting the external, 'mystical shell' of Hegel's philosophy of the Absolute Idea. Referring to Hegel's system, Lacan concludes: "when one is made into two, there is no going back on it. It can never revert to making one again, not even a new one. The *Aufhebung* (sublation) is one of those sweet dreams of philosophy".

Freud discusses the formation of a bounded sense of self, of the 'ego', and the separation of the ego (subject) from the external world (object) as a process whereby:

> Objects presenting themselves, in so far as they are sources of pleasure, are absorbed by the ego into itself, 'introjected'...........while, on the other hand the ego thrusts forth upon the external world whatever within itself gives rise to pain (the mechanism of projection).

According to Lacan, prior to the onset of the 'mirror stage', the child is completely devoid of any sense of itself as a 'unity', and lacks a fixed sense of itself as possessing a coherent 'identity' separate from whatever is 'other' or external to it. A transformation takes place, however, with the arrival of the mirror stage, when the child, like the legendary Narcissus, falls in love with the reflected image of itself, and identifies with this illusory 'other' as an ideal image of wholeness and 'subject hood'. Lacan describes the mirror stage as the ineluctable unfolding of a drama:

> The *mirror stage* is a drama whose internal thrust is precipitated from insufficiency to anticipation - which manufactures for the subject, caught up in the lure of spatial identification, the succession of

> phantasies that extends from a fragmented body-image, manifested in dreams as the individual's aggressive disintegration, in the form of disjointed limbs, or of those organs represented in exoscopy, growing wings and taking up arms for intestinal persecutions - the very same that the visionary Hieronymus Bosch has fixed, for all time, in painting, in their ascent from the fifteenth century to the imaginary zenith of modern man.

A drama that commences with the infant's emergence from an undifferentiated state of insufficiency (the body in bits and pieces) into an orthopaedic 'form', which is then 'finalised' in the fixed position of a unitary 'subject', in conjunction with the formation of a protective armour: the isolating "armour of an alienating identity, which will mark with its rigid structure the subject's entire mental development". The armour of an alienating identity that compares with the carapaces of insects and the rigid, undifferentiated, automatic (and 'unfeeling') nature of their stimulus and response motor reactions towards the pressure of instinctual drives triggered by external events.

A paroxysm or 'reification' of consciousness, spreading outwards from within; a consciousness externalised to become frozen in behaviours rendered ever more precise, involving organic adjustments resulting in a somatic morphology where individual particularities disappear. Where operations, once performed, seem to become charged with habit and are hardened into mechanical reflexes or instincts narrowly canalised, materialised into a series of rigid arrangements akin to the operations of a machine.

Thus the machine-like automatism of the 'ichneumonid wasp' (a group of several hundred related species of wasps), which instinctively seeks out and encounters either a cricket or a caterpillar, paralyses the 'host' insect with its sting, and then inserts its eggs into the host's body. When the larvae hatch they eat the living, paralysed body of the host from the inside out - carefully avoiding the vital organs in order to extend the life (and agony) of the host for as long as possible lest its body decay prematurely, spoiling the meat . For Charles Darwin, a man who at first writes that he does not "in the least doubt the strict and literal truth of the Bible", the sight of Ichneumons "tearing their prey to bits" precipitates a crisis, forcing him to pose the theological question: "How could a beneficent God have willed it so"? In contrast, the entomologist William Kirby esteems the ichneumonid wasp most highly for its judicious husbanding of its economic resources:

> In this strange and apparently cruel operation one circumstance is truly remarkable. The larva of the Ichneumon, though every day, perhaps for months, it gnaws the inside of the caterpillar, and though at last it has devoured almost every part of it except the skin and intestines, carefully all this time it avoids injuring the vital organs, as if aware that its own existence depends on that of the insect upon which it preys!

With equal respect, the entomologist J. M. Fabre describes with horrified fascination and in meticulous detail how the lava of the Ichneumon manipulates the movements of its cricket host:

> One may see the cricket, bitten to the quick, vainly move its antennae and abdominal styles, open and close its empty jaws, and even move a foot, but the lava is safe and searches its vitals with impunity. What an awful nightmare for the paralysed cricket!

The ability and the calculated precision of the Ichneumon are not acquired through practice - it is an inflexible 'instinctual' response to external stimuli, a biological quality inherent in the wasp. As a matter of fact we know that the outstanding difference between human beings and their fellow animals consists in the infantile morphological characteristics of human beings, in the prolongation of their infancy. This prolonged infancy allows for a certain plasticity whereby the rigid motor responses of instinctual behaviour are superseded by the transmission of culture and the capacity to 'learn', adapt to and modify the external environment. This explains the traumatic character of sexual experiences not shared by our animal brethren, and the existence of the Oedipus Complex itself, which is a conflict between the instinctual drives of the Id and the demands of cultural adaptation, expressed as an internalised conflict between archaic and recent love objects. Finally, the defence mechanisms themselves owe their existence to the fact that the human 'Ego' is even more retarded than the instinctual 'Id'; hence the immature 'Self' or 'Ego' evolves defence mechanisms as a protection against libidinal quantities which it is not prepared to deal with:

> In man, however, this relation to nature is altered by a certain de-hiscence at the heart of the organism, a primordial Discord betrayed by the signs of uneasiness and motor unco-ordination of the neo-natal months. The objective notion of the anatomical incompleteness of the pyramidal system and likewise the presence of certain humoral residues of the maternal organism confirm the view I have formulated as the fact of a real *specific prematurity of birth* in man. It is worth noting, incidentally, that this is a fact recognized as such by embryologists, by the term *foetalization,* which determines the prevalence of the so-called superior apparatus of the neurax, and especially of the cortex, which psycho-surgical operations lead us to regard as the intra-organic mirror.

The theory of retardation is also put forward from another point of view by Robert Briffault:

> It has been seen that the power of nutrition and of reproduction decrease in the cell in proportion to the degree of fixation of its reactions, that is, in proportion to its differentiation and specialization.....The higher the degree of specialized organization and differentiation which the cells of the developing being have to attain, the slower the rate of growth. Hence it is that the higher we proceed in the scale of mammalian evolution, the longer is the time devoted to gestation. Even more important is the fact that, although the time of gestation is thus lengthened, the rate of individual development becomes slower as we rise in the scale of

> organization and the young are brought into the world in a condition of greater immaturity.

Infantile or foetal characteristics which are temporary in other animals therefore seem to have become stabilised in the human species. In *Race, Sex and Environment,* Marett makes bold as to speculate that the causes of human retardation can be traced back through psychology and the endocrine system to minerals available in the soil. According to Marett, "Lack of any structural material would seem in the long run likely also to result in a slow rate of growth." "Lime deficiency is thus thought to encourage femininity, and iodine shortage to favour fetalization. Yet since many of the aspects of youth and femininity are similar, it will not be easy to distinguish between the two possible causes of a similar state." Regardless of the validity of these conjectures, *fetalisation* or *paedomorphosis* are generally acknowledged as one of the processes whereby human characteristics have emerged in evolution.

The structural anthropology of Claude Levi-Strauss focuses on the analysis of the 'synchronic' structures characteristic of 'cold' or 'primitive' societies designated as timeless and static, and permanently stabilised in the reproduction of one and the same cycle. In contrast, the 'diachronic' sequences of 'hot' or 'advanced' societies considered as evolving 'in history', involving processes of movement and change, seem to elude the grasp of Levi-Strauss' structural analysis. It appears that events already frozen in the historical past survive in our consciousness only as myth, for it is an intrinsic characteristic of myth (as it is also of Levi Strauss' system of structural analysis) that the chronological ('diachronic') sequence of events is irrelevant. The analysis of structures is strictly designed to determine how relations which exist in Nature (and are apprehended as such by human brains) are used to generate cultural products which incorporate these same relations.

Against the philosophical 'idealists' who contend that Nature has no existence other than its apprehension by human minds, Levi-Strauss' approach is 'materialist': Nature is for him a genuine reality 'out there'. A Nature governed by natural laws which are accessible, at least in part, to human scientific investigation. But our capacity to apprehend the nature of

Nature is severely restricted by the nature of the apparatus (the human brain) through which we do the apprehending. The structural analysis of 'primitive' myths, by carefully examining the classifications and resulting categories used in the processes of apprehending Nature, attempts to gain an insight into the workings of the 'universal' codes and structures that govern the mechanisms of our thinking. Accordingly, social structures mirror the structures of the mind, replicating those of the brain, itself a part of the matter in which the whole of the cosmos is in turn reflected:

> Thus simultaneously the myths themselves are generated by the mind that causes them, and through the myths is generated an image of the world that is already inscribed in the architecture of the mind.

On the face of it, Levi-Strauss' notion of a fundamental divide between 'myth' (the synchronic) and 'history' (the diachronic) seems to share an affinity with Julia Kristeva's perspective on the division between the cyclic or monumental time of motherhood and reproduction, and the linear, historical time of production and the symbolic discourse of language, considered as the enunciation of an ordered sequence of words. However, Kristeva transforms this division into a complex dialectical relationship and reciprocal interaction between, on the one hand, a polymorphously perverse and chaotic semiotic realm, "detected genetically in the first echolalias of infants as rhythms and intonations", and, on the other hand, the symbolic order and fixity of the speaking 'subject'.

A division that compares with the philosopher Friedrich Nietzsche's duality of the Dionysian element of raw chaotic sensual power versus the balanced order and organisation of the Apollonian aesthetic (and the synthesis of the Dionysian with the Apollonian in the culture of the ancient Greeks), or the philosopher Henri Bergson's duality of the spontaneous and creative flow of interpenetrating qualities which he terms 'duration', in opposition to the 'geometric' order of well-defined elements organised in accordance with definite rules. For Leon Trotsky the powerful flow is by its very nature a primordial rawness prior to any organised structure. Moreover, it expresses a protest against artificiality, a move away from the static rigidities and impositions of an outworn established order: "While in our uncouth Russia there is much barbarism, almost zoologism, in the old bourgeois cultures of the West there are horrible encrustations of fossilized narrow-mindedness, crystallized cruelty, polished cynicism".

In accordance with this view, civilisation establishes an elaborate code of distinctions, and these distinctions govern everything. As distinctions exhaust their power to distinguish, new ones are employed. The tendency is toward finer and finer discrimination and increasing attention to detail, to the point of decadence. A view taken up by Roland Barthes who contends that 'myth', like a parasite, saps the living energy of history:

> For the very end of myths is to immobilise the world: they must suggest and mimic a universal order which has fixated once and for all a hierarchy of possessions. Thus, every day and everywhere, man is stopped by myths, referred by them to this motionless prototype which lives in his place, and stifles him in the manner of a huge internal parasite assigning to his activity the narrow limits within which he is allowed to suffer without upsetting the world.

The civilising process is directed towards self-restraint, as Norbert Elias so clearly shows. The ways in which this restraint is marked - the specific forms, details and nuances - give class culture its distinctive flavour at each point in history. Habituated and internalised, the emotional economy of social nicety creates thresholds of embarrassment that shift. Practices once considered perfectly acceptable, such as wiping the hands on the table cloth, are later experienced as disgusting. Nowhere is taste so vividly inscribed as on the body, which the good manners of polite society systematically deny. The body in good taste is conceived as self-contained, whole and complete (or is discreetly altered to appear so). It derives from the values propagated by the European Enlightenment - reason, moderation, classical formality, individual autonomy and monadic self-sufficiency. But there is also a grotesque body, which, according to Kristeva's study of Mikhail Bakhtin's work on the writings of Francois

Rabelais, is "not a closed completed unit; it is unfinished, outgrows itself, transgresses its own limits. The stress is laid on those parts through which the world enters the body or emerges from it, or through which the body itself goes out to meet the world. This means that the emphasis is on the apertures or the convexities, or on the various ramifications and offshoots: the open mouth, the genital organs, the breasts, the phallus, the potbelly, the nose".

Thus the critical theorist Theodor Adorno argues that the stereotypical Jewish nose produces the virulent hatred of the anti-Semite towards the persecuted:

> The nose - the physiognomic *principium individuationis*, symbol of the specific character of an individual, described between the lines of his countenance. The multifarious nuances of the sense of smell embody the archetypal longing for the lower forms of existence, for direct unification with circumambient nature, with the earth and mud. Of all the senses, that of smell bears closest witness to lose oneself in and become the 'other'. When we see we remain what we are; but when we smell we are taken over by otherness. It is the trend to lose oneself in the environment instead of playing an active role in it; the tendency to let oneself go and sink back into nature. Freud calls it the death instinct, Roger Caillois *'le mimetisme'*. This urge underlies everything which runs counter to bold progress, from the crime which is a shortcut avoiding the normal forms of activity, to the sublime work of art. A yielding attitude to things, without which art cannot exist, is not so very remote from the violence of the criminal. Hence the sense of smell is considered a disgrace to civilization, the sign of lower social strata, lesser races and base animals.

According to Freud the replacement of smell by sight as the dominant and superior sense occurred at a stage in human evolution when "as a result of our adopting an erect gate, we raised our organ of smell from the ground". The adoption of an upright posture visibly exposed the vulnerability of the human genitalia, necessitating the development of a protective sense of shame associated with the emergence of an 'organic repression', ultimately resulting in the foundation of the family unit and civilised society. Freud associates the diminution of the olfactory sense with the "cultural trend towards cleanliness", resulting in general feelings of disgust directed towards bodily excreta. The residual coprophilic instinctual components of the body are in turn derided by society as perverse and incompatible with the norms of civilised 'human' behaviour and the refinements of culture. But the instincts remain active, which is why; still, "the excremental is all too intimately and inseparably bound up with the sexual". Freud concludes that the net effect of society's repression and sublimation of these bodily instincts can be detected in a general lack of sexual satisfaction and in a corresponding increased incidence of mental disorders and neurotic illness.

Julia Kristeva's celebration of ugliness as thematised in the writings of Mikhail Bakhtin and Charles Baudelaire, signifies an eruption of the sensual and erotic drives of the semiotic body in protest against its repression on the part of the rational ego, which belongs to the established order of the 'symbolic'. As such, the thematisation of ugliness represents a direct assault on enlightened subjectivity's horror of the unformed, its aversion in face of that which has escaped the levelling, identitarian stamp of 'civilised' life. The aesthetics of ugliness, therefore, reminds civilisation of a stage of development prior to the rational individuation of the species in face of primordial nature, the stage of its undifferentiated unity with nature, a moment of 'weakness' and 'vulnerability' civilisation has attempted to repress from memory. For civilisation is seized by an overwhelming fear of relapse into that primordial, pre-individualised state against which it struggled so concertedly to free itself that it has become tragically incapable of releasing itself from the rigidification of the ego synonymous with the principle of rational control. For in order to elevate itself above the level of a merely natural existence and thus arrive at self-consciousness as a species, humanity is required to subjugate its own inner nature, that is, become attuned to the renunciation of the instinctual drives of the semiotic body demanded by a 'reality principle' necessary for the level of cooperation required for the conquest and subjugation of external nature.

For Kristeva, the 'pre-symbolic' realm of nature is synonymous with the 'pre-symbolic' semiotic space/time of the child's initial fusion with and dependency upon the body of its m(other). The dialectic or process of self-consciousness which enables self-identity (the same) to distinguish itself from what is 'other', that is, the formation of subjective and objective identity, necessitates the denial and repression of this pre-symbolic state of fusion with the maternal body. The repression of the maternal body in turn provides the foundations for the social and symbolic mastery of nature, the body, of the non-identical, and of the heterogeneous. According to Kristeva, "Fear of the archaic mother proves essentially to be a fear of her generative power. It is this power, dreaded, that patrilineal filiation is charged with subduing".

Yet, in the end, the rigidification of the ego required for this purpose is ultimately so extreme that the original goal of the process, the eventual pacification of the struggle for existence and the attainment of a state of reconciliation with nature, is eventually lost sight of; and the means to this end, the domination of nature, is enthroned as an end in itself. For once the 'subject' comes to perceive itself as absolute and its 'other', the maternal body of nature, as merely the stuff of domination, this logic ultimately exacts its revenge upon the 'subject', which has somehow forgotten that the 'other' is a moment internal to itself, in other words, that humanity, too, is part of corporeal nature and is consequently a victim of its own ruthless apparatus of control. A tragic dialectic ensues, whereupon "Man's domination over himself, which grounds his selfhood, is almost always the destruction of the subject in whose service it is undertaken; for the substance which is dominated, suppressed and dissolved through self-preservation is none other than that very life as a function of which the achievements of self-preservation are defined; it is, in fact, what is to be preserved".

Reason abstracts, and seeks to comprehend through concepts and names. Abstraction, which can grasp the concrete only insofar as it reduces it to identity, also liquidates the otherness of the other. By making ugliness thematic, the poetry of Charles Baudelaire gives a voice to those oppressed and non-identical elements of society anathematised by the dominant powers of social control that are commonly denied expression in the extra-aesthetic world. Baudelaire's poems articulate the right of the other, of the non-identical, to be. It accomplishes this task by rejecting the burden of the concept and returning to the word's forgotten, repressed meanings through the agency of metaphor. The significance of ugliness, the tendency toward the incorporation of increasingly ignoble, unrefined themes in art, in contrast to the consistently more exalted concerns of classical art, is clearly expressed in the title selected by Baudelaire for his major collection of poems, *Les Fleurs de mal.*

The notion that something ugly can be 'beautiful', that in fact in can be beautiful precisely because it is ugly, tests the boundaries of the permissible, opening up immense, previously untapped reservoirs of experience. Poking fun at those painters who find nineteenth-century dress excessively ugly, Baudelaire celebrates the black frock-coat and dress-coat as "the necessary costume of our time" expressing the intimate relationship of modernity with death: "The dress-coat and frock-coat not only possess their political beauty, which is an expression of universal equality, but also their poetic beauty, which is an expression of the public soul - an immense cortege of undertaker's mutes (mutes in love, political mutes, bourgeois mutes). We are each of us celebrating some funeral."

Baudelaire cites the example of the artist Constantin Guys, a spectator and collector of modern life's curiosities: "this solitary, gifted with an active imagination, ceaselessly journeying across the great human desert - the last to linger wherever there is a glow of light, an echo of poetry, a quiver of life or a chord of music; wherever a passion can pose before him, wherever natural man and conventional man display themselves in a strange beauty, wherever the sun lights up the swift joys of the depraved animal."

Julia Kristeva shares Charles Baudelaire's fascination with the combined figures of the dandy and the *flaneur*, the artist and the poet, keenly receptive and perfectly at home in the streets, drifting through the crowded boulevards, painting in colours and in words the sensory array and variegated experiences of modern life. The artist adrift, acutely sensitive to the sadness of loss and the inevitably of decay captured in the fading and fragile beauty of each fleeting moment; a sadness reflected in the momentary glance of every stranger briefly encountered while passing through the city's crowded streets. The wandering poet whose artistic creations disrupt the fossilised social conventions of the symbolic order by resurrecting through the colour and play of words the memory of the semiotic experience: a feeling of bliss and unity, an ecstatic dissolution of the boundaries and divisions that separate, a sensation of 'oceanic' oneness; feelings and sensations synonymous with that original state of fusion of the infant's body with the body of its mother. The restoration of a 'love' experienced as the extinction of otherness; a love that the art of poetry articulates through the agency of 'metaphor', or the 'marriage' of one object with another; an analogical mode of thinking defined by the poet Stephane Mallarme as the secret to the 'mystery' of poetic creation: "Herein lies the whole mystery: to pair things off and establish secret identities that gnaw at objects and wear them away in the name of a central purity."

The *flaneur* or dandy, immersed in the flux of each passing moment, produce themselves as objects of a continual aesthetic elaboration whereby their passions, their behaviours, and their very lives, become works of art in a perpetual process of formation. Charles Baudelaire, poet and dandy, exemplifies for Kristeva her notion of the 'subject-in-process', with "flowing locks, pink gloves, coloured nails as well as hair", who produces himself through the very act of writing his poetry. Poetry that dissolves and then merges objects together again into one harmonious unity of the senses: a 'synaesthesia' of the senses consisting in the disintegrated displacement and reassembled condensation of sensations fused together into a unity; a process amounting to the poetic re-enchantment of the everyday, familiar world. Poetry that evokes for Kristeva "that archaic universe, preceding sight, where what takes place is the conveyance of the most opaque lovers' indefinite identities, together with the chilliest words: 'There are strong perfumes for which all matter is porous. They seem to penetrate glass'."

Mikhail Bakhtin traces the historical process by which images of fundamental bodily processes like "eating, drinking, copulation, defecation, almost entirely lost their regenerating power and were transformed into 'vulgarities'." Thus a hierarchy is established between the high and the low, the official and the popular, the classical and the grotesque, the top and the bottom, the face and the body's nether regions. Bakhtin celebrates the festivities of the carnival and the antics of the carnivalesque as the symbolic inversion and cultural negation of traditional distinctions between the 'high' and the 'low', leading to the negation and inversion of established social and political cultural codes and norms.

The grotesque body of the carnival is the corporeal body of the multitude, associated with the 'low' and the base, with orifices that leak and drip, with impurity, disproportion, immediacy, and with the porousness and indeterminacy of abject materiality. This is the material body, the direct antithesis to the classically beautiful, ideal body, which is culturally defined as symmetrical, elevated and refined. An ideal body conceptualised as a sealed, self-contained vessel, with a protective shell, or shield, serving to conceal (and deny) its material, corporeal aspect. A bodily ideal verging on the spiritual, symbolising a set of ordered and hierarchical relationships serving to maintain secure and impervious boundaries separating vital distinctions between such designated terms as inside and outside, proper and improper, order and disorder, ugliness and beauty, the corporeal and the spiritual.

In contrast, Bakhtin and Kristeva celebrate the grotesque, lower bodily stratum, expressed in the antics of the clown and the frivolity of the circus, and in the folk imagery contained in Rabelais' joyful descriptions of the medieval carnival. Images of bodily satisfaction and sensual gratification preserved within the oral language traditions and festivities of the common people, and recorded in historical texts concerning antique satiric drama and ancient practices such as the Roman Saturnalia. This is a history that affirms the material principle of the body's resurrection as the location and promise of a utopian alternative. The 'primary processes', subterranean drives, rhythmic pulsions, and libidinal connections of the semiotic body continuously irrupting, subverting, destabilising, and threatening the rigidities and stases of a socio-symbolic order that in turn endeavours to recuperate and contain these potentially destabilising affects by incorporating them into its very structure, in what can only be described as a dialectical conflict and provisional unity of opposites.

For Julia Kristeva, "The semiotic (body) is articulated by flow and energy transfers, the cutting up of the corporeal and social continuum as well as its ordering in a pulsating *chora,* in a rhythmic but nonexpressive totality." Mikhail Bakhtin's image of the grotesque body is Kristeva's semiotic body, the earthly element of the maternal womb, epitomising the cycles of life, death and renewal, terror and delight, as it flowers into new life. For Kristeva (following Bakhtin) the world of Francois Rabelais is an ever-present memory, the return of the repressed, marking the temporary suspension of hierarchy and prohibition, accompanied by the 'unofficial truth' of laughter and freedom from everything that oppresses and restricts; a topsy-turvy, inside-out, back-to-front world. A union of opposites where the top and the bottom change places, where the spiritual is displaced onto the physical, and the superiority traditionally attributed to the mind is overthrown in favour of the 'lower' bodily processes of humanity's supposedly 'animal' functions.

This connects with Kristeva's exploration of the notion of transgression, where to break with conventional cultural boundaries of order and acceptability runs the risk of being designated as 'other' or 'abject': the 'difference' or 'dissidence' associated with deformity, disease, formlessness, disintegration and decay. Where people considered as somehow indeterminate or marginal, that is, as a threat to a culture's definition of what constitutes its notion of secure borders, either geographically (ethnic minorities, refugees), or psychologically (the sexually transgressive, outsiders, the disabled, the sick, women), are liable to be victimised and persecuted in order to preserve an illusory sense of social 'order'.

Arguing against the type of abstract rationalism and 'monological' discourse that recognises only one kind of truth, Bakhtin's and Kristeva's celebration of the grotesque and the carnivalesque affirms the indeterminate, the intermixed, the paradoxical, and the ambivalent. The grotesque body exists as a fluid, split, multiple self; an unfinished and desiring subject-in-process; a corporeal entity open to the processes of reciprocal interaction and exchange occurring within the surrounding environment. In contrast, the classical bodies of the bourgeoisie are described as closed, centred, symmetrical and homogeneous.

Threatening the symmetrical proportions of the classical body and the centrality of the self-contained ego, the 'grotesque' body expresses the supposed vulgarity of corporeality: the physicality and materiality of the 'grotesque' body marginalised and excluded from the privatised interior realm of the privileged and the culturally refined. Accordingly, the materiality of the grotesque and the vulgar is designated as 'other', occupying a low and dirty periphery or 'outside', which, in turn, guarantees a coherent identity to the 'inside'. Ironically, however, the identity formation of the monadic 'subject' is dependant upon this very 'other' which is excluded as an inferior object of disgust (and desire). Thus the 'ideal' realm of 'high' culture, rationalism and civilisation, is based upon psychical processes of disavowal, denial and projection, where it is always someone else who is possessed by the grotesque, never the 'self'.

Moreover, with the extension of the civilising process there arises the necessity for greater controls over 'lower' bodily functions and emotions, producing changes in conduct and manners which heighten the sense of disgust directed towards the direct expression of bodily needs, desires and emotions. Mikhail Bakhtin builds his conception of the polyphonic 'multi-voiced' novel upon a fundamental break with this notion of a self-contained monadic subject, the narrative 'I' with a 'single voice'; instead, characters are conceptualised as nothing more than multiple points of view, a continuous intermixture, a dispersal and provisional reassembly of diverse 'subject positions'; culminating in the open ended freedom of Kristeva's 'subject-in process'. The separation of oneself, as a 'subject', from others and the environment, as 'objects', this differentiation makes culture (the symbolic order of language) possible: "I am not part of the street - no, I describe the street. One splits off, therefore."

Kristeva affirms Bakhtin's determined celebration of "the explosive politics of the body, the erotic, the licentious and semiotic" against the "official, formalistic and logical authoritarianism whose unspoken name is Stalinism." A formalistic style, along with its attendant hierarchy, detected in the novels dissected by Leon Trotsky, the exiled revolutionary opponent and critic of a "degenerated workers' state", the reflux of a revolutionary movement usurped by a "parasitic bureaucratic caste", led and personified by Stalin:

> The normal bourgeois novel has two floors: emotions are experienced only in the *bel-etage* (Proust!), while the people in the basement polish shoes and take out chamber-pots. This is rarely

> mentioned in the novel itself, but presupposed as something quite natural. The hero sighs, the heroine breathes; it follows that they perform other bodily functions too; somebody, then, has to clean up after them. I remember reading a novel of Louys called *Amour and Psyche* - an unusually sham and banal concoction, completed, if I am not mistaken, by the unbearable Claude Farrere. Louys puts the servants somewhere in the nether regions, so that his enamoured hero and heroine never see them. An ideal social system for amorous idlers and their artists!

The inversion of hierarchy is celebrated in Artaud's description, in 'The Race of Lost Men', of the Tarahumara Indians, along with their style of begging in the city streets of Mexico. Artaud applauds the Tarahumaras' display of "supreme contempt. They have an air of saying: 'Since you are rich, you are a dog, I am worth more than you, I spit on you'".

Julia Kristeva supplements the materialist dialectics of Marxism with psychoanalytical theories in an attempt to bridge the gulf separating the 'external', the 'objective' and the 'social' from the 'internal' processes of continual dissolution and reconstruction of the 'subject' conceived as a fluid entity. The result is Kristeva's 'subject-in-process', an inversion of the philosopher Louis Althusser's notion of 'history' as a 'process without a subject'. In this way we arrive at two antithetical systems which internalise and reflect one another's qualities:

On the one hand, we are presented with the view, espoused by Louis Althusser, of the individual as a 'sub-jected' social entity or 'object' of the social ('symbolic') order, allocated a fixed 'subject-position' objectively determined by the dominant mode of production. A process achieved through the mechanism of an ideology designed to constitute individuals as imaginary 'subjects' - centres of free initiative - *of* society, in order to assure their real subjection *to* the social order, as blind supports or victims of a 'closed system' where the worker as the occupant of a predetermined function or position is no longer individually differentiated as a 'work in progress', subject to the processes of change and renewal, but instead is compelled to operate within the rigidly circumscribed and narrowly specialised demands of their particular function and fixed subject-position without ever achieving the opportunity to open themselves up (amorously) to the 'other' as the creative and artistic being s/he potentially is.

On the other hand, we are presented with Kristeva's alternative of a 'living' or 'open system' combining the amorous and the artistic in the mutable form of the 'subject-in-process', conceived as an effective agent of social transformation, heterogeneous and open to the play of difference, exploded, multiple, and fluid, whose transgression of established boundaries is an expression of the *jouissance* embedded in the continuity of self and other that is repressed by the Law of the Father but is never totally destroyed. The organised stability and fixity of society and the 'subject' are revealed as based upon a somewhat tenuous symbolic control over the polymorphous pleasures and the dispersing impulses of the semiotic drives, which threaten apparent unities and stabilities with disruption and dissolution. There is thus a dialectical conflict and resolution of opposites at work; consisting, on the one hand, of drives and impulses belonging to the realm of the semiotic and the biological, and, on the other hand, of organised family and social structures belonging to the symbolic and the social.

The formalism of refined culture, and discourse designated as elevated, dignified and refined, feed voraciously upon, and are nourished and replenished by, the experiences of those designated as low and base, vulgar and exorbitant. Ironically, the socio-symbolic order of 'high' culture thrives upon, articulates, refines, codifies and preserves, in a coherent form, that very 'body' of impure and messy semiotic matter from which it seeks to cleanse itself. Kristeva explores relationships not only of production (cultural and technological), but also of reproduction (corporeality) - "survival of the species, life and death, the body, sex and symbol".

Julia Kristeva's fascination with the conflict, unity, and oscillation between such dualisms as sameness and difference, unity and dispersion, continuity and disruption, sexual desire and death, is an effective reworking and elaboration upon themes explored by the surrealist writer, Georges Bataille. Drawing upon the works of de Sade, Bataille writes of the fundamental link "between death and sexual excitement", adding, "In essence, the domain of eroticism is the domain of violence, of violation". In exploring the perverse and violent nature of sexuality, Bataille rigorously avoids any association or contamination of human eroticism with anything to do with what might be called purely spiritual concepts of ideal beauty, love or romance. Instead, Bataille revels in the connections he painstakingly establishes between eroticism and the more earthly concerns of ripeness and decay, the cycles of sexual expenditure, discharge and release, and 'abject' feelings of repugnance and disgust.

For Bataille, "Eroticism springs from an alternation of fascination and horror", a fascination expressed in the seductive nature of the monstrous and the grotesque. The goal of course is the attainment of unity through the symbolic fusion of two individuals in a sexual embrace that collapses social boundaries and constraints while at the same time destroying for the participants the 'isolation' and 'self-contained character' of their 'normal' lives as 'discontinuous individuals'. An erotic union that completely breaks down the distinction of self and other through a process of the inside collapsing into the outside producing "a feeling of profound continuity"; where the individual, who would normally regard themselves with the utmost importance and their sexuality, as a means, like any other, for their own satisfaction, become conscious of themselves from a biological standpoint as only a brief episode in a succession of generations, as merely a short-lived appendage to a germ-plasm endowed with virtual immortality.

Plato's *Symposium* recounts the ancient Greek myth of the Orphic Eros, simultaneously male and female. A perfect unity expressing the original harmony and unity of the universe:

> In the beginning.............there were three sexes, not as there are now two, male
> and female, but there was also a third which constituted a synthesis of the two others..............It was 'androgynoid', i.e. man-woman, inasmuch as it had the appearance and name of both the male and female sex.

According to Plato's account, as recounted by Aristophanes, this primeval race of androgynes, the ancestors of us all, were bizarre creatures with two faces looking in opposite directions, and with two sets of each pair of limbs: four arms, four legs, two heads, and two sets of genitals. Endowed with this remarkable collection of body parts, and with the back and sides of their bodies forming a perfect circle, they could move either forwards or backwards with incredible speed, rolling around performing cartwheels with the agility and athleticism of circus performers. Zeus, the primal father of the gods, threatened by the might, skill and strength of this race of androgynes, acted to diminish their power and self-sufficiency by splitting them in half "like a sorb apple which is halved for pickling, or as you might divide an egg with a hair." Thus split into two halves, and forever driven by the desire for reunion, each half seeks the other half; a desire only partially and temporarily fulfilled in the unity of the sexual embrace - as if a person looking into a mirror were able to merge with their idealised reflection, becoming one with it. Resulting in a coupling that allows the two separated halves of humanity an imaginary restoration of completeness and wholeness, which was ours originally before the inception of duality.

This division of an original unity is analogous to Theodor Adorno's description of the relationship between high art and popular culture: "torn halves of an integral freedom, to which however they do not add up." Or Kristeva's psychoanalytical reflections on the overt bisexuality of children: that is to say, a girl not only possesses an affectionate attitude ('object-choice') towards her father and an ambivalent attitude towards her mother, but at the same time she also behaves like a boy and displays feelings of jealousy and hostility towards her father and a corresponding affectionate and 'masculine' attitude towards her mother; a process through which 'female' 'subjectivity' is born. This corresponds with Freud's speculations concerning bisexuality and its role in the development of the male-female polarity; speculations that go back to the very origins of his psychoanalytical theories. For instance, in a letter to his friend and collaborator, the nose-and-throat specialist Wilhelm Fliess (who influenced him greatly on the topic), Freud writes: "Bisexuality! I am sure you are right about it. And I am accustoming myself to regarding every sexual act as an event between four individuals."

The ancient Greeks were keenly aware of the crucial importance of clearly defined boundaries as guarantors of human order. Women were regarded as individuals especially lacking in control of their own boundaries. The ancient Greek natural philosopher and physician Hippocrates attributes the difference between male and female to the following:

> The female flourishes more in an environment of water, from things cold and wet and soft.............The male flourishes more in an environment of fire, from dry, hot foods and mode of life.

According to Hippocrates, the condition of dry stability characteristic of the male body is something never attained by the female physique, which remains cold and wet all its life. Due to her innate wetness, women were considered more prone than men to liquefying incursions upon the integrity of their bodies and minds, especially those of love and emotion which were thought to be particularly endangering forms of wetness. The emotions associated with female *Eros* are considered as especially liquid and liquefying, acting to soften, loosen, melt and dissolve physiological and psychological boundaries which men prided themselves on being able to resist.

The clean and proper body for the (male) social subject is therefore based on the exclusion of 'abject' substances that threaten to break boundaries, on the principle of identity without intermixture, the condemnation of hybrids, and an obsessive fear of the threat of undifferentiation. Fluids attest to the undignified material attributes of a bodily existence: to the body's permeability, its vulnerable dependence on an outside, and to the precarious division between the body's inside and its outside; and the ever present danger of its complete collapse into this outside (which is what death represents).

Female sexuality is regarded as an uncontainable flow, associated with what is unclean and contaminating (such as the menstrual flow), with infection, disease, and decay. Liquids are devoid of shape or form. Bodily fluids flow, seep, and infiltrate; their control is a matter of perpetual uncertainty. For Julia Kristeva:

> These body fluids, this defilement, this shit are what life withstands, hardly, and with difficulty, on the part of death. There I am at the border of my condition as a living being................. Excrement and

> its equivalents (decay, infection, disease, corpse, etc.) stand for the danger to identity that comes from without: the ego threatened by the non- ego, society threatened by its outside, life by death.

Artaud celebrates the gestural immediacy and vitality of a theatre that will obliterate the 'spiritual':

> A theatre of blood,
> A theatre where at each performance
> Something
> Will be won
> *Physically.*
> In reality, the theatre is the *birth* of creation.
> That will happen.

The artist Jana Sterbak's *Vanitas: Flesh Dress for an Albino Anorectic*,(1987), an installation consisting of approximately fifty pounds of ageing meat (flank steak) organised by the National Gallery of Canada and presented in Ottawa in 1991, visibly portrays the relationship of meat with the female body as an object of consumption. The decaying meat combined with images of rotting fruit and vegetables, and flowers long past their bloom, suggests the cycle of fertility, birth, ripeness and decay, with its attendant intimations of human mortality. The work plays with the binary distinctions of wet and dry, animal and human, inanimate and animate, body and garment, interior and exterior, life and death. The fifty pounds of decaying meat enclosed within the space of an art gallery also recalls Theodor Adorno's discussion of the unpleasant undertones associated with the German word for museum (*'museal', 'museumlike'*) and its phonetic association with the word 'mausoleum', where "objects to which the observer no longer has a vital relationship are in the process of dying. Museums are like the family sepulchres of works of art. Art treasures are hoarded in them, and their market value leaves no room for the pleasure of looking at them."

In response to Sterbak's installation, the newspapers *Toronto Sun* and *Ottawa Sun* launched a negative campaign against the 'wastefulness' of the exhibition. This included a digitally manipulated image of the flesh dress alongside a recommendation from the editors urging the readers to cut the image out and then mail it to the curator responsible for the exhibit - Diana Nemiroff (address supplied) - suitably smeared with the most disgusting materials possible. Over two hundred readers responded. Some of the mailed images were smeared with excrement, and the gallery's mailroom staff were obliged to sort and open all incoming mail with rubber gloves for weeks on end.

The negative reaction to Jana Sterbak's installations suggests that her flesh dress did not accord with conservative tastes and was perceived as a transgression threatening certain acceptable boundaries. The sheer corporeality of Sterbak's installation shocked a conservative viewing public, and suggests numerous implications. In her book *The Sexual Politics of Meat,* Carol Adams writes:

> People with power have always eaten meat. The aristocracy of Europe consumed large courses filled with every kind of meat while the labourer consumed the complex carbohydrates. Dietary habits proclaim class distinctions, but they proclaim patriarchal distinctions as well. The sexism in meat-eating recapitulates the class distinctions with an added twist: a mythology permeates all classes that meat is a masculine food and meat-eating a male activity. Women are more likely to eat what are considered second-class foods, vegetables, fruits, and grains rather than meat.

The words 'matter' and 'material' come from the Latin word *'materia'*. But *'materia'* is derived from *'mater'*, meaning 'mother'. The material out of which everything is made is, as it were, a mother to it. Male and female are matter and also mater, flesh of their mother's flesh - the male in the early embryonic stages of his development is originally a female, too; and then becomes a variation or possibly even a mutation of the female. Whatever man is, however, woman is not; and with this imposition of the principle of sexual opposition comes the gradual historical definition of man as monopolising all the human skills and abilities, with an emphasis on thought as dominating, and altogether more noble and important than woman conceptualised as the half-formed, imperfect opposite.

This hierarchy of mind over body is duplicated in the hierarchy of male over female, humans over animals. It is also duplicated in the class hierarchy of rulers over workers. In ancient Greek society slaves were the human tools from whom wealth was extracted through exploited labour, preserving aristocratic leisure and culture for the rulers. For Adorno, 'pure culture' is based on the freedom of mental pursuits and their radical separation from the necessities and constraints of physical labour. The ancient slave-owning Athenians despised work, and held their slaves in contempt. Yet the rulers suffered an uneasy conscience which they dispelled by projecting it upon their slaves, thereby confirming the abject 'baseness' of physical labour.

The philosophies of Plato and Aristotle both assert the primacy of disembodied mind or intellect over the 'base' physicality of the sensate, corporeal body. A philosophy organised around two gendered concepts: form and matter. Form is defined as masculine, and is regarded as active, rational, and superior. Matter is designated as feminine, and is regarded as passive, chaotic, and inferior. We therefore have two essentially different worlds confronting one another with no passageway in-between them. A dualism that leads to the splitting of the human being into a divine immortal soul and an earthly corruptible body, degrading the fecund and ever-changing corporeal world of nature into abject materiality. A polarisation or split between the flesh and the spirit, the carnal and the divine, masters and slaves; and a division of the sexes in which men are associated with the divine qualities of spirit and transcendence while women are associated with an inferior and degraded material realm encompassing the body, flesh, carnality, nature, and the earth.

The violence implicit in this philosophy is expressed in the form of a hierarchy that asserts the superiority of men and the mind over an inferior realm encompassing women, slaves, and corporeality, in a chain of being that stretches from immaterial mind or Logos at the upper end of the hierarchy, to unformed matter at the lower end. This fetishisation of disembodied intellect is expressed in Aristotle's demotion of women to mere passive material receptacles of a spiritually transcendent male potency. According to Aristotle, woman "is matter waiting to be formed by the active male principle. Of course the active elements are always higher.......and more divine. Man consequently plays a major part in reproduction; the woman is merely the passive incubator of his seed.......the male semen cooks and shapes the menstrual blood into a new human being." The female herself is a result of a maternal failure in this process of formation, in which the female as matter is left incompletely formed by the male potency; a potency synonymous with pure thought as spiritual, dominating, and altogether nobler than woman as the half-formed, material opposite.

The Neo-Platonist philosopher Plotinus accentuates this hierarchy of ideal form over formless materiality, rational thought over bodily sensuality. For Plotinus, Absolute Being, or the One, is a realm of light and intelligibility distinct from the confused darkness and multiplicity of materiality. The divine soul is imprisoned within the body and the sensory world, an evil from which it endeavours to free itself in its eternal quest for reunion with the Absolute. Matter, isolated from the beneficial influence of the Ideal Principle, is described as "ugliness, utter disgracefulness, unredeemed evil."

For the Neo-Platonists, the material, corporeal world represents a descent, a falling away, from a primordial unity with the One: it is efflux, detritus. There is also an association with the phallus in this ancient philosophy:

> The secret phallus of philosophy, the one that transpired in Plotinus' discourse as a metaphor of the One............As the male organ of generation, the phallus is therefore essentially *logos* or source of the *logos*: rational power, or intelligible reason......the integration of rational power and the phallus.......The masculine organ is spiritualized, idealized, to the point of becoming a sign of intelligence.

The philosopher Karl Marx, commenting on the social conditionality of the scientific discoveries that find application in technology, includes in a footnote the following question:

## K. Osmosis

> A critical history of technology would show how little any of the inventions of the 18th century are the work of a single individual. Hitherto there is no such book. Darwin has interested us in the history of Nature's Technology, *i.e.*, in the formation of the organs of plants and animals, which organs serve as instruments of production for sustaining life. Does not the history of the productive organs of man, of organs that are the material basis of all social organisation, deserve equal attention?

Darwinian science investigates the following question: At what point in their biological evolution did our anthropoid ancestors acquire their present, quite human hands, which have exercised such a remarkable influence in promoting the success of the human 'intellect'? The philosophical 'materialist' would argue that they were probably formed due to certain peculiarities of the geographical environment which made useful a physiological division of labour between the front and rear limbs. Accordingly, the development of the human intellect appeared as the consequence of this division and became in their turn the immediate reason for the appearance of humanity's artificial organs, the use of tools. These new artificial organs furthered the development of the human intellect, and the successes of the 'intellect' again reflected themselves upon the organs.

A lengthy historical process emerges, in which cause and consequence are constantly alternating. Thus human society adapts itself to nature, and strives towards equilibrium with it by extracting energy from it through the process of social production. In the process of adaptation, human society develops an industrial technology (a 'second nature') consisting of an artificial system of organs - prosthetic enhancements designed to extend the range and capabilities of the human organism: developments that progressively eliminate the distinction between subject and object, culminating in the final union of "the *human* essence of nature" with "the *natural* essence of man." Freud agrees: "Man has, as it were, become a kind of prosthetic God. When he puts on all his auxiliary organs he is truly magnificent." An optimism contradicted by Christian Bok who predicts a very different vision of a near-future where the corporeal substance of the human organism is progressively extinguished and then superseded by the externalised artificial exoskeleton of its technology: "As Alfred Jarry observes, 'the machine is born of the ashes of the slave'. Like a dangerous supplement, every machinic tool augments, and then replaces, the anthropic limb that wields it. Each limb that constructs a limb for itself risks not self-emendation but self-amputation."

In conjunction with the accelerated development of cybernetics, human beings and the natural environment increasingly fuse as part of a self-regulating system as information-exchanging internal elements. While this cybernetic sociobiogeosystem is self-regulating, its internal elements (humanity and nature), taken separately, progressively lose their capacity for independent self-regulation. Nature exists no longer as something external, but is progressively internalised as a component of a self-contained technological system. Humanity and nature prove to be mere sub-systems of a universal cybernetic sociobiogeosystem.

This amounts to the realisation of a technology 'confronting' nature to a technology incorporating it; a technology encompassing and transforming not only the natural environment but humanity as well. "The human cortex is the most complex material organisation that we know; the machines it engenders are extensions of it; the network they will form will be like a second and even more complex cortex" ultimately superseding the first, resulting in a conclusive "final blow to humanity's narcissism." Reflecting upon the magnitude of these technological developments, and its possible impact upon the human form, the performance artist Stelarc concedes that the impact will be 'traumatic', where the human body as 'subject' will be reborn as a designed artefact or 'object': "the body is traumatised to split from the realm of subjectivity and consider the necessity of re-examining and possibly re-designing its very structure."

A technology fully self-contained, subsisting on its own wastes; a condition Marx predicted when he writes that as science and technology progress, they will be able "to throw the excrements of the processes of production and consumption back again into the circle of the process of reproduction", and that, he suggests, "without any previous outlay of capital, creates new matter for capital." This is the transition from simple mastery and utilisation, to maximum optimisation and reproduction, resulting in a complete reconstruction (not only systemised but integrated) of all scientific and technological activity. Culminating in the fusion of beauty, fashion and function, art and industry, the senses and the machine; collapsing the distinction between the senses and their objects, inside and outside.

Simultaneously, through technology and its link to art and sensation our unconscious is in the process of reconstructing itself in bits and pieces outside us. Technology breaks down the unconscious and then recombines it in forms that restructure the 'external' world. Just as the technical world and the world of commodities and objects become anthropomorphic, so the human world becomes technomorphic. What follows is the neotechnic adaptation of technology to biology: "instead of mechanism forming a pattern for life, living organisms begin to form a pattern for mechanism." Leading to confusion; a blurring of traditional distinctions between the animate and the inanimate, suggesting links between Freudian and Marxist theories on the nature of fetishism. Thus, Freud's definition of the sexual fetish as an inanimate object invested with the sexual appeal of a human, combined with Marx's analysis of the commodity fetish as possessing human characteristics: "far more wonderful than if it were to begin dancing of its own free will."

We can no longer confine ourselves to the customary thesis that the object exists outside the subject and that the subject transforms the object. When we examine the history of humanity's evolution as a whole, experience coincides with activity and merges into the aggregate of social practice. The concepts of practice and sensation reflect different aspects of the interaction of subject and object that are a unity.

In other words, the concept of practice characterises the interaction of subject and object from the side of its continuity, while the concept of sensation illustrates this interaction from the side of its intermittency, lack of continuity, and discreteness. It is often argued that humanity's central position is ensured in subjective idealism at the price of losing the subject's connection with the real world, and reducing it to an aggregate of sensations. The most extreme type of this variant of anthropocentricism is solipsism, which denies the existence of all other people. Conversely, we are presented with the danger of a 'materialist' homofundamentalism positing maximum penetration of the object by the subject in order to achieve a maximum convergence of the 'subject' with the 'external' 'real' world.

Humanity is, as it were, shaping its environment, and indeed, the environment of a given generation of people is largely the product and results of preceding generations. Differentiation of the interaction of the subject and object, the pulsations and instinctual drives of the semiotic underlying the static forms of language and culture (the order of the symbolic), makes it possible to disclose certain features involving the accumulation and transmission of experience and culture in human society in contrast to the biological laws of the transmission and relay of life from generation to generation. If the chaotic, polymorphous drives of the semiotic were not objectified in material and linguistic (symbolic) form as 'its other', yet differing from the drives themselves as their 'quiescent' or objectified result, the transmission and accumulation of socio-cultural and historical experience would be impossible.

Kinaesthetic sensations unite various sensations in the integral image of an 'object' as distinct from the experiencing 'subject', which is an important aspect of the living organism's attempts at differentiating itself and maintaining its internal coherence and integrity in relationship to its surrounding environment. For example, among single-celled or unicellular organisms, the protozoa, there exist two regions: an outer, clear and relatively homogeneous layer, or ectoplasm, forming a barrier separating the protozoic cell from its surrounding medium or environment; and an inner 'core' or endoplasm. The outer ectoplasm consists of a plasma membrane or 'skin', which forms a permeable, mutable boundary allowing for the diffusion of materials into and out of the cell. In particular, protozoa readily change their shape by protoplasmic flowing into forms exceedingly diverse allowing for the permutation and realisation of every possible form; a complicated mix of polymorphic life cycles including parasitism and a variety of variations in reproduction and sexual differentiation, complicating and bringing into question the very concept of 'individuality' in the protozoa just as it does in plants and animals.

## K. Osmosis

In accordance with Julia Kristeva's interest in "the 'open systems' of which biology speaks concerning living organisms that live only by maintaining a renewable identity through interaction with another", these unicellular organisms are fluid, mobile and increasingly complex, moving towards increasing the differentiation of their internal components and the diversity and dissemination of their external forms and relationships in the course of ontogenesis and phylogenesis. However, as in all animals and plants, the reproduction and proliferation of protozoa is dependent upon cell division.

The two most common types of cell multiplication in the single-celled protozoa are binary division and budding. Binary division involves the division of the cell into two essentially equal daughter cells that grow into replicas of the parent, making each half into a whole. The dissolution and extinction of the original parent cell is followed by differentiation in the daughter cells, such that the daughter cells are essentially two new organisms. In contrast, 'budding' allows the parent cell to retain its continued existence as a separate entity while producing by division one or many daughter cells. Sometimes the bud is nearly as large as the parent, so the result is nearly the same as binary fission except that parent and offspring can be distinguished; but usually the bud is much smaller, less differentiated, and gradually assumes the form of the parent after freeing itself from the parent's body. In some species of protozoa the buds arise on the surface of the parent; in others the buds are nurtured as developing 'embryos' inside invaginated chambers from which they escape at 'birth'.

For Julia Kristeva the body's boundaries are in a continual process of production and transformation. There is a constant interchange between the subject and the world in the ways in which the body's boundaries shrink or expand, incorporates objects into itself, or expels impulses and substances emanating from within. Relations between the body and its surrounding environment are blurred and confused - the outside environment is not distinct from the body but is an active internal component of its 'identity'. The borders of the body are not fixed or confined to its anatomical 'container', the skin. The boundaries are extremely fluid and dynamic, and there is an ongoing interchange between inside and outside.

The plasticity of our conceptions of the body and its boundaries is indicated by what many social scientists are currently describing as a pandemic in what they call 'body dysmorphic disorder'. People suffering this disorder feel that their bodies are somehow incomplete or imperfect. The illness generally manifests itself in the form of the more common eating disorders, such as bulimia or anorexia nervosa; but there are also patients with an obsessive desire to acquire extra body parts, or to have otherwise healthy limbs surgically removed because they perceive them as somehow ugly, abject, or extraneous.

According to Dr Joseph Rosen, Associate Professor of Plastic and Reconstructive Surgery at Dartmouth Hitchcock Medical Centre, New Hampshire, our limbs are intimately connected to neural networks or maps within our brains which possess the capacity to contract or expand. When we have a limb amputated, it takes considerable time for our neural map of that limb to contract or fade (hence the phantom limb effect). And if we acquire an extra body part, our neural map expands accordingly. For Dr Rosen, this discovery opens up infinite possibilities for the reconstruction of the human body.

Dr Rosen believes, with surgical techniques now in existence that can rearrange rib bones and stretch torso fat, that within five years he will be able to create wings for the human body. Although we would lack the ability to fly, we would resemble angels, and our wings, hanging flaps of boned tissue, would possess full sensation. He is also currently developing methods of equipping the human body with tails and enhanced hearing. In response to criticisms at a conference of plastic surgeons last year, Dr Rosen posed the question:

> Why do we only value the average? Why are plastic surgeons dedicated only to restoring our current notions of the conventional, as opposed to letting people explore, if they want, the possibilities?............Human wings will be here; mark my words............If I were to give you wings, you would develop, literally, a winged brain. Our bodies change our brains, and our brains are infinitely mouldable.

There is also, however, the danger that the human intellect, increasingly divorced from the body and reproductive nature, will become sterile. In order to be an effective organ of domination, thinking transforms itself into a self-sufficient, automatic process, becoming like the machines which itself produces so that eventually the machines will replace it. The computerisation of labour includes those activities which pose as purely conceptual. Whether this results in the eventual merging of body and machine into some kind of hybrid - that is, whether the body will take on the qualities of the machine (the 'cyborg') or whether the machine will take on the qualities of the human body ('artificial intelligence') remains uncertain. Artificial-intelligence proposes formal patterns as the be-all and end-all of intelligence: where the virtual mind, finally divorced from the body and nature is transformed into an information processor. For Olive Schreiner, this final sterilisation of thought from contamination with abject materiality presents a problem:

> Will humanity at last break out into one huge blossom of the brain - and perish? Like one of those aloes, which grow for three hundred years, then break out into one large flower at the top of their stem and die!

The internal coherence, integration, and completion of the human 'subject' is based upon a subject/object divide such that the image of external objects forms a secure foundation for the stability and fixity of the 'subject', and ultimately the definite wholeness and static stability of the 'object' itself. As such, our perception of external reality consists of mentally visualised images of an aggregate of sensations built up and then crystallised into 'objects'.

Accordingly, if we consider humanity as the 'formed' result of a succession of generations, of a 'history', then we must consider the sensory aggregates and mental images that make up our current notions of reality to be the end result of aggregations of sensations and mentally visualised images accumulated by countless preceding generations; an accumulated wealth of information passed on and incorporated into the 'subject's' 'own' 'individual' experience. An anti-humanism that dispenses with the notion of the individual 'subject' as the sole author or originator of ideas in favour of a 'geological' and historical conception of human knowledge consisting of accumulated deposits and sedimentary layers of experience, life and language borrowed from a succession of generations.

An anti-humanism complemented by the theories of the mineralogist and crystallographer Vladimir Vernadsky, who argues for an end to the distinction between biology and geology, giving detailed descriptions of life as a type of mineral, its cellular structures fusing, splitting and proliferating, coalescing and disseminating, merging and diverging; and his analysis of the endless process of biomineralisation of living organisms, or rather, organic minerals, as they eke out and assimilate into their physical structures, and then leak out and environmentalise, minerals temporarily borrowed from the earth.

Accordingly, Vernadsky reproduces his History in ultra-materialist order: the earth, micro-organisms, plants, articulated skeletons, animals, and finally 'humanity', in a perpetual reference to the reciprocal interactions between animate and inanimate matter. For Vernadsky, "Life is not life but rock endlessly rearranging itself under the sun."

An anti-humanism akin to Julia Kristeva's, Roland Barthes', Louis Althusser's and Michel Foucault's notion of the 'subject-individual' as merely the ensemble of material and social relations mediated by history and the material, concrete processes of language; and their debunking of the essentialist notion of the 'subject-author' as the sole originator of ideas. According to Michel Foucault:

> This thin surface of the original is populated entirely by those complex mediations formed and laid down as sediment in their own history by labour, life and language so that what man is reviving without knowing it, is all the intermediaries of a time that governs him almost to infinity.

•

An objective law is a boundary separating the possible from the impossible. Rudolf Carnap stresses that a law generalising empirical facts or more particular laws formulated earlier provide the answer to why a particular phenomenon is possible. If we cease to recognise this kind of explanation as the basis of 'laws', we arrive at the liberating (and 'pataphysical') science of imaginary solutions, where 'everything is possible in the world', which is equivalent to the statement 'nothing is impossible in the world'.

Natural 'laws' are therefore not final, once and for all dividing the possible from the impossible, and the 'laws' themselves are mutable, and possibly even cyclic. This connects with Julia Kristeva's notion of the maternal body as a space or location where the apparent stasis of cyclical or 'monumental' time exists in combination with the dynamics of a linear or 'developmental' time consisting of genealogical and grammatical changes and mutations. Rudolf Carnap duly hypothesises:

> The actual world is a world that is constantly changing. Even the most fundamental laws of physics may, for all we can be sure, vary slightly from century to century. What we believe to be a physical constant with a fixed value may be subject to vast cyclic changes that we have not yet observed.

The inner logic of the development of science and technology - the drive to penetrate further and deeper into matter - is leading in fact to a discrepancy with the corporeal needs of the vehicle of science itself, namely, humanity; this, moreover, is not a refined need of some sort, but a grossly palpable need to survive in a technically reconstructed environment. The inanimate once seemed the immutable basis of changing life, fixed once and for all. But now, under the impact of technology, the biosphere's inanimate parameters themselves are becoming considerably disordered.

For "natural science to lose its abstractly material - or rather, its idealistic - tendency, and become the basis of *human* science", it has to set broader aims than simply the intensified growth and consumption of matter, energy, and information. As technology becomes ever more powerful, becoming an end in itself, the fragility of nature is exposed, and its destruction becomes a real possibility, wiping out the very material foundations of the being of humanity itself. For we are witnessing a transition from an environment developing in a pro-anthropic direction to one taking an anti-anthropic path that could result in the destruction of all 'organic' forms of life. The transition through infinite accumulation of wastes is a form of losing the biosphere's qualitative definiteness, a form of transmutation into something opposite.

Norbert Wiener looks at the problem in accordance with the laws of thermodynamics:

> As entropy increases, the universe, and all closed systems in the universe, tend naturally to deteriorate and lose their distinctiveness, to move from a state of organisation and differentiation in which distinctions and forms exist, to a state of chaos and sameness.

In relation to the species *Homo-sapiens* this means that we are hastening the process of entropic dissolution by introducing regressive and chaotic elements into the environment. This has led some theorists to the proposition of humanity's parasitic essence in relation to nature. Jean Dorst, for instance, compares humanity with "a maggot in a fruit", or "a moth in a ball of wool", gnawing away "at his habitat, while exuding theories to justify his existence." A complete abjection "where man frightened, crosses over the horrors of the maternal bowels" and is completely engulfed in a technology parasitically consuming the corporeal body of maternal nature. The human species transformed into a "great greedy parasitic worm, blind and degenerate, snug in excrement, isolated in a seething mass of eroticised abjection, which he substitutes for the other. The secret life of Technocratic Man."

In response to a technological and disenchanted view of nature as just so much dead stuff, narrowly quantified in accordance with the laws of computation and utility as simply raw material for profitable exploitation, and the implacable imperatives of a technology and its impetus towards the wholesale subjugation of nature, like "some huge engine which has senselessly seized, cut to pieces, and swallowed up - impassively and unfeelingly - a great and priceless Being", Julia Kristeva opts for an interpretation of Marxism based upon a combination of production and reproduction; and a labour process centred upon the libidinal intensities of the corporeal body as the underlying form for the realisation of a qualitative, reciprocal, non-utilitarian, aesthetic and eroticised relationship between subject and object, humanity and nature.

Thus Kristeva defines productive activity and the labour process along the lines of reproductive sexuality as a relation between the worker's body and the body of nature, involving an expenditure or discharge of human energy. Humanity and nature are therefore considered as two equally necessary halves of a single entity. The union of the two is considered by Kristeva as an act of love, where subject and object are conjoined through the dynamics of the forces and relations of production, in combination with psychic processes of introjection and incorporation, osmosis and identification. Where, in place of the existing model of economic production, with its notions of scarcity, an asceticism of labour, and its emphasis upon an endless accumulation of surplus value, Kristeva asserts the need for the construction of a new 'science' of economy based upon notions of reciprocity, of the gift, expenditure, bodily enjoyment, play, unification and communion, expressing an awareness of the shared possession of a common substance. Kristeva illustrates her proposition with a quotation from Marx: "As William Petty puts it, labour is its (wealth's) father and the earth its mother."

In occupying a position of political opposition and criticism towards the established socio-symbolic order, Kristeva samples, combines and re-mixes ideas extracted from a variety of sources. These include the theories of psychoanalysis in combination with the philosophical systems of Hegel, Marx and Lenin. For instance, Kristeva displays an interest in the theory and application of dialectical materialism when she writes "the Hegelian conception of negativity already prepares the ground for the possibility of thinking a materialist *process*."

Kristeva's dialectical method serves to connect any two opposed terms or positions; it functions to unite, or to separate and divide, thus undermining stable unities. This is a dialectic that consists of an open-ended, continuous flux; a continual becoming that abolishes all classification, culminating in the disappearance of strict lines of demarcation. This amounts to an all-pervasive dynamism, where the distinction between the container and the contained becomes irrelevant. Where seeing, thinking, dreaming, and writing are interrelated; and the subject of writing and the subject who writes alternately fuse and fission, in conjunction with a materialised process of creation involving the inseparability of object and subject, and multiple juxtapositions and dislocations of texts involving the fusion of seemingly unrelated themes. This is a process that obliterates limitations and classifications, producing poetry that evolves not in accordance with any regular progression; but instead, through the recurrent use of metaphors and motifs, achieves coherent form. Where the body ceases to be circumscribed by barriers that artificially separate the self from the other, or from the external world.

The nature of this dialectical and materialist conception of the world as a continual process of movement and change, perpetually in conflict with the encrustation of the mechanical in the living, and the tendency towards sterility, inertia and rigidity symptomatic of the socio-symbolic order, is succinctly defined by Kristeva with a quotation from Lenin: "The splitting of a single whole and the cognition of its contradictory parts is the essence of dialectics." Everything is, therefore, to be understood as a unity of contradictory or opposed elements; everything, in the language of dialectics, is a unity of opposites. It is the insistence that change must eventually confront the finite elasticity of all things and all structures, effecting a fundamental transformation of their very nature. Accordingly, beneath the appearance of every seemingly stable and unified thing there lies constant tension and opposition.

The focus is therefore not on the outward appearance of stability and permanence, but on the underlying reality of internal conflict and permanent movement. Where the unity of subject and object, and the relativity of the antithesis between matter and consciousness, is expressed in Lenin's declaration: "We must dream"! "Man's consciousness", Lenin contends, "not only reflects the objective world but creates it." And he points out that the idea of the ideal turning into the material is a very profound one, for we are constantly witnessing complicated processes of the material being transformed into the ideal and of the ideal being transformed back into the material. These complicated and contradictory mutual transformations of the material into the ideal and vice versa demonstrate the relativity of the contrast between spirit and matter. According to Lenin, human consciousness is therefore not simply "a *reflection* in a mirror but a complex act.......which includes the possibility of an imaginative flight from life; and, even more, it includes the possibility of a transformation of the abstract concept into an imaginative fantasy (which ultimately = God)."

Karl Marx also appreciates the allure of fantasy expressed in the "youthful and fantastic dream" of Hegelian philosophy, and he aspires to bring reality into harmony with that idealised image of a world that philosophy had hitherto realised only in thought. In a spirit of optimism, he proclaims that the world "has not yet become clear to itself. It will then turn out that the world has long dreamt of that of which it had only to have a clear idea to possess it really". For Julia Kristeva dialectical theory equally applies to Freud's interpretation of the 'dreamwork'. Particularly in the way that dream symbols, through the processes of condensation (metaphor) and displacement (metonymy), can say one thing and, at the same time, mean the opposite. Freud's 'Dream-work' provides Kristeva with "a theoretical concept that triggers off a new research" that places the dream in opposition to the prosaic world of conscious activity, providing an alternative model of production, a "playful permutation" whereby things a given a new form.

Kristeva incorporates Freud's definition of the dream as the symbolic fulfilment of desires denied satisfaction in the real world, along with the inevitable conflict that ensues between, on the one hand, the body's demands for a pleasurable satisfaction of its desires and, on the other hand, a disagreeable reality that obstructs the gratification of these desires. A conflict ameliorated through the construction of an interior world of 'phantasy', described by Freud as a kind of 'nature reserve' where humanity's unfulfilled desires are protected, providing the blueprints and building blocks for the construction of a new reality to replace the old.

A process where the subject-positions of 'normality' and 'psychosis' merge together in the common goal of transforming reality in accordance with the wishful constructions preserved in phantasy. Resulting in two different approaches: in practical action directed towards the outside world designed to achieve the remoulding of objective reality in favour of erotic desires previously denied (Freud's "alloplastic adaptation"); or in a 'psychotic', philosophically Idealist approach, concentrating upon passive, internal changes, amounting to the construction in thought of an ideal reality as a substitute for the partial or complete denial of the existence of the real external world (Freud's "autoplastic adaptation").

Kristeva forcefully proclaims the notion of art as constitutive of the subject, rather than constituted by the subject:

> It's necessary to see how all great works of art – one thinks of Mallarme, of Joyce, of Artaud, to mention only literature – are, to be brief, masterful sublimations of those crises of subjectivity which are known, in another connection, as psychotic crisis……….It is, very simply, through the work and play of signs, a crisis of subjectivity which is the basis of all creation, one which takes as its very precondition the possibility of survival

Julia Kristeva's analysis of the painter Giovanni Bellini's ideological and cultural (or 'symbolic') articulation of the mother/child relationship, includes a detailed examination of the psychological, social, economic, historical, and artistic practices that together combine to determine the 'personality' of the painter Giovanni Bellini as a historical 'subject', grappling with the artistic dilemma of representing the unrepresentable - the shared bodily space of mother and child. For Kristeva:

> An artistic practice...not only operates through the individual (biographical subject) who carries it out, but it also recasts him as an historical subject - causing the signifying process that the subject undergoes to match the ideological and political expectations of his age's rising classes....One cannot understand such practice without taking its socio-economic foundations into account; nor can one understand it if one chooses to reduce it solely to these foundations thereby bypassing the signifying economy of the subject involved.

Kristeva's essay on Bellini is a project that incorporates and recombines semiotics, psychoanalysis, Hegelianism and Marxism to produce a 'semanalysis' that provides "dialectical logic with a materialist foundation - a theory of signification based on the subject, his formation, and his corporeal, linguistic, and social dialectic." Accordingly, Kristeva opts for a form of (Marxist) historical materialism involving a subtle and complex appreciation of the relations between the forms of social consciousness (and the signifying practices of the cultural 'superstructure') and their material and economic basis. For Kristeva society consists of a complex and dynamic system of interacting elements, each influencing the other - a system where the economic factor is the determining one only in the 'last instance'. A complex unity and mutual interchange of distinct, necessarily related but relatively autonomous practices, where the signifying practices that make up the cultural superstructure actively influence the material basis from which they arise, forming an organic whole. One in which the 'symbolic order' of the 'superstructure' - culture, politics, ideology, language - and the corporeal (the 'semiotic') are treated as specific instances of a complex totality, articulated upon each other and upon the economy. Where, to quote the philosopher Louis Althusser:

> The economic dialectic is never active in *the pure state;* in History, these instances, the superstructures, etc. are never seen to step respectfully aside when their work is done, or when the time comes, as his pure phenomena, to scatter before His Majesty the Economy as he strides along the royal road to the Dialectic. From the first moment to the last, the lonely hour of the 'last instance' never comes.

According to Kristeva: "Love replaces narcissism in a third person....Hence, 'God is Love': it is for this very reason that he does not exist, except to be imagined as child for a woman." Kristeva's emphasis on the social primacy of love is therefore completely at odds with the type of 'vulgar' Marxism that would compare copulation to the drinking of a glass of water: where the experience of love is disenchanted to the point where it loses its poetry, and is rendered purely instrumental. Kristeva is therefore opposed to a type of Marxism that reduces love and sex, the amorous and the artistic, to the biological and the economic by stripping away the cultural accretions that tend to glorify and preserve the poetry of existence. A Marxism that reduces everything cultural directly to its economic basis; a type of Marxism vehemently opposed by Lenin:

> This "glass-of-water-theory" has made part of our youth completely crazy. Its advocates contend that it is Marxistic. No thank you, for such a Marxism which makes all phenomena and all changes in the ideological superstructure of society derive directly and immediately from its economic basis. Things are not as simple as all that..................To try to reduce these ideological changes, divorced from their context with the total ideology, to the economic basis of society would be rationalism, and not Marxism. Surely, thirst demands to be quenched. But will a normal individual, under normal circumstances, lie down in the gutter and drink from a puddle? Or even from a dirty glass? What is more important than anything else is the social side. Drinking water is an individual act. Love requires two people and may result in a third life. This fact contains a social interest.

The ancient Greeks developed their thought around beliefs concerning body heat, and its role in determining the differentiation of the sexes. Foetuses well heated within their mother's womb were born as males; foetuses lacking heat were born as females. The female was a creature "softer, more liquid, more clammy cold, altogether more formless than were men."

The philosopher Aristotle investigated this inequality of heat, and drew a connection between menstrual blood and sperm: menstrual blood was cold blood, sperm was cooked blood. Sperm was superior as it created new life; menstrual blood was considered inferior as a substance passive and inert. For Aristotle, the male possessed the principle of movement, action and creativity; in contrast, females he defined as identical with the formless passivity of flesh and materiality.

Aristotle also investigates the role of heat in the development of melancholia. According to Kristeva:

> Aristotle breaks new ground by associating melancholia with heat, considered to be the

> regulating principle of the organism. This Greek conception of melancholia remains alien to us today; it assumes a properly balanced interaction of air and liquid. Such a white mixture of air (*pneuma*) and liquid brings out froth in the sea, wine, as well as the sperm in man. Indeed, Aristotle links melancholia to spermatic froth and eroti, with explicit references to Dionysus and Aphrodite. The melancholia he evokes is not a philosopher's disease but his very nature, his ethos. It is what strikes the first Greek melancholy hero, Bellerophon, who is thus portrayed in the *Iliad*: 'Bellerophon gave offense to the gods and became a lonely wanderer on the Aleian plain, eating out his heart and shunning the paths of men'. Self-devouring because forsaken by the gods, this desperate man was condemned to banishment, absence, void.

Aristotle's association of heat with the melancholic disposition of male philosophers and heroes, his conception of blood as either cooked or uncooked, and the role of blood and body heat in determining the differentiation between the sexes, relates to an even older tradition which ascribes "the bones to the male principle and the flesh to the female". In accordance with this tradition, bone marrow is derived from semen, which is cooked blood, while the fat in flesh is derived from uncooked blood, which is cool and female.

In *The Raw and the Cooked*, Claude Levi-Strauss explores the binary opposition between Nature and Culture, and the function of cooking as a universal means by which raw Nature is transformed into Culture. The ancient differentiation between flesh and bone, hot and cold, blood cooked and uncooked, male and female, is analogous to Levi-Strauss' notion of experience as organised along the lines of binary opposites. Accordingly, Aristotle's conception of the female as 'uncooked' equates women with Nature, while his conception of the male as 'cooked' equates men with Culture.

The philosophy of Georg Wilhelm Friedrich Hegel represents nature as the 'alienation' and abject degradation of the Absolute

Idea or Spirit. Hegel provides a lengthy and detailed description of the processes through which this Absolute Spirit externalises itself into the objects of the material world for the purpose of self-realisation, culminating in a climactic resolution to the conflict between spirit and materiality, mind and body, subject and object. According to Hegel, the anatomical distinctions between male and female exemplifies a hierarchical principle privileging activity over passivity, and productive form over chaotic materiality. Hegel thus attaches considerable importance to the anatomical distinction between the testicle, the ovary and the clitoris, with the female genitalia considered as an inside-out version of the male: internalised, hidden and enclosed, rather than outward and exposed. This represents for Hegel an interior-exterior barrier that determines the difference between Being-For-Itself from Being-In-Itself; the distinction between human, conscious existence and the existence of mere 'things'. Nature (as female) is conceived as a lifeless, dispersed mode of existence awaiting the purposeful, projective activity of the (male) Spirit to bring it to fulfilment. A trace of the ancient conception of the active male principle as synonymous with the bone is expressed in Hegel's declaration: "The being of Spirit is a bone."

Thus for Artaud:

> To live,
> You have to be somebody,
> To be somebody,
> You have to have a BONE,
> And not be afraid of showing the bone,
> And losing the meat in the process

The philosopher Karl Marx, expressing his impatience with Hegelianism, declares philosophy to stand "in the same relation to the study of the actual world as onanism to sexual love". In his own words, he puts Hegel's philosophy "on its feet" by recognising that matter is the stuff of all existence and that all mental and spiritual phenomena are its by-products. Henceforth, Hegel's self-realisation of the Spirit is replaced with the notion of a progressive, historical development of the material forces of production. A process of development where the 'humanity' of "man's relation to nature" can be gauged by "the relation of man to woman." In this respect it is interesting to compare Marx's (philosophical materialist) attempt to stand the absolute idea of Hegel's philosophy "on its feet" with the relentless materialism expressed in Georges Bataille's essay "The Big Toe", where he concludes: "Human life entails, in fact, the rage of seeing oneself as a back and forth movement from refuse to the ideal, and from the ideal to refuse - a rage that is easily directed against an organ as *base* as the foot."

In her article 'Thin is the feminist issue', Nicky Diamond quotes the actress Jane Fonda, her body honed down and stripped away through bodybuilding, declare: "I like to be close to the bone." Like the world champion female bodybuilder Lisa Lyon, who posed for a series of black and white pictures by the photographer Robert Mapplethorpe titled *Lady: Lisa Lyon,*(1983), Jane Fonda's desire 'to be close to the bone' suggests an attempt at containment, a fixing of boundaries and the removal of 'fat' as excess, surplus matter in an attempt to realise the ideal of the essential, integral self. The achievement of this ideal of closeness to the bone means that the skin surface that forms the body's outside tightens and enfolds itself around the skeleton that forms the body's inside. While the philosophical idea may be that of the container and the contained, there may also be an allusion to certain psychoanalytic theories of an early 'skin-ego', conceptualised as a 'psychic envelope'.

Marx's exploration of the 'anatomy' of society leads to his assertion of the determining role of the material, economic 'base' in shaping the cultural and ideological 'superstructure'. This connection of cultural forms to an underlying material, economic structure is further explored in the writings of the Marxist philosopher Antonio Gramsci. In a rather curious passage from *The Prison Notebooks,* Gramsci employs the female body as a metaphor to illustrate a more complex understanding of the relationship between base and superstructure against a Marxism that treats culture as simply an epiphenomenal reflex of the 'economic':

> We cannot say, with regard to the human body, that the skin (and the type of beauty prevalent at a particular time) is mere illusion and that the skeleton and anatomy are the sole reality; however, for a long time something similar has been

> maintained. Questioning the role of the anatomy and the functions of the skeleton does not mean claiming that men........can live without them. Continuing the metaphor, we can say that it is not the skeleton (in the narrow sense) which makes one love a woman, but we understand how much the skeleton contributes to the grace of her movements, etc.

Julia Kristeva's study of motherhood expresses an excess that converts the order of the patriarchal family into a disorder that blurs the boundary between narcissism and object-love, verging on the breaking of the incest taboo. Amounting to a re-activation of the relationship between the maternal and the sexual - from the vantage point of the mother and her retention of (or return to) some of the characteristics of infantile sexuality, rather than that of the child and his/her development toward heterosexual 'normality'. An androgynous or same-sex embrace, an asexual union that breaks down the distinction of inside/outside, in so doing revealing the process of the inside turning into the outside producing a hybrid. The liminal space of hybridity, where gender and cultural differences touch, abolishing the binary oppositions and distinctions that account for the divisions of gender: Artaud's 'Body-Without-Organs' – the liberation of uncodified desires; and a disintegration of 'normalised' identities; obliterating the civilised 'ego', and the 'stratifications' of all systematic organisation.

# Fervent Machines

by Robert Lort

"There can be no art without pain,
there can be no pain without art".
-- Alexandro Jodorowsky

Friedrich Nietzsche does not close the shutters when he hears the cries of "solitary and agitated minds", Nietzsche listens to the shrieks and bellows of madmen,"'Ah, give me madness, you heavenly powers! Madness, that I may at last believe in myself! Give deliriums and convulsions, sudden lights and darkness, terrify me with frost and fire such as no mortal has ever felt, with deafening din and prowling figures, make me howl and whine and crawl like a beast...'" No Nietzsche does not close his shutters, he knows that, "Almost everywhere it was madness which prepared the way for the new idea."[1] Nietzsche knows that traversings through destruction and tragedy seem almost always embedded in the lives of exemplary individuals. He knows how the madman turns on his squeaky heals, to merge with another circle, always widening and furthering his departure. But he knows also of the dangers, the threats - madness, depression, addiction, anorexia, sado-masochism. The dangers which he himself, Vincent Van Gogh, Antonin Artaud, Jackson Pollack, Charles Baudelaire and William Burroughs, to name only a few, have had to struggle against, which has been as much their source of brilliance as a threat to it. The pertinent question then is, how to avoid an impending collapse? This is the question that all fervent bodies face, how to destroy the wall that confines and trammels their desire, without simultaneously falling into a black hole and a hole of self-destruction, that is no longer productive.

This is what confronts the central character in Werner Herzog's *Woyzeck,* what makes this character exceptional is his oblivious incomprehension of anything to do with marriage, money, fatherhood and the law. It is his insensible indifference to these social codes that is at the core of his rebellion. He is forced to endure the ridicule, from those that enforce them, so he instead continually scurries away on a line of flight, into a vast space. But those that taunt him, push his escape out too far, it becomes cornered, and blocked on all sides, it cannot be maintained, and so it reaches its collapse.

The fervent body, or as Deleuze and Guattari call it, "a full Body without Organs," is a body that is permeated with a deterritorializing force, a feverous and inflamed kind of desire, it is a cathartic body that utilises and engages with a very specific kind of intensified energy. Deleuze and Guattari describe this type of body in terms of individuals like Nietzsche, Artaud, Kafka and Van Gogh, but there are many different types of these bodies. Fervent bodies are also like the music-bodies of Jimi Hendrix, Iggy Pop, Patti Smith, Ian Curtis and Nick Cave, they are also the film-bodies like Pier Paolo Pasolini, Jean-Luc Godard, Jan Svankmajer and Andrei Tarkovsky. The fervent body exists by its degrees of movement and rest, speed and slowness. But all this only exists at a later point, the fervent body must be formed, from a body that is stationary and immobile. The fervent body is a deterritorialized surface, it is a line of flight, but what is important is what this body encounters, what its line of flight always intercepts, for it reaches a kind of wall, which determines its success or failure. What is critical is whether the fervent body succeeds in smashing apart this wall, both traversing it and undermining it. The task is to smash this wall, to break through it, to upturn the barricades. Smashing through this wall engenders the collapse of subjectivity; the face is shattered, leaving no longer a rigid "face" defining and categorising the subject politically, historically, sexually, familiarly and aesthetically. All these precepts become supple and fluid variables, unknown before, and unknown after. Smashing the wall engenders the collapse of the signifier; expression is no longer delimited by the rigidities of grammaticality, notation and signifiance. Intensities existing outside the wall engender spaces where the formations no longer abide by these imposed rigidities. The language system instead outsteps itself, it begins to stumble, and waver, the entire system gives way to allow movements of flux and deterritorialization, it becomes imbued by flows and continuums, and is no longer divided into discrete units of definition. The music-machine similarly overstrains itself, by reaching the limit that borders the outside, where it will confront intensities of silence, and brut noise. The image is no longer bounded by pictorial objectification, it moves into spaces outside; a minimalist space, a dada machine, a Pollack swirl. The artwork becomes no longer an objective representation but a frantic form, an abstraction that integrates disparate elements, joining and merging them together. The art work instead advances to a scream, a wail of despair, an accusation against the system.

The fervent body is always the furtherest, the outermost, it will succeed if it breaks through the wall, otherwise it fails and turns into a breakdown, wallowing in self destruction, suicide and overdose. But the breakthrough and the breakdown are not necessary opposite, indeed they seem almost inseparable, almost indistinguishable. In any case venturing beyond this wall is no simple task, few men or women have ventured beyond this limit. To pass outside or beyond this wall demands a certain disembodiment, a becoming incorporeal, an abstract metamorphosis. Venturing to intensities beyond this limit necessitates and consequences a careful and prolonged process, risking self destruction. But there are still other ways of conceiving this barrier to our line of flight. Antonin Artaud conceives of this wall as "a huge malleable sheet in osmosis with all the rest of reality."[2] Reverse osmosis is a process which effectively filters a liquid by passing it through a semi-permeable membrane, it is commonly used to separate salt from sea water. For Artaud, this wall is then a filter on reality, situated at the interface between the body and reality, that allows only the passage of specific segments of reality to pass through, and blocks the passage of other segments. This wall is simultaneously the skin, the bodies sensors and the logic motors. Antonin Artaud is a body-sieve, all that he does is multiply the number of his little holes, or similarly alter their size - allowing the passing through of that externality, that meta-reality which was previously blocked. What we must do is to meddle with our filters, find and connect up those flows more subtle and anomalous, smash our walls, and connect with the alterity.

"Beauty will be convulsive or not at all"

-- Andre Breton

Body arts convulsive engrossment in castration, crucifixion, sexual perversion, suicide, state oppression and mental illness has been a long and insistent attack against the current institutions of authority. Many of the these artistic events have aimed at exposing and outwardly enacting the crisis of the individual, subjected to exploitation and organised and oppressed by prevailing authorities. Their methods employ unremitting and shocking depictions of pain. Of many performances perhaps some of the most notorious include; Chris Burden's *Shoot* (1971), where the artist had himself shot through the left arm by a friend facing him from a short distance; Vito Acconci's "semen(al)" public masturbation in *Seedbed* (1972); the infamous Rudolf Schwarzkogler, who in 1969 fabricated a spectacular simulation of castration; Otto Muehl's scathing attacks against the debilitating and alienating sensibilities embodied in bourgeoisie social and sexual aesthetics; and the dionysian animal sacrifices performed by Hermann Nitsch.

Austrian born artist Gottfried Helnwein's work is also of exemplary value, beginning with bandage action events (documented by the artist appearing in cafe's and lying in the street with his "wounded" head and face bandaged). His work depicts physical injuries which are metaphors for far deeper existential, psychological and human tragedies. Medical injuries, facial deformities and abused children proliferate throughout his work evoking primary internal anxieties. The inhumane acts of violence (child abuse, war atrocities, state oppression) and frightening images of familial estrangement that are presented in his work, constitute events which are preferred forgotten, like the Nazi era, or preferred left unspoken such as familial traumas like child abuse. Helnwein also conducts a probing analysis of the individual and the self through an abundance of self portraits, each obscured by hideous facial bandages, his facial muscles, lips and eyes are stretched apart, torturingly, by varied medical instruments, now made famous by the Rammstein covers. All his images in some way evoke associations with mutilation, anguish or internal alienation. The works (frequently paintings appearing remarkably like photographs), boldly put forward social unacceptabilities never before portrayed so lucidly and so confrontingly. The many intensities produced in the work are profoundly disturbing, the impressions - uncomfortably eerie, electrocuting the eyes with a rush of haunting spatiality.

The performance group Coum Transmissions, featuring members of Throbbing Gristle, brought into the art gallery the underground, in the same way that Warhol cinema had a decade earlier, but managed to once again challenge the previous subversions, with their explicit and confrontational approach to crime, prostitution, pornography and sado-masochism. Their performances seemed to draw straight out of the pages of a Marquis de Sade novel. Genesis gives a description of their performances, "Then I got a 10-inch nail and tried to swallow it, which made me vomit. Then I licked the vomit off the floor and Cosey helped me lick the vomit off the floor... And each day it got heavier, so that on Easter Sunday I was crucified on a wooden cross, whipped with 2 bullwhips, covered in human vomit and chicken wings and chicken legs... And then I urinated down Cosey's legs while she stuck a lighted candle up her vagina... Just ordinary everyday ways of avoiding the commercials on the television..."[3] The work is innovative and commendable for its intentional disruption of authority, especially censorship and aesthetics; its stretching of, or redefining of the enclosing limit, a limit which defines specific activities outside or beyond it, as pornographic or obscene; and the performance of acts exposed to public view (as opposed to private view) which might otherwise bring police arrest. These masochist bodies are also releasing the surging, bellowing flows of schizo desire, flows of urine, wax, vomit, dismembered flesh and corporeal asignifying expressions. These are the flows that potentially exceed the socius own degrees or limits and thus threaten the equilibriums established by the system.

Jill Scott's early San Francisco performances, *Taped* (1975), *Boxed* (1975), *Tied* (1976) and *Strung* (1976) demonstrate aspects of the human condition and perhaps from a specific female condition. In *Taped* Jill Scott's body was constrained in an elevated position against the vertical exterior of a city building, precariously secured against the wall by lengths of adhesive tape stretching across her back and limbs. *Tied* involved the artist being gruesomely tied to a telephone pole, by reams of cord encircling her body from foot to head. *Strung* was again similar, wherein her body was confined against the *Golden Gate Bridge*. These works are not bound within the gallery space and for this reason enable the confronting of a public audience who may not normally encounter such artistic practices. The performances express the bodies incarceration within the city's architecture, alienated to it and oppressed by it. The organic body becomes immured within the cities inorganic structures: fences, parking spaces, walls, power lines, freeways that criss-cross like shadows over the body.

The artist Stelarc has for some time been intensely involved in rearticulations of the body, and the discourses surrounding the bodies emerging takeover by machines. Stelarc's performances are frequently challenging, he describes one of his early experiences, "Leading up to the first suspension event I had done some sensory deprivation pieces that were demanding. I occupied a gallery for a week in Japan. I sewed my lips and eye lids shut with surgical needle and thread. I was tethered to the gallery wall with a pair of cables which connected to two hooks in the back of my body."[4] He is most renowned for his suspension events which entail the body being gorily suspended above ground by multiple cords connected to his naked body by hooks which penetrate beneath the skin. The raw, intense confrontation is a bodily transformation, seeking the disembodiment of subjectivity, to eject from the body and make blurry the distinctions between what is part of the body and what is not part. It entails the dismantling of the organism, "opening the body to connections that presuppose an entire assemblage, circuits, conjunctions, levels and thresholds, passages and distributions of intensity..."[5] The suspended body becomes a body without organs, obsolete and dysfunctional, the body is forced to plug into alterier realms. Stelarc experiences the body as raw, in its most molecular form, as networks of veins, blood pressure and stretched cells.

Stelarc is the frontiersman of the assimilation, hybridisation and connection of the body into the arrays of multiple and unfixed corporeal capacities facilitated by technological advances. The artist's previous ingenuity has involved sound amplifications of his body (muscle movements, bloodflow, heartbeat and brainwaves), the development of a robotic arm attached at his elbow, laser attachments to his eyes, and the filming of the interior of his stomach. With each machinic-attachment the body becomes further adaptable, extendable and mutable, merging with the tools and machinery, which become integral parts of the body.

It can be deliberated that the invention of the tool, disengaged the body from any conventional biological evolution.

The forklift, the diving suit, the horseman's stirrup all enable the body to engage with, perform and move within its environment, in ways that the uncoupled, untooled body itself cannot. Development thus becomes independent of biological evolution and the tool becomes an extension, and component of the body. Originally, evolution transformed the human bodies two forward limbs effectively from feet to hands, developing the bodies bipedalism, or two legged upright movement. This effectively freed up the two forward limbs to be used as tools, feelers and mechanisms of interaction. Stelarc's own performances appear to extrapolate from our present evolutionary plane into post-evolutionary planes. A way of speeding and tangling things up. His suspension events where the body effectively floats, may then be described as a-pedal, states of zero gravity. His third robotic arm events similarly represent a further artificial extrapolation of evolution, the development of further multiple limbs of interaction. The characteristic significance of the third arm is the way that the body becomes unbalanced and asymmetrical. Stelarc's artistic practices can easily be described as processes which deterritorialize the body; too many arms become wings, that draw lines of flight.

The fixed organic bodies immersion and incorporation within expanding technological terrains, increasingly engenders the bodies obsolescence. The body, because of its redundancy and ineffectiveness in comparison with machinic and robotic capabilities becomes substitued by machines. The body becomes idle. With the obsolescence of the body, the subjectivity of the individual is increasingly disengaged and moved to places outside the physicalities of the organic body. The "I" becomes uncontained by the body, separated from it. A still further consequence of the obsolescence of the body is an apparent imploding of the two poles of masculinity and femininity.

The technology-machine which engenders the obsolete body and the disembodiment of subjectivity, arises from outside the state apparatus and is continually reabsorbed and appropriated into the state, to neutralise its deterritorializing force. If the technology-machine remains external to the socius, it threatens to destabilise the system as a whole. A consequence of this effect, was the engendering of a technology race, which seeks to avoid the threat of superior technological advancement arising in a rival, which would threaten and potentially disrupt a socius's existing coagulations of power. Technology is therefore not generically a component of the state used against its citizens, as is commonly thought. It instead originates from outside and against the state. It is only found within the state apparatus, as a result of its appropriation and absorption. The deterritorializing effects of the technology-machine; relinquishing of the states absolute need for workers, surplus production and mass information and cultural exchange are then always reterritorialized through levels of bureaucracy, demands for full employment, internet regulation, monopolisation and regulation of the means of information exchange. The state is therefore forced to appropriate, and reterritorialize the technology machine, to minimise its propensity to disruption. We will not position technology onto an apocalypse/utopia styled dichotomy, technology is neither generically oppressive nor liberating, nor is it generically masculine, it is only under specific regimes and uses that it can become either. What is paramount is enabling individual manipulation and reconfiguring of its modes of production, engagement and activation. To elicit its capacities for multiplicity and to configure its deterritorializing effects in modes counter to the state.

Mike Parr is another performance artist who has endured a turbulent trajectory, winding amidst pathways of the subconscious, in pursuit of a forever elusive self. For an artist with a congenitally unformed arm, his most representative performance has to be his *Cathartic Action: Social Gestus No.5* (1977). In this performance the artist sitting at a table, raised a meat cleaver in one hand and hacked off an arm-like prosthetic attached at his shoulder. The dismembered arm spewed forth blood and flesh, causing a traumatic response in the audience. The performance sought to invoke a fragmenting of the body, a dissociative state similar to how the body exists before it is conditioned and manipulated into a structured and cohesive whole by authority. Other performances involving members of his own family, especially his father, entailed the decapitation of roosters in the performance space, which both alluded to Mike Parr's upbringing on an isolated poultry farm, and again confronted symbolically, anxieties of castration associated with the absence of his arm. The acts of butchery elicited the splattering of the blood, entrails and feathers of the birds. In this way the performance confronted the tensions and oppressions located within the family structure, and sought to viciously release and therefore disrupt the patriarchal structures. His performance piece, *The emetics: primary vomit. I am sick of art (red, yellow and blue)* (1977) engaged the artist first consuming coloured food dye and then disgorging the contents of his stomach in the performance space. It characterises the artists distaste of dominant aesthetic values and artistic codes. The vomitory act seeks the release of unobstructed flows, that invade the cleansed, quiet and cordial spaces of the gallery. The event muddles the flows; the signifying enunciation is replaced with an outpouring of vomit; he egests a foul vomit of words, and thus empties and voids himself. The enunciation becomes the gesticulatory motions of an anorexic, "to speak" and "to eat" are merged and no longer segregated, both at once. To speak with your mouth full!

Mike Parr is keenly perceptive of how the body is socialised and organised into a form. Through his *Self Portrait Project,* he attempts to counter the dominance of the face over the body.[6] The portraits taking after the automatistic drawings of Antonin Artaud, scatter the embodied memory, disgorging it onto the page and dissociating its traces, stammering all the traces of reflection. The present is always disassembled by an absence of memory, the self always merging in another direction, fragmenting and eddying the contours of the formation. It is evident that the face as socially constructed dominates the body, this is most exemplified in the media and advertising where the mask dominates the body like a commanding despot forming a paranoiac and despotic relationship with the remaining torso, limbs, organs and genitalia. This remainder is exiled, concealed behind clothing, plasticised and nullified against the omnipotent facial mask. What is left is the body reduced to a face, the facial mask. Mike Parr counters all of this by developing a body with faces, a plurality of unrecognisable and unperceived faces. He submerges everything in a mire of heavy blackened streaks, tremulous smudges and abrasive outlines. The portrait becomes a facial-surface, a face merging with the landscape, a face obscured and unreachable, a face that is a black monochromatic void. There is no origin connected to this face, it is the dissolution of the self, the self without origin, that is unmappable and imperceptible. He stammers everything producing not images of pictorial clarity and exactness, but inundating them with splutters, upheavals and flurries.

In Deleuzian/Guattarian terms the convulsive, scarifying, burning and masochistic nature of these various artistic probings can then be read as a process of scribbling over and decoding the inscriptions that are impressed by social institutions onto the body and into our minds. Such work implies that the inscriptions cannot be simply and painlessly erased, implying the tattoo nature and permanence of the inks. Nor can one succeed by over-inscribing the institutionalised inscriptions with textual and signifying codes (as opposed to asignifying scribbles) as this would result in the artists themselves still remaining trapped and entangled within orthodox slogans, leaving the body still bounded and composed of singularities and bi-linearities. The abject and purgative directions of these artists are then justified due to their engendering of a body composed of continuum's, of flows and intensities, or what Deleuze and Guattari term the Body without Organs, the organism without parts. This Body without Organs, is understood as a surface or plane upon which organs, machines, limbs, part(ial) objects and so forth, interconnect and assemble in a multiplicity of formations and regimes. Both fascist and anti-fascist or similarly paranoiac and schizophrenic Bodies without Organs are possible. But what differentiates the fascist from the anti-fascist or similarly the paranoiac from the schizophrenic Body without Organs is the manner and degree in which the regime or assemblage is capable of multiple interconnections; of engendering multiple and continuous conjunctions and disjunctions, connections and reconnections; of effecting multiple arrangements and continuous rearrangements between the organs, machines, objects and adjacent planes. It is the fascist body that is incapable of multiple connections, it is a sterile and unproductive body: "no mouth, no tongue, no teeth, no anus". The fascist rejects the organs in the same manner as the priest, while the schizo body attracts the organs, moulding them over his/her surface, interchanging them and reforming them. Further differences unravel, the Body without Organs of the fascist is clothed, differing from the schizo body which is naked. On this point, the said "nakedness" of the schizo body should not be interpreted as affiliated to the plasticised images typical of pornography, such images are in various senses still *clothed*. The fascist body remains repulsed at its corporeality, its physicality and especially its genitalia. The fascist remains horrified at the bodies capacities and functions: defecation, urination, bleeding, ejaculation, breast feeding, birth and menstruation. See for example the quaint inversion of the aesthetics and mannerisms associated with the seemingly opposite bodily functions of defecation and ingestion in Luis Bunuel's, *Phantom of Liberty*.

The Body without Organs that is developed, even if ephemerally, through these artistic pursuits is one that is capable of forming a multiplicity of connections. Deleuze and Guattari have delineated various revolutionary pathways, or "becomings" for cultivating the schizo Body without Organs, including; becoming woman, becoming child, becoming animal... and becoming imperceptible. Becomings are methods for engendering the abstract metamorphisis of the body. In Franz Kafka's *The Transformation* the body of Gregor Samsa awakes one morning from troubled dreams to find himself transformed into a monstrous insect. Gregor is certainly one such body, a Body without Organs having engendered a veritable becoming animal. Einstürzende Neubauten's *Zum Tier Machen* (Changing to animal) is a similar instance of a becoming animal. One might even say that the animated objects in the films of the Czechoslovakian filmmaker, Jan Svankmajer demonstrate so many examples of becomings. Each object "comes to life", developing an alterity through miraculous becomings that cumulate into a chimerical assemblage or Body without Organs.

For you can tie me up if you wish,
but there is nothing more useless than an organ.

When you will have made him a body without organs, then you will have delivered him
from all his automatisms and restored him to his true freedom.

Then you will teach him again to dance wrong side out
like in the frenzy of dance halls
and his wrong side out will be his real place.

-- Antonin Artaud

The becomings of the Body without Organs are revolutionary since they are always dominated by dismantlings of signifiance (grammaticality and the regime of signs), disassemblings of subjectification (the self, memory and consciousness), and deterritorialization of the body. While the Body without Organs has in part its origins with Antonin Artaud's, *To Have Done with the Judgement of God,* a text by William Burroughs is perhaps most demonstrative, "but no organ is constant as regards either function or position... sex organs sprout anywhere... rectums open, defecate and close... the entire organism changes colour and consistency in split second adjustments... "[7] But it should be noted as it is in Deleuze and Guattari's writing that like the masochist, the paranoiac and the hypochondriac, the drug addict forms what is called an emptied or fascist Body without Organs. This type of Body without Organs is unable to connect in a multiplicity of combinations, it is empty rather that full. The junky develops the experimental Body without Organs which is "botched", in this instance the body falters in the attempt to effect a full body populated by multiplicities. What remains is a fascistic and empty Body without Organs. The junky's body is instead reduced to a single organ - the vein. The masochist uses suffering to force a Body without Organs into existence, a body that is consequently incapable of accommodating anything other than the sole intensities and waves characteristic of pain, and for this reason is also, likewise botched. The full Body without Organs does not exist unless it productions are multiplical.

The artist navigates through the unexplored plateaus and planes of the Body without Organs forming full Bodies without Organs, but also at times, forming botched Bodies without Organs. The task is phenomenally difficult, the map, the inclination is always fluctuating, continuously assembling into new unpredictable anamorphic formations. It is in this way that I believe the schizo artist can inadvertently fall into botched Bodies without Organs, but at other times it appears that the artist deliberately enters drugged or masochistic bodies, ephemerally with various intentions; to experiment, to examine potentials of passing onto still other plateaus, to use it as an intermediate for projecting oneself onto a full Body without Organs, to gain from one plateau experience or knowledge that can be of benefit in another. Intermittent fallings into botched Bodies without Organs may even be unavoidable.

It is a problem which Deleuze and Guattari are very much aware of, "It is a struggle and as such is never sufficiently clear. How can we fabricate a BwO [Body without Organs] for ourselves without its being the cancerous BwO of a fascist inside us, or the empty BwO of a drug addict, paranoiac, or hyperchondriac? How can we tell the three bodies apart? Artaud was constantly grappling with this problem"[8]. What remains is a degree of uncertainty and confusion of how to discern the full Body without Organs from its empty doubles. One may yet be able to avoid emptying and botching the productions of the Body without Organs, by simply maintaining ephemeral and perpetually transitory movements. So long as what is produced remains multiplical then the Body without Organs has not been botched. But it is apparent that the Body without Organs is nearly always threatened by this cancerous collapse, that its existence remains perpetually unstable, it appears to be always warding off its own collapse. "We have to move quickly, we mustn't linger on something that might bog us down",[9] like a death-fixation, a drug dependence, sadism, phallocentrism. Deleuze and Guattari's position is however not a value laden strategy, the Body without Organs will traverse and encounter all of the these disparate forms, what is important is that it will avoid *always* being drug addicted, or *always* masochistic, or *always* self-destructive. The Body without Organs is always moving on a line of flight that continually re-groups and assimilates diverse features.

The process of becoming is described as an individuated undertaking, it is a solitary task, but it is one that inevitably leads to the collective, to the crowd. On this matter, Deleuze describes the solitude or reclusivness of Jean-Luc Godard as "an extraordinarily populous solitude"[10]. This populousness is manifested in the diversity of components that enter each of his films; literature, film history, art, documentary, music, political theories - all broken and blurred within interspersed clusters.

It must also be affirmed that the formation of the Body without Organs in no way concerns itself with biological evolution. The Body without Organs is not defined by any physicality, it is defined conceptually; by modes of engagement and degrees of multiplicity. The body without Organs and its construction, implies actions that are here and now, possibilities that always exist in the present.

The wall and filter that I spoke of previously are inextricably linked to the formation of the Body without Organs. In order to traverse onto or reach this Body without Organs, one must first shatter the barricading wall. You will never find your Body without Organs unless you dismantle the wall, or similarly meddle with your filter. Vincent Van Gogh is certainly one of the dissociated individual who has run up against this wall, Artaud another. The crucial question is how does one destroy this wall, without plummeting into despair? How does one deterritorialize without collapsing into a cancerous inertness. Deleuze and Guattari assert that one cannot succeed in bursting through this wall by violently impacting against its surface. A too sudden deterritorialization can be fatal, even suicidal, a too sudden deterritorialization will also botch the Body without Organs. They provide the advice of Vincent Van Gogh, "How does one get through this wall, for it is useless to hit it hard, it has to be undermined and penetrated with a file, slowly and with patience, as I see it"[11]. Vincent Van Gogh's dejected life, cumulating in his own tragic ending only points out that there are no certainties and no assured methods. Antonin Artaud's attempt is also similar, an opium addict for most of his life and an eventual death in an asylum at Ivry outside Paris. The task of schizophrenization as described by Deleuze and Guattari certainly proceeds by way of destruction, the task necessitates the destruction of the molar assemblages, the structures and organisations of power, both within and outside the body. But it is however certain that there are imminent dangers, risks and consequential cautions that must be taken - there is always the risk of too much damage, achieved too quickly, leaving only a cancerous, emptied body.

Deleuze/Guattari's explanation of the Body without Organs revels that it is not at all organless but forms a very distinct relationship to the biological organism. The Body without Organs remains opposed to territorialized formations of the body, fixed stable structures that are typically binary as opposed to the multiplical connections privileged by the Body without Organs. The Body without Organs "is not at all the opposite of the organs. The organs are not its enemies. The enemy is the organism. The BwO is opposed not to the organs but to that organisation of the organs called the organism...[what is opposed is] the organism, the organic organisation of the organs."[12] For this, the Body without Organs attracts and arranges all the organs; eyes, tails, ani, wings... deterritorializing them; attracting and connecting, releasing and searching. What is formed and produced through the Body without Organs becomings is no less real because it is unreal, or rather it is real to the individual as the real itself. Becomings are perfectly real even if what one becomes is not.

What is then the outcome, what is asked of us? Make for yourself a Body without Organs, find your Body without Organs. "Lodge yourself on a stratum, experiment with the opportunities it offers, find an advantageous place on it, find potential movements of deterritorialization, possible lines of flight, experience them, produce flow conjunctions here and there, try out continuums of intensities segment by segment..."[13]

---

Notes

1. Hollingdale, R J (ed and Trans) referencing Nietzsche's "Daybreak": 14 in *A Nietzsche Reader* Harmondsworth, Middlesex, Penguin Books, 1977, pp. 88-90
2. Antonin Artaud, *Artaud Anthology,* ed. Jack Hirschman, San Francisco, City Lights Books, 1965, p. 33
3. Throbbing Gristle interviewed by Re/Search, "Throbbing Gristle," *Re/Search Industrial Culture Handbook,* issue #6/7, San Francisco, 1983, p. 17
4. Stelarc Interviewed by Martin Thomas: "Just Beaut to Have Three Hands," *Continuum, Electronic Arts in Australia,* Vol 8, No.1, Ed. Nicholas Zurbrugg, Perth, 1994, p. 383
5. Gilles Deleuze and Felix Guattari, *A Thousand Plateaus, Capitalism and Schizophrenia,* p. 160
6. Graham Coulter-Smith and Jane Magon, "Mike Parr's Self Portraits: Unma(s)king the self" in *Eyeline #5,* Brisbane, p. 22
7. William Burroughs *Naked Lunch,* Hammersmith London, Paladin, 1992, p. 22 or New York, Grove Press, 1966, p. 8,

quoted by Deleuze and Guattari in *A Thousand Plateaus Capitalism and Schizophrenia* p. 153

8. Gilles Deleuze and Felix Guattari, *A Thousand Plateaus Capitalism and Schizophrenia* p. 163
9. Felix Guattari, Chaosmosis, an *Ethico-Aesthetic Paradigm,* Sydney, Power Publications, 1995, p. 84
10. Gilles Deleuze, "Three Questions About "Six Fois Deux,"" in Raymond Bellour and Mary Lea Bandy (Eds), *Jean-Luc Godard, Son + Image 1974-1991,* New York, Museum of Modern Art, 1992, p. 35
11. Vincent Van Gogh, "Letter of September 8, 1888", cited in Antonin Artaud, *Artaud Anthology,* ed. Jack Hirschman, San Francisco, City Lights Books, 1965, p. 150, and quoted by Gilles Deleuze and Felix Guattari in *Anti Oedipus, Capitalism and Schizophrenia* p. 136.
12. Gilles Deleuze and Felix Guattari, *A Thousand Plateaus Capitalism and Schizophrenia,* p. 158
13. ibid p. 161

# Rhizomatic Ontologies

by Robert Lort

"There is no ontology of essence, there is only ontology of sense."

-- Deleuze

Deleuze and Guattari develop the concept of the rhizome in their introduction to *A Thousand Plateaus, Capitalism and Schizophrenia.*[1] Although a rhizome is conventionally thought of as a root like stem, Deleuze and Guattari have a different or indeed a broader conception of it. For Deleuze and Guattari the rhizome is a conception of space, an understanding of the immense number of interconnections, assemblages and arrangements of matter, machines, lines, bodies, sounds and so forth. The Rhizome is an expanse of deterritorialization, a deterritorialized plane of flux.

The rhizome is composed of a multitude of dimensions, lines and degrees of intensity. It's form has no beginning and no end, what exists is the middle, the inbetween. "The rhizome is an antigenealogy. It is a short-term memory, or antimemory. The rhizome operates by variation, expansion, conquest, capture, offshoots."[2] The rhizome is deterritorialized space, a multiplicity of *n* dimensions, it's effects are disorganising, non-hierarchical, and decentralising. The rhizome has no unity, form or fixivity. It operates by forgetting, by fragmenting, by diversifying.

The rhizome is made of lines in motion as opposed to stationary points, it is an anti-structure. Lines of the rhizomatic type are always twirling, folding, unravelling and disaligning themselves. These lines form what are called "lines of flight", or movements of absolute deterritorialization. The rhizome is characterised as swarming indefinite space, of multiplicity and ephemerality of arrangements. In principal it disables the formation of power centres, it is anti-hegemonic. A rhizome structure is flat, rather than tall, ordered and hierarchical, its capacities and affects always engender and enable heterogeneous forms. The rhizome itself has no centre of origin, what exists is only the inbetween.

Insurgent crowds, such as the crowds in Sergei Eisenstein's *October* (also known as *Ten Days that Shook The World*) are characterisations of a rhizome. The images of revolutionary masses scurrying, surging, flooding, scrambling and upheaving, in every way exemplifies a rhizomatic understanding. The crowds abound in rhizomatic movements, movements that are impulsive, spontaneous and haphazard, motions and gestures always denoting fleeting lines of flight. Collisions and flurries never cease to exchange assemblages and to engage with offshoots of vectorial spasms. The infamous image of ants scurrying over the palm of the hand in Bunuel and Dali's *Un Chien Andalou* are equally demonstrative.

Einstürzende Neubauten are the devisers of rhizome music. In their description of the formation of the musical piece *Wardrobe* they write; "N.U. played the wardrobe. It features our longest tape loop (30 seconds), Alex's dog Lola, singing chainsaws, a rank of 3m high airducts arranged like dominos, snapping wood and water dripping on a hot stove"[3]. The formation constitutes a Neubautenesque desiring machine, a rhizome machine par-excellence.

The rhizome may be contrasted with what Deleuze and Guattari call the strata. The strata defines a space of organisation and fixivity. Such spaces are said to be stratified, and are characterised by their immobility and their linear structures of a hierarchical and binary nature. These spaces are distinguishable by their solidity as opposed to the fluidity of the rhizome. Not surprisingly, the objective of any revolutionary movement is one of destratification and deterritorialization, movements attaining rhizomatic conceptions.

Deleuze and Guattari have identified two points in their discourse that are in disagreement with the work of their contemporary Michel Foucault. The second is of significance in this context, for which Deleuze/Guattari write: "the diagram and abstract machine have lines of flight that are primary, which are not phenomena of resistance or counter attack in an assemblage, but cutting edges of creation and deterritorialization."[4] The important word here is "primary", which forms the core of their disagreement. Foucault, by contrast insists that there is nothing "primary" or innate to the conception of the power assemblage ("diagram and abstract machine"). This disagreement or difference is not even minor, almost the contrary. It seems that for Deleuze/Guattari there are primary positions of revolt (contrary to Foucault) and similarly primary locations of repression, what determines the difference is their relative degree of deterritorialization. This is why we must find our most deterritorialized flows, and avoid those that are reterritorializing. But still it is less than simple, repressive machines can also be highly deterritorialized.

The denial of any kind of essentialism at all, is to fall into a dead end anthropocentric idealism. But present perceptions regarding ontology still offer no assurances. They are not only exceedingly restrictive, but are fundamental components to the agencies of repression which act to restrict and hold back the movements of absolute deterritorialization. For Deleuze and Guattari, ontology is neither generically liberating, nor generically oppressive. It is not about discovering some pre-technological ontology which has been repressed in modern society, that would potentially restore freedom. Nor is ontology a fixed and rigidified form which would subjugate (women for example) to fixed and invariable modes of being. Deleuze and Guattari offer a Spinozist inspired conception of ontology. "Bodies are not defined by their genus or species, by their organs and functions, but by what they can do, by the affects of which they are capable - in passion as well as in action."[5] A body is defined by what a body can do, by the connections it enables, by its degrees of movement and speed, by its capacities and affects. It is defined by engagement and action, and not materialism. What is important is how the ontology is assembled and utilised, together with the extent that it engages with and allows integrations and connections with multiplicities. The full Body without Organs realises a rhizomatic ontology, it brings forth and engages rhizomatic intensities, and is itself installed and comprised within the interstices of such a rhizomatic ontology.

The crucial question becomes how to constitute political, social, sexual, work and familial relations in the assemblage of a rhizome. How to assimilate these components into a plane of consistency, the surface that brings forth a rhizomatic ontology. The plane of consistency is the field of immanence of desire, it is the Body without Organs. "The plane of consistency of Nature is like an immense Abstract Machine, abstract yet real and individual; its pieces are the various assemblages and individuals, each of which groups together an infinity of particles entering into an infinity of more or less interconnected relations"[6]. The plane of consistency is comprised of a rhizomatic nature, of intensities and surfaces, movements of rest, speed and slowness that comprise an infinite number of assemblages and an infinite number of interconnections between parts.

The plane of consistency is an asignifying surface, it can be constructed in innumerable ways. The members of Einstürzende Neubauten sit around their empty table, their "Tabula Rasa", their slate/table is wiped clean, engendering their plane of consistency. It is a surface upon which any sound can enter, any conglomeration of emergences can take hold. The plane of consistency itself is infinite, one can effect it a thousand different ways, it can form a thousand different arrangements and assemblages of objects, limbs, machines, flows, sounds, whatever. "We must try to conceive of this world in which a single fixed plane... is traversed by nonformal elements of relative speed that enter into this or that individuated assemblage depending on their degrees of speed and slowness. A plane of consistency peopled by anonymous matter, by infinite bits of impalpable matter entering into varying connections."[7]

The plane of consistency is however the first conception of the plane, for there is a second kind of ontological plane, this plane is called the plane of organisation. This type of plane "is structural or genetic, and both at once, structure and genesis, the structural plan(e) of formed organisations with their developments, the genetic plan(e) of evolutionary developments with their organisations. These are only nuances of the first conception of the plane. To accord these nuances too much importance would prevent us from grasping something more important..."[8] What is important is how the two planes are formed and interrelate, what they produce and enable and what they block and disallow, the assemblages and interconnections that are effected and the extent to which the Body without Organs approaches and derives the rhizomatic nature of a full Body without Organs. Whether the body becomes immured and oedipalized in the plane of organisation or engenders the becomings and lines of flight of a Body without Organs installed in a plane of consistency.

The plane of organisation acts as a surface of stratification, it is always acting against the plane of consistency, always trying to reorder the movements of divergence, always trying to restratify and recentre the flows, always pulling back the deterritorializations. But on the other hand the plane of consistency is constantly pulling in the other direction, always struggling to extricate itself from the plane of organisation, always collapsing stratifications and scattering particles further afield, always assembling lines of flight that merge with the anomalous, always releasing flows and engagements of deterritorialization.

But herein lies the problem, for the plane of consistency is never provided from the outset, at birth it remains separated from the individual, as yet unconnected and unfound. "[T]he plane itself is not given. It is by nature hidden."[9] We must find and activate our plane of consistency. It is found as a part alongside, and adjacent, but never given in the first instance. "The egg is the BwO [Body without Organs]. The BwO is not "before" the organism; it is adjacent to it and is continually in the process of constructing itself."[10] The plane of consistency must be discovered and effectuated, it must be constructed as a separate plane above the plane of organisation. We must discover our unconscious, feel it and activate it, but it is not at all a matter of returning to it. You did not lose your full Body without Organs at the earliest stage of childhood, for you had not yet even found or discovered it. But it is however certain that the majority of adults are further from the full Body without Organs, than they were in their childhood. In this sense the child is still privileged as nearer to fully effectuating the full plane of consistency, the Body without Organs. You must find the plane before you can make it work, this is the same as forming the Body without Organs, the same as smashing through the wall, and meddling with your body-sieve. We are always deterred and hindered from finding and actualising the plane of consistency, the stratified agencies of the socius are always curtailing and limiting the unboundedness of the ontological expanse. The ontological field is ceaselessly reduced to those modalities, those engagements, territories and assemblages conductive or aligned with capitalist functionings of enabling profit. The plane of organisation will always obscure and conceal the plane of consistency, always leaving us trapped and at an impasse, which we must overcome. The plane of consistency, like the Body without Organs is grasped and revealed through movements of deterritorialization, it is always constructed.

The interpretation is that the body begins blank or neutral, a mass adjacent to the plane of consistency which subsequently begins to acquire and gain connections and conjunctions, eventually effecting a complete destratification to form a multiplicity in the case of the full Body without Organs. But this is not at all the case for most bodies, as we know very few presently succeed in forming or constructing a full Body without Organs. Instead most bodies form only the most rudimentary of connections - far, far too few! The few connections that are formed are those that are the least deterritorialized, those immediately adjacent the body and those principally binary and stratified. Connections of this kind remain comparatively rigid, hierarchical and organising. They form the connections of the organic strata, the oedipal connections, the connections of the capitalist socius, connections which subordinate to a singly focused identity and subjectivity.

All the warnings, "do not deterritorialize past this point", "do not venture that plane of consistency!" Even the schizo, the annihilator of the oedipalizing self, must traverse across this milieu, beginning by moving outwards across the plane of consistency, fleeing fugitively from claustrophobia, always propelled at a tangent to the enclosing circles. The schizo accelerates outwards in a mad haste, always out-distancing the reductive oedipalizations. The schizo is always unwrapping a new ontological realm.

The plane of consistency brings about the coexistence of disparate forms; conscious and subconscious, real and imagined, masculine and feminine, organic and inorganic - without incorporating or installing them into a system of privilege, valorization or hierarchy of one over the other. It is a dissolution of the dominant hierarchies, by collapsing them into a planar coexistence of interweaving assemblages. The plane of consistency is not so much the elusion of what is pregiven but a full effectuation of what is pregiven, *Oedipus is then just a speck in the true scope of ontology.* The rhizomatic ontology once understood revels that essence and nature are then alterable and in every way mutable and adaptable, capable of movements in all directions, any kind of becoming or creation is possible. The only problem is starting it, of trigging the Body without Organs.

---

Notes

1. This introduction is published separately by Semiotext(e), see Gilles Deleuze and Felix Guattari, *On The Line,* New York, Semiotext(e), 1983.
2. Gilles Deleuze and Felix Guattari, *A Thousand Plateaus Capitalism and Schizophrenia,* Minneapolis, University of Minnesota Press, 1987, p. 21
3. The liner notes to Einstürzende Neubauten's *Wardrobe* from the double CD, *Strategies Against Architecture II.*
4. Gilles Deleuze and Felix Guattari, *A Thousand Plateaus Capitalism and Schizophrenia,* p. 531 Note 39
5. Gilles Deleuze and Claire Parnet, *Dialogues,* New York, Columbia University Press, 1987, p. 60
6. Gilles Deleuze and Felix Guattari, *A Thousand Plateaus Capitalism and Schizophrenia,* p. 254
7. ibid, p. 255
8. ibid, p. 265
9. ibid, p. 265
10. ibid, p. 164

# A Thousand Tiny Sexes

by Robert Lort

What is needed so urgently are new conceptions of sexual becomings, connectivities and desires, combined with the deployment and development of sexualities that dismantle and discontinue the foregoing dominance of oedipal and patriarchal despotic centres. What is needed is the conception of the multiplical sexuality.

### *Difference*

The negation of sexual difference is still an unbalanced equation. Difference will manifest itself in revolutionary terms, which eschew implying deficiencies and inadequacies. Difference is not a definition of the women's role and subjectivity, by contrast it will assert the unlimited, molecular-woman. "Equality in difference"[1] builds itself on a pluralistic expansion of all possibilities of deviation from the normal and patriarchal, a revolutionary equality of expanding dissimilarity and difference.

Of greatest significance is the desire for conditions which do not elicit new intolerances to difference. "Equality in difference" posits itself in radical opposition to normalisation, fixivity and tyrannical sameness. To cause change in any system an element of difference must be introduced. Any attempt at resolving gender binarism by asserting a singularity; masculinity and femininity as social constructs and an "inbetweenness" as yet another dismal essentialized fixivity, is itself problematic, and reinventing in a new form what it attempts to disavowal of. A move towards a multiplicity, an encouragement and acceptance of all positions, *n* positivities of equal sexes, an argument not of unity but in favour of diversity and difference, a difference that subverts, expanding rather than contracting, becomes the revolutionary process.

The intent is to not only affirm difference but to proliferate and expand it in all possible directions, the counter movement to positions which rather, reduce the existing binarisms onto sameness and absolute singularities. Equality in difference seeks to understand "woman" in indeterminant and multiplical terms, rather than explicit one meaning definitions of the sort; woman = lesbian, woman = man, woman = nurturer and so forth. To instead form definitions which yield *n* meanings, *n* contiguities of engagement. One meaning definitions of the sort described, only render new blockages and new limits binding women's subjectivity. Equality in sameness seeks to reduce everything down to a common centre, a central fixed core upon which everything is equalised. Whereas equality in difference delineates the non-reductive, non-contractible surface that is the equality of multiplicity. In this instance there is no longer a unique and single solution, but multiple (and dissimilar) positions of equality.

Is sameness a necessity to equality? The French Feminist Luce Irigaray agreeably shows that "at the level of a superficial cultural critique" affirmative answers to this question, "are well founded, but that as a means of liberating women they are utopian. Women's exploitation is based upon sexual difference; its solution will come only through sexual difference. Certain modern tendencies, certain feminists of our time, make strident demands for sex to be neutralised" (ie crushed down to a single core). "To wish to get rid of sexual difference is to call for a genocide more radical than any form of destruction there has ever been in History... It is vital that a culture of the sexual, as yet nonexistent, be elaborated, with each sex being respected."[2] The only flaw in this argument is Irigaray's conception of the human species as divided into two distinct genders; masculine and feminine. While it is true that masculine and feminine exist on the ontological level, (that of the organism) of which she speaks of, it is also true that there exists many more, (ontology also consist of what is not of the "organic organisation of the organism"). Following Deleuze and Guattari, sexuality is a thousand tiny sexes, it is not binary (two disparate sexes), it is not singular (a single sex divided by power), it is always *n* tiny sexes.

***The two codes normal and abnormal.***

For the revolutionary movement to achieve genuine equality and the cessation of oppression, it is critical that its framework discontinues the dichotomy normal/abnormal. Any continuation of this dichotomy, constitutes a propensity to re-continue, and re-establish mechanisms of repression. In this frame current radical initiatives must avidly seek the disintegration of this dichotomy. Without successfully carrying this out progressive movements risk establishing a simultaneous deterritorialization and reterritorialization of both men's and women's sexualities; a simultaneous liberation and re-repression; or said otherwise, a de-aestheticizing followed by a re-aestheticizing. Progressive movements must therefore continually eschew the re-creation of deviational, incorrect, and abnormal categorisations of all kinds. Any continuation or redefining of the relational categories normal/abnormal, consequently threatens to carry forward repression. A revolution which engenders new orders, ideals and ethics, is no revolution at all.

Current movements should instead continually expand and broaden the category of normal, by continually enlarging and extrapolating its territory, in ways that conquer and flow into the territory of abnormal, until a dichotomy (normal/abnormal) per se no longer exits. The process is the exact converse of the disciplinarian process of normalization, which establishes a fixed and immovable territory denoted as "normal", and seeks to continually reintegrate the deviant into this centralised and universalised territory. Deviations are then always pulled back inwards, as opposed to anti-normalization which continually dislodges any partition between normal and abnormal and engages flows that encounter an unbounded field of flux.

What is strived for is no ideal, correct or totalising conception of sexuality (of any form), but a multiplicity of differences, a terrain of coexistent and pluralist forms of diversifying sexualities. We cannot achieve a revolutionary schism by simply rearranging and reordering the categories of normal and abnormal, nor by simply inverting the dichotomies, either way the general frameworks of repression remain perfectly intact. To effect a break from the dominant structures we must not error in reforming those structures with the indices repositioned. We must smash the dichotomies in their entirety. We must pull apart the oedipalized subjectivity of judgement, that is omnipresently prevalent throughout the entire socius, making everyone a judge. Oedipus makes everyone a judge, from priests, to the parent, to certain prudish feminists. No more sign posts, "you will not past this point", "you will not deterritorialize beyond this circle", "you will not make for yourself a schizo body".

Bursting open the hard rock of Oedipus is the same as breaking the hard rock of patriarchy. We must in every way send the shards flying! But we must eschew the re-establishment of new ideals, the remaking of hard rocks, of new fixative stratas. Overall, we must not seek to unify things, even at ulterior points. "It is surely absurd to hope to overthrow the power of the bourgeoisie by replacing it with a structure that reconstitutes the form of that power."[3] Many social and political movements continually seek to recontain present conceptions of being, knowing and value amongst new equilibriums, be they political, sexual, aesthetic or whatever. This effectively astringes all the intensities, flows and motions, through the reconsolidation of the forms. Against such reconsolidating movements, rhizomatic analyses engender depositionings, which alternatively, always seek the infinite disequilibriums, rhizomatic analyses seek to perpetually smash apart all the centres of identity, value, unity and knowledge, which continually act to fetter the complete release. In this context, the downfall of movements such as surrealism, communism, even punk[4] can be seen as being due to the movements re-establishing fixed equilibriums of ethics, aesthetics and value, which ultimately fettered further progression. Revolution is not a march to an end point or attainable conclusion, revolution is the interminable scurry that is a schizo-stroll. It is paths or lines that stumble, weave, and wobble.

### *Becoming-Woman*

"nur sie wird das Licht als erste sehen..."
(only she will see the light first)
-- Einstürzende Neubauten

Becomings are the very functions and productions of the full Body without Organs. All becomings begin with and pass through a becoming-woman. This becoming engenders the connectors that first reveal the contiguousness and adjacency of disparate segments. In general, becomings follow a kind of sequence, for which becoming-woman is only the first becoming.

Becoming-woman leads to the other becomings which follow; becoming-child, becoming-animal, and onwards until becoming imperceptible. For the present I wish only to focus on an introduction and examination of the first becoming; for its relation to feminist positions and because the development of this becoming serves as a requirement to the development of the successive becomings.

Becoming-woman, like all becomings is a process of deterritorialization, it is a line of flight that activates segments of a rhizome. Becoming-woman engenders a fluid and heterogeneous plane of multiple sexualities, a variable, de-hierarchized, and destabilised field. Becoming-woman is a destratification, it embarks into the spaces between strata, engendering the expansive plane of pluralised and deterritorialized sexualities of a Body without Organs. But most of all, becoming-woman smashes apart the dualisms of patriarchal sexuality, it is the force that produces a thousand tiny sexes.

Deleuze and Guattari make a distinction between two kinds of sexualities, the human and the non-human. Human sexuality is the capitalist representation of sexuality that is imposed on the subject. It is a sexual identity that is consolidated and territorialized onto the individual under the manipulations of the socius. It is as much organismal as it is commodified. It is human sexuality that crushes and amputates desire, "desire finds itself trapped specifically limited to human sex".[5] It causes the full multiplicities of desire to become truncated and blocked on either side, binarized and entrapped within the great oedipal dichotomy, masculine/feminine. This is why revolution entails eliciting the surging uncontrollable becomings of a non-human sex, precisely what is a becoming-woman.

Sexuality can immure itself in a strata; a biological strata, a commodity fetishism or a nullification, but it can equally move in another direction, a direction of destratification. Sexuality can territorialize and oedipalize all its flows and connections, but it can just as easily draw a line of deterritorialization that elicits the line of flight of a becoming-woman. What a becoming-woman produces is a molecular-sexuality. All becomings are molecular, they are always tangential movements bursting out from what is molar. Becomings always involve a fragmenting of the molar, an emission of micro-particles, the shattering of strata. "What we term a molar entity is, for example, the woman as defined by her form, endowed with organs and functions and assigned as a subject. Becoming-woman is not imitating this entity or even transforming oneself into it."[6] Becoming-woman is not about resembling or simulating the molar woman, becoming-woman produces the molecular woman, what is a non-oedipal woman. The molecular woman is the anomalous, most women (and even more of men) have not as yet found their molecular becoming. A molecular sexuality is a thousand tiny sexes, its nature is such that each of us can mutate and venture over to any other of the thousand different sexualities.

While it is certain that the intention is for men to effect a becoming-woman, it is also made very clear that not only must men effectuate a becoming-woman, but women must also. Women must just as much find their destratifying path out of patriarchal indoctrinated subjectivities. The man must become-woman no less as much, as the woman herself must become-woman. "Becoming is always double, that which one becomes becomes no less than the one that becomes..."[7] Becomings are in a sense always dual, "A woman has to become-woman, but in a becoming-woman of all man."[8] A woman becomes-woman through the becoming-woman of a man, a man becomes-woman through the becoming-woman of a woman. What is found and utilised is an outer medium, or a third medium, which is neither man nor woman, but a space inbetween the binarism and simultaneously a space outside the binarism. A becoming always sets both points in motion, setting into motion, not only the one who becomes but also what one becomes. Becoming-woman is not simply a male point which is moved to intercept with a stationary female point. Becomings set both points in motion, becoming-woman sets both the male point and the female point in motion, a movement of flux, a line of flight. "A line of becoming has only a middle. The middle is not an average; it is fast motion, it is the absolute speed of movement. A becoming is always in the middle; one can only get it by the middle. A becoming is neither one nor two, nor the relation of the two; it is the in-between, the border or line of flight or descent running perpendicular to both."[9] A becoming-woman encounters the interstices, the crevice or abyss between the stratas that elicits the thousand tiny sexes, the schizo surface of multiplicity.

"There is no becoming-man because man is the molar entity par excellence, whereas becomings are molecular."[10] The reason why there is no becoming-man, is because "man" represents sexuality reduced to a gigantic struggle for the phallus, a gigantic anthropomorphic conception of sexuality, which situates the phallus at the genesis of all forces and relations, and situates lack and castration as underlying every desire. Man is the molar conception of sexuality; it is singularity, it is Oedipus, it is a need to entrap everything in a homogeneous centre. Masculinity forms the undifferentiated core, the strata and nucleus from which one flees, to initiate these becomings. This fleeing suggests a traversing across a plane, always with our backs to that which is less differentiated, always our chests toward that which is more differentiated. Becoming-woman is not a single directional movement, that merges and aligns bodies into a confluence, a sequential tiered movement, that might restrict other becomings, other offshoots. Becoming-woman is entirely unlike that, becoming woman is by nature *n* directional, comprised of an infinite number of lines of flight. Neither is becoming-woman a reduction to one human sex, just as becoming-animal is not a reterritorialization onto one animal being. Becoming animal is in many ways a becoming inanimate, just as becoming-woman produces a non-human sex. All becomings are multiplical, they never involve the engendering of singularity as lasting or final. The becoming-animal for instance consists of continuous transformation, wolf to fish, fish to insect, insect to amoeba... and for this reason can be said to be inanimate. Becomings are always decentring and never involve recentrings on an organism or a single and unchangeable gender. The organism and the single gender are exemplary of singularity, whereas becomings are always multiplical.

Becoming-woman by no means reduces sexuality to a single sex, it is not at all the binary being reduced to the single, but to the contrary, it expands and facilitates all the possibilities and divergences, the outcome is always the production of a thousand tiny sexes. Becoming-woman begins the proliferation of sexuality beyond and outside existing binarisms (man/woman). A further misconception is that there is a hidden woman already inside every male (and vice-versa), that is continuously concealed and held in dire secrecy, as though we might all eventually reveal our bisexuality that we had always concealed. Becoming-woman instead always involves a finding, an activation of what is contiguous, a connecting up to something that has not previously been located. It is not something we return to, something already inside us that has been suppressed, but on the contrary, it is outside, it is yet to be found.

What is additionally important are the relationships and connections formed between the becoming-woman and other strategies of deterritorialization. The becoming-animal that is attached to male masochism (fur, dog collar, horse whip), effects a deterritorialization of patriarchal sexuality, through the interruption of the conventional positions of dominance and submission. But while masochism accomplishes a deterritorialization of the dominance of the father-figure, it is still accompanied by a reterritorialization on the mother-figure and thus re-establishes dominance, in an inverted form. This is why it botches the Body without Organs. Sadism on the other hand could never be considered to contain any degree of deterritorialization, as the father-figure still maintains the position of dominance. Homosexuality is another approach to deterritorializing patriarchal sexuality, it can engender a becoming-woman, but homosexuality can still just as much reterritorialize on itself, and block further lines of flight, pulling itself back onto a strata. What will determine the success or failure of a becoming-woman is the intensities and degrees of multiplicity that are assimilated, exactly as what determines the success or failure of a Body without Organs.

The movements of a becoming-woman position non-conjugal relations and connections between bodies, that derive a rhizomatic nature. Conjugations between bodies are characterised by non-oedipal flows; connections that break and reform, that distribute and reassemble, always emerging amongst new offshoots and engaging with a decentring line of flux. Here the junctions and indices between bodies are always migrating, always proliferating, they are made up of fleeting and transversal attachments. Joinings are always ephemeral, never hardening or petrifying into the oedipal rigidities. To venture a becoming-woman is to produce the non-oedipal woman, "a daughter born without a mother"[11] The non-oedipal body is always an orphan, eternally a foreigner, she/he exists constantly outside the borders. Above all the non-oedipal body does not delimit, does not erect borders, partitions, territories or limits, neither around or over themselves nor around or over others. The non-oedipal body is always unowned and unowning. The schizo body that is engendered by these forces of becoming, is a body uprooted and evicted from any origin (sex, class, nationality... ), it's body is originless, a body without a mother and a body without a father. The non-oedipal woman is epitomised by outsider women. Women who are anti-moulds, women like Kathy Acker, Patti Smith, Yoko Ono or Anna Kavan, women which regrettably some quarters of the feminist movement have been continually trying to restratify.[12] We must not recentre these fervent lines of flight. We must not reintegrate or solidify these flows. Schizophrenic women have always been outsiders to the feminist movement, their movements have always been clashing against its walls and homogenisations.

The writer, Anna Kavan, cleverly characterised as Kafka's sister, fills a most remarkable position, gathering around her all the mysteriousness that Franz Kafka was himself so apt at finding. A registered heroin addict for some thirty years, she died holding the battered syringe, she so enigmatically nick-named her "Bazooka". A woman who by deed poll changed her name, adopting the name of a character in one of her earliest books[13]. This woman with "machines in the head", that wake her every morning beginning their incipient grinding cacophony; "The cogs are moving, the engines are slowly gathering momentum, a low humming noise is perceptible even now. How will I recognise every sound, every tremor to the laborious start... intolerable and inescapable at the same time, like sickness inside the blood... The wheels revolve faster, the pistons slide smoothly in their cylinders, the noise of machinery fills the whole world."[14] A woman who writes of leopards that come and sit down beside her, of flowers and of childhoods. But Anna is not in need of a cure, anything but! Her quick compulsive shifts from realm to realm, her hasty impulsions, the machinic urgencies, these may burn up at times, but at other times they uncoil and intersect with the most diverse distances, detaching strange becomings, triggering the opening of the co-existent universes that surround us.

Women too know how to liberate the schizophrenic flows, the libidinal intensities and the multiplicities of desire. A desire that is both convulsive and anti-aesthetic, subverting and empowering. The poet and musician, Patti Smith prefigured riot gurrl near ten years before any such notion existed. A woman who erupted and blasted on stage, a feverish and intense woman, arms flaying, the first woman to truly play with her amplifier up too loud, lying on her back with the guitar butt between her legs. She is intensity, she overflows with an incredible mixture of rigidness and suppleness. Her lines of flight emerge amongst her distinctive characteristics; dark glasses, scruffy slipshod blackhair, a white face with giant's eyes, wide lips, shabby black coat and tight jeans. These are the eccentric traits that Robert Mapplethorpe must have been instantly attracted to, and which eventuated in several photo sessions. Her skinny, limp corporeality, comprising textures simultaneously hard and soft are what make her unavoidably illfitting, from which emanates all of her overflowing awkwardness - not forgetting that fully exposed hairy armpit on the front cover of the *Easter* album. In her own words, "These ravings, observations, etc. come from one who, beyond vows, is without mother, gender, or country." It is assured that Patti never wanted to be at the centre, she always wanted to be peripheral, to remain on the verge. "I am a night rope walker."[15] She abandons to walk along the connecting rope that spans between the two dipoles (masculine and feminine, resembling the two ends of the tight rope between which she walks), and knows that the next step is to fly. She is a Body without Organs, becoming nigger, becoming sexual nomad.

These intensities are equally found in the sexual scatologies of Kathy Acker. In Kathy Acker's, *In Memoriam to Identity*, Rimbaud excitingly declares, "Language is alive in the land of childhood. Since language and the flesh are not separate here,... This society hates and locks up its madness because they hate and lock up themselves. I know the system of schizophrenia."[16] The language of childhood is so alive, a language that embraces Artaud, it is a language that is non-inscriptive, it is of the body, emanating from the body and exciting the body. The language of childhood escapes the tyranny of the signifier, it doesn't form signifying identities upon the body's corporeal surface. The language is instead erratic, non-narrative, automatistic, variable, grammatically incorrect and freed from the restraints of paranoiac despotism.

Elizabeth Grosz in her text *Volatile Bodies, Towards a Corporeal Feminism,* initiates many theoretical investigations which provide and propose questions well worth pursuing and interrogating through to their ends, mostly in the framework of probings and suggestive rethinkings. On sexual difference she asks, "Is it that there is a sexual continuum - a (quasi-biological or even natural) continuum of sexual differences between bodies, which power divides and organises in historically and culturally variable forms?"[17] While it is certain that sexuality is something produced and created, and not something that "is" as an underlying "truth" in each individual, the extent that it is produced and created is somewhat frustratingly fettered, not only by the effects of capitalist subjectification but also by the conditioning effects of the organism. A thousand tiny sexes seeks to elude the territorialisations that act against it, it seeks to encounter an ontological vastness, a rhizome of sexuality, that does not adhere to, nor privilege any so-called "true" sexuality, but instead only encourages and opens out its unending potential for mutation and deterritorialization. What happens when we go so far as to encounter the complete abandonment of human sexuality? What do we find? But overall, this quasi biological continuum is not a fallacy, but the real emphasis is to understand that such a quasi biological continuum only constitutes an ontological strata that is one *tiny* facet or component of the complete or full scale of possibilities of ontology. For it must be clearly stressed that ontology also includes the possibility of destratified fragments, that enable movements and lines of flight that eject themselves outside such a tiny continuum. There is simply no singular ontology, it is always multi-ontology. There can never be an ontology of fixed essence, only ontologies of sense.

Ongoing scientific research is presently finding bio-psychological and essential differences both between men and women, and between homosexuals and heterosexuals. These findings purport aspects such as homosexuality and sex inbetweenness (individuals who may be described as either butch or effeminate), as biologically formed and part of a natural biological diversity, rather than the result of complex social influences, often attributed to poor parenting, teenage rejection, sexual confusion and so forth. Does the homosexual choose his or her subjectivity out of rebellion against sexual norms? Or was it there from the start? In practice these findings, in the correct context can be potentially beneficial, since the claims attest that, even biologically, there is substantial crossing over, overlapping and blurring of sexual difference, rather than the existence of disparate and distinct categories, others will however emphasise the potential negativity, since it (supposedly) implies limitations on the potential for political change. But otherwise, it consequently comes as little surprise that sections of gay and transgender political discourse are already making ample shouts of "I was born gay/transgendered". But still the context and positions relating to feminists are still different, and dissimilar. While tentatively tracing this line of thought, we see that, disciplinary power divides, tortures and mangles this quasi-biological continuum, scarifying and punishing those individuals who violate the binarized and value centred dipoles that are established by the socius and inflicted on the subject. Mechanisms of social repression are then effecting a corruption and subordination of the quasi-biological sexuality, accompanied with the development of a "produced sexuality", as a new strata, which establishes segregations and inequalities between the sexes as secondary.

But even while such a quasi-biological continuum seems more deterritorialized, and therefore more favourable, than the hugely disparate and binarized poles that the socius continually segregates and confines us to, ultimately this is not what Deleuze and Guattari have in mind, for it is still far too constrained, since our unloosening from cultural determinisms has only been subsequently regrounded in the biological. Any so called quasi-biological continuum falls way short of producing the thousand tiny sexes of a non-human sex. The biological stratas, the centres of organisation and the points of subjectification (advertising, nightclub, magazine) are what bind and fixate sexual subjectivity - but ontology also includes the spaces inbetween and outside these points, that are lines of flight, movements of destratification, rhizome spaces, positions which are denaturalised. We will not restrict ourselves to the sexualities consisting in the organism - we will go still further and beyond these territorialized and stratified forms. We will not only drift in the space between the dipoles (masculine/feminine, and for that matter heterosexual/homosexual as well), gliding and shifting about on the connecting cable that stretches from one end to the other, but we will also slip off, leaping off on a line of flight perpendicular to this cable, departing entirely from this line, into rhizomatic becomings, moving beyond and outside these categorisations and fixed subjectivities.

I must stress that it is a mistake to reduce ontology down to mere biology, and make crude statements like man=hunter, woman=nurturer. The body cannot be entirely reduced to biological determinisms, and nor can it be reduced entirely to social conditionings. The body must be understood as a complex intermeshing engendered by multiple forces. We will always make a blunder when we reduce all the points of influence to a single code. Masculinity and femininity are socially conditioned, in the sense that the entire ontological field of *n* sexes is reduced and astringed to just these two possible locations. Masculinity and femininity are therefore not a social construct, they existed long before any socius of authority and regulation, but they are the only accepted realms for the deployment of sexuality. Biology is certainly a constituent of ontology, but that it is the only constituent is entirely a lie, there is simply much more. It is only one *tiny* facet amidst many others. Ontology will be reconfigured, collecting up planes, flows and rhizomes, and not just stratas, objects and materialities. A rhizomatic ontology is not something fixative and immutable, it an ontology that is an agency of multiplicity. A rhizomatic ontology will always remain in antithesis to what is called biological determinism. Biological determinism represents; (1) singular subjectivity, either you are man, or you are woman, (2) exclusivity, masculinity can only be in the male, and femininity can only be in the female, (3) immobility, what is initially biologically determined is indispensable and unable to be altered or mobilised, (4) universalist conceptions that delineate what is male and what is female, and (5) value determinism, male is superior to female, thus establishing a primacy of inequality and binarised difference. A rhizomatic ontology is by contrast, representational of multiple subjectivities, non-exclusivity, mutation and becoming, deconstruction of universal valorizations and the primacy of multiplicities of difference.

It is not that we are all "born" butch/effeminate or bi-sexual, the body is initiated alongside and adjacent the plane of consistency, at a zero level of connectivity. Sexual orientation is produced, within the first year the body becomes defragmented and connected to the biological continuum, to the parental milieu and so forth. The bodies implantation in the biological stratum establishes a sexual positioning, but other stratums, the capitalist stratum, the religious and the technological stratum for instance will also coextensively influence this positioning. But still, we must recall that there is always the other side, where the body eludes the totalisations of the stratas, and makes the transversal connections that form a free Body without Organs.

Conceptions which speak of a single-inbetween sexual subjectivity common for both men and women, which becomes divided and bifurcated by capitalist mechanisms of conditioning and internalization is still asserting an essentialism, even if it be unlike the essentialism they quite correctly disapprove of. But this single-inbetween subjectivity still constrains the possibilities of being and subjectivity that women might wish to effect, trammelling women's selfhood in whole new ways. It condemns masculinity and femininity, as socially constructed, and valorises that inbetween them. We will achieve nothing until we go beyond good and evil. Multiplicity achieves just that, it is an unvalorized position, accepting and encouraging of all positions as equal. But yet, certain theorists will still go on enforcing the imperative of obliterating the two ends of the dipole (masculine/feminine) to collapse and astringe everything in a homogeneous centralised core.

Becoming-woman does not disavowal and condemn masculinity, multiplicity will always mean that shards of masculinity will get swept up, and put into operation. The point is that it will at some point, always be put down again to try a new direction, be remixed and exchanged for another desiring function. Kathy Acker's desiring production incorporates and integrates masculinity, her affinities for body building, motorbikes and tattooing, are not incompatible to a Deleuzian/Guattarian becoming-woman. For Patti Smith, her becoming woman is uniquely ajoined to the becomings of homosexual men. I am referring here to her fondness for homosexual men, eg Mapplethorpe, Burroughs and Rimbaud. It is always a question of the degree of deterritorialization, and the degree that it facilitates multiplicities. Becoming woman then does not impede feminist type appropriations of the masculine. Our becoming-woman will even fail if all we do is respond passively, behave ladylike, unassertively and politely. Becomings always fail when they form rigidities and orthodoxies that constrain and disallow the flows.

***Torrential Desire.***

In the prevailing circumstances the need is for continual revolution, entailing the unending extension of the peripheral and what is excluded. The way forward demands revolutionary actions eliciting the detachment of anti-oedipal flows, actions disconnecting, de-aestheticizing, decoding and deterritorializing - with wounded flesh, schizophrenic flesh, dissimilar flesh, machinic erogenous flesh. For these are the types of flesh inherently obscene to the socius. "The only possible attack on this totality is the exhibition of intolerable bodies"[18] - saturate with burnt flesh, menstrual blood and faeces - overflow the system. "A flow moves, irresistibly; sperm, river, drainage, inflamed genital mucus, or a stream of words that do not let themselves be coded, a libido that is too fluid, too viscous: a violence against syntax, a concerted destruction of the signifier"[19]. For the signifier was always dead flesh, a mannequin, a body hanging from the gallows. The only escape, the true emancipation from primal and despotic consciousness is to the body of the hermaphroditic schizophrenic, the gegensex (othersex)[20], the Deleuzian/Guattarian non-human sex. It is our duty to extricate the unconscious and release all forms of untrammelled desire.

---

Notes

1. The term originates in Gilles Deleuze and Felix Guattari's *Anti-Oedipus Capitalism and Schizophrenia* Minneapolis, University of Minnesota Press, 1983, p. 295
2. Luce Irigaray *Je, Tu, Nous, Towards a Culture of Difference,* London, Routledge, 1993, p. 12
3. Felix Guattari, *Molecular Revolution, Psychiatry and Politics,* New York, Penguin, 1984, p. 63
4. In Jello Biafra's characteristic manner, he speaks mockingly against punk fundamentalism, "If you're not vegetarian then you're EVIL! If you're not homosexual then you'r homophobic!"

5. Gilles Deleuze and Felix Guattari, *Anti-Oedipus Capitalism and Schizophrenia,* p. 323
6. Gilles Deleuze and Felix Guattari, *A Thousand Plateaus Capitalism and Schizophrenia,* Minneapolis, University of Minnesota Press, 1987, p. 275
7. ibid p. 305
8. ibid p. 292
9. ibid p. 293
10. ibid p. 292
11. Gilles Deleuze and Felix Guattari, "Balance Sheet-Program for Desiring-Machines", *Chaosophy,* New York, Semiotext(e), 1995 p. 130 and Semiotext(e), *Anti-Oedipus,* Vol 2, No 3, 1977, p. 123.
12. I must stress that feminism is of course an encouraging and indispensable component in fighting patriarchal fascisms. But feminism is no less susceptible, progressive movements of all types, can quickly plummet into cancerous and despotic regressions. This is why the task constantly facing feminism is one of extricating itself from the orthodoxies and (so called) radical feminisms of the Andrea Dworkin and Catherine MacKinnon type. For feminism to wrest itself from the stratifications that immure its intense line of flight, and elicit its Body without Organs.
13. Anna Kavan is a character in *Let Me Alone* (1930), which was published under her then name, Helen Ferguson.
14. Anna Kavan "Machines in the Head" from *Asylum Piece and other stories,* London, Peter Owen Ltd, 1972, pp. 116 and 118. This work was originally published in 1940, reflecting her duration spent in a mental hospital.
15. Patti Smith, *Early Work 1970-1979,* New York/London, Norton, 1994, pp. 35 and 14.
16. Kathy Acker *in memoriam to identity,* Hammersmith London Flamingo, 1990, pp. 89 and 92.
17. Elizabeth Grosz, *Volatile Bodies, Towards a Corporeal Feminism,* St Leonards, Allen and Unwin, 1994, p. 156. This book provides an excellent analysis of the works of Nietzsche, Foucault and Deleuze/Guattari as a framework for developing contributions to feminist discourse.
18. SPK "The Post Industrial Strategy", Re/Search *Industrial Culture Handbook,* issue #6/7, San Francisco, 1983, p. 104

19. Gilles Deleuze and Felix Guattari, *Anti-Oedipus Capitalism and Schizophrenia,* p. 133
20. "Ich bin die umstrzlerische Liebe / Der gegensex" (I am the subversive love / the othersex), the opening lines to *Seele Brennt* (Soul Burns) by Blixa Bargeld, *Stimme fribt Feuer,* Berlin, Merve Verlag, 1988, p. 126. Seele Brennt appears on Einstürzende Neubauten's CD *Halber Mensch* (Half Man).

# From Cut-Up to Cut and Paste, Plagiarism and Adaptation: Kathy Acker's Evolution of The Cut-Up Technique of William Burroughs and Brion Gysin

by Edward S. Robinson

Although many writers have cited celebrated Beat Generation author William S. Burroughs as an influence, few have followed his lead to the extent that Kathy Acker has. Fewer still have been so open about the degree to which they have drawn upon his ideas. During her career, she frequently acknowledged her indebtedness, citing him as her central influence.[1] Acker often wrote using methods derived from Burroughs, taking *The Third Mind* (1978) as her inspiration.[2] This is noted by Peter Wollen, who observes, 'it was not one of the master's more straightforwardly literary works – *The Naked Lunch*, for example – which intrigued her the most, but a much more formally extreme and experimental text.'[3] Acker herself described how she 'used *The Third Mind* as experiments to teach myself how to write.'[4]

Born in 1948, Acker grew up in New York City.[5] According to Calcutt and Shepherd, the uncertainty regarding her age is 'indicative of a contrary writer committed to both the destruction and creation of identity,' a suggestion which is relatively accurate in describing at least one of Acker's primary preoccupations.[6] Although she would later return to an academic environment in a teaching capacity, while initially at college she studied a number of writing courses – all of which she 'hated:'[7]

> I took a lot of writing courses when I was in college… They were just torture… I reacted in this kind of this radical anti-authority stance,

> anti-right rules of writing. I started off by saying 'no' to everything. My whole identity as a writer was in saying 'no,' in reacting. So in my first books I refused to rewrite. I wrote as fast as possible. I refused to have any consideration for proper grammar or proper syntax. In a way, [those books] were very easy and what they were was experiments.[8]

That Acker should describe those early works as experiments is noteworthy, as much of the experimentalism was based on the practices detailed in *The Third Mind,* breaking down the flow of narrative to create a discontinuous, cut-up style of prose. Having studied classical literature as an undergraduate as Brandeis University, Acker possessed a knowledge of canonical literary texts, and was therefore 'qualified' in academic terms to rebel and experiment.[9] Moreover, her formal education left her disaffected: Avital Ronell suggests that 'as far as Acker was concerned... universities have peculiar transmission problems: they transmit stupidity,' and this led her to write against all she had learned.[10] This involved relinquishing authorial control, 'a commitment to the avant-garde tradition' and the distribution of her writing in serial form as part of a Mail Art network[11]

Leaving home at 18, she worked in a sex show and became involved in the New York art scene, and in time began writing. Her involvement with the art scene was primarily of a poetical persuasion, particularly the Black Mountain poets, and this too proved to be a great influence on her early writing, as she told Karl Schmieder: 'The first book – it wasn't a novel – was called *Politics*. That was a bunch of prose pieces with poetry surrounding the prose pieces. It was very much a Burroughs-like diary. Kind of *Interzoney*.'[12] This text effectively set the blueprint for the first stage of her career, which can be roughly divided into three. The first runs from the late 1960s to the mid 1970s, and is defined by the incorporation of passages created using the cut-up method as detailed by Burroughs and Gysin in *The Third Mind*. The texts of this period include *Politics* (written circa 1968, privately published 1972, and not republished until 1991); *The Burning Bombing of America: The Destruction of the U.S.* (1972) and *Rip-Off Red, Girl Detective* (1973), which she describes as 'a pornographic mystery story.'[13] The second phase of her career is one of transition, and is marked by a shift from syntactic cut-ups toward outright plagiarism and a method that could be more accurately described as cut and paste than cut-up. In the texts of this period, as exemplified by *The Childlike Life of the Black Tarantula by The Black Tarantula* (1973) and *The Adult Life of Toulouse Lautrec by Henri Toulouse Lautrec* (1975), Acker intercut larger sections of narrative from different sources. Where she overtly plagiarised from her source texts, by simply copying sections of them out, she sought to 'represent' the texts, and address the question, 'if I repeated the same text, would it be the same text?'[14] In this way, she addresses the issues of ownership and authorship. Significantly, she can also be seen to be using a method based on 'cutting up' existing texts to apply the type of 'appropriation [that] has been some sort of postmodernist technique in the arts for a number of years' to writing, thus returning to the point which inspired the cut-up method, namely to apply 'the montage technique to words on a page.'[15]

The later works of this phase saw the introduction of illustrations and diagrams to create multimedia texts with a collage-like feel, as represented by *Blood and Guts in High School* (1978). Here, as Wollen observes, she incorporates 'calligraphy, self-drawn dream maps and Persian and Arabic script... she simply added these new techniques to her ongoing concern with experimental writing.'[16]

The texts of her third and final phase continue to reflect this concern with experimental writing, and incorporate elements of the preceding periods. These later texts are, however, distinguished by a more prominent focus on narrative. The works of this period, which include *Empire of the Senseless* (1988); *In Memoriam to Identity* (1990) and *Pussy, King of the Pirates* (1996), use longer sections of interweaving narrative to reflect switches between speaker, time and location.

Her first 'novel,' *The Childlike Life of Black Tarantula by the Black Tarantula* was published in 1973.[17] Her breakthrough to public prominence came with *Blood and Guts in High School.* Between then and her death from breast cancer in 1997, she published a considerable volume of novels, collections of essays and a number of short stories which appeared in various anthologies and small-press magazines.

In this essay, I shall devote a section to each phase of her career. Because of the volume of work Acker produced, and also because of the nature of her works, which is intended to confuse and to raise more questions than answers, I will be focusing on specific texts which best exemplify the ways in which the cut-up approach has been manifested within her output. To this end, I will first discuss *The Bombing Burning of America,* with a view to establishing the origins of Acker's interest in cut-up modes of narrative. I will then move on to examine her transition from cut-up to more elaborate variations on the technique, with particular attention to her mixed-media works, as represented by *Blood and Guts in High School,* and explore the ways in which these experimental collage texts draw from Burroughs' experimental works of the 1960s and 1970s, in particular *The Third Mind* and *The Book of Breeething* (1975, republished 1979 as part of *Ah Pook is Here and Other Texts*). In the third section of the essay, I will consider Acker's later work in the form of her final novel, *Pussy, King of the Pirates.*[18] In this section I will examine her writing's continued evolution, and consider the significance of pirates and piracy, and the question of 'myth.' I will also be addressing the way in which the developments in Acker's later works reflect the ways in which she adapted and evolved her own modes of cutting up narrative.

### *Early Cut-Ups: Acker and the Third Mind*

*Politics* represents Acker's first attempt at writing, and was only commercially published posthumously.[19] The scenes and locations shift without clear distinction, and the narrative is unconventional and non-literary, with her disregard for 'proper grammar or proper syntax' clearly evident. The punctuation is minimal, creating a rapid, almost jumbled stream rather than a smooth flow in sequential or syntactic terms, and reflects her interest in 'doing everything I wasn't supposed to do. And writing badly.'[20] The following passage is exemplary:

> after we had dinner at this god awful chinese restaurant fake chinese gardens the waiter shit wouldn't give another bowl to us for the winter melon soup for two on the menu Mickey was barely able to kiss Mark goodbye we went to Mark's house 13th and A stories about how If

> you venture out there after dark one block or more you automatically get raped mugged castrated we smoked went into the bedroom to see the new waterbed[21]

The events depicted are in themselves unremarkable, and with only minimal detail. Where detail is provided, it serves to accentuate the negative: 'fake chinese;' 'the waiter shit.' Moreover, the *fake* chinese hints at the artifice Acker would focus on in her later works as she strove to construct and destroy – often within the same text – distinctions between reality and fiction. The lack of punctuation and regular capitalisation produces a jumbled, disorientating narrative, in which is unclear at which point the reader is to 'break' or breathe – an effect also common to cut-up texts. This was clearly Acker's intention, as she recalls writing *Politics* by 'cutting in tapes, cutting out tapes, using a lot of dream material, using other people's dreams, doing a lot of Burroughs experiments.'[22] The Burroughs-style experiments may not be overtly apparent, but this passage clearly shows a mode of writing that attempts to break down the conventions of grammar and punctuation. Such disregard for these conventions represents a challenge to accepted notions of literary writing, and in this way *Politics* was emblematic of Acker's desire to attack not only 'the establishment,' but also the control mechanisms embedded within the established protocols of language. She further explained the reasoning behind her early writing style as follows: 'I came out of a poetry world... But I didn't want to write poetry. I wanted to write prose and there weren't many prose writers around who were using the ways of working of poets I was influenced by.'[23] Of the prose writers she did feel an affinity with, she cited Burroughs as her 'first major influence,' stating, 'I love to read Kerouac, but Burroughs is the more intellectual. He was considering how language is used and abused within a political context. That's what interested me...'[24] *The Burning Bombing of America* clearly illustrates this, developing from the stream of conscious narrative of *Politics* to a clear adoption of the cut-up method.

> all plants and animals burst into flames/light through the hole   the circle of waters   we walk to the New City at night   flamethrowers colour

> bombs   cats fly through your hair   governing
> men   the Tao Te Ching   like governing horses
> we are ready   the images are ready   we are
> ready to move at the first sight of morning[25]

This passage is typical of *The Burning Bombing of America* as a whole, combining fragments that appear to be drawn from news items, poems and a miscellany of other sources at random. The recurrent juxtaposition of objects – plants, animals, flamethrowers – with synonyms for explosions and fire provides a thematic unity and creates an apocalyptic scene that suggests what the destruction of America might be like. The reference to images can be seen to allude to the text's own construction as a sequence of images, and this clearly illustrates how closely Acker followed Burroughs' lead, not only in terms of applying the cut-up method, but in the selection of some of her source materials. Both the content and rhythm of *The Burning Bombing of America* is extremely close to Burroughs' cut-up works, and also to those of Weissner and Pélieu that most rigidly follow the directions in *The Third Mind*. Indeed, some sections bear a remarkable similarity to Burroughs' Nova trilogy, suggesting the possibility that Burroughs' texts, along with other Beat writings, may have provided source material.

> 1920   Free all prisoners   leave people's minds
> alone   only our personal life exists   fish leap
> through our hair   our limbs tangle we mutilate
> each other   take guns slash off our heads   long
> orange machetes [...] not now known   I lonely
> praise   Gertrude Stein   Walt Whitman   Allen
> Ginsberg   the women of you   American
> apocalypse   visions   who fly to the raging
> beams   moon   revolution every 1/3 second
> faster than any dynamite thought [26]

The way in which the fragmentation of phrases reveals new phrases and new images shows a concerted attempt to test the replicability of Burroughs and Gysin's initial experiments. Phrases like 'fish leap through our hair' and 'long orange machetes' echo curious abstractions like those which fill the works of other writers who followed Burroughs' lead, the likes of Claude Pélieu in his cut-up novel *With Revolvers Aimed... Finger Bowls* (1967).[27] Such phrases link back to Gysin's suggestion that cutting up could produce 'abstract prose,' and also highlight the Surrealist lineage of the original cut-ups which appeared in *Minutes to Go* (1960). However, Acker's punctuation – or lack of – does mark a point of difference between her cut-ups and those of her precursors. Whereas Burroughs and those practitioners who immediately followed in the 1960s nearly all marked the intersections between the fragments of text with various typographical characters, including em dashes and ellipses, Acker simply uses additional spacing. This achieves an effect of reduced separation: the fragments run together more in the absence of concrete visual breaks, creating more of a continuous flow of 'narrative.' A focus on building narrative and on using different narrative voices would become a prominent feature of the next stage in her literary development.

### *Blood and Guts*: Cut and Paste

Although Acker referred to herself as a plagiarist, conceding that 'if I had to be totally honest I would say that what I'm doing is breach of copyright,' her writing does not comply with the strictest definition of plagiarism.[28] 'I change words,' she explains, and Wollen notes, 'it wasn't really plagiarism because she was quite open about what she did,' and she never attempted to pass the works of others off as her own.[29] 'I have been very clear that I use other people's material... I've always talked about it as a literary theory and as a literary method,' she says.[30] As she also wrote, 'I do not write out of nothing, or from nothing, for I must write with the help of other texts' (*Bodies of Work: Essays p.* 100). Here, she alludes to the complex relationship between creativity, influence, authorship and ownership. She contends that identity is 'questionable', and that ownership 'must be questioned' (*Bodies of Work: Essays p.* 100-101). As Robert Lort writes: 'Kathy Acker's pseudo-plagiarism is a method she uses in which she appropriates texts from different sources and proceeds to then deconstruct them by playing with them, modifying them, layering, rearranging, rewriting and fragmenting the original texts.'[31] This 'pseudo-plagiarism' is sometimes apparent from the titles of her works alone: *Great Expectations; Don Quixote: Which Was a Dream;* and *Hannibal Lecter, My Father* provide just three examples of titles drawn from precursive texts, and illustrate just one way in which she 'undermined the staple myths of originality, of literary ownership and reliable reference.'[32] *Great Expectations* was written by 'cutting it up, not even rewriting, just taking it and putting it together again, like playing with building blocks.'[33] Such an approach shows the common ground shared with Burroughs and Gysin, and practically demonstrates the way a writer does 'choose, edit and rearrange words at his disposal' and manipulate words as an artist would paint.[34] This method of appropriation succeeded her initial cut-up approach, and represents the beginning of the second stage of her career. More than this, it represents her first move away from simply using Burroughs' methods for her own ends, and her first contribution to the evolution of the cut-up technique.

Much of Acker's 'plagiarism' served as a means of exploring the relationship of her own writing with canonical texts, and as a way of discovering her own identity. As she explained in *Bodies of Work* (1997), 'in my confusion, I look to older writing, as I have often done when I am confused. I look to find a clue about my writing' (Bodies of Work: Essays p. 98). This 'older writing' ranged from Faulkner, Artaud and Cervantes, to Genet and Dickens. Burroughs, however, proved a constant source of reference: 'I keep returning to American literature [and] to the books of William Burroughs', she said (*Bodies of Work: Essays* p. 6). To this end, *The Childlike Life of The Black Tarantula* sees Acker apply a cut-up approach to sections of narrative, splicing and interweaving 'very direct autobiographical, just diary material, right next to fake diary material. I tried to figure out who I was and who I wasn't and went to texts of murderesses. I just changed them into the first person... and put the fake first person next to the true first person.'[35] This practice of directly copying and making minor alterations to existing texts represents the application of a lesson she learned from one of her early mentors, poet David Antin, who, aware of his students' lack of life experience, would tell them, "don't be afraid to *copy it out*... Kathy really took that ball and ran with it."[36]

*Black Tarantula* opens with a diary entry dated June 1973, which begins, 'I become a murderess. I'm born in the autumn or winter of 1827. Troy, New York... My name is Charlotte Wood.'[37] The chapter continues with Wood's brief biography, interspersed with fragments that stand at odds with the tone and structure of the linear chronological narrative: 'Do you want me to call you yes. I call Friday call Saturday Sunday this is Kathy O uh do you want to spend a night with me again are you too busy I'm too busy uh goodbye.' These fragments, with their unpunctuated anti-literary style distinguish the sections of diary material from the 'copied' sections. Wood's biography is followed by a series of brief biographies of other women. These biographies appear as straightforward narratives, detailing family life, encounters and relationships. However, intercut paragraphs appear incongruous to the overall flow of the narrative:

> when I sit on my waterbed where I write the material of the crotch of the pants presses against my cunt lips I'm always slightly hot I masturbate often when I write I write a section 15 minutes to an hour...'[38]

Such inclusions break the continuity of the narrative, and one is frequently compelled to question precisely who is speaking, and to consider whether or not the scene is factual or fictional. At the end of each chapter, Acker places an endnote listing the sources appropriated in the construction of the text. The endnote to chapter one states that 'events are taken from myself, *Enter Murderers!* By E.H. Bierstadt, *Murder for Profit* by W. Boltholio, *Blood in the Parlour* by D. Dunbar, *Rogues and Adventuresses* by C. Kingston,' disclosing her method.[39] Elsewhere, Sade's *Justine*, Alexander Trocchi's *Helen and Desire* and *Thérèse and Isabelle* by V. Leduc are listed as sources alongside 'my past, and my fantasies.'[40] Through the application of this technique, Acker exposes the way in which identity is not fixed, as the 'narrator' is revealed to be a shifting succession of narrators spliced to create a single, but not necessarily unified 'whole.' The end result is a cut-up composite character, or, perhaps more accurately, a composite narrator formed with facets if numerous characters. Acker thus presents a composite personality, rather than a composite 'being' to speak of. Acker's 'split' composite narrator, upon whom facets of murderesses are amalgamated within and superimposed upon the single speaker, explores her interest in 'the model of schizophrenia.'[41] She explained her interest in identity arguing that 'it's a thing that's made. You create identity, you're not given identity per se... texts create identity.'[42] Acker's composite narrator shares common ground with the film Burroughs made with Tony Balch entitled *Bill and Tony*, in which the speaking heads of Burroughs and Balch swap names and voices, creating a third mind / body of sorts. Yet in other ways, the composition of *Black Tarantula* represents a completely new development within the evolution of the cut-ups, not least of all in the way that the appropriated texts are purposefully altered.

*Blood and Guts in High School* continued to develop the incorporation of diary material alongside pieces of texts appropriated from other sources by introducing graphic and visual elements, and became Acker's first book to be published in Britain, appearing in a single volume alongside *Great Expectations* (first published 1982) and *My Death, My Life* (1983) in *Blood and Guts in High School Plus Two* (1984).[43] This publication garnered considerable attention and brought her fame and notoriety in almost equal measure. Such polarized critical reception of her work persisted throughout her life, and even beyond. 'In the canon of cult fiction, there are few writers who have proved so controversial that their death has prompted a sheaf of for and against letters in a national newspaper, as occurred in the *Guardian* after Acker's untimely demise,' note Calcutt and Shepherd.[44]

As much a loosely-ordered sequence of scenes, dreamscapes and psychodramas as a novel in the conventional sense, *Blood and Guts* invites comparison to both *Naked Lunch* and the works that followed the *Nova* trilogy for its experimental formulation and modes of presentation. The book follows the central character, Janey, from her home with her father to Tangier in the company of Jean Genet and beyond. Initially the most striking feature of the book is the presentation. The text is interspersed with sketches and illustrations, maps and diagrams, and uses a broad range of different typefaces. Many of the sketches, which predominantly feature in the book's first section 'Inside High School,' take the form of crude line drawings depicting erect penises and open vaginas. These are intended to be shocking and serve to set Acker's anti-literary, 'radical anti-authority stance, anti-right rules' agenda from the outset.[45] In addressing the non-conformist stance presented within the book's formulation,

Niall Lucy encapsulates the way in which Acker's work divided the critics more generally:

> To say... that *Blood and Guts in High School* shouldn't be undervalued for not meeting a standards of literature defined by novels like *Jane Eyre* would not be to say that, simply because of its nonconformity, therefore it represents a radical challenge to that standard or exposes the oppressive illusion that literature could ever be understood in terms of standards. (Sometimes a cigar is just a cigar, and the nonconformity of Acker's novel could just be the consequence of bad writing rather than transgressive writing.[46]

Such criticisms overlook Acker's extensive knowledge of classical, canonical and avant-garde literature, and in this context it is less problematic to accept *Blood and Guts* as simply transgressive. The book is essentially a collage, incorporating calligraphy, sketches and broken *mise en page*. The sections 'The Persian Poems' and 'The World,' the latter of which consists purely of annotated diagrams and illustrations, exist almost wholly separately from the main narrative and apart from the loosely-structured, fragmented 'plot.' In this way, Acker's indebtedness to cut-up and multimedia texts like *The Third Mind*, *White Subway* (1965) and *The Book of Breeething*, is immediately apparent.[47] That *Blood and Guts* is constructed from a series of discontinuous short passages is significant also, bearing structural similarities to *Naked Lunch.* Burroughs famously remarked that 'you can cut into *The Naked Lunch* at any intersection point,' and Acker believed the same to be true of *Blood and Guts*, responding to Lotringer's suggestion that 'I don't think you would expect your readers to read your novels from beginning to end' by commenting 'no, on the whole they can read wherever they want... you could read pretty much anywhere.'[48]

To consider *Blood and Guts* in a loosely chronological order remains the most logical approach here, however. The book opens with a brief introduction of the central character, Janey Smith. We are informed that she is ten years old, and that her mother died when she was a year old. As a result, she 'depended on her father for everything, and regarded her father as boyfriend, brother, sister, money, amusement, father' (*Blood & Guts p.* 7). Immediately we learn that 'Janey and Mr Smith had been planning a big vacation for Janey in New York City in North America. Actually Mr Smith was trying to get rid of Janey so he could spend all his time with Sally, a twenty-one-year-old starlet who was still refusing to fuck him' (*Blood & Guts p.* 7). The prose style is simple, the declarative sentences basic, paratactic in formation. The phraseology and limited use of punctuation renders the style simplistic to the point of appearing naive: the prose possesses an unedited roughness, even an almost child-like quality.

Less simple is the relationship between Janey and her father. Within the first three paragraphs, it is apparent that their relationship is not 'normal.' That Janey should bestow upon her father so many roles is indicative of a twisted psychology, while her father's plan to 'get rid of Janey' suggests he is at best a poor parent. That Janey calls him 'Johnny,' and 'fucks him even though it hurts like hell 'cause of her Pelvic Inflammatory Disease' (*Blood & Guts p.* 10) further illustrates the unusual and deeply disturbing nature of their relationship. The similarity of the two characters' names is of interest, suggesting something of an interchangeability between the two, a cut-up composite character of sorts. Janey's direct descendance from Johnny is highlighted by this association, their genetic connection accentuated by the similarity of their names, while at the same time the subtle difference between their names serves to also illustrate the variations in their genetic makeup. The connotation of the 'father figure' is also significant, as the traditional role of the father figure is one of authority. The relationship is emblematic of Acker's own difficult and complex relationship with authority, through which she consciously rebelled against authority in the form of her college tutors and her literary forbears.

It is evident that the relationship between Janey and her father involves mutual abuse and that the sexual aspect is far from loving: there is a distrust between the characters. That this 'family unit' exists, even within a fictional context, serves to challenge the idea of 'norms.' The relationship between Janey and her father questions the idea of social norms as exemplified by the traditional nuclear family. Perhaps what renders the depiction of their relationship most shocking is the matter-of-fact tone of the narrative.

Echoing the satirical passages of *Naked Lunch*, which saw Burroughs' text on trial for obscenity, Acker passes no authorial comment on the morality of the scenario, and she consequently found *Blood and Guts* the subject of legal scrutiny in Germany in 1986. The Federal Inspection Office for Publications Harmful to Minors commented in its report on the text, 'it is confusing in terms of sexual ethics.'[49] The report also records that 'the structure of the plot is in part quite difficult to understand. It is partially very hard or completely impossible for the reader to see whether we are dealing with the protagonist's imagination or real events.'[50] Herein lies a key issue of the text's structure: not only is the narrative broken syntactically by fragmentary sentences and ambiguous punctuation, but it is also constructed from larger fragments which disrupt any overarching narrative continuity. In this sense, Acker can be seen to be applying the principles of the cut-ups to blocks of text, on a narrative rather than textual level.

The relationship between Janey and Johnny also represents a feminized adaptation of the Oedipal myth. This represents a common theme in Acker's work, namely the practice of revising existing texts and stories, often by inverting and reversing gender roles, and demonstrates her knowledge of classical literature. The significance of Oedipal conflict and the connotations of this particular myth to Acker was considerable, on account of the great influence it has had over the psychoanalysis of male / female and familial relations from Freud to the present. The version of the family portrayed by Acker in Janey and Johnny a possible outcome of when Freud's 'tripartite formula – the Oedipal, neurotic one: daddy-mommy-me' is deviated from.[51] Also connected to the Oedipal mode of discourse is the idea of 'Anti-Oedipus,' put forth by Deleuze and Guattari, which proved to have a profound effect on Acker as Lort notes:

> Acker was very influenced by French intellectual thought, particularly feminist thought, and was on familiar terms with Bataille and de Sade (writers considered

> dubious by most other feminists). But… it wasn't until she had read *Anti-Oedipus, Capitalism and Schizophrenia* by the radical French philosopher Gilles Deleuze and his accomplice Felix Guattari and other works by Michel Foucault that she finally understood on a theoretical level what she had been doing intuitively. Only then did she finally have words to describe what she had been doing.[52]

Acker's work prior to her reading of *Anti-Oedipus* can be seen not simply as 'experimental,' but as the open workings of an author trying to understand herself, her ways of thinking and the context in which these exist. The narrative switches, interchangeable identities and confused roles are perfectly matched to the schizophrenic tendencies Deleuze and Guattari identify and both endemic within and symptomatic of modern consumerist society. Deleuze and Guattari observe how Freudian psychoanalysts have 'often tried to lead the schizophrenic down the road to ego formation, and normality [which] has often meant forcibly imposing the Oedipal cycle, which is supposedly characteristic of normal psychic development.'[53] In *Anti-Oedipus,* Deleuze and Guattari consider the connection between late capitalism and schizophrenia. As Jonah Peretti argues, the current consumerist climate not only accelerates the flow of capital, but also the rate at which subjects assume identities. To this end, the schizophrenic state is, if not an 'ideal' state, then one which is closely linked to postmodern society, in which advertisers or 'production machines' require the consumer to act as a 'desiring machine,' and to assume and dissolve identities at a pace in keeping with the rate that images and advertisements are bombarded at them. Acker describes reading *Anti-Oedipus* as a revelation, stating, 'when I read *Anti-Oedipus* and Foucault's work, suddenly I had this whole language at my disposal.'[54] It is apparent that, even prior to her reading of *Anti-Oedipus,* Acker was instinctively writing against the 'normative' Oedipal cycle, and also demonstrating a postmodern or schizophrenic approach to the formation of shifting identity, but her discovery of the text brought about a greater degree of self-awareness in her writing.

Through her portrayal of the Janey and Johnny, the use of language and the phraseology, the narrative is within itself representative of a challenging of (literary) norms and is demonstrative of the rebellion which lies at the heart of Acker's work. Acker's refusal to have 'any consideration for proper grammar or proper syntax' is evident.[55] One can almost sense her refusal 'to rewrite,' and that the writing was done 'as fast as possible,' supporting her claim that 'I write to get it out of me. I don't write to remember it.'[56]

In keeping with her determination to write against convention, *Blood and Guts* skips between narrative voices and modes of presentation frequently and in rapid succession. This shows a continuity within her work, as the splicing of different narratives in *Blood and Guts* represents a fairly straightforward development of the way different texts were intercut in *Black Tarantula* and *The Adult Life of Toulouse Lautrec*.[57] Her method of 'collaging' different narratives shows a clear lineage from the original cut-up method, as well as a distinct development in its application, the transition from cut-up to 'cut and paste.' After just half a page of narrative prose, there is a switch to an alternative method of presentation as she turns to dialogue presented in script form.

> **Janey**: You're going to leave me. (*She doesn't know why she's saying this.*)
> **Father:** (*dumbfounded, but not denying it*): Sally and I just slept together for the first time. How can I know anything?
> **Janey:** (*in amazement*) She didn't believe what she had been saying was true. It was only out of petulance: You ARE going to leave me. Oh no. That can't be.
> **Father:** (*also stunned*): I never thought I was going to leave you. I was just fucking.
> (*Blood & Guts p.* 7)

This exchange of dialogue further highlights the strangeness of the relationship between Janey and her father, and is indicative of the multiplicity of roles her father plays in Janey's life: he is, in effect, a cut-up composite of many characters within a single 'shell.' Through the scripted dialogue we see the mechanisms of the relationship between Janey and her father, and the way in which insecurity and confusion provide its basis. In this sequence, we see further evidence of the duality of Janey's relationship with Johnny as a dual metaphor for Acker's exploration of male / female relations as well as her own complex relationship with her literary forebears. As Acker noted, 'the canon' was created by male writers, and throughout her career she worked to establish, or, moreover, to understand her place as a woman writer. 'From the time of my high school days, I have known, in the way that one knows the streets of one's city and the laws of one's culture, the names of those in the pantheon of great... American writers. The big men. There weren't many, any, women,' she wrote (*Bodies of Work: Essays* p. 1). Like Burroughs before her, Acker believed that language equals power; therefore, that the canon is a male creation is a signifier of male dominance within culture and society.[58]

The use of the script format is most unusual within the context of a novel, and it is most likely that Acker adopted the style of presentation in light of Burroughs' use of script dialogue in *Naked Lunch, The Wild Boys,* the *Nova* trilogy and *The Last Words of Dutch Schultz*. Unlike Burroughs' scripts, there is little sense of the filmic in Acker's script. However, she had previously written performance pieces, including *The Birth of the Poet,* which includes lengthy sections of language exercises and translations in Arabic which are not readily performable.[59] Nevertheless, Acker's incorporation of script passages do serve the function rendering the editing of text analogous to that of film, and in this way continuing to pursue the objectives of the cut-ups of her literary precursors, namely to bring the act of reading closer to that of real life.

In terms of directions, Acker's 'script' contains no 'movement.' The characters make no gesticulations, and so appear static within their location. Because of this, the entrances and exits of characters from scenes are somewhat problematic. Janey is shown to speak 'as her father was leaving the house.' A page on, he speaks again, without seemingly re-entering. There is no mention of his return, and nor is there any mention of where he goes to when he leaves. In *Blood and Guts,* we do not always know precisely how the characters arrive at a given location. We do not see them leave scenes, and how they appear at the next scene, we know not. Such discontinuity presents little problem in the context of a cut-up narrative, the function of which is to dispense with the need to detail movement, and Burroughs contended that 'the reader can fill those gaps.'[60] Acker's contention, too, was that the transportation of the characters and such things didn't matter. Moreover, she was of the opinion that the very sequencing of events within a book could be more or less arbitrary. This would suggest that Burroughs' prediction that 'new techniques, such as cut-up, will involve much more the total capacity of the observer' (*The Third Mind* 6) had been fulfilled and that the cut-ups had finally resulted in the re-education of writers, if not readers. Perhaps for this reason, the narrative continuity, in terms of sequentiality and 'speaker' is questionable in *Blood and Guts*. For example, upon her father's leaving the house, Janey calls her father's best friend. Their conversation is continued within the same continuous sequence of dialogue, and so effectively merges two separate locations within a single setting, cutting through the artificial time / space sequencing commonly imposed upon events within conventional narrative, and which Burroughs strove to dispense with through the development of the cut-ups. Elsewhere, the events which serve to move the plot along (develop would be a rather inappropriate choice of word) are confined to the briefest of inclusions. 'Mr Smith puts Janey in school in New York City to make sure she doesn't return to Merida.'(*Blood & Guts p.* 31) 'She left high-school and lived in the East Village...' (*Blood & Guts p.* 44). Acker explained her approach to sequential narrative thus:

> I certainly don't believe linear time is adequate. So you don't need to structure a novel according to linear time or even according to memory, flashbacks plus linear time. I don't think that's the kind of world that I live in. So, if I'm going to do anything that has any relation to my own life, which it has to, I'm not going to write in terms of linear time.[61]

By taking this stance, Acker can be seen to be attempting to address the problem of conventional narrative that the cut-up technique was devised to address, namely that of creating a mode of narrative that brings writing closer to reality, echoing Burroughs' assertion that 'consciousness *is* a cut-up; life is a cut up.'[62]

The arbitrary approach to sequence within *Blood and Guts* is nowhere more strongly evidenced than in the 'letters' from Erica Jong to Janey that appear amidst the pages of Janey's diary in the section 'A journey to the end of the night' (*Blood & Guts p.* 125-6) – which also appeared as a separate volume, under the title *Hello, I'm Erica Jong* (1982). These letters both mimic and parody the author, combining 'factual' elements such as the title of the book that brought her to the public's attention with fictitious parody of her style.[63]

> HELLO I'M ERICA JONG. ALL OF YOU LIKED MY NOVEL *FEAR OF FLYING* BECAUSE IN IT YOU MET REAL PEOPLE. PEOPLE WHO LOVED AND SUFFERED AND LIVED. MY NOVEL CONTAINED REAL PEOPLE. THAT'S WHY YOU LIKED IT. MY NEW NOVEL *HOW TO DIE SUCCESSFULLY* CONTAINS THOSE SAME CHARACTERS. AND IT CONTAINS TWO NEW CHARACTERS. YOU AND ME. ALL OF US ARE REAL. GOODBYE. (*Blood & Guts p.* 125)

Passages such as this, in the form of 'fake' letters from a 'real' author, not only blur the boundaries of reality and fiction, but serve to expose the artifice of the format and linearity of 'the novel.' Ultimately, Acker raises more questions than answers, but succeeds in provoking thought concerning the point at which the author and reader engage, and the idea that the authorial voice is only as 'real' as the characters portrayed. Moreover, the inclusion of such elements add to the scrapbook effect, and illustrate just how the cut-up technique had been advanced to a new level of sophistication. If the early cut-ups were intended to expose the mechanisms of control and the ways in which language can be manipulated to create 'fiction' and 'history,' then Acker's methods of appropriation, alteration and collaging explore precisely how complex those mechanisms of manipulation really are.

In *Blood and Guts* the plot soon becomes buried amidst a lengthy sequence of sketches and maps, poems and language exercises in which the male world is attacked from various angles. The line-drawings of open vaginas and ejaculating penises at once celebrate female sexuality whilst also highlighting the 'phallic-oriented' nature of Western culture. These drawings, inserted at seemingly arbitrary points within the text, break the vague continuity of the narrative with quite incongruous-looking visual diversions. These images physically cut through and fragment the flow of the narrative. Placed in juxtaposition with the text, these images function quite differently from the seminal media-interrogating collage works of Marshall McLuhan, as they do not appear to reflect a concern with producing a new 'message' through the contrasting words and images in altered contexts. Instead, in conjunction with the notes which accompany the sketches (these include 'my cunt red ugh' and 'girls will do anything for love' beneath a pair of parted legs displaying an open vagina), the purpose of the sketches, apart from to shock and to attack the boundaries of literary acceptability, is to explore pictorial language, as Burroughs had in *The Book of Breeething*.

Acker's interest in the construct of language is nowhere more apparent than in the 'Persian Poems' section of *Blood and Guts.* Consisting of some twenty-three pages of 'hand-written' text, 'The Persian Poems' take the form of a series of exercises.

This passage shares common ground with Gysin's permutational poems which appeared in *Minutes to Go, Exterminator* (1960) and *The Third Mind,* taking the form of simple repetitions with the word order being altered, a word at a time, in each line. Although not running through every variation of a single phrase, Acker's 'poems' do demonstrate the way in which changing a single word within a phrase can substantially alter its meaning. Thus the language / vocabulary exercises explore the way in which word selection and ordering is integral to communication, and is a significant factor in the manipulation of language. These exercises also demonstrate a struggle of sorts, as Acker, through Janey, addresses the issues of the functions language, and of 'naming,' which Kristeva identifies as the beginning of all control and repression: 'Naming... and hence differentiating... amounts to introducing language, which, just as it distinguishes pleasure from pain as it does all oppositions, founds the separation inside/outside.'[64] The parallels between Kristeva's theory and Burroughs' ideas are drawn by Robin Lydenberg, and when placed in the context of comparative readings of Acker's common recourse to Burroughs' work, the continued trajectory of these theories embedded within literary practice is rendered clearly apparent.[65] The similarities between Acker's 'Persian Poems' and pages 113 and 114 of *Cities of the Red Night* are incontrovertible:

*Porque ne tiene* Because he doesn't have
*Porque la falta* Because he lacks
*Marijuana por fumar* Marijuana to smoke[66]

Janey's language exercises represent the learning of a new language and the relearning of linguistic formulation. The parallel between the character's attempts to relearn formulae for expression with the author's is obvious, given Acker's stated intention to 'create a new language' – 'trying to find a kind of language where I won't so easily be modulated by expectation… looking for what might be called a body language' – and to appropriate a means of expression which fulfilled her purposes as a female writer.[67] This purpose was, she believed, not so much to reclaim language from the male domain and 'feminise' it, but to degender language and literature, to remove the gender specificity inherent in writing and literature. 'Until I met Sylvère Lotringer, I didn't understand a lot of the reasons I wrote the way I did,' she told Andrea Juno. 'But I think the reason was probably my *hatred of gender*... a hatred of the expectation that I had to become my womb. My hatred of being defined by the fact I had a cunt.'[68] It is interesting, then, to note that Janey's exercises, while opening new doors in terms of scope for expression, show that all languages are built upon the same formulation, and have the same capacity to propagate the same power structures endemic in all societies. The language is formulated so as to create a hierarchy which creates social divisions, differentiating not only 'this' peasant from 'that' peasant, and a 'good' peasant from a 'bad' peasant, but also creating social divisions: 'peasant,' 'man,' 'woman.' These exercises serve to demonstrate the fundamental truth that language equals power, and in whatever language phrases are learned, those phrases still set the coordinates of power and perpetually reinforce social order – an order built on dominance and control over the collective individual.

The section entitled 'The World,' which appears almost as an appendix to *Blood and Guts*, located after the end of the narrative, is also concerned with the way in which language is used to order the world around us through the ascription of names to objects, etc., and combines pictorial and textual elements. Here, there is a definite narrative aspect to the alphabetical writing, but the illustrations could be taken independently to convey the story. The presentation of this section is indicative of Acker's far-ranging interest in language, language formation and language conditioning, as well as her taking not only the original cut-up, but also the variations and extensions of the technique as a starting point for her own exploration. The parallels with *The Book of Breeething* are clearly apparent, Acker herself acknowledged the fact that Burroughs' work in which he was 'dealing with how language and politics come together, the kind of language, what the image is' was an inspiration.[69] The cutting words and images together in 'The World' functions in the same way as *The Book of Breeething*, namely to extend writing beyond verbal or alphabetic methods of communication.

'The Persian Poems' and 'The Word' sections create a sense that the reader is not reading a novel, but flicking through someone's personal belongings, a collection of diaries and school exercise books. In this way the purpose of *Blood and Guts* as a collage, a large-scale cut-up or cut-and-paste, becomes apparent, again evidencing not only the continuities within Acker's work in its incorporation of 'real' diary material and 'fake' diary material, but also the progression of her narrative from her earliest cut-up experiments that so closely emulated the works of Burroughs and Gysin. It is interesting to note that 'The Persian Poems' was also published as a separate volume, retaining the title *The Persian Poems* (1980).[70] This edition takes the 'notebook' idea to its logical conclusion, appearing in an embossed stiff card cover, held together with staples rather than a more conventional perfect binding, and with the pages unnumbered. Like Burroughs' *White Subway, The Persian Poems* is presented as a series of experiments and exercises, a scrap-book or exercise book of sorts, showing the mechanisms and the workings of the author – although in *The Persian Poems*, there remains a greater degree of artifice in that the author is not Acker, but Acker writing as Janey.

Elsewhere in *Blood and Guts* we find dialogue which makes explicit Acker's view of the function of language and the way in which the control of language represents the ultimate power:

> **Mr Fuckface:** You see, we own the language.
> Language must be used clearly and concisely
> to reveal our universe.
> **Mr Blowjob:** Those rebels are never clear. What
> they say doesn't make sense.

> **Mr Fuckface:** It even goes against all the religions to tamper with the sacred languages.
> **Mr Blowjob:** Without language the only people the rebels can kill arethemselves.
>
> (*Blood &Guts p.* 136)

Here, we see 'two Capitalists' discussing the way in which they use language as a mechanism for control. This exchange reiterates Burroughs' opinion that to control language is to control society. Acker can also be seen here to be allying herself with the 'rebels,' and addressing the issues of her own rebellious 'anti-literary' stance on writing. Borne out of frustration with the writing courses she took (and hated) whilst in college, her rebellious intent was to 'tamper' with language and its use within literature. By incorporating the type of criticism leveled at her work and work like it – 'what they say doesn't make sense' – within the script, Acker not only diffuses the criticism, but reverses the target of the criticism, highlighting the narrow-mindedness and conservative nature of 'the establishment.'

One of Acker's primary objectives was to liberate language in some way. But while Burroughs used the cut-up in connection with his preoccupations with the mechanisms of control and the ways in which language and control are significantly intertwined, Acker was of the opinion that language was reactive to society and culture, and not vice versa.

> Language is that which depends on other language. It's necessarily reactive. An isolated word has no meaning. Art, whether or not it uplifts the spirit, is necessarily dependent on contexts such as socio-economic ones. What can this language be which refuses?
>
> The only reaction against an unbearable society is equally unbearable nonsense.
>
> (*Bodies of Work: Essays* p. 4)

Within the parameters of reactive language, she strove to break down the language-controlled barriers between the classes in British society, and to challenge the accepted orders of art and literature without producing 'unbearable nonsense'.

The themes of male dominance and 'the big men' of literature are themes which recur throughout *Blood and Guts*, as is evidenced in Janey's relationship with Jean Genet, whom she encounters after escaping from kidnappers who abduct her subsequent to her leaving school and living in the West Village. That Janey should arrive in Tangier at this point is significant. Having long been considered by many to be an exotic 'never-never land of international intrigue, shady financial dealings and esoteric sex for sale or rent... seedy, salacious, degenerate,' Tangier is also a place to which writers and artists gravitate.[71] As Iain Finlayson explains, the Moroccan city's reputation developed from the seventeenth century, from which time it was ruled by European and American consuls. This served to render Tangier a place apart, and an International Zone. 'Tangier was innately corrupt, and... its reputation was condoned by the city authorities… Undoubtedly, some control existed, but it was principally and superficially directed at keeping the peace rather than cleaning up any perceived immorality or enthusiastic free enterprise.'[72] Many writers, including Burroughs, Bowles and Genet have written in, on and about Tangier, portraying a city rife with drugs and sex which could readily be bought, and cheaply. Tangier was the inspiration for Burroughs' otherworldly city of Interzone in which much of *Naked Lunch* takes place. Its amalgamative naming, reflecting the city's status as an inter(national) zone, was no accident.[73] Within the context of Acker's writing, then, Tangier is more than simply a location providing a backdrop to her character's activities, as a location with strong associations to the authors she saw as her literary forebears.

At the beginning of their time together, Janey talks to and learns from Genet, but the relationship ends badly, with Janey imprisoned for stealing '*two copies of* Funeral Rights [Genet's 1947 novel] *and hash*' (*Blood & Guts p.* 133) from Genet. In short, Janey steals from her mentor and is punished. Acker punctuates this section of the book with extensive quotations from Genet's work, and in doing so clearly invites parallels to be drawn between Janey's story and Acker's own theft / plagiarism from her own influencers. Indeed, she comments that 'it's at the end of *Blood and Guts in High School* when I start *really* [my italics] using plagiarism, with the Genet stuff.'[74] Having already plagiarised heavily from other sources in the past, Acker can be seen to locate this as the point at which she specifically draws together the act of plagiarism with the creation of 'fiction.' The Janey / Kathy 'parable' bridges the gap between the constructs of the fictional time / space continuum (Janey's actions) and the present (the book itself). More significantly, however, is the strongly implicit concern with influence and theft, or plagiarism, and Acker's choice of Genet as a character is significant for a number of reasons, not least of all because he is one of the authors she cited as a major influence on her work. For Acker, influence and plagiarism are almost interchangeable, and that she should 'steal' or appropriate from Genet, a literary forebear who was a thief in the literal sense – his autobiographically-inspired *The Thief's Journal* (1949) requiring little by way of an explanation here – seems entirely appropriate. Having taken all she can from Genet in terms of discussion and transmitted knowledge, Janey resorts to simply taking – stealing – objects, at which point Genet rejects her, and, once rejected, she in turn rejects him. It is interesting to consider that the way on which Acker's literary influence-relationship with Genet is translated in an almost allegorical manner, and Janey's relationship with Genet in many ways parallels her relationship with Johnny, which is also built around a twisted mutual reliance of sorts.

The similarities between the fiction and the reality are such that, in truth, only the names have been changed – slightly – and that the final theft and rejection in the narrative is literal rather than metaphorical. That Acker has incorporated this influence allegory into the text is indicative of the way in which her own life experiences inform her writing. This is a literal adoption of Genet's personal belief that a writer becomes a writer 'at birth,' something Burroughs also believed.[75] The phonetic similarity of Janey's name to and Genet is difficult to ignore, and serves to render explicit the notion that the influencee absorbs greatly from the influencer. Herein lies a suggestion that Acker felt a degree of anxiety regarding her influences, and the way in which influence has a bearing on authorial and individual identity. In her questioning her identity, Janey, and, in turn, Acker feel it necessary to reject the father figure, the influencer. Despite her lifelong connection to Burroughs, there were times at which Acker felt compelled to 'reject' him, saying '20 years ago, everyone thought that

Burroughs was some kind of way-out science fiction writer, but now he looks a bit tame.'[76] This statement could be interpreted as simply a comment on the development of literature and society and the ways in which Burroughs' apocalyptic future has become the real present. It could also be interpreted as a comment on how the avant-garde becomes accepted within society, and the way in which once society becomes accustomed to something it ceases to be shocking.

Acker further addresses the issue gender relations and social hierarchies variously, returning to the script as a method of dialogue presentation frequently throughout *Blood and Guts*. This is nowhere more apparent than in her trial for stealing from Genet:

> **Judge 1:** You're a woman.
> **Judge 2:** You whine and snivel. You don't stand up for yourself. You act like
> you do totally to please other people. You're a piece of shit. You're not real.
> **Judge 3:** You're a whore a thief a liar a smelly fish a money dribbler an egotistic snob.
> **Judge 4:** You have every vice in the world.
> etc.
>
> (*Blood & Guts p.* 133)

It is clear that this scene and the characters of the Judges as much vehicles for addressing the issues central to Acker's personal agenda as they are devices of plot, and in this way this scene functions in much the same way as Burroughs' 'routines.' That Acker uses judges to express anti-female opinions is interesting on a number of levels. First and foremost there stands the issue of a judge's social function, that of arbiter of social justice. Judges are supposed to be free from prejudices: the judges in this scene clearly are not. Not only, then, is Acker highlighting, in a satirical fashion, the problems women face in a world in which gender bias remains rife, but she is also attacking the inherent flaws of the 'justice' system. It is also interesting to observe that the first-mentioned judge is noted as being female. Conceivably, Acker is suggesting that to succeed in a male-dominated profession in a male-dominated society, a woman needs to discard her feminine traits and take on male opinions, even if this means to betray her own gender as well as her unbiased, objective perspective. Of course, all of this is implied, as the dialogue is presented without the framing of authorial opinion or overview. It was Acker's opinion that such a lack of context for the 'MTV generation' posed no problem, again reflecting her alignment with Deleuze and Guattari.

> We all come out of MTV, so what's the problem? But it's an old conservative crowd that runs the literary world and they haven't quite gotten that we were all brought up on MTV and we have no problem with this. We don't need things to be continuous. I don't need to be told what the meaning is every 5 minutes. I like garbage. I like noise.[77]

As Acker comments, writing for her, must have relation to her own life, and to this end strove to represent 'reality.' She saw her work's place, stylistically speaking, as being within the realms of the contemporary 'reality,' and placed her cut-up, montage approach firmly in the postmodern context of the fast cuts, edits and the rapid succession of images which proliferate in pop music videos – after all, 'we all come out of MTV, so what's the problem?' In making this statement, Acker is essentially asserting that her writing, in its non-sequential ordering, in part reflects her life in postmodern society, in which we all now live. The reality of modern living is that we are subjected to a bombardment of images, music videos with fast edits, random and unconnected images and sounds, people and cars passing by, litter, peripheral and meaningless miscellanea and extraneous background noise. But Acker was always keen to subvert any accepted form, and to simply reflect was not the purpose of her writing. As Kathleen Wheeler writes, Acker 'sought to reveal the fact that familiar order and logic are much less native to our experience than we realise, whether we mean inner mental experience or the apparent order of nature and the "external" world. Sanity is, arguably, merely the most familiar form of irrationality.'[78] What Acker is also stating is that her writing is, in turn, contributing to that garbage and noise. Even Acker's more linearly-developed passages are subject to deliberate interruption as the text is interspersed almost at random by the sketches and diagrams which appear to only have limited relevance to the text they appear beside. In this sense, the very formulation of Acker's work simultaneously embodies and perverts both the contemporary cultural reality and the nature of memory, echoing Burroughs' opinion that 'life is a cut-up.'[79] Moreover, Acker's work illustrates the symptoms of that time and society in a 'schizo' manner as theorised by Deleuze and Guiattari: 'The schizophrenic deliberately seeks out the very limit of capitalism: he is its inherent tendency brought to fulfilment, its surplus product, its proletariat, and its exterminating angel. He scrambles all the codes and is the transmitter of the decoded flows of desire.'[80]

Acker strongly believed that it was vital for art, in all its forms including writing, to have a close connection to the culture in which it is created. 'If it wasn't for certain community consensus as to the meanings and usages of words, words would be nonsense. Language, then, is deeply discourse: when I use language, I am given meaning and I give meaning back to the community,' she wrote (*Bodies of Work: Essays* p. 4). 'Posmodernism,' she continues, 'for the moment, is a useful perspective and tactic. If we don't live for and in the, this, moment, we do not live at all' (*Bodies of Work: Essays* p. 5). As her career progressed, she became increasingly interested not only in the meanings ascribed to language, but also in the way that 'this moment' in which we live is coloured by history, which is constructed and circulated through the formation of myths and mythology. In the final section of this essay, I consider the way in which she drew on models of mythology and popular genre fiction to explore the notions of twentieth century myths.

### *Pussy, King of the Pirates*: Piracy, Plagiarism and Myth.

Commonly aligned with postmodernism, Acker has also been named by some as a primary exponent of the 'cyberpunk' genre. A subgenre of Science Fiction, another genre with which Acker's work is frequently aligned, other writers whose works are commonly considered to be exemplary of the genre include William Gibson, Bruce Sterling and Rudy Rucker. Dani Cavallaro, author of *Cyberpunk and Cyberculture,* differentiates cyberpunk from SF and defines it thus:

> Cyberpunk foregrounds the provisional status of all definitions of value, rationality and truth in a radical rejection of the Enlightenment ethos. It amalgamates in often baffling ways the rational and the irrational, the new and the old, the mind and the body, by integrating the hyperefficient structures of high technology with the anarchy of street subcultures.[81]

This definition provides the reasoning behind the term 'cyberpunk' by noting that there are two distinct component elements to the genre. Namely, we can see that the 'cyber' aspect refers to all things 'cyber': cybernetics, 'cyberspace' and all associated hardware and peripherals connected to the high technology with which the world of the Internet and global culture, while 'punk' calls to mind the rebellious, anarchic DIY ethos of the music of the punk era of the late 1970s. Cavallaro adds that 'cyberpunk bears many points of contact with postmodern fiction. Indeed, cyberpunk novels are often taught on courses on Postmodernism.'[82] Acker's part animal / part human pirates are a curious breed, who in part signify a regression from civilised society, and in equal part can be seen to exemplify the cyberpunk idea of 'posthumanism.'[83] *Pussy, King of the Pirates* certainly warrants is place within these categories, crossing and breaking genre divides as it does by retelling *The Story of O* (1954) and recounting the life of Antonin Artaud, all within a loose framework based on a feminised version of *Treasure Island* (1883).[84] Acker summarised the plot and its inspiration thus:

> *Pussy, King of the Pirates*, takes two girls from an Egyptian whorehouse to an island where they fight with female pirates. It's loosely related to Robert Louis Stevenson's classic *Treasure Island,* and the whole idea was triggered after I saw a great Japanese film. In my book the characters enjoy themselves in a landscape that doubles for the female body.[85]

The book's preface begins with Artaud narrating O's story in a style reminiscent of a children's story or a tale recounted orally:

'When O was a young girl, above all she wanted a man to take care of her...' (*Pussy, King of the Pirates* p. 3). Such an introduction sets Acker's agenda from the outset, illustrating the ways in which traditional fairytales and children's stories reinforce gender stereotyping and, according to many feminist theorists, socialise children into adopting conventional gender roles. Thus, the control of individuals through linguistic programming and conditioning can be seen to begin at a young age, and by subverting the conventions of the medium through which this conditioning takes place – namely the children's story – Acker uses *Pussy* as a vehicle to attack the control mechanism.

The narrator switches between the voices of Artaud and O every two or three pages during the book's opening sequence, breaking the continuity of each of the narratives. These rapid changes between the speakers, which reduce to sections as short as two lines toward the end, fragment two narrative strands, effectively cutting them up, not on a syntactic level, but on a narrative level, with the changes occurring very rapidly in a manner analogous to the editing of a pop video or television commercial, appropriate to the MTV generation's style of viewing.

The main body of *Pussy* is divided into two primary sections: 'In the Days of Dreaming' and 'In the Days of Pirates.' Here, we find a map of Pirate Island, featuring conventional genre trappings, including places marked 'treasure' and 'dead men coast.' However, there are also areas labelled 'the places for transformations' and 'the repository of dreams' which illustrate the elements Acker introduces from other sources. It is here that we are also presented with a 'manuscript' containing a history of the pirates and told in 'our scummy pirate language' (*Pussy, King of the Pirates* p. 68) and are introduced to King Pussy's story. We learn from the outset that she 'always lives inside her own head' (*Pussy, King of the Pirates* p. 72). Thus the narrative that follows, in conjunction with the map and the manuscript, presents the reader with a dreamscape in which it is impossible to distinguish the 'facts' from the narrator's imagination. This narrative, which consists of short scenes in which 'reality' and 'imagination' are blurred to the point of indistinction, conveys a history whilst simultaneously revealing, as the early cut-ups did, the problematic nature of the construction of history. Being composed of 'documents' as well as events, both internal and external, as recalled by an unreliable narrator, the text questions the authenticity of 'the document' and idea of a credible unified history, and so addresses the notion of 'history as myth.'

In her narrative, Pussy recounts her experiences of pregnancy, abortion, casual sex with drug addicts, and her separation from society that ultimately leads her from being 'a nice girl' (*Pussy, King of the Pirates* p. 72) to becoming the King of the Pirates. The pirates are presented as not only separate from society, but, quite literally, a breed apart:

> Only the woman is doing the cooking because the man's sexist. Since she's a pirate, she won't have anything to do with the humans: either she's cooking for animals or she's cooking up an animal. One is the same as the other.
> Right now, her version of cooking is to make animal food out of catshit.
> (*Pussy, King of the Pirates* p. 112)

Part animal, part human, Acker's pirates in part signify a regression from civilised society, and in equal part can be seen to exemplify the cyberpunk idea of 'posthumanism.' Yet once again, the characters in Acker's work do not fit perfectly into this category, replacing the popular 'cyborg' element of the posthuman with a regressive animalism. If, as Walter Truett Anderson believes, technology has altered the relationship between humans and the planet and "*Homo sapiens* becomes a different kind of animal, struggling to comprehend and manage a new relationship between planet and people" (2004: 103), then Acker presents us with an image of a culture that emerges when the relationship falls apart.[86] Acker's pirates show one of the possibilities for the future if, as Fukuyama states, 'Huxley was right, that the most significant threat posed by contemporary biotechnology is the possibility that it will alter human nature and thereby move us into a "posthuman" stage of history.'[87] Perhaps Acker's brand of cyberpunk fiction is closer to Mark Fisher's assertion that 'cyberpunk is a convergence: a crossover point not only for fiction and theory, but for everything that either doesn't know its place or is in the process of escaping it.'[88] The simple fact is that however one attempts to categorise

Acker's work, it does not fit neatly into the definitions of any one genre.

It is questionable whether this tendency to create an ever-increasing array of new and unusual, not to mention increasingly esoteric and intricately defined subgenres reveals more regarding the present nature of fiction or the present nature of criticism, a field Acker felt at odds with on many levels, writing, 'I've never been sure about the need for literary criticism' (*Bodies of Work: Essays* p. 6). Throughout her career, she wrote and spoke openly of her feminization of classical mythology in the creation of her own texts. Although not alone in this practice, Acker was without doubt a leader in this field.[89] In interviews, she was always wholly open about her drawing from classical literature and 'classics,' even going to far as to suggest that appropriation and the (instinctive) use of other texts is vital for the evolution of literature:

> If a work is immediate enough, alive enough, the proper response isn't to be academic, to write about it, but to use it, to go on. By using each other, each other's texts, we keep on living, imagining, making, fucking... (*Bodies of Work: Essays* 6)

In *Pussy* we see a considerable evolution within her work, whilst simultaneously representing the culmination and assimilation of many of the themes which recur in her previous works, and a continued use of 'other texts.' Cut-up passages are also to be found, showing that while making the transition to a more narrative-based approach, she continued to use earlier methods.

> . . . vast memories of sacred cities have become lands in themselves . . . strewn across deserts most of whose shifting grounds no human will ever touch . . . traces where there were once no traces . . . these are dreams. (*Pussy, King of the Pirates p.* 112)

Used sparingly to convey dreamscape imagery, the cut-up passages fit comfortably with the fragmentary narrative, which incorporates many of the features common to *Blood and Guts*:

diagrams, maps and *mise en page*. That the same text would appear in excerpt form accompanied by illustrations in a separate volume entitled *Pussycat Fever* only highlights the way in which Acker attempted to cut up the narrative not only syntactically, but also by physical or visual means.[90] Furthermore, by re-presenting a segment of text from the novel – her own novel – Acker returns to her earlier question 'if I repeated the same text, would it be the same text?'[91]

Switches of narrator and diary extracts also feature throughout the book. 'You don't read Acker the way you read traditional novelists; you read Acker the way you watch TV, only Acker won't let go of the remote. In *Pussy,* as in her other works Acker makes plot subsidiary,' comments Brad Tyler.[92] However, despite its fragmentary nature, in keeping with the narrative style of *Treasure Island, Pussy* reflects a concerted attempt to use a more cogent, conventional narrative form:

> Lately I've been working on narrative... But I'm starting to worry about self-censorship... I might be writing what people expect me to write, writing from that place where I might be ruled by economic considerations. To overcome that, I started working with dreams, because I'm not too censored when I use dream material.[93]

Clearly, she felt as though her shift toward 'proper' narrative could be perceived as a shift toward commercialism, and a rejection of her rebellious principles. Reviews of her later work suggest she need not have been excessively worried however, as Gérard Murphy's appraisal reveals: '*Pussy* does not engage us in conventional or formal narrative pleasure; which is not to say that we are not indulged in other ways.'[94] Her use of dreams, then, provided a means of retaining her sense of creative freedom and to prove - as much to herself as her critics - that she had not 'sold out.' She explained her increasing interest in dreams to Karl Schmeider.

> I began looking for the source of dreams, what makes a dream. I realized a dream is a pure movement of desire. And in a dream, you're just watching without judgement, without stoppage,

> which is what you do when you're not dreaming. Lacan says [the] object of desire is never there. It's an absence and to look for the real meaning of a dream, you have to look for the one point where the dream doesn't make sense, where there is something missing. That will tell you what the dream means. And that fascinated me.[95]

Of interest here is the theoretical approach Acker took in her approach to considering dreams, in that she makes recourse to Lacan, with whose ideas on 'the imaginary' Burroughs' work draws certain parallels, as Timothy Murphy observes.[96] Burroughs was clear in the direction his exploration of dreams led: 'I am quite deliberately addressing myself to the whole area of what we call dreams. What precisely is a dream?' (*The Third Mind p.* 1). Acker closely echoed Burroughs' opinion when she wrote, 'without dreams, our desires, especially sexual desires, we will die' (*Bodies of Work: Essays* p. 3).[97] But of the greatest significance here is the fact that Acker uses dreams as another means of relinquishing authorial control over the writing and returning to one of the original functions of the early cut-up, namely to bring writing closer to the subconscious mind. By using dreams as a source of inspiration and attempting to replicate the dream experience in narrative, she necessarily arrived at a narrative that moves between locations without the requirement of explaining the details of precisely how the characters are transported from place to place, and unencumbered by the dictates of lineal time or fixed single perspective. To this end, a fragmentary narrative formulated from sections of text that do not necessarily follow sequentially – a cut-up of sorts – represented the most appropriate mode of narrative for her purpose.

Another key motif of *Pussy* is that of the outsider, as exemplified by the appropriately-named Ostracism's diary excerpts:

> Pages torn out of my first school diary:
>
> (no date)

> school is a dairy
> because all headmistresses are cows
>
> Now that I'm in school, I'm never again going to be alone.
>
> I used to hate girls. I remember. *Girls are stupid, girls always lie...* What I meant was that I was from a different race than all of them. Because the same blood wasn't in me that was in them, I was awkward. I wasn't right.
>
> (*Pussy, King of the Pirates p.* 113)

O's awareness of the difference between herself and the girls in school places her apart from them. The image of 'the outsider' brings with it implicit associations of the exile, the outlaw. Like Burroughs' pirates in *Cities of the Red Night,* there is a degree of idealism, of utopianism, about Acker's pirates, who can be seen to represent the type of 'outsider' figure Acker herself could relate to. When questioned by Ellen Friedman about her 'new direction' which began with *Empire of the Senseless,* Acker summarised the shift in her approach as 'the search for a myth to live by... I'm looking for a myth. I'm looking for it where no one else is looking... The myth to me is pirates.'[98] She continued:

> It's like the tattoo... it concerns taking over, doing your own sign-making. In England the tattoo is very much a sign of a certain class and certain people, a part of society that sees itself as outcast. For me the tattoo is very profound. The meeting of the body and, well, the spirit... So that's what I'm saying about looking for the myth with people like that – tattoo artists, sailors, pirates.[99]

The significance of her remarks on the symbolism of pirates is relevant on a number of levels, not least of all in that she makes a specific connection between the idea of pirates and myth. On one level, this idea of searching for a myth to live by and having recourse to the historical – the conventional image of pirates remains rooted in the historical tradition of which *Treasure Island* is a part – would seem to go against all that is contemporary, postmodern and progressive in literary terms, i.e. the things with which Acker is associated. Yet, on another level, pirates match her literary position perfectly. In the first instance, as Acker notes, there is the idea of the pirate as 'outcast,' or, perhaps more accurately, 'outlaw.' 'Not just outcasts – outcasts could be bums – but people who are beginning to take their own sign-making into their own hands. They're conscious of their own sign-making, signifying values, really,' she said.[100] This focus on sign-making and the suggestion that the tattoo functions as an ensign is of interest here, because it relates back to the concept of non-verbal or pictorial communication methods. As such, it illustrates Acker's all-encompassing interest in modes of communication and the ways in which her narrative style and the incorporation of images as well as her collage approach echo her concerns; that is to say, the form reflects the content in *Pussy*. It is a logical step to make the transition from the idea of pirates to piracy, and to consider this in the context of Acker's celebrated career of plagiarism of precursive texts, as Lotringer notes, commenting that plagiarism is when you 'pirate someone else's text. Or rather hijack it, which is the etymology.'[101] The significance of pirates to Acker on a personal level becomes plainly apparent in this context. If Burroughs' *Cities of the Red Night* represented a shift from active piracy (of other texts, in the form of the cut-ups) within the Burroughs *oeuvre,* then Acker's *Pussy* makes an explicit and all-encompassing link between plagiaristic piracy and piracy in all other, broader senses. Having hijacked the works of others previously, *Pussy* sees Acker not only hijacking more traditional genre fiction and selectively retelling the story of Antonin Artaud, but also moving into the realms of 'pirate' radio, recording an album to accompany the book with UK new wave act The Mekons.[102] The record itself represents another act of piracy, hijacking musical styles from corruptions of traditional shanty songs to tribal drumming via 'pseudodisco.'[103] The record is not a simple spoken-word reading of the book with background music, but something of a soundtrack inspired by scenes and characters from the book, and in keeping with Acker's exploration of identity, the recording personnel are all credited under appropriate pseudonyms.[104]

Elsewhere, we find other references to piracy also. 'The décor in the room pirated that of a 1950s New York City apartment: roses papered the walls' (*Pussy, King of the Pirates* p. 86). Such details lend the text a thread of continuity which runs thematically if not in terms of narrative flow, by illustrating a further way in which 'piracy,' 'plagiarism,' 'pastiche' and 'theft' are all closely connected. The suggestion that a style of décor can be 'pirated' reinforces the idea that a style of art or writing can similarly be mimicked. Moreover, by describing a room which is a facsimile of a room from another period, the text reminds us that we should not trust what we see; that surfaces can be deceptive, and that history can be recreated and thus altered.

Further on, Acker returns to dialogue in the script format to further expose the artifice of character:

> Now I'm going to interview myself.
> Questioner: Did the ointment smell of her?
> Me: Yes.
> Questioner: How can you best describe the odor?
> Me: Like a witch who's just died.
>
> (*Pussy, King of the Pirates p.* 148)

In creating a situation in which Ostracism interviews herself, Acker is projecting through her character the interrogation process a writer undertakes when deciding how to render the sights, sounds and smells within a given scene. This achieves a dual result; in the first instance, it reveals character and dialogue to be as much a fictive construct as plot or sequential, linear narrative, while in the second, it also further demystifies the creative process, the way in which a writer does 'choose, edit and rearrange the words at his disposal.'[105] In this way, Acker uses the medium of writing against itself, employing a range of techniques to destabilise the 'author' figure and to promote reading as an activity which requires participation instead of passive observation. As such, we see Acker engaging with literary theory within her writing: just as Roland Barthes suggested that 'it is language which speaks, not the author,' and that 'the birth of the reader must be at the cost of the death of the author,' so Acker diminishes the 'mystery' of writing and thus diminishes the power of the omnipotent authorial 'voice.'[106]

Just as Burroughs approached his creation of 'a new mythology for the space age' by rewriting the past, so Acker too presents her 'posthuman' society through a narrative with a historical context.[107] By this, I mean that Acker employs genre trappings and conventional narrative styles as a means of creating a new 'myth' born out of the old:

> "Here are the girls I told you about. The ones for whom you and what's-her-name have been looking. They even have a captain named Pussy."
> I must have been looking a bit disapproving 'cause then she said that, though the girls look like alcoholics, I had to learn that when it comes to the sea, appearances are deceptive. Actually they were the toughest old salts she had ever met. They even had an available ship whose name was *Mary* and they had rigged it as well as any vessel, even in the past, has been prepared for the roughest and most treacherous seas. (*Pussy, King of the Pirates p.* 218)

Here we see Acker's use of more developed narrative, which could actually be considered 'conventional.' Again, genre trappings and phrases which are traditionally associated with such tales are present: 'old salts' and 'roughest and most treacherous seas' border on cliché, but serve the purpose of placing 'the old' in a new context, revising the past in preparation for the future, and the creation of the new myth. Moreover, the phraseology is derived heavily from *Treasure Island*, and characters such as Silver are lifted directly – and then altered slightly – from the source text.[108] Other examples of 'plagiarism' include the shanty which recurs throughout *Treasure Island*. White *Treasure Island* features the refrain 'fifteen men on the dead man's chest — Yo-ho-ho, and a bottle of rum!' (pp. 1, 4, 6, 60, 144, 206) the verse appears in *Pussy* as 'Two girls lost on a dead man's chest... and all that's old has turned to scum' (*Pussy, King of the Pirates p.* 220).[109] The 'musical' refrains in *Pussy* not only draw on and alter the 'songs' which appear in *Treasure Island*, but also serve to render explicit the analogy between the composite text and musical composition that Burroughs had previously observed as a facet of the cut-ups. The musical comparison was one Acker also saw as relevant to her version of the cutting up:

> What's fun is when you start playing with a text, it's just like jazz riffs, you go back and forth and down and around... I was talking with a friend about appropriation in music, all these scratched records... I think it's great![110]

In this context, the plagiarised sections in Acker's texts are analogous to longer samples – equivalent to a chord sequence – whereas the original syntactic cut-ups can be seen as shorter samples – equivalent to a few notes or a drum sound. If the initial purpose of the cut-up technique had been to bring writing more into step with developments in painting, then Acker's development of the method can in part be seen as an attempt to keep writing abreast of contemporary culture. It was because of her desire to update and recontextualise existing texts in a modern framework that the idea of a 'new' myth became so important to her during the final stage of her career. In her attempt to create the new myth, Acker makes some dramatic revisions to the past. For example, Burroughs' pirates, with the exception of the Fuentes (Iguana) Twins, are all essentially 'classic' historical characters: Acker's pirates, on the other hand, are all distinctly unlike any classic or historical characters: part-human, part animal, desocialised mutants who live like wild dogs:

> A few days later, I saw bad Dog chewing on a rat. I thought, it must be dinnertime. At the same time, because mutt-girl was no longer available to clean our deck, a three-foot-long rat stepped over my foot… my vision of Bad Dog munching on a rat, for unknown reasons, had made me hungry. (*Pussy, King of the Pirates* p. 224)

Bad Dog would appear to be a corruption of Black Dog from *Treasure Island* and elsewhere we see the pirates involved in animalistic, frenzied orgies reminiscent of the homoerotic scenes which proliferate in Burroughs' homotopian novel *The Wild Boys* (1971). If Burroughs and many popular science fiction writers depict the future as post-evolution, then the landscape of *Pussy* stands out as presenting a form of regression. And yet it remains a utopia of sorts, in that *Pussy* shows a society – however broken down – in which the outlaws, the misfits, the pirates, are able not only to survive, but to unite and thrive. Indeed, the society Acker portrays in *Pussy* can be located within the realm of what Kumar terms 'feminist utopias.'[111] 'It was perhaps inevitable that women should take to utopia,' he writes, continuing, 'where else would they be free and equal? No known society in history has allowed them material or symbolic equality with men.'[112] Given Acker's feminist credentials, it should be of no surprise that she should use her novel, set in the traditionally male domain of pirates and within a retelling of what is traditionally considered a 'boys book' in the form of *Treasure Island*, as a vehicle by which to portray an alternative future whereby female outsiders are central characters. By developing this alternative history / future by means of documents, diaries and multiple narrators, the way in which Acker contributes to the evolution of the cut-up technique becomes clear. Combining a variation of the syntactic cut-up in its irregular punctuation, the narrative cut-up created by the frequent and discontinuous narrative switches, the fragmentation of the larger narrative segments through the inclusion of maps, script-format dialogue, diagrams and 'manuscripts,' *Pussy, King of the Pirates* draws together all aspects of the cut-up previously employed by Burroughs over the span of his entire career, as well as those used by Acker across her previous works, within a single text.

Acker's work, in its concerted attempts to defy convention, betrays a defiance of genre definition. Coming 'out of MTV,' her discontinuous narratives both reflect and draw upon contemporary mainstream culture, culture beyond literature, and for this reason her work commonly finds itself in the 'postmodern' category. But while the common perception of postmodern fiction is that of a celebration of depthlessness and superficiality, in Acker's hands these methods of fragmentation – both of narrative and of character, and in which linear continuity is eschewed in favour of rapid 'channel-hopping' edits – become a means of grappling with the deeply personal. In this way, her modes of writing are symbolic of her struggle to channel the words at her disposal into forms which have real meaning for her as a writer and serve to accurately reflect her life experience and perception of the world. Rather than hiding a lack of sincerity behind a veneer of structural and presentational 'special effects,' Acker embraced these techniques and used them as vehicle not for self-expression so much as self-exploration. On one level, this focus on the self, the author, would appear to contradict the idea that the cut-up approach – applied at whatever level – is primarily a device for removing the author from the creative process. But to subscribe to such a line of thought would be to overlook the way in which Burroughs, as the technique's leading innovator, had drawn on, and then cut up, his own biography in order to write a new, mythologised author / narrator figure, cutting the past not to reveal, but to rewrite the future.

Acker saw that 'the academy' and publishers of fiction remained fundamentally conservative in their approach. Although she was certain that the reading populace would be able to accept and accommodate her radical modes of writing, there remained an obstacle between her work and the world in that publishers needed to be convinced of the marketability of such (anti-)literature.

> What they want a novel to do is to teach you how to think and act properly according to the dictates of your class and money and all that. This is very clear in England. So you learn this is a novel of manners: This is the right way to talk, this is the right way to show your emotions, this is the right way to conduct yourself, this is the right way to deal with things such as sexuality, this is the right way to act to those who have more or less money than you. I think that they get very angry at novels that don't teach that.[113]

Clearly, Acker's novels teach none of these things, but instead represent an alternative to all of them. Acker's work exists in diametric opposition to the accepted norms of social structures and the dictates of class. In doing so, she was once again aligning herself with the tradition of literary outcasts, those writers who existed on the fringes of literary acceptance for whom success was achieved on their own terms, without compromise and without adapting to meet the expectations of the mass market.

Similarly, her plagiarism from a notably broad range of sources, while generating an intertextuality which is integral to her work in a manner in keeping with prevailing postmodern modes, represents anything but a celebration of the death of originality. Like Burroughs, Acker saw existing texts simply as building blocks for new texts. By inverting the gender aspect of *Don Quixote,* a whole 'new' and 'original' text is created. Of course, there is a counterpoint regarding the originality of the 'original' text, the 'original' *Don Quixote* which needs noting here. If, as Burroughs, and subsequently Acker, argued, there are no 'original' words and that a writer merely edits and assembles using available materials, then *Don Quixote* itself cannot be considered an 'original' text. Consequently, to rewrite and revise *Don Quixote* – or *Great Expectations, Treasure Island, The Story of O* or large sections of Genet's output – would not be to produce an 'original' text, but simply a 'new' text.[114] Acker contended that her appropriation represented a type of 'liberation' of the words, and that such practices reflected her self-professed 'post-modernist' position.[115]

The key issue here is not the relation between Acker's texts and the texts from which she so heavily and openly plagiarised, but the inspiration for her plagiarism. It is clearly apparent that Acker's wide-scale borrowing from existing sources represents a following of the directions for writing laid out within the bodies of Burroughs' fictive texts and in *The Third Mind*. Knowing as we do the extent to which Acker felt herself inspired by and indebted to Burroughs and his work, this in itself requires little further qualification. I would argue that this mode of assimilation does not sit within the 'anxiety' framework of influence manifestation put forward by Bloom. Yet nor is it simply an example of postmodern sampling or pastiche, despite her tendency to 'copy it out' and despite her claims that she 'never did find' her own authorial voice.[116] That said, as with Burroughs, Acker's most distinctive work is that which draws most heavily on existing texts. As she comments,

> I found my voice was a reaction to all that stuff... I've been told by some of the writers in

> the generation above me: You'll be able to write when you've found a voice. And I couldn't find one – and I kinda didn't want one. So I just invented ways to write without having a voice then everyone said: Oh! It's really clear what your voice is![117]

Through these very public attempts to tackle the issues of identity and authorship, Acker's body of work signifies a substantial range of developments in cut-up methodology. In short, what we see in Acker's writing is a significant contribution to the ever-changing signs and meanings within language, and within the form of 'the novel,' and, ultimately, a major development in the (re)volutionary objectives which lie at the heart of the cut-up.

---

Notes

1. One leading example of this citation is the essay 'William Burroughs's Realism,' written in 1990 and contained in *Bodies of Work: Essays*. Serpent's Tail, London, 1997 (hereafter referred to within the text as *Bodies of Work: Essays*). The essay 'A Few Notes on Two of My Books' is another example, as Acker speaks more of Burroughs and his influence than her own books. Published in *Review of Contemporary Fiction*, vol. 9, no. 3., Fall 1989.
2. *The Third Mind*, a collaboration between Burroughs and Gysin collected previously published cut-up texts, originally published in *Minutes to Go* (1960) and elsewhere, plus other previously unpublished works, as well as interviews and texts which detailed the precise methodology for the production of cut-up texts.
3. 'Don't Be Afraid to Copy it Out.' Peter Wollen, *London Review of Books*, Vol. 20, No. 3, February 1998.
4. 'Devoured by Myths: interview by Sylvère Lotringer.' Hannibal Lecter, My Father. New York: Semiotext(e) 1991, p. 4.
5. Some sources state that Acker was born in 1944, although the majority give her year of birth as 1948, which is the

date given in the publication details of her books. However, the Mark/Space biography of available at http://www.euro.net/mark-space/bioKathyAcker.html (accessed 30 January 2004) gives a third alternative of 1945.

6. Andrew Calcutt & Richard Shephard, *Cult Fiction.* Prion Books, London, 1998, p. 1.
7. Karl Schmieder interview with Kathy Acker, Ilato.org: July 25, 1991, Naropa Institute, Boulder, Colorado.
8. Ibid.
9. Peter Wollen. 'Kathy Acker.' *Lust for Life*. London and New York: Verso, 2006, p. 11.
10. Avital Ronell. 'Kathy Goes to Hell.' *Lust for Life*, p. 15.
11. Peter Wollen. 'Kathy Acker.' *Lust for Life*, p. 5. Stewart Home defines Mail Art as the practice whereby art or writing 'rather than being sold as a commodity it is usually mailed to friends and acquaintances.' Stewart Home. *The Assault on Culture: Utopian Currents from Lettrisme to Class War*. London: Aporia Books & Unpopular Press, 1988, p. 69.
12. Karl Schmieder interview with Kathy Acker. See also *Hannibal Lecter, My Father*, in which Acker discusses her early biography in detail.
13. 'Devoured by Myths: interview by Sylvère Lotringer.' *Hannibal Lecter, My Father*, p. 2. *Rip-Off Red* and *The Burning Bombing of America* were published posthumously in a single volume. New York: Grove Press, 2002.
14. Ibid., p. 8.
15. Ibid., p. 13. Burroughs, 'It Belongs to the Cucumbers.' *The Adding Machine: Selected Essays*, p. 52.
16. Peter Wollen, 'Kathy Acker.' *Lust for Life* p. 4.
17. This book was published under the name of Black Tarantula. This use of the pseudonym, which is the same name as that of the eponymous central character of the book further illustrates Calcutt and Shephard's observation regarding the creation and destruction of identity, something Acker would pursue throughout her career. *The Childlike Life of Black Tarantula by the Black Tarantula* was reprinted in the Acker anthology *Portrait of an Eye – Three Novels*, which collects this volume along with *I Dreamt I Was a Nymphomaniac: Imagining* and *The*

*Adult Life of Henri Toulouse Lautrec by Henri Toulouse Lautrec*. New York: Grove Press, 1998.

18. Hereafter referred to within the text as *Pussy, King of the Pirates*.
19. Written when Acker was 21, *Politics* remained unpublished until 1991 when it was published by Semiotext(e) imprint. Excerpts of the book are also contained in *Euridice in the Underworld* and *Essential Acker*.
20. 'Devoured by Myths: interview by Sylvère Lotringer.' *Hannibal Lecter, My Father*, p. 8.
21. from *Politics*. *Essential Acker*, New York: Grove Press, 2002, p. 2.
22. 'Devoured by Myths: interview by Sylvère Lotringer.' *Hannibal Lecter, My Father*, p. 5.
23. Ellen G Friedman, 'A Conversation with Kathy Acker.' *The Review of Contemporary Fiction*, Fall 1989, Volume 9.3, p. 14.
24. Ibid.
25. Acker, *The Burning Bombing of America*. p. 165.
26. Acker, *The Burning Bombing of America*, pp. 180-182.
27. During the 1960s, a number of Burroughs' disciples (often correspondents and associates of the author) produced their own cut-up prose pieces, poems and novels published through underground press outlets. Less edited and therefore more spontaneous than Burroughs' published cut-up works, Pélieu's book is in many ways typical, with bizarre images and Surreal juxtapositions being central to its formation.
28. 'Devoured by Myths: interview by Sylvère Lotringer.' *Hannibal Lecter, My Father*, p. 12.
29. Ibid., p. 12. Peter Wollen, 'Kathy Acker.' *Lust for Life*, p. 4.
30. 'Devoured by Myths: interview by Sylvère Lotringer.' *Hannibal Lecter, My Father*, p. 13.
31. Robert Lort, 'In Memoriam to Kathy Acker: A Deleuze and Guattarian Approach by Robert Lort. *Paroxysm* Adelaide: Paroxysm Press, 1998, p. 192.
32. Avital Ronell. 'Kathy Goes to Hell.' *Lust for Life*, p. 23.
33. 'Devoured by Myths: interview by Sylvère Lotringer.' *Hannibal Lecter, My Father*, pp. 15-16.

34. Eric Mottram. 'Rencontre avec William Burroughs.' *Conversations with William Burroughs*. p. 15.
35. 'Devoured by Myths: interview by Sylvère Lotringer.' *Hannibal Lecter, My Father*, p. 7.
36. Peter Wollen, 'Kathy Acker.' *Lust for Life*, p. 4.
37. *The Childlike Life of the Black Tarantula by The Black Tarantula. Portrait of an Eye: Three Novels*. New York: grove Press, 1998, p. 3.
38. Acker, *Portrait of an Eye*, p. 11.
39. Ibid., p. 21.
40. Ibid., p. 40.
41. 'Devoured by Myths: interview by Sylvère Lotringer.' *Hannibal Lecter, My Father*, p. 7.
42. Ibid., p. 7.
43. London. Pan Books, 1984, hereafter cited in the text as *Blood & Guts*.
44. Calcutt & Shepherd, *Cult Fiction: A Reader's Guide*, p. 2.
45. Karl Schmieder interview with Kathy Acker.
46. Niall Lucy. 'Introduction: (On the Way to Genre). *Postmodern Literary Theory*, p. 33.
47. Originally published 1965 in a limited edition of 1,000 copies by Aloes, London, republished without illustrations and photographs in *The Burroughs File*, San Francisco: City Lights Books, 1984.
48. Burroughs, *Naked Lunch*, p. 187. 'Devoured by Myths: interview by Sylvère Lotringer.' *Hannibal Lecter, My Father*, p. 15.
49. Report by The Federal Inspection Office for Publications Harmful to Minors, Germany, 18 September 1998, reproduced in translation in *Euridyce In The Underworld*, pp. 144-150
50. *Euridyce In The Underworld* p. 146.
51. Gilles Deleuze & Félix Guiattari, *Anti-Oedipus: Capitalism and Schizophrenia*. London: Althone Press, 1984, p. 23.
52. Robert Lort, 'In Memoriam To Kathy Acker: A Deleuze and Guattarian Approach.' *Paroxysm*, p. 190.
53. Jonah Peretti. 'Capitalism and Schizophrenia: Contemporary Visual Culture and the Acceleration of Indentity Formation / Dissolution.' Available at http://www.datawranglers.com/negations/issues/96w_peretti.html, accessed 6 January, 2004.

54. 'Devoured by Myths: interview by Sylvère Lotringer.' *Hannibal Lecter, My Father*, p. 10.
55. Karl Schmieder interview with Kathy Acker, Ilato.org: July 25, 1991, Naropa Institute, Boulder, Colorado.
56. R. U. Sirius, 'io' magazine, reproduced at http://www.altx.com/io/acker.html (consulted 1 May, 2003). This approach to writing shares common ground with Kerouac's 'first thought, best thought' dictum, as well as Burroughs' belief that his writing was a type of purging himself for the accidental shooting of his wife, Joan Vollmer.
57. In conversation with Sylvère Lotringer, Acker recalls how she ran into trouble for the use of a four- page section of *The Pirate* (1975) by Harold Robbins within *The Adult Life of Toulouse Lautrec. Hannibal Lecter, My Father*, pp. 11-15.
58. This theme is discussed in detail in the essays contained within *Bodies of Work*.
59. *The Birth of the Poet*, first performed in New York City on 3rd December 1975 is contained in full in *Hannibal Lecter, My Father*, pp. 75-103, and also in *Eurydice in the Underworld*, pp. 77-105. Act Three, 'Ali Goes to the Mosque' contains large amounts of Arabic script, and was published separately as 'Ali and the Mosque' in *RE/Search* (no issue number or date) in 1981, pp. 20-21.
60. Burroughs, 'My Purpose is to Write for the Space Age,' *The New York Times*, 19 February 1984, pp. 9-10.
61. Karl Schmieder interview with Kathy Acker, Ilato.org.
62. Burroughs, 'The Fall of Art.' *The Adding Machine*, p. 61.
63. 'In 1973 Erica Jong published *Fear of Flying*, the novel for which she is probably best known, and a novel that would take the public by storm for its explicit treatment of women's sexuality. The novel was greeted on publication with high praise from such prominent writers as John Updyke and Henry Miller.' From the official Erica Jong website, available at http://www.ericajong.com/abouterica2.htm (consulted 23 July 2007).
64. Julia Kristeva, *Powers of Horror: An Essay on Abjection* (tr. Leon S, Roudiez). New York: Columbia University Press, p. 61.
65. Lydenberg, *Word Cultures*, p. 123.
66. Burroughs, *Cities of the Red Night*, p. 112.

67. Interview by R. U. Sirius, *io magazine.*
68. Andrea Juno. *Angry Women*. San Francisco: Re/Search Publications, 1991, p. 177.
69. 'Devoured by Myths: interview by Sylvère Lotringer.' *Hannibal Lecter, My Father*, p. 4.
70. New York: Bozeau of London Press, 1980.
71. Iain Finlayson. *Tangier: City of the Dream*. London: Flamingo, 1993, p. 4.
72. Ibid., p. 331.
73. Burroughs provided the foreword to the 1974 book by Mohamed Choukri, *Jean Genet in Tangier*. New York: Ecco, 1974. The translation of this text into English was done by Paul Bowles.
74. 'Devoured by Myths: interview by Sylvère Lotringer.' *Hannibal Lecter, My Father*, p. 10.
75. As Burroughs recounts, 'Someone asked Jean Genet when he started to write, and he answered "at birth." A writer writes about his whole experience, which begins at birth. The process begins long before the writer puts pencil or typewriter to paper.' Victor Bockris. *With William Burroughs: A Report from the Bunker*. Revised edition. New York: St. Martin's Griffin, 1996, p. 1.
76. Karl Schmieder interview with Kathy Acker, Ilato.org.
77. Karl Schmieder interview with Kathy Acker, Ilato.org.
78. Kathleen Wheeler. 'Reading Kathy Acker,' *Context* no. 9, 1991.
79. Burroughs, 'The Fall of Art.' *The Adding Machine*, p. 61.
80. Deleuze and Guatarri. *Anti-Oedipus*, p. 35.
81. Dani Cavallaro. *Cyberpunk and Cyberculture*. London and New Brunswick, NJ: The Athlone Press, 2000, p. xi.
82. Ibid., p. 10.
83. This term is defined and discussed in detail by Daniel C. Uist in the essay 'What is Posthumanism?' available at http://home.teleport.com/~jaheriot/posthum.htm, accessed 10 November 2003.
84. Originally published in French as *Histoire d'O* by Ann Desclos, under the pseudonym Pauline Réage.
85. *Internet*, 18 May 1996, quoted by Henry W. Targowski at Mark/Space Interplanetary Review, available at http://www.euro.net/mark-space/bkPussyKingOfThePirates.html, accessed 30 January 2004.

86. Walter Truett Anderson, *All Connected Now: Life in the First Global Civilization*. Boulder and Oxford: Westview Press, p. 103.
87. Francis Fukuyama, *Our Posthuman Future: Consequences of the Biotechnological Revolution*. London: Picador, 2003, p. 7.
88. Mark Fisher: 'Writing Machines' from *Word Bombs,* available at http: / / www,altx.com / wordbombs / fisher.html, accessed 6 January 2004.
89. Writers such as Jean Rhys and Angela Carter are obvious examples of feminist writers who have 'updated' fairytales, classics and myths in a contemporary, feminized way. Carter's *The Bloody Chamber* is actually a feminist retelling of *Bluebeard*.
90. Edinburgh: AK Press, 1995.
91. 'Devoured by Myths: interview by Sylvère Lotringer.' *Hannibal Lecter, My Father*, p. 8.
92. Brad Tyer, 'Pussy Galore.' Review of *Pussy, King of the Pirates*, reproduced at http: / /hotwired.com / books / 96 / 12 / index4a.html, accessed 16 November 2003.
93. Interview by R. U. Sirius.
94. This review first published in *CTHEORY*, and was subsequently reproduced online reproduced at http: / / acker.thehub.au.martin.html, accessed 23 August 2003.
95. Karl Schmieder interview with Kathy Acker, Ilato.org.
96. Timothy Murphy. *Wising Up The Marks*, p. 40-41.
97. Burroughs had previously written, 'Recent studies of dream and sleep have yielded a wealth of date that was not available in Freud's day. Perhaps the most important discovery is the fact the dreams are a biological necessity. Deprived of REM sleep, experimental subjects show all symptoms of sleeplessness, no latter how much dreamless sleep they are allowed. They become irritable and restless and experience hallucinations. No doubt prolonged deprivation would result in death.' 'On Freud and the Unconscious,' *The Adding Machine*, p. 95.
98. Ellen G Friedman, 'A Conversation with Kathy Acker.'
99. Ibid.
100. Ibid.
101. 'Devoured by Myths: interview by Sylvère Lotringer.' *Hannibal Lecter, My Father*, p. 13.

102. London: Quarterstick Records QS36, 1996. Formed in Leeds in 1977, the Mekons are renowned equally for their overtly political nature and their musical eclecticism. During their 25-plus year career have released over a dozen albums. In *Rock: The Rough Guide* (2nd Edition), (London, Rough Guides Limited, 1999, p. 633) Huw Bucknell (accurately) describes *Pussy, King of the Pirates* as 'a startlingly off-kilter album backing the spoken word narration of postfeminist American writer Kathy Acker.'
103. Brad Tyer, 'Pussy Galore.'
104. Kathy Acker is named as 'The-More-than-Able Seaman Acker,' while musicans on the record include 'Midshipman Roche,' 'Captain Morgan of Gwent,' 'Pricey Pugwash,' 'Tom the Cabin Boy' and 'Seaman Stains.' – taken from the sleeve notes of the album.
105. Eric Mottram. 'Rencontre avec William Burroughs.' *Conversations with William Burroughs*. p. 15.
106. Roland Barthes, 'The Death of the Author.' *Image, Music, Text*. London: Fontana, 1977, p. 143.
107. See Burroughs, 'My Purpose is to Write for the Space Age.' *The New York Times*, 19 February 1984, pp. 9-10.
108. In *Treasure Island* Long John Silver is male. In *Pussy*, the character is simply known as Silver, and is female.
109. Robert Louis Stevenson. *Treasure Island*. London: Penguin (Popular Classics series), 1994.
110. 'Devoured by Myths: interview by Sylvère Lotringer.' *Hannibal Lecter, My Father*, p. 13.
111. Krishan Kumar. *Utopianism*. Milton Keynes: Open University Press, 1991, p. 102.
112. Ibid., p. 102.
113. Karl Schmieder interview with Kathy Acker, Ilato.org.
114. William Burroughs. 'Cut-Up Method,' quoted by Murphy, *Wising Up the Marks*, p. 105.
115. Karl Schmieder interview with Kathy Acker, Ilato.org.
116. Marita Avila and Cheryl Meier. 'Consorting with Hecate,' available at http://members.aol.com/MeierAvil/acker.html, accessed 5 January 2003.
117. Ibid.

# Mobile@ngel

by Kenji Siratori

abnormal living body of a chemical=anthropoid-modem=heart of the hybrid corpse mechanism that turned on technojunkies' ill-treatment to the terror abolition world-codemaniacs of the chromosomal aberration that was controlled FUCKNAMLOAD****the acidHUMANIX infectious disease archive of the biocapturism nerve cells nightmare-script of a clone boy to the super-genomewarable to the feeling replicant living body junk of her digital=vamp cold-blooded disease animals reptilian=HUB ultra=machinary tragedy-ROM system to the brain universe of the hyperreal HIV=scanner form murder game of the dogs@tera DNA=channel of the drug fetus of the trash sense is debugged!

terror fear=cytoplasm gene-dub of the drug fetus of the trash sense is debugged to the paradise apparatus of the human body pill cruel emulator corpse feti=streaming of the soul/gram made of retro-ADAM::data=mutant of her abolition world-codemaniacs feeling replicant ecstasy system of the acidHUMANIX infectious disease archive_body encoder that BDSM plays a chemical=anthropoid to the brain universe that was processed noise hunting for the grotesque WEB to the genomics strategy circuit of the biocapturism nerve cells mass of flesh-modules of the hyperreal HIV=scanners that turned on the ill-treatment of the corpse city reptilian=HUB of a clone boy=joints....

I turn on ill-treatment to the DNA=channels of the biocapturism nerve cells abolition world-codemaniacs that was processed the data=mutant of her ultra=machinary tragedy-ROM creature system corpse feti=streaming of a clone boy****the gene-dub to the paradise apparatus of the human body pill cruel emulator that compressed the abnormal living body of a chemical=anthropoid-brain universe of the terror fear=cytoplasm that was controlled the acidHUMANIX infectious disease of the soul/gram made of retro-ADAM@trash sense of drug fetus feeling replicant of the hyperreal HIV=scanner form tera of dogs were installed to the reptilian=HUB_modem=heart that hung up non-resettable murder game.

reptilian=HUB_modem that crashed to the paradise apparatus of the human body pill cruel emulator murder-gimmick of the soul/gram made of retro-ADAM chemical=anthropoid=cardiac covered that mass of flesh-module hunting for the grotesque WEB=joints acidHUMANIX infectious disease archive of the biocapturism nerve cells to the brain universe of the ultra=machinary tragedy-ROM creature system that was processed the technojunkies' data=mutant nightmare-script of a clone boy is debugged to a hybrid corpse mechanism insanity medium of the hyperreal HIV=scanners that was send back out to the feeling replicant living body junk@digital=vamp cold-blooded disease animals era respiration-byte of the corpse city is aspirated acid.

# Mechanical Hunting For The Grotesque An Interview with Kenji Siratori

**Robert Lort:** Which city in Japan do you live in? How does Japanese culture imbrue your writing? Why do you write in English and not Japanese? Deleuze and Guattari have developed a concept of minor literature which talks of writers, who write in a major language living within the context of a minor language, the strident example is Kafka as a Czech, writing in German. The essence is to write like a foreigner, to disrupt the major language with new grammatical and stylistic variations, vernacular slang and displaced linguistic idioms. How do you think this relates to what you are doing?

**Kenji Siratori:** I live in Kashima recently. The Japanese chaos makes my writing the gene-dub to the composition of Antonin Artaud and William Burroughs. Because my writing is the primitive remix of nerve system. I use the primal noir language by the digital-perversion. It is the queer voice that was turned Kafka's hypertext and the cruel emulator that turned podcast of Artaud's body. I set up the genomics strategy circuit that chemical=anthropoid escaped to the language system. For example, Marilyn Manson's industrial BDSM play, guerrilla desire and humanworm installation. I practice grammatical survival to WWW.

**Robert Lort:** From first glance your work draws comparisons with the sexual scatologies of Pierre Guyotat, the deranged tirades of Antonin Artaud and the perverse texts of Jake Chapman. "Meatphysics" by Chapman has been described as "Windows source code as hacked by Gilles Deleuze,"[1] which seems absolutely appropriate to describing the high speed linguistic wrap-arounds, erratic discontinuities and sporadic hypertext you employ. Do you share sensibilities with these writers?

**Kenji Siratori:** I hyperlink to the writers of speed. It brings about the generation change of acidhuman. Like Chuck Palahniuk's transgressive fiction. And the speed of my writing is absorbed by an industrial BDSM play in this abolition world. Guyotat's 21st century noise dashes on J.G. Thirlwell's corpse feti streaming circuit. My writing speed rapes the industrial mass of flesh-module of a drug fetus. Generate Kafka's biocapturism guerrilla apparatus!

**Robert Lort:** What are your current thoughts on the state of the publishing industry? In the information overload age, why have you chosen to effectively self-publish through iUniverse? When will Creation Books be releasing "Acidhuman Project" and what can we expect from this new book? Do you think that pdfs will become the mp3s of books?

**Kenji Siratori:** I deconstruct the objective corpse feti=streaming circuit of a chemical=anthropoid. The icon of self-publish is in creative demand. The larvas of the digital contents must be aspirated acid like Alt-X. "Acidhuman Project" is the manual regarding the guerrilla=sex of a drug fetus. To send back out the modem=heart of 21st century Kafka era respiration-byte. And to ill-treat on the transgressive abolition world-codemaniacs that chemical=anthropoid was installed. R.U. Sirius manufactures the new podcast-mind of a chemical=anthropoid recently. It is the bioware of acidhuman. I manage the transgressive genomics strategy circuit of a chemical=anthropoid as the fictional bioware.

**Robert Lort:** Your writing appears to take the Burroughs and Gysin cut-up technique onto new levels. Do you still draw on the original form of the cut-up as described by William Burroughs? Do you use a computer program that does cut-ups to Xenakis polynomials? Is it nano-cut-ups? What is your process of writing? What techniques are you using? What are you trying to achieve?

**Kenji Siratori:** The primal word of a chemical=anthropoid is in Francis Bacon's picture. As if the mass of flesh-module of the hyperreal HIV=scanner form of the drug fetus that was cut the suicide-code of the abolition world is manufactured. The dogs of tera exterminated William Burroughs's objective brain universe. Plug-in Antonin Artaud's body encoder to this abolition world! Genomics strategy circuit of a chemical=anthropoid is open to Artaud's podcast-mind and Burroughs's guerrilla sex generation.

**Robert Lort:** There are innumerable musicians who have taken to writing, but few examples of writers who have taken to music. Your *Bizarre* CD is injected with influences from Merzbow, Foetus, Meat Beat Manifesto, Frontline Assembly... Do you think sampling technology and programmed music is closer to your writing style? What techniques have you brought from writing to music and vise-verso? What kinds of music are you listening to?

**Kenji Siratori:** I sample the transgressive genomics strategy circuit of a chemical=anthropoid. Industrial quickening of the abolition world is notified in my writing. Life=noise of a drug fetus corrodes the brain universe that tera of dogs were ill-treated on biocapturism. I praise Foetus's work. Foetus transplants the drug fetus army to a nerve cell. I am J.G. Thirlwell's literary apprentice. My ear scratches William Burroughs's psychedelic placenta. As an exception, Marilyn Manson, the reptilian=HUB_modem of a drug fetus=cardiac covered that mass of flesh-module abolition world in hunting for the grotesque WEB=jointed and the living body junk feeling replicant who turned on the ill-treatment of a chemical=anthropoid guerrilla.

**Robert Lort:** Similar to Burroughs, you have also become recognized as an artist, what relationship exists between your visual artwork and your writing?[2] What artists or genres prove significantly fertile? Do you work purely in the realm of digital art?

**Kenji Siratori:** My writing invades into industrial BDSM play of the abolition world. I output Antonin Artaud's nerve struggle to the 21st century corpse feti=streaming circuit of a drug fetus. Digital-Artaud and Digital-Bataille parasitize into the hybrid corpse mechanism cultural context of a chemical=anthropoid. I am interested in Douglas Rushkoff recently. Douglas Rushkoff HIV=scans the gene-war of a chemical=anthropoid, the digital=chimpanzee's deconstruction declaration. The genomics strategy circuit of Rushkoff's hyperreal HIV=scanner form amputates the neuromatic suicide-code of the abolition world. The dogs of tera will send back out the mass of flesh-module of digital art era respiration-byte.

**Robert Lort:** The postmodern age has declared the death of the Author, "writing is the destruction of every voice, of every point of origin... the negative where all identity is lost"[3] (Barthes). Just as Stelarc proclaims the obsolescence of the body, we are simultaneously faced with the obsolescence of the text. Your texts appear to have mutated into pure data streams, as something to be downloaded or plugged into. The conventional linear-narrative archi-text, what Reza Negarestani characterized as an "egocentric disease,"[4] is here relentlessly shredded and stripped of its authorial subject, what remains is an acephalous corp(u)s, a schizo-machine text. Is there a point where a text becomes just complete chaos, utterly non-sensical?

**Kenji Siratori:** The text is attached to invade fate. A word ill-treats on the hyperreal HIV=scanner form body encoder of a chemical=anthropoid. Chuck Palahniuk's text cries out the throes of death. Exterminate the philosophical corpse feti=streaming circuit that tera of dogs were excreted! Mashup Antonin Artaud's living body junk modem=cardiac in the textual brain universe of a chemical=anthropoid! The DNA=channel of the abolition world is broadcast to a hybrid corpse mechanism. To digital=vamp the scatologic corpse feti=streaming circuits of the postmodern age, from Stelarc's obliqueness.

**Robert Lort:** Deleuze has described how the new Control Societies are taking over from the old disciplinary societies considered by Foucault. Deleuze remarks that the locus of revolt in Control Societies "may be to create vacuoles of non-communication, circuit breakers, so we can elude control"[5] The traces of cross fire in an information war might unfold with the hijacking of the sound and image barrage, hacking the circuity to revert the control systems upon themselves or the anti-muzak tactics of the "Decoder" film. Do you think that your texts are playing a part in this new subversion?

**Kenji Siratori:** To debug the abolition world is achieved the super-genomewarable violence of a chemical=anthropoid abnormal living body-by controlling. My guerrilla writing uploads the hyperreal HIV=scanner form genomics strategy circuit of a chemical=anthropoid to the corpse feti=streaming pituitary of the abolition world through Digital-Artaud. Deleuze-machine continues to amputate the chemical=anthropoid's suicide-code that inheriteded.

---

Notes:

1. http://quimbys.com/product_info.php/products_id/6158
2. http://www.inter-zone.org/kenjigal.html
3. Roland Barthes "The Death of the Author" *Image, Music Text,* New York, Hill And Wang, 1988, p. 142.
4. Reza Negarestani *Technodrome* http://www.3ammagazine.com/litarchives/2005/oct/technodrome.shtml
5. Gilles Deleuze "Control and Becoming" in *Negotiations 1972-1990,* New York, Columbia University Press, 1995, p. 175.

# Geoffrey Schmidt, *The Atrocity Exhibition*[1]

by Robert Lort

"The performance explores the inner and outer landscapes. The character is schizophrenic, his landscape is splintered and magnified. His ambiguous personas pursue their fetish existence, magnification of human surface, sexual fulfilment through metal objects penetrating, encasing or touching soft flesh. Objectifying and isolating body parts to medical terms and purely functional commodities. Measurement, manipulation and study of body postures as answers to psychological questions. Science as Pornography."[2]

Geoffrey Schmidt enters the stage and stands behind a semi-opaque screen. He is wearing black leather S&M trousers, on his head is a revolving helmet. Behind him, on the wall above his head appears a large computer animated image of a blue head revolving against a blue sky. To the left and right of this central image are slides unfurling fetishistic and perverse imagery. Further to the left and right of the slide images are two video monitors which depict close-up images through a screen which Geoffrey is behind. Like voyeurs our eyes penetrate eagerly through the screen. A soundscape of freeway noise, birds and machine noise pervades the entire performance.

The performance develops as Geoffrey begins to moves his fingers over his back. He pulls and caresses at his skin, centring on the edges of the tattooed spine on his back, loosening the skin as though the skin might eventually separate from his inner flesh, as though the tattooed spine might pull out and release his body in some way, disentangling it from its organic configuration. He progress by attaching long black feathers to the soft flesh on the underside of his arms and evoking a common S&M practice he attaches lines of pegs to himself which pinch the skin of his chest. Seemingly demonstrating his completed shamanic becoming or alterification, he outstretches his arms/wings. He then detaches the pegs and feathers from his body and transfers them to the helmet. The performance itself, in the context of its schizophrenic allusions, tends to evoke what Deleuze and Guattari delineate as a process of becoming, in this case, a becoming-bird. The schizo-transformation is quite evident in the way the pegs become plumage in the final chimerical form.

The performance probes the myriad of sexualities present in *The Atrocity Exhibition,* a book by J.G. Ballard. The performance specifically probes the way that sex exists in the "inbetween", mediated through a third but distant component, plugged into depths of alterity and surface/depth-becomings. The way that the characters sexual desires for each other become intensified and stimulated, by way of their partners contiguous sexual liaisons. How their desires do not exist in binary isolation, but are intricately connected to vast external networks of criss-crossing and mutating desire. Where each desire becomes fragmented and displaced as it is infused in and between other desires. The intensification of desire is fulfilled through the alterification and subjective becomings of the partners. In *Crash,* it is emphasised in the way that Catherine pursues a sexual fantasy of Vaughan, via an imagined homosexual encounter between her lover and Vaughan. It traverses the *inbetween,* where her lover is becoming Vaughan, as much as she is becoming her lover. And similarly how Catherine's lesbian fantasy with her secretary Karen, becomes inserted into the sexual relation between her and her male lover. It is the enigma and perversity of the situation that inspires them.

Geoffrey Schmidt's performance points to the way that the schizo-body becomes a surface. This surface is punctured and penetrated, bruised, pierced, concealed and marked with tattoos. It is a surface which is nolonger invalidated against the overriding significance of the principal sexual orifice. These surfaces are allowed to desegregate and merge into one another; surfaces of motorways, chromium auto-surfaces, surfaces of human bodies. By conceptually demolishing the surface of the skin, by pulling it apart and puncturing it like a metal vessel, the schizo manages to blur the segregation between what is internal to the self and what is external. The surfaces can then merge and fold in on one another; self and non-self, biological and technological, viscera and motorway. A Deleuze/Guattarian

Body without Organs is produced, a body that consists of nothing but depth.

As Ballard points out in *The Atrocity Exhibition,* in the face of AIDS desire becomes ineluctably entwined with death, which has the effect of displacing sexuality amongst new loci. Sexuality increasingly becomes conceptual and displaced into a detached perversity. When genital penetration becomes life threatening, desire is forced off course into ulterior spaces. Desire when it breaks with it's genital fixation, it becomes heterogeneous. "...it's an interesting question - in what way is intercourse per vagina more stimulating than with this ashtray, say, or with the angle between two walls?"[3] In accordance with this, the organs are abandoned, and desire is compelled to extend, stretch and delve into new intensities. It is the schizo sexuality that abandons monomorphous sexual desire (ie desire constrained to a single sense, a single desire and a single outcome) to encounter a realm of polymorphous sexual desire (ie desire that functions as an assemblage of surfaces, as zones of depth and intensity, eliciting innumerable outcomes and movements of becoming). Monomorphous sexuality is characteristically linear, in this instance, desire repeatedly follows a normative and defined sequence of events and spatial encounters, functioning according to pre-defined stages and levels of intensification. A polymorphous sexuality is by contrast directly engaged in and productive of a non-linearity, that engages directly with movements of duration and spatiality, employing these elements as variable and heterogeneous components of the intensification. The schizo's production of a multiplical sexuality, engages a poly-perversity that continually strives to encounter and produce different feelings, different events, arrangements and outcomes and the unending evolution of its complexification and sophistication. It is a sexuality of transitoriness, that emerges in complex and proliferating impulsions and segmentations.

Geoffrey Schmidt's performance is also directly impregnated with processes of becoming and mechanisms of subjectification. These are processes involving the transformation of "self" - Deleuze and Guattari have described these as becoming woman, becoming child, becoming animal and so forth. These processes of subjectification are adjoined and not dissimilar to those associated with perverse sexual acts, where participants adopt set personifications. For Geoffrey, as it is for the characters in *The Atrocity Exhibition*, these processes produce a splintering of the "self", a facelessness, a subjectivity that functions by displacement, intensification, forgetting of self and abstract fetishization. The heterogeneity of these processes are however constantly threatened by oedipal impasses, which coerce them into becoming formulaic and fixated, imbued by oedipal identifications, phallo-centric fixations, reduced of their plurality through a retracting into dominance and submission dualisms. There is always the danger that these negative effects can take hold and jeopardise things, plugging the flows and potentially reterritorializing the vivaciousness of the engagement.

Imaginary sex organs that sprout up anywhere, a visceral cut-up of flesh, interchangeable features that flicker and heave amidst moving mirrors, frenzied excrescences that flourish in surface cracks, clattering noise and electronic murmurs, organs having neither continuity of function nor conformity of positions and subject-relations, a changeling surface, dynamically transforming structure and re-configuring enhancements in swift machinic fluctuations, instantaneous modification and non-stop adjustment. Desires bursting and coming apart, projecting, swelling, congealing, coalescing and unfolding.

When the body no longer has a surface, as when the surface is penetrated, (physically and abstractly), the skin no longer functions as partition between what is of the self and what is not, and the body becomes suddenly immersed in zones of depth and nearnessness, the body is intensified and no longer impermeable to the flows of desire, other bodies penetrate it, and it others, coexisting and merging with the foreign parts. Other bodies become incorporated in and fill our bodies, just as our bodies become dissociated and dispersed between others. A schizo sexuality brings forth a non-human sexuality pervaded by imaginary sexual perversions and the production of paradoxical sexual assemblages. Foucault envisions S/M as, "the real creation of new possibilities of pleasure... I think it's a kind of creation, a creative enterprise... These practices are insisting that we can produce pleasure with very odd things, very strange parts of our bodies, in very unusual situations, and so on."[4]

Duchamp's, *The bride stripped bare by her bachelors, even* (aka *The Large Glass)* is a complex and perplexly/perversely wonderful contraption, it demonstrates how Duchamp could envision sexuality in terms of networks of surfaces, volumes, movements, flows and assemblages. These desiring-machines elicit desires that traverse outside the dominant oedipal and patriarchal desires. They make possible the production of surfaces of intensity, of strange appendages and the synthesising of desires as yet, impossible and seemingly paradoxical.

Obsessions with modern violent death, recalls Vostell's 1958, *Das Theatre is auf der Strasse II* (The Theatre is in the Street II) where, the "sculpture is made by putting all the parts from an automobile accident onto the street or at a busy intersection and repeating this act, "with accident after accident until traffic is impossible"".[5] By analogy, one could almost imagine multiplying vistas of fake sex acts, repeated one after another, until 'real' sex is impossible.

In the schizo-terrains of *The Atrocity Exhibition,* (both Geoffrey Schmidt's and J.G. Ballard's) we are confronted with the production of amorphous, fluid, inchoate and indeterminate sexualities. Sexualities, where desire is not essentialised but actively produced through processes of experimentation, creativity and interconnection, rather than as something that "is", as an immutable individuated "truth," that is supposedly liberated and succumbed to. Desire is no longer rigidly confined and repeatedly played out within a narrowly bounded territory, but immersed in its own becoming, as a perpetually evolving experimentation and augmentation, that no longer separates the sexual from the asexual. It assembles desire where the outcome or conclusion is not known in advance. It is a fetishized assemblage, a multi-erogeneity that evokes a pre-sexual and non-human sexuality, that probes into the raw, fleshy and ontological depths.

Notes

1. The germination of this piece originally came from a review I wrote of Geoffrey Schmidt's *The Atrocity Exhibition,* a performance art event, performed at the Queensland Art Gallery on 27 and 28th April 1996. My review, although initially accepted for publication, was unfortunately never published.
2. Artists statement by Geoffrey Schmidt
3. J.G. Ballard Re/Search *The Atrocity Exhibition,* San Francisco, 1990, p. 61
4. Foucault, "Sex, Power and the Politics of Identity," in *Foucault Live,* New York, Semiotext(e), 1996, p. 384
5. Schimmel, *Out of Actions: Between Performance and the Object, 1949-1979,* MOCA Los Angeles, Thames and Hudson, 1998, p. 80.

# From The Keller <S.P.K.>
# Gilles Deleuze and Francis Bacon: The Logic of Sensation

by K. Osmosis

*Francis Bacon: The Logic of Sensation* traces the philosopher Gilles Deleuze's encounter with the paintings of Francis Bacon. Deleuze interprets Bacon's paintings as an investigation of the body as meat, expressing the confrontation between flesh "as the corporeal material" and bone "as the material structure". This dichotomy of flesh and bone has a long tradition in the history of Western philosophy.

The Ancient Greeks developed their thought around beliefs concerning body heat, and its role in determining the differentiation of the sexes. Foetuses well heated within their mother's womb were born as males; foetuses lacking heat were born as females. The female is a creature "softer, more liquid, more clammy cold, altogether more formless than are men".

The philosopher Aristotle investigated this inequality of heat, and drew a connection between menstrual blood and sperm: menstrual blood is cold blood, sperm is cooked blood. Sperm is superior as it creates new life; menstrual blood is considered inferior as a substance passive and inert. For Aristotle, the male possesses the principle of movement, action and creativity; in contrast, females he defines as identical with the formless passivity of flesh and materiality.

This conception of blood as either cooked or uncooked, and the role of blood and body heat in determining the differentiation between the sexes, relates to an even older tradition that ascribes "the bones to the male principle and the flesh to the female". In accordance with this tradition, bone marrow is derived from semen, which is cooked blood, while the fat in flesh is derived from uncooked blood, which is cool and female.

In *The Raw and the Cooked,* the structuralist anthropologist Claude Levi-Strauss investigates the binary opposition between Nature and Culture, and the function of cooking as a universal means by which raw Nature is transformed into Culture. The ancient differentiation between flesh and bone, hot and cold, blood cooked and uncooked, male and female, equates with this binary opposition: Aristotle's conception of the female as 'uncooked' equates her with Nature, while his conception of the male as 'cooked' equates him with Culture.

In *A Thousand Plateaus,* Gilles Deleuze employs the metaphor of the 'tree' to describe the hierarchical dualisms characteristic of Western philosophy. For Deleuze, the 'philosopher-kings' are the functionaries of 'arborescent', despotic state machines. They are responsible for instituting fixed dichotomies between such terms as male and female, subject and object, spirit and matter, mind and body. The metaphor of the erect 'tree' illustrates the way these dichotomies are organised and stabilised. Upon the firm "root-foundation" of 'truth', a hierarchy is established privileging certain terms and positions over others regarded as 'inferior'. Accordingly, immaterial mind gains ascendancy over the corporeal body, 'civilised' culture over 'primitive' nature, the master (subject) over the slave (object), spirit over matter, male over female.

Arborescent culture's dualistic hierarchy duplicates itself in the top-down, 'stratified' organisation of the human body. The natural flows and intensities of desire that constitute the body prior to its articulation as a 'body with organs' are blocked, channelled and regulated. The 'abstract machine' of society, or the "socius", in the form of such repressive apparatuses as the state and the family, allocate to this organised body a fixed identity and position as a 'subject' separate from other bodies ('subjects') and opposed to the world of 'objects'.

These "forms, functions, bonds, dominant and hierarchized organizations" imposed upon the body, serve to "secure us, nail us down" to the repressive use of the body as a blunt instrument of labour within "the dominant reality" of a stratified society. It is a society based upon the fabrication of false needs and "the savage unity of desire and production" in the exploitation and subjugation of the earth and other human beings, within a dualistic framework that dissociates such terms as subject and object, spirit and materiality, mind (head) and body.

A hierarchical dualism articulated in Platonic philosophy, where an essential and 'true' world of imperishable Ideas or Forms is opposed to the 'untrue' visible world of sensory appearances. A dualism that opposes abstract thought to physical sensation; the immaterial mind (identified with the 'soul') to the corporeal body. Thus the phenomenal world of sensory appearances is but a dim and distorted shadow or copy of the 'real', suprasensory world of ideas. 'True' knowledge is achieved when the mind (*nous*) - "the eye of the soul" - detaches itself from the body and the impermanent, material world of sensible particulars, to contemplate the immutable, divine world of pure forms.

This distinction between divine mind or soul and the corporeal body, is further elaborated in Plato's *Timaeus*. Immaterial mind or consciousness is portrayed as immutable and good. In contrast, visible corporeality, the body and the flesh, is described as chaotic and formless, the source of mutability, sickness and mortality; and of moral error in the form of physical sensations and sensual appetites to be mastered by the mind. Humans participate in the divine, eternal, ideal realm through their possession of a thinking mind and the faculty of abstract, contemplative reason. Against this, the body remains "a confused speaker", and the corporeal world exists as "the failure of thought, its inert mass, stupidity".

In Plato's *Republic,* the primacy of mind over body corresponds to the hierarchy in society of master over slave, male over female, human over animal. The just and well-ordered society mirrors, and is sustained by, the hierarchy of the well-ordered self: the mind corresponds to the ruling class of philosopher-kings, the will to the class of guardian-warriors, while the base sensual appetites correspond to the slave class. The successful subjugation and control of nature is commensurate with the subjugation and control of the 'lower', sensuous and appetitive faculties of the body. And if the individual fails to exercise control over their sensual appetites, at death their souls are reincarnated either into the body of a woman or into that of a beast.

## K. Osmosis

In the *Enneads,* the Neo-Platonic philosopher Plotinus accentuates this dualism of ideal form and formless materiality, pure thought and bodily sensuality. Absolute Being, or the One, is for Plotinus a realm of light and intelligibility distinct from the confused darkness and multiplicity of materiality. The divine soul is imprisoned within the body and the sensory world, an evil from which it endeavours to free itself in its quest for reunion with the Absolute. Plotinus describes matter, isolated from the beneficial influence of the Ideal Principle, as "ugliness, utter disgracefulness, and unredeemed evil". The material, corporeal world represents a descent, a falling away, from a primordial unity with the Divine Absolute: it is efflux, detritus.

The Seventeenth Century philosopher Rene Descartes completes the Platonic dualism of soul and body, mind and materiality. Descartes proclaims the primacy of the thinking, unitary, individual (male) subject, who is the master – "the lord and possessor" – of all that he surveys, measures and represents, of the nature external to him. The subject, soul and consciousness are identified with incorporeal mind ('thinking substance', *res cogitans*) which stands over and against the body and nature, defined as 'extended substance' (*res extensa*).

For Descartes, nature is conceptualised as a mechanical device, infinitely divisible into discrete units; the cries and writhing of animals beneath the vivisectionist's scalpel merely mechanical reflexes. Disembodied intellect is the "eye of the mind"; it perceives and apprehends the world outside itself "clearly and distinctly" as manipulable stuff to be quantified in accordance with the rules of mathematics, geometry and mechanics.

In *Lying Figure,* (1969), and *Triptych Inspired by T.S. Eliot's Poem "Sweeney Agonistes",*(1967), Francis Bacon unashamedly displays the human Figure as formless, fluid, corporeal substance; voluptuous bodies revelling in their sensuality, challenging the ascendancy of mind over body, along with the 'well-ordered' hierarchy of the 'self'. In contrast to the rigidity of the Platonic/Cartesian 'subject', based upon the supremacy of 'divine' thought over bodily sensation, the Figures portrayed in Bacon's paintings unfurl themselves as liberated 'bodies without organs': disarticulated, de-subjectified, and freely disorganised. The dualism of spirit and corporeality, interior and exterior, surface and depth, 'self' and 'other' is obliterated in the body expressed as a fluid medium of desiring sensation.

In the *Dioptrics*, Descartes establishes a hierarchy of the senses, with sight declared to be "the noblest and most comprehensive". For it is through the eye that the immaterial mind of the unitary 'subject' clearly apprehends, as an abstract, visual spectacle, the world of extended, material substance. In contrast, the senses of touch, taste, hearing and smell are demeaned as opaque and corporeal. This hierarchy of the senses duplicates itself in the hierarchical domination and control exerted by a detached, thinking 'subject' over the physical world of external, material 'objects'.

Against this hierarchical stratification of the senses, Gilles Deleuze discovers that the "multi-sensible" figures depicted in Francis Bacon's paintings express "a kind of original unity (synaesthesia) of the senses". In paintings such as *Three Studies of George Dyer*, (1966), and *Portrait of Isabel Rawsthorne*, (1966), this synaesthesia of the senses is expressed in Bacon's depiction of the human head disintegrating; where eyes, ears, nose and mouth seem to meld together into a polymorphous unity, and individual sense organs lose their specific functions and become mobile 'conductors' of bodily intensities and desiring flows. The head ceases to function as the 'face' or persona of an identifiable 'subject', and is depicted simply as an extension of the body. This non-hierarchical, polymorphously perverse body is a surface upon which desiring intensities flow, "an absolute outside that knows no selves because interior and exterior have fused".

The philosophy of Georg Wilhelm Friedrich Hegel represents nature as the 'alienation' and abject degradation of the Absolute Idea or Spirit. Hegel provides a lengthy and detailed description of the processes through which this Absolute Spirit externalises itself into the objects of the material world for the purpose of self-realisation, culminating in a climactic resolution to the perennial conflict between spirit and materiality, mind and body, subject and object. According to Hegel, the anatomical distinction between the sexes exemplifies a hierarchical principle privileging activity over passivity, and productive form over chaotic materiality. Hegel thus attaches considerable importance to the anatomical differences between the testicle, the ovary and the clitoris, with the female genitalia considered as an inside-out version of the male's: internalised, hidden and enclosed, rather than outward and exposed. A fact that represents for Hegel an interior-exterior barrier that determines the distinction between Being-For-Itself from Being-In-Itself; a distinction that corresponds to the difference between human, conscious existence and the existence of mere things. Nature (as female) is conceived as a lifeless, dispersed mode of existence awaiting the purposeful, projective activity of the (male) Spirit to bring it to fulfilment. A trace of the ancient conception of the active male principle as synonymous with the bone is expressed in Hegel's declaration: "The being of Spirit is a bone".

In *Anti-Oedipus*, Gilles Deleuze cites the transvestism of Freud's patient, Judge Schreber, as an alternative to this hierarchical dualism. The dichotomy and ensuing conflict between the active male principle, Spirit or Ideal Absolute, with the passive materiality of the corporeal world, is resolved at a crucial stage in Judge Schreber's psychoanalytic cure when Schreber "becomes reconciled to becoming-woman and embarks upon a process of self-cure that brings him back to the equation Nature = Production (the production of a new humanity)". It is a celebration of schizophrenia as "the process of the production of desire...............the process of production wherein Nature = Industry, Nature = History".

The philosopher Karl Marx, expressing his impatience with Hegelianism, declares philosophy to stand "in the same relation to the study of the actual world as onanism to sexual love". In his own words, he puts Hegel's philosophy "on its feet" by recognising that matter is the stuff of all existence and all mental and spiritual phenomena are its by-products. Henceforth, Hegel's externalisation of the Spirit is replaced with the notion of a progressive, historical development of the material forces of production; a history where the 'humanity' of "man's relation to nature" can be gauged by "the relation of man to woman".

For Marx, "The forming of the five senses is a labour of the entire history of the world". Accordingly, the naturalisation of humanity and the humanisation of nature - "of nature developing into man" - is commensurate with the replacement of the "crude eye" and the "crude ear" with the "human eye" and the "musical ear". It is the replacement of senses crudely instrumental with senses capable of purely disinterested, complex and aesthetic appreciation of a humanised nature's "beauty of form".

Marx's exploration of the 'anatomy' of society leads to his assertion of the determining role of the material, economic 'base' in shaping the cultural and ideological 'superstructure'. The economic base constitutes, as it were, the bones upon which the "drowsy flesh" of the cultural superstructure depends.

This connection of cultural forms to an underlying material, economic structure is further explored in the writings of the Marxist philosopher Antonio Gramsci. In a rather curious passage from *The Prison Notebooks*, Gramsci employs the female body as a metaphor to illustrate a more complex understanding of the relationship between base and superstructure against a Marxism that treats culture as simply an epiphenomenal reflex of the 'economic':

> We cannot say, with regard to the human body, that the skin (and the type of beauty prevalent at a particular time) is mere illusion and that the skeleton and anatomy are the sole reality; however, for a long time something similar has been maintained. Questioning the role of the anatomy and the functions of the skeleton does not mean claiming that men.......can live without them. Continuing the metaphor, we can say that it is not the skeleton (in the narrow sense) which makes one love a woman, but we understand how much the skeleton contributes to the grace of her movements, etc.

For Gilles Deleuze, paintings such as Francis Bacon's *Figure at a Wash Basin,* (1976), and *Lying figure with hypodermic syringe,* (1963), illustrate this complex relationship between the body and its supporting material structure, the flesh and the bone. In these paintings, "the bones elevate themselves above flesh..........from which the drowsy flesh seems to descend". According to Deleuze, this primacy of bone over flesh "is specific to Bacon and differentiates him from both Rembrandt and Soutine".

For example, in Chaim Soutine's paintings, such as *Woman in Pink* and *Woman in Red,* the bones are dissolved into the flesh. In *Praying Man,* (1921), Soutine's neglect of the material element is taken even further: the clothing on the Figure erases the presence of both bone structure and flesh. If we designate Francis Bacon, with his emphasis on the determining role of bone structure in the articulation of the Figure, as a materialist, then we may define Soutine, with his neglect of the role of the material element and his concentration on the outward, surface appearances of flesh tone and clothing, as a philosophical Idealist. It is a view supported by the art historian Alfred Werner, who writes:

> As elsewhere in Soutine's work, bone structure, flesh, muscles are obliterated by the clothing; this, too, might be related to the attitude of the Ghetto Jew, who often treated everything strictly corporeal as unimportant and even irritating, and put the stress on the immaterial, the intellectual, the spiritual.

Francis Bacon's *Triptych: Studies from the Human Body,* (1970), exemplifies Deleuze's celebration of the 'body without organs': a body disorganised, "smooth, slippery, opaque", existing as an uninterrupted flow "of amorphous, undifferentiated fluid". The Figure in Bacon's study conforms to Deleuze's description of the body without organs as a 'desiring machine': a bodily plexus of libidinal flows - "thrusts and pulsions" - spasmodically seeking out new connections and new lines of escape, within the confines of the circular expanse of colour that constitutes the Figure's supporting material structure. The Figure "spreads itself out along the entire circumference of the circle, the centre of which has been abandoned by the ego".

Freud discusses the formation of the sense of self, of the 'ego', and the separation of the ego (subject) from the external world (object), as a process whereby:

> Objects presenting themselves, in so far as they are sources of pleasure, are absorbed by the ego into itself, 'introjected'.........while, on the other hand, the ego thrusts forth upon the external world whatever within itself gives rise to pain (the mechanism of projection).

The ego is "first and foremost a bodily ego". Accordingly, our 'highest' thoughts are linked to corporeal sensations entwined with infantile phantasies of incorporation, ejection and penetration. It is a theme that has been developed by the Kleinian school of psychoanalysis:

> Owing to these mechanisms (of introjection and projection) the infant's object can be defined as what is inside or outside his own body, but even while outside, it is still part of himself, since 'outside' results from being ejected, 'spat out': thus the body boundaries are blurred. This might also be put the other way round: because the object outside the body is 'spat out', and still relates to the infant's body, there is no sharp distinction between his body and what is outside.

For Deleuze, the figures that move rhythmically and amoeba-like across the surface of Bacon's canvases, experience their bodies and external objects as "'accumulated' or 'coagulated' sensation". As crystallisations of desiring sensation, things appear as 'subjective' (inside) or 'objective' (outside) in accordance with whether they are attracted to or repulsed from the body.

In *Anti-Oedipus,* Deleuze goes on to describe how 'mental' phenomena differ from 'physical' ones only inasmuch as the latter are produced collectively ("the social production of reality"), while the former are produced by individuals ("desiring-production"). As sensation, the 'stuff' of mental and physical phenomena are identical; there is no fixed space of interiority or 'subjectivity', only the provisional discordance between the desiring-production ('phantasy') of individual desiring machines, and the social production ('reality') of technical and social machines.

In each of the three panels that compose Francis Bacon's *Triptych* (1973), a single Figure is reproduced. The individual panels possess distinctive environments, and individually compose the fluid body of the Figure into shapes and forms specific to these environments. The reproduced Figure appears isolated and disconnected from its replicas in each of the other panels. This has the disturbing effect, for the viewer, of breaking down the continuity of the 'narrative' that the triptych is traditionally designed to recount. Thus the notion of a unified ego, or 'subject', possessing clearly defined boundaries, a secure foundation, and a fixed identity, is brought into question.

The Figure portrayed in the three, disjointed panels of *Triptych*, is no longer a single entity, but three: a multiple effect of the environments that capture and mould it, and of which it forms an integral part. The traditional notion of the individual as a unitary subject with a fixed essence and origin, the cause of a narrative, sequential unfolding of events, is lost. This fragmentation of the individual into a multiplicity of subjectivities, accords with Deleuze's definition of the liberated 'schizo-subject':

> With no fixed identity, forever decentred, *defined* by the states through which it passes..........born of each state in the series.........continually reborn of the following state that determines him at a given moment, consuming-consummating all these states that cause him to be born and reborn (the lived state coming first, in relation to the subject that lives it).

Against the dualism of Western thought, with its propensity to establish hierarchical oppositions between fixed terms, is the attitude of the schizophrenic, as recorded in the pages of *Anti-Oedipus*:

> Whereas the "either/or" claims to mark decisive choices between immutable terms (the alternative: either this or that), the schizophrenic "either . . . or . . . or" refers to the system of possible permutations between differences that always amount to the same as they shift and slide about.

A schizophrenia that amounts to a rejection of philosophical binaries, replacing the dualistic model with a pluralistic and polyvocal account of experience that is not closed and hierarchical, but inclusive of a multiplicity of differing terms and distinctions that fluctuate in accordance with contextual shifts and the play of chance. A disjunctive synthesis between desiring-production and social production, Figure and Structure. A synthesis that never resolves itself into a static unity, but is forever breaking down, unleashing libidinal flows, fluxes, intensities and becomings, perpetually at odds with "the dualisms that are the enemy, an entirely necessary enemy, the furniture we are forever rearranging". Exemplified in Francis Bacon's *Crucifixion,* (1965), where the meat on the sacrificial body is presented as "that state of the body in which the flesh and the bones come to a local confrontation instead of composing themselves into a structure."

# Collapsing Neu-organs Einstürzende Neubauten And The Body Without Organs

by Robert Lort

Einstürzende Neubauten (Blixa Bargeld, F.M. Einheit (Mufti), Andrew Chudy (N.U. Unruh), Alexander Hacke and Mark Chung, the title of the group translates as "collapsing new buildings") know nothing of compromise, nothing of aesthetic conventions, nothing of correctness; they understand the condition all too well. A band which has no influences, that takes their instruments of scrap sheet metal, pipes, jack hammers, angle grinders, drills, springs, air conditioning ducts, shopping trolleys and water towers.... to the most extreme anguished and intensified sounds. They know nothing of limit, wall or of barrier, they themselves show no restraint, in the forming of their deliberately unstructured, actionist musical forms. Einstürzende Neubauten push everything to the limit, the boundaries simply crumble and then vanish. For them there is no restriction, no limit, a band that exceeds beyond belief, beyond all the boundaries.

Einstürzende Neubauten appear on the horizon like a feverish volcano, a force pulverising and pounding against the earth's crust, collapsing and crumbling all the fragile and unstable conventions, tearing down all the pedestals. Their assaults of cathartic aggression are breathtaking relentlessness, the sounds crashing and atomising against your ears. The volcano approaches - blackening, smothering and asphyxiating - disgorging and spilling everything out of its viscous sound inferno. Its energy flows as from a giant carcass, horrifying, and imminent. Einstürzende Neubauten are a sublime work from the burnt and inflamed soul, the denudated ruin, truly the ineffaceable and unexceedable.

Always the question: how to diffract the sound, how to deterritorialize? How to connecting things up in new ways, to constitute new sonic spaces, terrains and territories, to activate the spaces between the connections. Einstürzende Neubauten have continued the diffraction of music's grammaticality, its notational structure of ordered signs and symbols, its measured timing, by finding the spaces between the notes, the fissures and accelerations between the keys on a keyboard; the spaces outside, those of silence and deafening noise, the rhythm created by sliding from one position to another, the shattering burst of "inbetween". Linear timing is splintered and stammered through bursts, accelerations, movements of chaos and discontinuity. It is rhizome music, composed entirely of intersections of speeds and slowness, movement and rest, duration and intensity. It has neither beginning nor end, it exists for the moment, unrepeatable, it is never the same again. It exists in contrast to signifiances and virtuosity, to linearity and permanence, where each sequence is always determined in relation to the preceding.

Keine Schönheit ohne Gefahr No beauty without danger

The body of Einstürzende Neubauten's work is a planar expanse of ruins, of guttered and collapsed structures, of flattened hierarchies. They state their objective as a process of stretching music out until everything is music, a practice of expanding the territory of music until an outside no longer remains, until there is no longer an extremity containing the excluded and unincorporated. To reach a plateau where the statements "everything is music" and "there is no music" combine to mean the same thing. The strategy is one of desertification. It is breadth, and not height that interest Einstürzende Neubauten. It is the plane of variable and de-hierarchized forms that are of interest, in contrast to fixed centres of vertical and valorised forms.

What began with initial experiments in atonal music forms in the early eighties have feigned, 20 years later a whole new music category, that of industrial music, but Einstürzende Neubauten do not stop here, they do not settle into a predictable terrain or established principle, but instead continue to diversify, extrapolating and trajecting onto still unexplored strata, still avoiding categorisation as simply "industrial". A categorisation which is now divested of its own virulent beginnings. Einstürzende Neubauten chose to continually traverse outwards, never settling or concluding their radical engagement with the rupturing of sound. They ceaselessly find more strata to take apart. In their more recent releases, what has attained greater dominance has been music-assemblages of sand, stone, fire, obscure electronic resonances, flowing liquids, chugging machines, silences, memory-mantras and rumbling vocalisations. In their theatrical production of Goethe's *Faust* it was music-machines of books, furniture, and giant guitars. From whatever is discarded and abandoned, they locate within it an individuated plateau of poetics, shrill harmonics and chromatics. Einstürzende Neubauten exemplify the development of an art constituted as uncontrolled, as dangerous and as a process of expanding towards untrammelled infectious desire. The connections, both lyrical and musical, are continually altered by spontaneous interruptions, employing elements of chance divergence and augmentations engendering contrast and difference.

For Einstürzende Neubauten construction is enabled by means of *Kollaps*. Through the collapse, the segments are dislodged and detached from the fixed centres, the sound segments are dismantled and demolished, disembowelled from the body so that they can move and traverse over an external field, a body without organs. With each collapse the pieces fragment into yet smaller and smaller imperceptible units, it is the construction of nothing but space, the sound of chaos. The particles scatter into the darkness, ricocheting off one another, bellowing and bursting, in cacophonous flight. Everywhere disconnected fluxes spin off from the harder fragments, deterritorializing shards fly off from the rigid strata, and enter new spaces. No form is incessant or final, no walls are remade, that are not subsequently demolished. The process is characterised by modes of synthesis, arrangement and selection, that maintain ephemeral and multitudinous directions. Each collapse leads in another direction, each disassemblage multiplies the fragments and broadens the territory. Einstürzende Neubauten proceed by detaching found objects (drills, hammers, angle grinders, walls, stones, furniture) from their dominant modes of utility and connectivity, to engender previously unfound enunciations, breaking objects from their territories and pushing them into fields of sonority and variance. So that the objects effectively cross a threshold, escaping from their singularised actuality or essence, to traverse heterogeneous spaces - intensities of alterity, machinic multiplicities.

Music emerges from among the strongest forces of deterritorialization, which causes the line of flight in music to always encounter, "the danger of veering toward destruction, toward abolition." The ruination that seems to assimilate itself into the work of Einstürzende Neubauten seems a direct result of these intensities embodied in music. The overdriven fury of some of their performances, which have on occasion escalated into setting stages on fire during performances, seems to emerge from the release of these forces of deterritorialization, that turn music into a war-machine. Einstürzende Neubauten seem to embrace exactly what Deleuze and Guattari have in mind when they say, "Music has a thirst for destruction, every kind of destruction, extinction, breakage, dislocation."[1]

What sets Einstürzende Neubauten out from all of their contemporaries is that Einstürzende Neubauten are quite simply unashamed to venture into madness, to be outsiders, to be anomalous. These aspects are most lucidly represented in songs such as *Hören mit Schmerzen* (Listen with Pain), *Tanz Debil* (Dance of mental illness), *Sehnsucht* (Longing) and *Armenia*. The lyrics to *Sehnsucht* speak of the energy, *die Sucht* (addiction) that Einstürzende Neubauten have:

Sehnsucht
Sehnsucht kommt aus dem Chaos
Sehnsucht ist die einzige Energie
Meine Sehnsucht
Meine Sucht
Sehnsucht ist die einzige Energie
Chaos => Sehnsucht/Energie[2]

Longing
Longing comes out of chaos
Longing is the only energy
My longing
My addiction
Longing is the only energy
Chaos => longing/energy

"Sehnsucht", is normally translated as "longing", but it is translated, somewhat suggestively by Blixa Bargeld himself, as "addicted to desire"[3]. It is revealed that Sehnsucht was written at night, under a shower with a fever, "every word like lead"[4]. This "Sehnsucht", is not merely an addiction, it is fervent intensities, a body addicted to desire. It is desire for an energy that is assembled in chaos, that breathes between centres, swallowed by thirsty abstract particles, composed from desiring-machines. It is found:

| | |
|---|---|
| zwischen Mikrophon und Makrokosmos... | between microphone and macrocosm... |
| zwischen Plankton und Philosophie... | between plankton and philosophia... |
| zwischen c" und vitamin C... | between [high] c and vitamin c... |

- a random selection of lines from Einstürzende Neubauten's *Die Interimsliebenden* (The Interimlovers).

What emerges is a deterriorialized body of sound that has abandoned fixed coordinates, linear measure and regular arrangements. A flux is released from the body that follows a line of flight, towards abolition, ejaculation, implosion, Bavarian bees, black holes, library music, becoming-animal. The atomisation of sound into micro-vibrations, micro-chromatics and micro-durations, brings about the ecstatic convergence of the atomic and the cosmic. Ejected from the body without organs is an eviscerated sonority; to not play, not eat, not sleep... to be no part of it (*kein Bestandteil sein*). The scream folds back and becomes a black hole through which the body escapes on its line of flight.

| | |
|---|---|
| Wir reissen die entzündeten Organe aus | We rip the inflamed organs out |
| Körper ohne Organe[5] | Body without Organs |

The introduction of *Zebulon* offers us:

| | |
|---|---|
| Lass meine Mitte deine Achse sein<br>um die dein Leib sich windet<br>Lass dein Mitte meine Achse sein<br>um die dein Leib sich windet | Let my centre be your axis<br>around which your body turns<br>let your centre be my axis<br>around which your body turns |

The orbiting motion recalls Nietzsche's eternal return, as it facilitates a divergence, the eternal return that can lead to difference and diversity, the mechanism that enables becomings. The introduction makes us aware that a transfiguration is taking place, an exchange between a feminine axis and a masculine axis, a masculine axis that is becoming-woman. The concept of the decentred subjectivity appears also in *Fiat Lux*:

| | |
|---|---|
| Inmitten meiner Kreise<br>doch deren Mitte bin ich nicht | In the middle of my circles<br>but their centre I am not |

The Nietzschian *Halber Mensch* (Half Man), begins a search for another half, but it is a search not out of lack, not even to become whole, but to become unwhole. To find that doorway or threshold into chaos. To snap off all the transmitters and wires, the organs and veins that truss and fasten the body, restricting and fettering all the becomings, that could occur, that might transform our subjectivity; becoming animal, chrysanthemum, stone, hospitalised child or a lizard that lives in fire (Salamander). The deconditioned body as Einstürzende Neubauten see it, is a fluid amorphous structure. Such a body is comprised of a spaghetti-DNA, a central nervous system that dances, it has nine arms.

Possibly the only just comparison to the scream that opens Einstürzende Neubauten's *Armenia*, is Antonin Artaud's squelling caterwaul in the French radio broadcast of *Pour en finir avec le jugement de dieu* (To Have Done with the Judgement of God). In this regard, Einstürzende Neubauten's work between music and theatre is highly relevant to their line of flight from contemporary music, the most significant works being *Die Hamletmaschine* (with Heiner Müller) and *Faustmusik* (with Werner Schwab) others include *Andi* (with Peter Zadek) and a raudy midnight theatrical procession along the Vienna ring-road *Das Auge des Taifun* (The Eye of the Typhoon) (with Heiner Müller) from which emerged the original version of *Headcleaner*. The song *Sie* (She) from *Tabula Rasa* even includes theatrical directions. Between music and dance they have worked with the ballet troupe La La La Human Steps, from which several songs have emerged. Their work with the Japanese butoh troupe Byakko Sha formed part of the music-video/documentary *Halber Mensch*. It re-enacts their earlier impulsions for colliding and beating their own bodies and implements (drills and hammers), against the walls and floor of the performance space. An attempt at literally breaking down the segregations and walls between the performance space, the audience and the outside. A desire to adjoin the music space with this outside. At numerous live performances, audiences have been known to join in as performers. The intent is similar to the way that Antonin Artaud connected theatre up with an outside - an a-signifying noise or expressivity that entirely evades the signifier, the brut noise of gesticulation. This evasion of the signifier facilitates the continuous rewritings and reassemblings that they introduce to their songs, enabling each songs evolution through unending and spontaneous mutations and variations that occur with each performance.

The achievements of Einstürzende Neubauten only too well demonstrate the senselessness of reliance on musical notation. It is quite evident that it appears near impossible to transcribe their productions into the conventional signifying codes of musical notation. For Einstürzende Neubauten the sound is always positioned outside the signifier, in an unpositioned space. "Der Mund ist die Wunde des Alphabets,"[6] (The mouth is the wound of the alphabet), the signifier will only be a wound, that expresses redundancies, unless it is made vertiginous, made to stammer[7].

It should not be surprising to find astronomy listed as one of the three thematic metaphors used by Einstürzende Neubauten, the remaining two being fire and biology.

Astronomy constantly demands the rupturing of time and space as linear entities. *Die Explosion im Festspielhaus* from *Ende Neu* offers this example:

| | |
|---|---|
| Aberjahrmilliardenwirbel | Endless trillions of years of spin |
| Myriaden Wonnefeur | myriads of fiery rapture |
| heraus- | hurled out hurled in |
| hineingeschleudert | Milky Way cum shot |
| Milchstrassencumshot | lava flow ejaculation |
| Lavastromejakulat | |

This astronomical theme originates in pieces as early as, *Kalte Sterne* (Cold Stars) to *Letztes Biest (am Himmel)* (Last Beast (in the Sky)) and to the more recent, *Total Eclipse Of The Sun*, *Beauty* and *In Circles*. The fascination with astronomy, with its orbits, pulses, stretched time and multi-dimensions, is one that also captures the great father of electronic music and tape cutting, Karlheinz Stockhausen, who originated his own "star music". It was the premiere of Varèse's *Déserts* (Deserts) (1951/54) (with Stockhausen as tape operator) which first brought about the eruption of noise with its inclusion of recorded sounds from factories and foundries. On *Tabula Rasa*, Einstürzende Neubauten respond with their own *Wüste* (Desert) inspired from a concert in the American desert, complete with burning oil and sand.

Always the question what remains? (was bleibt?/was ist übrig?). Each time, after all the strata have been shattered new reverberations, decaying, whispering and gravitation are revealed. After having ripped off layer-by-layer the indestructible core of oneself is laid open and exposed, but yet still unapproachable for infinite more layers, becoming-imperceptible. In *Redukt* the organs are discarded like a needless encumbrance weighing us down like lead, pegging us to the ground. It seeks to find where the elusive "I" is located within the DNA.

| | |
|---|---|
| Bin ich, ist Ich in jeder Zelle? | Am I, is me in every cell? |
| Wohl kaum ist „Ich" die | Though hardly "I" is the |
| Summe des genetischen | sum of the genetic |
| Materials... | material... |
| Gibt es Überflüssiges oder | Is there anything redundant, |
| Festgewordenes... | solidified... |
| das sich abwerfen lässt wie | that can be discarded like |
| Ballast, wie Sandsäcke aus | ballast, sandbags out of a |
| einem Freiballon? | free balloon? |

In the womb of Einstürzende Neubauten the machines of desire are constantly laid bare, like a fulminating factory, constantly bursting and colliding, brimming with the anomalous, falling out of orbit, a wounded song, a shooting star, a scorched sense, une dent-de-lionion (dandelion).

---

Notes

1. Gilles Deleuze and Felix Guattari, *A Thousand Plateaus Capitalism and Schizophrenia*, Minneapolis, University of Minnesota Press, 1987, p. 299
2. Blixa Bargeld, *Stimme frisst Feuer* p. 44. There are several different versions of Sehnsucht, two appear on the live 2*4, an early version is on *Kollaps* (Collapse) and another on *Halber Mensch* (Half Man)
3. ibid p. 81
4. ibid p. 81 *Halber Mensch* was also written in this condition.
5. ibid p. 26 *Meningitis*
6. ibid p. 62, see also *Blutvergiftung* (Blood Poisoning)
7. To stammer not in one's speech, but in one's language, to be a foreigner in one's own language. Deleuze describes Godard, Kafka, Beckett and others as stutterers in their own language systems. They develop an unevenness and a brokenness in language that stammers. A prominent illustration of this stammering from Einstürzende Neubauten is the expression, "Ich steck' dich an", appearing in *Vanadium-I-Ching*, which means simultaneously "I inflame you" and "I infect you". One must also mention their multi-lingual capacity - "I want to

mix German, English and Latin just as none of these language was my language." (sic) (Blixa Bargeld in Andrea Cangioli (ed), *Einstürzende Neubauten*)

References

Blixa Bargeld, *Stimme frisst Feuer*, Berlin, Merve Verlag, 1988

Blixa Bargeld, *Headcleaner, Text für Einstürzende Neubauten - Text for Collapsing New Buildings*, Maria Zinfert (ed), Berlin, Die Gestalten Verlag, 1997, German/English

Klaus Maeck, *Hör Mit Schmerzen (Listen with Pain), Einstürzende Neubauten 1980 - 1996*, Berlin, Die Gestalten Verlag, 1996, German/English

Andrea Cangioli (ed), *Einstürzende Neubauten*, Stampa Alternativa/Nuovi Equilibri, Collana Sconcerto, Prima Edizione Gennaio, 1993, Italian/English

Audio Visual References

Sogo Ishi, *Halber Mensch* (Half Man)

Paulus Manker, *Das Auge des Taifun* (The Eye of the Typoon)

Klaus Maeck & Johanna Schenkel, *Liebenslieder* (Lovesongs)

Uli M Schppel, *Der Platz*

Hubertus Siegert, *Berlin Babylon*

Birgit Herdlitschke and Christian Beetz, *Einstuerzende Neubauten: listen with pain*

# The Space of Absence in the Music of Giya Kancheli

by Dylan Trigg

Long renowned as his greatest film, Andrei Tarkovsky's *Stalker* (1979) is a visceral illustration of the relationship between intimacy and estrangement. This is immediately evident when we consider The Zone, Tarkovsky's metaphysical centrepiece of the film. Tarkovsky's prophetic vision of a post-industrial wasteland littered with the remains of relics from an absent space was later realized by the fallout of Pripyat, the abandoned city on the fringes of Chernobyl. Like Pripyat, The Zone is a space marked by lost presence and arrested decay. In each space, the human desire to be orientated is disarmed by radical ambiguity that carries with it a particular aesthetic experience.

As an illustration of absent space, Tarkovsky's *Stalker* is a paradigm. Alongside Tarkovsky, this relation between intimacy and alienation is realized in musical silence. Consider how the possibility of suspending and distorting time is possible through the medium of music. Composers have long sought to meditate passages between absence and presence. Indeed, the dynamic is itself a leitmotif, which induces feelings of either solemn profundity or garish discomfort. One of the reasons why Bruckner's oeuvre, for example, is either loved or loathed is because it relies so earnestly upon an escalating structure, in which the human becomes "spiritual." What is dated in Bruckner, therefore, is a spiritual aspiration toward anonymity and absence.

Today, Bruckner's spiritual epistles have been outmoded by the work of Giya Kancheli. Giya Kancheli is a Georgian composer whose musical landscape derives from a world that unfolds alongside the fall of the Soviet Union. The gradual fall of the Soviet Union and the rise of *glasnost* enabled Kancheli to confer titles upon his work that hitherto had seemed overly political: *Bright Sorrow, Mourned by the Wind, Life Without Christmas*. Though, rather than being of a political content alone, the potency of Kancheli's resides in its existential expression: the political *becomes* the existential and in turns sounds the voice of revolt, anguish, and loss. Symbolism then - the clothing of the idea in a visible form - becomes the means through which the Soviet composer was forced to communicate. Indeed, during the height of censorship, such was the language of Soviet music that to misunderstand the inherent symbolism within the music would be to omit the music itself.

We are, of course, in an age where symbolism is no longer needed. Generally, the artist is able to reproach his land in an explicit manner without fear of retribution. In a post-Soviet era, musicians of a once oppressed land are thus now finding their poetic fruition through means of contemplation, reverie, and nostalgic lamentation. This is perfectly pronounced in the works of, amongst others, Schnittke, Silvestrov, Artyomov, and Gubaidulina. In Kancheli, the sense of lamentation, both for a land torn by oppression and for the exile this entails, reaches an apotheosises. But Kancheli's appeal is not limited to space and time. The composer's music is understood best, not necessarily from within the context that it derives from, but as a permanent structure of consciousness itself. About this timelessness, Schnittke writes of Kancheli thus: "In the relatively short period of 20-30 minutes of slow music, we experience a whole lifetime, an entire history; at the same time, the drag of time is absent - we glide high over centuries as if in an aircraft, with no sensation of speed."

As Schnittke indicates, central to the logic of Kancheli's music is the disembodiment of time. From this disruption, silence and presence conspire, producing a vastness parallel to Tarkovsky. Even in the early compositions, the vacillating polarities between presence and absence, which would later adopt the form of an explicit *dynamic stasis* consisting of abrupt orchestral attacks preceded by mournful silence, are implicitly announced. In the case of Symphony Three (1973), then we are already in a tonal landscape which alters violently between the stampede of feet and wordless chants sung by the Georgian singer, Gamlet Gonashvili. The silence emerges in the space in-between, in the occasion where the march gives rise to an absence, whose intimacy is suspended by the presence of the voice. That the Third Symphony was composed in 1973 whilst Kancheli was still in residence in his teaching post at the Tbilisi Conservatory, is perhaps indicative of its symbolic content. We are never entirely sure quite what the respite in sound conveys, or, what the subsequent outbursts allude to.

The Third Symphony ends with a protracted coda, a reluctance to dissolve. At the same time, this dissolution is counterbalanced by tenderness toward loss. The loss is thus purgative and mournful concurrently. In this way, the silence becomes mediated by the musical landscape that preceded it. Every instant of presence is also an instance of absence. Such a landscape is the ground in which Kancheli's music is rooted. His is a music that dwells in the space in-between: between memory, between place, and between time. Fundamentally interstitial in character, his music disarms boundaries and leaves the listener both disorientated and drained.

Kancheli's compositions frequently lean toward memories that have their place in the home. Because of this attachment to home, a logic of disruption runs throughout his work. In the case of his especially pessimistic Fifth Symphony (1976), then the role of the negative is brought to a visceral climax. Contrasting childlike passages on the harpsichord with sharp glissando passages on the strings, the impression is of lost purity, an absence of hope, and a retreat into a resigned fatalism: short-lived passages that endeavour to ground themselves in harmony, wistful passages raped by the shriek of self-consciousness. Even more explicit than in the Third Symphony is the implosive desire to unite both hope and failure. The dejection of hope is contrasted perfectly by the volatile oscillations between semi-baroque passages that lead only to discordance and strife. Here, the aesthetic underpinnings of Kancheli lend themselves to an ethereal disharmony that is only possible within the landscape of the familiar. Like both Max Klinger and Alfred Kubin before him, Kancheli takes full advantage of placing common objects in unfamiliar contexts, in turn producing an uncanny sorrow that plays on both the nostalgic and the melancholy. It is only when the listener is close enough to perceive the perversity in the composition, that its otherworldly disjunction becomes wholly apparent.

There is a further disjunction in architectural terms between the Classical formalism of Kancheli's compositions and the absent space in which they inhabit. The use of tonality and overt structure establish a context in which objects can be freely displaced or otherwise distorted. It is an architecture that is entirely recognizable in its form and yet lacks the detail which renders it homely. Like the paintings of de Chirico, Kancheli lingers in a period that verges on dusk without actually succumbing to it, and as such protracts itself upon its own demise. We hear rustles, distant voices murmuring, the furrowing of pages, the dirge of movement, silence paraded like a funereal parade bloated in its own grief. The dark territory of Kancheli, which reaches its summit in his Sixth Symphony (1981), is founded in this emergence from the negative, from the space in-between - that is, as the absent aesthetic.

In replacing the positive with the negative, Kancheli's music frequently slides into pessimism. Pessimistic because the objectivity of absolute value is reduced to an artifice that at best attains the momentary transience of a subjective claim. The stance of pessimism does not preclude nostalgia, and if anything serves to prolong a sense of nostalgia which is founded in a space still flourishing with the chime of hope. The recourse to a single boys voice in the conclusion of his *Life Without Christmas* cycle (1990-94), acts as a refrain which serves to remind us of a hope that is never realized; it is a voice that is hinted but never fully comes into fruition, as such induces a dynamic of thwarted hope. Likewise, the kitsch passages of *Trauerfarbenes Land* (1994) that are violated by fortissimo claps on the orchestra, suggest a reluctant nostalgia framed by the disparities between progression and regression. It is as though the nostalgic is defaced by the guise of the kitsch, and so must be annihilated in order to craft a space of production.

Returning to the spectacularly bleak Sixth Symphony, these elements of nihilism, pessimism, and absence unite in a eruption of grief, resignation and scorn. The complexity inherent in the Sixth Symphony owes itself to a distortion of form rather than a perversion of content. Indeed, in its sense of tonality and convention, there is something entirely conservative about the Sixth Symphony. Already in the Prelude, Kancheli has established a background in which silence becomes the form through which the slightest nuance of sound emanates symbolically against a plaintive backdrop. There is a motionlessness that is both mournful and nostalgic. The two viola players, each concealed behind a screen at the composers request, mimic the drone of a Georgian *chianuri*. An absence of movement, an absence of sound, the occasional flicker of the harp ascending a semi-tone: the evocation of subdued grief, each note seeking to dive deeper than its predecessor, is suddenly ruptured by the downward attack of the orchestra. The attack is so terse that when the violas reappear it as though nothing has changed. Henceforth, the aspiration towards ascent is gradually thwarted by the increasingly frequent staccato attacks of the orchestra, each of which nostalgically recollects what was previously destroyed. It is as though Kancheli is trying to establish his home in the space of absence, as though the emptiness is the conditions under which hope can flourish, Rilke:

*"Don't you know yet? Fling the emptiness out of your arms*
*into the spaces we breathe; perhaps the birds*
*will feel the expanded air with more passionate flying."*

The expanded air in Rilke's poem re-emerges in Kancheli as the negative space in which the composer seeks to dwell despite the onslaught of orchestral violence and splintered aspirations. The overwhelming absence of Rilke's poetry, its unremitting longing, finds it sonic counterpart in these passages of Kancheli that seek to convert the negative into the positive, each of which relies upon the other for its existence. Likewise, in Stalker the distorted trinity consisting of the Writer, the Professor, and the Stalker himself, forms a dialectic in which each aspect of negation reflects upon the other to produce a synthesis that is both positive and united. If we treat the Stalker as an impassioned Christ like figure who reproaches his motivations and desires, and as such is reduced to the martyr incapable of appeasing the ego, then we can equally correlate this figure to the childlike passages of Kancheli which seem self-consciously aware of their pious naivety. The Writer meanwhile, would seem to suggest the voice of experience: disillusioned and cynical, he reciprocates the Stalker's piety in a manner that only rejects his desire for salvation amongst the ruins. As an intercession between these polarities of 'surrender and abandonment', the Professor embodies the ethical stance, the self-reflective voice of morality that seeks to reason, by way of a formal narrative, the bridge between despair and hope. In the scene where the three figure travel to the Zone by cart, then despite (or perhaps because of) the persistence of silence, this disparate trinity seems to reconcile in an affirmation of negation and hope, as though the dynamic stasis between silence and violence is necessarily dependent upon the other for their endurance.

We might well hope to find some firm reconciliation between the polarities of grief and hope, as though by way of a Socratic dialogue the glimmer of truth might emerge. Turning to the composer, writer, or artist, then we expect to be pushed in the direction of truth, of eventual clarity. An austere truth, but truth nevertheless. It is perhaps our final aspiration to be at home, whether it is in the space of absence or amongst the façade of presence. Such things are no doubt reproduced aesthetically and in terms of architectural form. How to learn from the space that has already been perverted by experience? This is a question which is as important as it is absurd. Yet despite our discomfort with torn landscapes we nevertheless persist in revisiting them as one might pay homage to a habit forsaken through conformity. In the same way, there is no space more alive, more foaming with truth, beauty, and vulgarity, than an empty space. Civility would increase were we establish homes in the space that no longer exists.

Kancheli, all too familiar with the potency of the distant, relies upon passages the evokes this theme. Bachelard writes: "Immensity is within ourselves. It is attached to a sort of expansion of being that life curbs and caution arrests, but which starts again when we are alone. As soon as we become motionless, we are elsewhere we are dreaming in a world that is immense." In the *Exil* cycle from Kancheli's recent ECM series, the frozen architecture between viola and soprano permits an immensity that is founded in both inertia and nostalgia. It proceeds to modulate nowhere whilst forever pointing to an elsewhere, a space that no longer is present.

Immensity, as Bachelard says, is always of an interior experience. Turning to a well known poem of Baudelaire's, *Le Cygne,* this abstract notion of self-vacuity is illuminated. The contrast between the land in which we inhabit and the space that is no longer, arouses a sense of impossible yearning through which no materiality can abate. In the case of Baudelaire, the impossible object of yearning is Paris itself.

*"The old Paris is gone (the form a city takes*
*More quickly shifts, alas, then does the mortal heart);*

*I picture in my head the busy camp of huts,*
*And heaps of rough-hewn columns, capitals and shafts,*
*The grass, the giant blocks made green by puddle-stain,*
*Reflected in the glaze, the jumbled bric-à-brac."*

What is notable about this excerpt from Baudelaire is the melancholy of detail, the mutable quality of the background: whilst the foreground seems engaged in progression and movement, it is amongst the alcoves of the forgettable that the essential emerges. And yet, what is profoundly intoxicating about the loss of a space is the inconsistency with which we react to such a bereavement - the mere transfiguration of time is neither absolute nor devoid of indifference As such, the possibility of returning to a space that accords itself with our own interior experience is an exception:

*"Paris may change, but in my melancholy mood*
*Nothing has budged! New palaces, blocks, scaffoldings,*
*Old neighbourhoods, are allegorical for me,*
*And my dear memories are heaver than stone."*

For Kancheli, homecoming marks a refusal to concede to the dissolution of time and a lament in the face of a frayed world. Nothing has changed, and yet nothing is present. The memento mori that emerges as the leitmotif in his *Vom Winde beweint* (Mourned by the Wind) (1984), fulfils the role of establishing a dissonant tonality that thwarts any subsequent aspiration to resolve itself. Aesthetically, the inertia of the viola implicates the fragility of life amongst ruin. Tentatively and without wishing to extinguish itself, the inhalations increase until there is almost a sense of catharsis, a renewal of courage against the memento mori of loss. The heavy air of Baudelaire's Paris hangs down upon Kancheli's Liturgy in resigned unison. It is a heaving sigh, repressed but violent, that every exile finds upon returning to his homeland. And suddenly, in the space of the elsewhere, the accelerated stagnation of time induces an immensity that is framed by an architecture that reveals a familiar form countered by a otherworldly content. Nowhere is this immense motionless more apparent than in the opening bars of Kancheli's *Vom Winde beweint*.

Kancheli's music disorientates the listener, presents an opaque disjunction between the conventions of tonality and the absolute refusal to submit to abstraction. Even so, like the archetype of Prometheus upon his rock, at points in time we are able to recognize ourselves in the face of the unknown. Certain historic figures reveal the shape of consciousness in a way that can only be articulated through violence or art, and when art and violence unite then the shape of this consciousness is able to rendered from afar, that is, as an object. Aesthetically, the space of absence has found its objectified essence through the music of Giya Kancheli. It is, to be sure, an essence that is as true as it is immense.

# Giya Kancheli and the Aesthetics of Nostalgia

by Dylan Trigg

*"Music is swansong"*

(Nietzsche)

The fate of the nostalgic is bleak. Longing for a space that no longer exists, he exerts his passion despite inevitable disappointment. Unable to dismiss the possibility of return, there arises an impossible impasse between desire and absence. As such, nostalgia is both alluring and terrifying. On the one hand, we allow ourselves, by way of reverie, to be transported to a space in which the familiar resides over the unfamiliar and hence enforces the impression of being at home; on the other hand, such an illusion only affirms the impossibility of ever returning to that space permanently.

Deriving from the Greek *nostos* 'to return home' and *algos* meaning pain, the term nostalgia was coined by a 17th Century Swiss medical student Johannes Hofer, who in his dissertation referring to Swiss mercenaries displaced from their mountainous homes, described it as homesickness to the point of pathology. He writes "a continuous vibration of animal spirits through those fibres of the middle brain in which the impressed traces of the idea of the Fatherland still cling."[1] Such was the danger of nostalgia, that Swiss soldiers were advised to avoid the sounds of cowbells and alpine melodies lest they were remained of their displaced home. To the purely physical diagnosis of nostalgia, the antidote of homecoming, or at least the promise of it, was thus an actuality attainable both in space and time. When in the late 18th and early 19th Century as the Romantic taste for subjective reflection supplanted the austere order of the Enlightenment's beacon of reason, so nostalgia changed its form. Through a displacement founded in both aesthetic and political taste, the exteriority of the Swiss mercenaries later became internalised as something inherent to the self. Accordingly, with the advent of Freudian psychoanalysis nostalgia became synonymous with regression, a craving for home that was thus indistinguishable from the desire for parental supervision. By post 1945, any such remedy for nostalgia prescribed by a prodigal 'homecoming' seemed at best an amiable whisper of speculation and at worst a vile echo of nationalism.

Despite the associations of nationalism, Postmodern pastiche, or regressive cravings, the desire towards the nostalgic gaze has not been abated. We are a nostalgic culture. When a society is in the throes of decline, then there arises a yearning for an elsewhere, a space that no longer exists and as such can be infused with aspirations that are immune to the taint of experience. We see this implicit sense of *Weltschmerz* politically, ethically and above all else aesthetically. The torture of the mind seeking to return to a time now dissolved whilst the body remains spatially fixed, is at the heart of this aesthetic. The impossibility of nostalgia is hence the impossibility of ever uniting space and time. And so, the inevitable emptiness that arises upon returning to ones birthplace is thus due to the disparity between space and time.. Time itself has moved on but the space has remained inert and as such there emerges a sense of the uncanny in that we are both somewhere that is simultaneously distant and familiar. It is a conflict between passion and absence: a conflict consummated through the music of the Georgian composer Giya Kancheli.

In exile himself, Kancheli's relationship to both his homeland and the home as an existential motif, is thus central to his composition: the presence of nostalgia is hence an *idée fixe* that acts as a locus for the majority of his pieces. Though this yearning for a lost home might be apparent in Kancheli's music, to suggest that this is a rigid dynamic or an otherwise purely introspective emotion would be misleading. Like Tarkovsky, Kancheli's understanding of nostalgia is both complex and equally reflective of a distinctly Russian problem, as Tarkovsky himself writes: "Our '*nostalghia*' is not your 'nostalgia.' It is not an individual emotion but something much more complex and profound that Russians experience when they are abroad. It is a disease, an illness, that drains away the strength of the soul, the capacity to work, the pleasure of living."[2] Despite this difference, both the sentiment of hope and the acknowledgment of an empty reality are entirely dependent upon one another, not only for the nostalgic himself, but also for the composer who seeks to portray nostalgia. To concede to despondency whilst in exile, to disarm the lure of hope, is to submit to annihilation. Nostalgia yearns, and to yearn one must still tinge with a trace of hope. Death, suicide, or a drive towards dissolution afford nothing to the exiled but an affirmation of their impossibility. The dualistic nature of nostalgia thus renders it a violent dynamic entirely capricious to the vagaries of reverie, a reverie which can be suspended only whilst the nostalgic maintains a tense distance between himself and reality. Musically, this dynamic is approached by Kancheli in such a way so as to establish a sense of homeliness before disjoining it with the sense of being-elsewhere. Unlike the self-consciously nostalgic compositions of the Ukrainian composer Valentin Silvestrov, Kancheli's composition do not permit an unfettered purity that is only content to wistfully invoke what has already passed. When Silvestrov has thus written how he deems his music as "not the end of music as art, but the end of music, an end which it can linger for a long time", then we know that for Silvestrov time no longer holds the possibility of returning. As such, for him all that remains is the "area of the coda", an area in which the remembrance of lost space fills the absence which emerges in the present. Kancheli equally locates himself in the "area of the coda" but enforces a sense of temporal deformation that renders his nostalgia both impulsive and dynamic.

Silvestrov's resolute nostalgia, his submission to absolute remembrance, is contrasted in Kancheli by a more complex arrangement that eventually leads to the *dynamic stasis* between lyrical passages of immense beauty and violent thrusts of the orchestra. The contrast between the two composers is important since it mirrors a fundamentally different approach to nostalgia framed by either surrender in Silvestrov or defiance in Kancheli. Sublime is the concession to the fate of the nostalgic: to exist in the throes of remembrance alone is no doubt an act of passive grandeur. But for Kancheli, remembrance alone lacks absolution. It is no more than an abstraction divorced from the present. When we consider a piece such as *Magnum Ignotum* (2000) then what is apparent is a disjunctive unity between the past and the present and between the present and the absent. That the piece develops in the manner of an archaeological dig, each relic recalling the other in its absence whilst simultaneously aspiring to progress in a deliberately affirmative fashion, is indicative of the ambiguous nature of nostalgia. This is particularly evident in *Magnum Ignotum* where the use of taped recordings of both a polyphonic Gurian song from the 1930's and Georgian folk music sung by the Rustavi Choir is contrasted with Kancheli's own live performance. The effect is such so as to establish a presence framed by a tonal centre before disjoining the centre through the introduction of distant voices that are both intimate and foreign. There exists modulation, but it is a thwarted modulation, tense with the foreknowledge that each movement is bound to recollection rather than pure experience. Listening to it, one is reminded of a poem by Rene Char where, like Kancheli, the home is founded in an inversion of emptiness so that the space of nostalgia becomes the home itself:

> *"Wait a while until I come*
> *To cleave the cold which holds us*
>
> *Cloud, in your life as threatened as mine*
>
> *(There was a precipice in our house*
> *So we left and set up home here)* [3]

The 'precipice' of Char's poem emerges in Kancheli's music as the dreadful weight of nostalgia. Throughout Kancheli's *Magnum Ignotum* there emerges an aspiration towards progression, towards a forgetfulness of the past so that the present can be lived only to once again fall back into contemplative reverie. It is, of course, part of the paradox of nostalgia that through aspiring to forget the origin of our nostalgia so that we can then embrace the present we thus lose the centre to which the nostalgic yearning has forged. We adjust to our anguish so much so that it becomes a symbol of familiarity. The longing protracts and in turn becomes a source of comfort. Nostalgia is as much as infatuation with one's longing as it is a longing from home itself, and when this longing is dissolved though forgetfulness then the nostalgic becomes exiled from nostalgia itself. The oscillating impasse is endless.

Against this nostalgic impasse, the function of musical form becomes essential. In its most deliberate attempt to 'begin again', Serialism sought to disrobe nostalgia so that the present would unfold in a specifically indeterminate manner. Privileging no specific tone from the chromatic scale, so that the possibility of there emerging a tonal centre would thus be annulled,

Serialism sought to achieve an absolute equality of musical form. A stance of negation hence emerges: the 'tone' of Serialism is characterised by what it seeks to avoid: tonality. For Schonberg in particular, the drive towards tonality is a drive towards exhaustion, a regressive and therefore nostalgic impulse towards sentimentality and degeneration. Speaking of the diminished seventh chord which would play such a momentous part in Wagner's work, Adorno writes thus: "Even the most insensitive ear detects the shabbiness and exhaustion of the diminished seventh chord and certain chromatic modulatory tones in the salon music of the nineteenth century. For the technically trained ear, such vague discomfort is transformed into a prohibitive canon."[4] Adorno is no doubt right to be scathing of "antiquated and untimely" sounds, but that Serialism would mark an absolute divorce with both tonality and nostalgia is manifestly wrong - since it is Serialism itself which has now become an object of both nostalgia and kitsch appreciation in the same way that diminished seventh chord was a generation before. From the vantage point of the present, we can now see that through the decline of Serialism how a re-emergence of a self-consciously nostalgic, inward music has re-appeared. Referring once again to Silvestrov, then the recourse to such traditional musicals forms as the sonata or more notably the symphonic-poem is used in such a way to enforce a sense of nostalgia that is both formal in structure and actual in content. For Silvestrov, it is as though Serialism never existed.

To consider Kancheli's use of form then, is to consider his distinctly complex views towards nostalgia itself. Uniting both the familiar and the unfamiliar, the splintered song-cycles we hear in Kancheli are indicative of a desire to distort an un-nostalgic form against a nostalgic content. In the case of his *Exil* cycle (1994) then this disjunction between form and content is particularly lucid. Set against the words of Celan, Hans Sahl, and the Psalms, *Exil* is perhaps Kancheli's most explicit expression of mourning. In *Exil,* Kancheli seduces us into a serenity, but it is a dangerous serenity that belies a deeper loss veiled by the beauty of the cycle itself. Here we a find a mood that is saturated in sparse resignation: cold, static and without a firm sense of modulation, only once is there an orchestral eruption, as though the reverie is suddenly shattered by the remembrance of *why* there is mourning. The deliberately cold posture resists the lure of emotivism in favour of detachment, reserve, and a dignified mourning framed by a Stoic resilience that nevertheless remains in conflict with itself:

> *"There's nothing left to say of that.*
> *Dust clouds abate.*
> *I've turned my collar up, pulled down my hat.*
> *It's getting late.*
> *The cable screams, They've buried him. He's gone.*
> *There's really nothing left to say of that*
> *Too late."*[5]

Sahl's poem echoes Kancheli's apprehensive Stoicism: to adopt a Stoic perspective is to admit to loss, to seek consolation in the determinacy of the nomadic self rather than depend upon a space that runs the risk of being robbed of its homeliness. For the nostalgic, Stoicism is the last resort since it aspires to render something homely from the estranged and as such renounces any such of hope of an absolute restoration: "I've turned my collar up, pulled down my hat" writes Sahl accordingly. Recalling Tarkovsky's remark that "Our 'nostalghia' is not your 'nostalgia,'" then we can perhaps infer that a Russian exile in the West is imbued with veiled connotations that are otherwise evaded by a Westerner. In this case, whilst Stoicism becomes a necessity rather than a choice, the nostalgic yearning simultaneously gathers intensity. The detachment in *Exil* then, is a defiance against yearning; an act of resistance that enables the exiled to resist nostalgia seeping through.

In her *The Future of Nostalgia,* Svetlana Boym has written of an approach to nostalgia that reflects Kancheli's own apprehensive Stoicism, the name she gives to it is 'diasporic intimacy'. She writes: "Diasporic intimacy can be approached only through indirection and intimation, through stories and secrets...diasporic intimacy does not promise an unmediated emotional fusion, but only a precarious affection..."[6] As with Kancheli, diasporic intimacy permits a seduction with lost memory, an indirect conflation of absence and presence so that the debilitating weariness of an explicit nostalgia can be avoided. The intimacy that is conferred upon the exiled is precisely that estranged familiarity that houses the self in a centreless space, as

Boym writes: "The foreign backdrop, the memory of past losses and recognition of transience do not obscure the shock of intimacy, but rather heighten the pleasure and intensity of surprise."[7] Boym would lead us to think diasporic intimacy in this sense resolves the impossibility of nostalgia. But can the mourning for a lost land ever evolve into a voice of purity so that the *vox angelica* can sing devoid of the taint of memory? We should like to think that if we persist in our mourning or otherwise accommodate it by rendering it intimate, then our nostalgia will subside, that the distillation of memory will result in a readjustment of both space and time so that our adopted country can then be transformed to our homeland. The remedy, however, is never that direct. Again we return to our memories, glide into reverie so that we can trace the origins of our loss, and when pure abstraction is not enough, then the compulsion to haunt spaces of absence thus takes precedence.

It is no doubt for this reason that Kancheli's recent piece *Little Imber* (2003) was a site-specific composition written as a eulogy for a deserted Wiltshire village. Against the backdrop of an abandoned village colonized by the American Army for military training in 1943, Kancheli's *Little Imber* reprises the nostalgic theme whilst simultaneously using the village of Imber as a medium to lament the loss not only of his own exile but also the exile of the 160 villagers forced to desert their home. That the event was advertised as a burial in which "Imber will finally lay its past to rest" is perhaps indicative of a false aspiration aided by a misunderstanding of nostalgia. Since it is not closure that is afforded by lamentation, but rather grief extended. Once again Kancheli returns to a landscape of loss, dislocation, and homelessness not merely to invoke the theme of nostalgia or to perform a requiem for a deserted village, but rather to express the impossible dynamic of nostalgia as conveyed between the polarities of passion and absence. Deserted space ensnares the nostalgic, and in turn serves to mirror an internalized absence rendered material. This is all the more appealing in deserted spaces that have yet to be physically ventured into since they afford a freshness of nostalgia that is otherwise annihilated by spaces already familiar to us. In foreign but vacant space, there exists the possibility of returning to our origins without explicitly embracing a form of regressive nostalgia that actively seeks to recreate the home itself. Kancheli's *Little Imber* seeks to disclose the essence of nostalgia from the vantage point of a space that can thus maintain its distance. Though, the splinter of relics - dislocated objects torn from the homeland that serve to induce a sense of longing - littered in the landscape, no doubt heighten the nostalgic aesthetic by imparting a sense of distant familiarity in the wastelands of absence. For this reason, during the performance of *Little Imber* we find the Rustavi Choir themselves parading the village of Imber in a ceremonial manner that suggests Kancheli rendering Imber his own.

Such is the burden of absence, that for the nostalgic the temptation to invoke a duplicitous representation of the former home is equally as appealing as encountering an absent space reflecting the contents of the exiled mind. One thinks of Miss Havisham from Dickens' *Great Expectations* preserving the home despite her abandonment. In that case, the home becomes the shrine of suffering through which the exterior absence is concealed by the drawn curtains. In the poems of the exiled Lithuanian writer Alfonsas Nyka-Niliūnas we find a similar approach to nostalgia whereby the poetic creation of an imagined world replete with objects of familiarity soothes an actual absence:

*"There stands a house with blue storm shutters, by itself;*
*The toys I left behind in childhood live in it;*
*My days are sleeping deep within the noonday silence,*
*Watched over by the wind with broken wings."*[8]

Faced with this dynamic between artificially creating an imaginative home or otherwise conceding to a loss that can never be resolved, the question of whether or not nostalgia results in either a pessimistic or optimistic conclusion becomes vital. Approaching this question, it is worth considering Tarkovsky's *Nostalghia* (1983) since there Kancheli's aesthetic between passion and absence, and the overall question of whether or not an artist can survive in a foreign country, is explicitly addressed. Framed in this context, the presence of dreams offers the nostalgic an essential point of guidance.

In Tarkovsky's *Nostalghia* we find the dreamscape extend to the point of intoxication. Andrei Gorchakov, the protagonist, is a Soviet musicologist researching the life of an 18th century

Russian composer whilst staying in rural Italy. Despite the fact the research has ended, Gorchakov remains in Italy lingering between intrigue and homesickness. Played out against his relationship with the Italian translator, Evgenia and a local reclusive, Domenico, *Nostalghia* thus represents the collision of desires between the love of one's homeland, the peculiar pleasure that resides in longing for that homeland, and the wilful desire to submit oneself to a vocation that will absolve desire itself. Through the figure of Evgenia, Gorchakov's relationship to Italy and thus exile, emerges as one of profound ambivalence taut with estrangement. As an expression of this ambivalence, we find Gorchakov's inability to relate to Evgenia coupled with the dormant desire to be seduced by her. Evgenia seduces. But against Gorchakov's estranged inertia, the seduction falters: "I'm tired of these sickeningly beautiful sights," he says towards the beginning, "I want nothing more just for myself. That's enough." It is reminiscent of Kancheli's aspiration to house himself in an abandoned space whilst simultaneously failing to reconcile his grief with a lost presence, a suspicion of a superficial beauty that might well veil a future loss

For Gorchakov (or Tarkovsky) the solitary experience of exile is not enough to give rise to resolution: a spiritual kinship between abandonment and surrender is required. Here the role of Domenico, the recluse who is portrayed as 'mad' through holding a pre-occupation with an unsung apocalyptic disaster before sacrificing himself by committing suicide on top of the statue of Marcus Aurelius, and who Gorchakov in turn identifies with, becomes pivotal. Domenico has faith: even when sacrificing himself, there exists faith in salvation, albeit a necessarily posthumous salvation. It is a faith that Gorchakov himself holds in esteem. In exile, separated from his family, his homeland, and thus alone, Gorchakov's nostalgia is projected into the Dionysian sacrifice that Domenico undergoes. As a consequence of this desire for faith, Gorchakov fulfils Domenico's outwardly illogical request to carry a lighted candle across a drained thermal bath. Twice he fails, twice the wind steals Gorchakov's faith until at last the candle, cupped in his hands, reaches the end of the bath at which point Gorchakov collapses. A poem by Tarkovsky's father, featured earlier on, suddenly resounds:

> *"I'm a candle burnt out at a feast.*
> *Gather my wax up at dawn,*
> *And this page will tell you the secret*
> *Of how to weep and where to be proud,*
> *How to distribute the final third*
> *Of delight, and make an easy death.*
> *Then, sheltered by some chance roof,*
> *To blaze, word-like, with posthumous light."*[9]

What we can infer from both Gorchakov and Domenico's sacrifices - the former a sacrifice involving faith over logic and the latter a sacrifice of passion for salvation - is that, for Tarkovsky any possibility of resolving nostalgia must involve what Nietzsche refers to as a pessimism of strength. The question of whether or not an aesthetics of nostalgia should result in either pessimism or optimism is perhaps a misleading question, since it is not a simple dichotomised either/or at stake but rather an approach that is defined by how much one is willing to sacrifice in order to evoke resolution, however tenuous that resolution may be. It is not that content of one's suffering is altered by way of a symbolic transfiguration but simply that the manner in which it is approached is either characterised by malaise or strength. For Tarkovsky, the rewards of sacrifice are posthumous: in the final sequence of the film we see a sublime landscape comprised of Gorchakov sitting by a pool in the foreground flanked by a Russian farmhouse and then enclosed by the ruins of a Roman cathedral. It is a nervous reconciliation between absence and passion, infused with the sepia hue of both hope and loss. Tarkovsky, like Kancheli, does not play down the torment of nostalgia - if anything the film is poem of suffering - but rather than retreating into a bitter *Weltschmerz,* the impossibility is faced through courage which avoids a necessary correlation between suffering and pessimism, as Nietzsche writes: "Is pessimism necessarily a sign of decline, decay, degeneration, weary and weak instincts...is there a pessimism of strength? An intellectual predilection for the hard, gruesome, evil, problematic aspect of existence, promoted by well-being, by overflowing health, by the *fullness* of existence?"[10] Nietzsche's solution to suffering was a sacrifice of the individuation for the absolute unity of the Dionysian revelry. The 'metaphysical comfort' of acknowledging the horror of existence before then submitting oneself to the cosmic dance whereby individuation is dissolved in the Heraclitean river of becoming over being is what Nietzsche means by a pessimism of strength. For the nostalgic this entails forsaking the pride in temporal dislocation, in favour of a spatial collapse defined by a sacrificial release. Making recourse to the extremity of choice, the aesthetic implications of nostalgia are precisely aligned to Nietzsche's perspective on Greek tragedy whereby "We are to recognize that all that comes into being must be ready for a sorrowful end; we are forced to look into the terrors of the individual existence - yet we are not to become rigid with fear..."[11] Like Nietzsche's depiction of Dionysian art, nostalgia, at its aesthetic apotheosis, invokes a tragic worldview where submission reigns sovereign over pure sentiment.

Returning to Kancheli, then we shall conclude by looking at a composition that unites the elements of Tarkovsky's *Nostalghia* whilst simultaneously flirting with the possibility of a Dionysian release: *Lament* (1999). Dedicated to the memory of the Italian composer Luigi Nono, *Lament* marks a paradigm in Kancheli's compositions if only for its breadth of dynamics alone. It is a movement devoid of exterior logic but rather structured in terms of quivers, reposes, and eruptions. Transparency falters when one seeks to abstract motifs from their context. As such, to interpret the score, dissecting motifs as though they were allegorical allusions or otherwise definite symbols pertaining to a lived experience, is to render it partial. Nevertheless, thematically we can understand the *Lament* in such a way so as to present a unity whereby nostalgia, grief, and sacrifice compound. When the first fragments of the viola flicker contemplatively against the desolate but arching soprano, then we are reminded of the static grief featured in the earlier *Exil* cycle. It is a grief rendered indeterminate by its depth, a searching that can no longer navigate itself without recourse to self-denial, and only when the fragile poise of mourning is ruptured by the initial orchestral outburst can this indeterminacy be charred. Initially, Kancheli contrasts these wistful moments of ethereal beauty in a typically reserved manner, evoking the nostalgic sepia so often a feature for Tarkovsky. A dialogue thus unfolds between sorrow and memory, between a contemplative loss characterised by restraint and the recollection of that loss expressed through bitter grief. In the context of the words of Hans Sahl, against which the movement is set, the piece suddenly takes on the form of a tense but determined pathway through which the restraint of pure memory must invariably fissure in a violent release:

> *"Quite slowly I am walking from the world*
> *into a landscape farther off than far,*
> *and what I was and am and shall remain*
> *as patient, as unhurried walks with me*
> *into a country never trodden yet."*[12]

This sudden release is marked by the furious *rondo* passage which occurs about half way through: it is a militant stampede acquired only through a suppression of grief and loss, and like the sacrifice in *Nostalghia* the sense of individuation is thus lost to a faith in the illogical. How can we begin to account for this passage without evoking the spirit of Dionysus? For Kancheli, it is as though the impossibility of return is a source of pessimistic strength through which the apotheosis of the dance reaches it virile conclusion in the Dionysian affirmation of unbridled unity, a unity that forces the nostalgia to sacrifice his loss so that the 'metaphysical comfort' of an unfaltering becoming transpires. Until finally, the clutching of a restorative hope gives way to a faith in "a country never trodden yet", a space that affirms the Nietzschean tragic worldview whereby submission to the unknown supplants the spurious possibility of a reasonable return to one's homeland. The question that arises in *Lament* is thus: how can a memory find resolution when its origin is no longer present? It is a grave question that pertains not only to the loss of a friend, but also to the loss of one's homeland. Kancheli's tentative response to this impasse of memory would appear to align with Tarkovsky's: that sacrifice affords a restorative opportunity whereby a destruction of the nostalgic self conceives a spontaneous self no longer determined by the structure of loss.

Until Kancheli's oeuvre is completed, then any understanding of an aesthetics of nostalgia is invariably a partial one. At best, we can gather sketches, allusions, and possibilities: a manner in which the impasse between passion and absence might be approached. But to adopt a firm stance is to run the risk of objectifying nostalgia itself, of giving it the false presence of yielding to a fixed centre. Memories elude, and their aspect is dependent upon the time of the day in which they are revealed. This variability renders nostalgia resistant to cures. For Kancheli, the very notion of nostalgia becoming aesthetic is indicative of an overcoming of its paralyzing aptitude. To render the terrible one's own through converting it to an object of aesthetic appreciation is no doubt to disrobe it of its estrangement. There, the source of loss becomes the object of poetic gain, a gain which is as dependent upon loss as it is on the propensity to sacrifice that loss for a higher aesthetic ideal.

---

Notes

1. Hofer, J *Medical Dissertation on Nostalgia* Trans: Kiser, C. from *Bulletin of the History of Medicine 2* (1934)
2. Tarkovsky in interview with Maurizio Porro (1983) http://www.acs.ucalgary.ca/~tstronds/nostalghia.com/TheTopics/Tarkovsky_Porro-1983.html
3. Char. R. 'On the Heights' cited in *The Dawn Breakers* Trans: Worton, M. (Bloodaxe Books, 1992) p. 97
4. Adorno, T. *Essays on the Philosophy of Music* Trans: Palmer, R. (Cambridge, 1985) p. 98
5. Sahl, H. *Exil* cited in "Giya Kancheli's 'Exil' by Hans-Klaus Jungheinrich (ECM Records, 1995)
6. Boym, S. *The Future of Nostalgia* (Basic Books, 2001) p. 252
7. Ibid. p. 255
8. Nyka-Niliūnas, A. 'The Symphony of Dispossession' cited in *The Perfection of Exile* (University of Oklahoma Press, 1970) p. 163
9. Cited in Le Fanu, M. *The Cinema of Andrei Tarkovsky* (1987, British Film Institute) p. 119
10. Nietzsche, F. *The Birth of Tragedy* Trans: Kaufmann, W. (New York, 2000)
11. Ibid
12. Sahl, H. Stanzas Trans: Hamburger, M. (ECM Records, 1999)

# Zoviet France, Leaky Frames, and Derrida: A Neo-Collagist Primer Polemic

by Kane X Faucher

***Fractalogue in Galactalogue***

This will have been a journey into syntax.

The attempt to employ either Derrida or the avant-noise ensemble Zoviet France as a kind of lever, fulcrum, pivot, thetical "corner" or any other such argumentation principle would be to construct a frame composed of Derrida occupying one corner (with two lines on a coordinate plane leading outward to form a right angle) and Zoviet France on the other (with an opposing coordinate plane leading outward to meet the initial right angle) would prove to be an instance of a highly bankrupt order. We would be called upon to discuss Derrida on his own "terms" (the one plane leading out) and Derrida in relation to Zoviet France (where the plane connects with the return movement of the inverted coordinates). We would also have to consider Zoviet France on their own terms and in relation to Derrida. But even in this process there will be leaks, this being an exemplar of just one of those leaks, a theoretical seepage from an imposed parergon. We have now considered and mediated what this is not, perhaps obliquely engaging our commitment to a phantom Hegelianism that we now "deconstruct" without remainder, without reserve.

Fractalogue. Soundscape. Avant-noise. Exoconsistency/ endoconsistency: a galactalogue, a non-partage, an opus, an oeuvre incomplete, yet whole in its singularity (and who could be satisfied here with an imaginary whole unless comfortable with thematic criticism?)-a becoming, a trace, perhaps even a constant de-lexicalization of the sonorous plane and a decentering of a portrait within a frame. We just might have to satisfy demands of providing a summary background on the lesser known of our two corners, Zoviet France, through a kind of exoteric exposition of the esoteric and obscurely marginal (and what is a margin if there is no center?) that highlights their historical significance to theory-later to be grafted on to the significance it has to Derrida (or vice versa). This graft, or weave, may place Zoviet France in a submissive, minor relation to

Derrida, in which we may have to slot in Zoviet France's works like a variable in an academic formula which more signifies the themes Derrida announces in his own plenum of texts. We here switch on the footlights to indicate with demonstrative rigour (itself playful and not to be taken too seriously, for to com-pose is to lay out the dead, and our subject is still living) to/upon Zoviet France.

There are no limitations to the adjectives and neologisms we could heap upon Zoviet France, a process of explication very common among music reviewers in marginal music periodicals that only a small percentage of the populace ever read. I could begin with describing them thus: angio-genetic, crypto-cacophonic, bifurcatory discord, hydra-dis-sonority, discursive, oncotextual fractamorphism, and so forth. But what would this reveal but an attempt to fill form with content, with descriptions, jarring motley of portmanteaus to explain or justify the meaning of the signifier. We are not restricted by our own sense of metastasizing wordplay on this front, but what I wish to retain in this flood of constructions, detours, apertures, lexical monstrosities, and other installations is the prefix "dys", for it is the trace of transgression and monstrosity. And, indeed, we will need to field monstrosity as such, monstrosity as the heart of demonstration-or, de-monster-ation: the point at which, ontologically, the aberrant, transgressive, trans-aggressive monster is restored to order by being indicated, its veils lifted to reveal it to analysis. And analysis always has the ability to transmute all our monsters into pets. Such efforts carry an incredible analytical weight that will not be divested for as long as we hold fast to an irate, intransigent moment of demanding fixity of the monster. But who makes the monster? Who judges the monster to be named as such? This act of naming precedes the de-monstering of the monster who was made so by being named as such. It is here that we invoke the overlap of two distinctive yet corresponding plateaus: monsters and margins.

A segue into "background information": and by background, we merely what is at play behind, events unfolding in the wings and folds. Robin Storey heads up the ensemble known as Zoviet France. He once headed up another ensemble by the name of Rapoon. Storey is or was an adamant user of intravenous drugs, but this is neither new nor interesting. More intriguing would be Storey's self-imposed musical asceticism.

That is, he denied himself all access to any new music produced during a one-decade long period. Was this for purity in creation? Did he desire silence? Did he discover in silence another kind of music, a naturally occurring John Cage 3:33? When examining the thematic (rather than historic) components and conceptual array, Zoviet France incorporates a great deal of traditional middle-eastern music interspersed with minimalist background noises and sound collages. One may obtain the impression that Zoviet France puts Rauschenberg to music. Or hooks Andy Warhol's "Factory" to a synthesizer in some comedic repetition of the repetition. The music is seemingly laconic and flat in parts, punctuated with a sort of style of resonance that calls to (my) mind experiences in a sanitarium-the incidental noises, the weakly defended and blurry line between sanity and its inverse double...where the doctors and orderlies become more like their patients and vice versa in a double movement. But that is just one paradigm among many that do not bring us closer to the music, but opens up another aqueous channel in which to appreciate its pluralist, heterogeneous, retro-reintegration. It is always problematic to write on music, for writing and memory are soundless, and to impose our memory upon the music is to admit a kind of deafness: we do not hear the music "on its own terms" if there are even terms to begin (or end) with. When our memory stands in place of hearing-truly hearing-we effectively become deaf. This is unavoidable. We are condemned to meaning, recall, and experiential re-memoration as an epistemological blockage to openness and newness. But it could also be that we are so accustomed to this deafness that we are deaf to even our own deafness.

Consider a poem, a recipe, a track listing on a CD, that I will advance as a playful explication which may be withdrawn or traced lightly upon a sonorous surface...Our attempt to write on music:

1-3

-Noise

-Van-garde/guard/ (a) van (t)-garde/ re-gard(e)

Silence/Noise (Sound). Presence +/-

4. "Collagerie": Plus/minus distinction under cancellation and erasure.

5. Pre/post/proto melodic order.

6. [dys]continuity. [dys]sonance.[dys]cord: SYNTAX.

7. Archive of singularities and traces,a moving archive (itself a trace) with no center, situated on a desert horizon of shifting sand.

8. Arche-noise II

9. Pediment, firmament - shiftings, overlaps, interweaves, hinges, rotations, circum-sonorities, nomadic (re)[dys]tribution, self-contained motility (unsteady monad becomes plural).

### *Archive, Frame, Circle*

"The archontic principle of the archive is also a principle of consignation, that is, of gathering together."[1] The arch-ontic of archive. Double signed as implied by a consigning (between a signer and signee-consignatory relationship). An ontologically binding contract. The contract gathers together its clauses, conceptual components and subjects (contraction, condensation) to derive a horizon of (allegedly) ineffaceable text. This is the production of the commandment, and it is the duty of the other to validate this through some jussive moment of commencement (to speak, as a kind of Christ, for an absent father the commandment of this contract). And even then, this "life will be verified only at the moment that the bearer of the name...will have died."[2] We have already invoked such problematic terms as "avant-noise" and "arche-silence." What of them? Where are they written? The first has been written as a popularization, a new convention of categorization by reviewers of obscure music. The latter is perhaps more elusive. Silence is heard as double: as absence, but also as spacing that makes the noise possible as a reception into the vestibule of the ear, its antre. Do we possess a contract that itself implies a consensus of these terms I have here invoked? Who will stand and be present to accountability for these terms? I, for one, will do so, but only provisionally, only insofar as I can play the miming role of a harlequin attempting to mime both a kind of music and its terms.

Avant-noise: understood in its framework, the term alludes to a period when improvisational "noise" or 1960s sound collagists were influencing the margins of music. A setting of "avant" implies another prefix wherein we could possibly state "post-noise" (would this not be silence?).[3] however, this prefix does not suit either the conditions of the term or the frame. Avantism is a leak, a subsitution or a placeholder that awaits final classification. It is yet to be categorized, and so the "avant" stands in (for the moment, or as relation to this moment). Noise is somewhat limiting as well, for the concept can be extended (literally) to all music. But noise in this context would be considered through a special filter: that which is not produced by conventional instruments or arranged in a conventional melodic manner according to conventional musical scales. But here the term is merely a shadow-component, a binary opposite of "music." My problem with the term "avant-noise" is now documented hic et nunc in the terms of this con-tract, and hence necessitated my earlier outburst of neologisms. But to name is not to give life to the work, for life and work appear to be contradictory elements that unite in the name.[4] However much jubilance it would bring one to smash the archive and commit infama (destruction of all records), we are still at least partially obliged to sift through these records, these categories, in order to choose exactly where in the frame a split may be realized. For this, we will need to (re)play the music. It must be reiterated to us to reveal the leaks in the frame it presents as it moves.[5]

Indeed, we will not be able to ascribe "nuclear meaning" (at once both new and clear meaning), seeing as the music under scrutiny will have been (at least externally) opposed by a logic of substitution.[6] An operation of logic would attempt to efface a virgin territory that is neither virginal nor non-virginal. There is a lateral undecidability at the heart of classifying such complex effects as Zoviet France, its music, and all its plural components (a task worthy of transcendental empiricism). This (non) virginal moment will have folded back in on itself through a series of blank silences, been remarked, and then open itself across a surface of multiplied blanks. If there is any archive at all that acts as a "guarantor" or some lexical "contract" which would determine (negatively, in Hegelian terms) Zoviet France as "avant-noise", then it is a false and playful archive.-Or some undecidable space that is playing at being an archive while at the same time withdrawing from any rigidifying signification or codification. This pseudo-archive will have inscribed within itself the record of Zoviet France, but this record will be in constant motion throughout its diaphanous "body". It is much akin to the flight of a single memo through a horribly disorganized and confused bureaucracy, except in this instance there is no central head, and the employees in addition to the offices are in constant rearrangement. This archive will not provide the suitable frame in which Zoviet France can be contained. Rather, Zoviet France will move in and out of the frame without there being a distinctive or serious "inside/ outside" relation.[7]

What is a frame? A frame abducts a "work" of art and sections it off from extrinsic characteristics of the outside such as its value, the audience, and so forth.[8] Even here, as we examine the music with the assistance of given concepts, the music itself remains in itself unaltered by our inquest (for it is the critic's job to declare the work dead, static, amenable to analysis or editorial, the critic's function as coroner of fortuitous expressions). However, what prohibits us from extending the "frame" to include this act of literature from being an extension of Zoviet France's music, as a kind of appendix? Is it impossible to believe that each of these words written down in the order and manner that they are, have letters, a through g, which we could capitalize and later play upon an instrument? Ah, onE woulD wonDEr whAt thAt woulD look likE. But this is another, cursory, oblique, and marginal matter. The frame is still under consideration at this point. The frame would trap the scene or event of music-even (and especially) music as a text. Outside Zoviet France's parerga would reside all the adjunct properties, the unobtrusive ornamentation that flanks, garnishes (but a garnish that adds rather than takes away), and buttresses the work of art. But let us consider a more physical, literal property of the frame and suspend what will inevitably become a logic of infinite conjunction...and...and...

Zoviet France occurs, musically, on a printed CD. The songs occupy a few millimeters of space each upon the circular surface. The constitution (perhaps in two senses) of the CD is replete with a series of multiple frames, like a Russian Doll, a mise en abyme. At the outermost ring is the CD case itself. As we proceed inwardly toward the center (where there is nothing but a hole, a blank, an absence, a non-territorialized space), we come across the title, the explanatory notes in the CD jacket, the outer ridge of the CD itself, and the poly-frames of each musical track in one circular totality. The musical "whole" is framed by these. But what of each musical selection? How is it that one piece of music physically constituted and inscribed as data upon the surface of the CD act as a frame for the piece next to it? Do tracks 1 and 3 cease to be artworks when framing (and listening) to track 2? Are these tracks true parergons (in the sense of par as equal and ergon as work) or mere transparent partitions only detectable by the subtle mechanism of a sweeping laser? Are all the tracks "equally working" as both frames and artworks? Certainly I have raised a crude and facile interpretation of the parergon in relation to music on CD, perhaps. Recall that, for Kant, in the third critique, he speaks freely of such physical objects surrounding the artwork as colonnades, drapery, gilded frames, and other such material framings. Why can we not invoke the same physicality in reference to the CD to indicate the undecidability of inside/outside, parergon/ergon? Let us not depart just as yet. What of the circular constitution of the musical track, or of the CD itself? The CD cannot be spliced at some radial point, stretched out into some convenient square to be placed in a conventional frame. The CD is housed in a square receptacle to facilitate transit, safe packaging, and easy storage (in considering pugilist sports, the common analogy is interestingly enough "squaring the circle"). We already can see how our listening can create a frame for music through the context we bring to it, but there is a conceptual ingredient missing to declare with any verity that the physical CD track is either framed or not. These physical properties of space can be considered mere ornament, but for this to happen the essential sonority circle or cycle must be squared. Circle$^2$ From here, we fade to black on this point... (or consider the encore of the music's true validation by the other as signed in this fashion: ©, the circled "c", c-note and circularly framed...or yet a broken circle within a whole circle. Musi©?)

In terms of the purely aural-which we can here suspend as a fiction, for the occupation of one sense organ does not limit the others from a polyglot of associations being received by eyes, mind, nose, tactility, etc.-it would appear that the "frames" surrounding and enshrouding the singular music track (or trace) is a border of silences. Does this silence constitute a frame, just as silence precedes and succeeds a piece of music and functions as a kind of partition or frame between musical pieces? How can a frame function as a frame and yet still be, according to the metaphysical pedagogy, absent? There would be as much sense pronouncing the silences around a track a frame as there would be in stating that the spaces between words delineate some unity of art in the one word, or that other paintings in a gallery serve as frames to the one painting being viewed in the present. Or at least in the case of the word that it some way may be calculated in terms of its stand-alone meaning-value...a prized activity among myopic semanticists, but not for someone like Derrida who utilizes non-lexicalized terms in an associative chain where to split them is to lexicalize them. But we are capable of making infinite cuts and infinite connections when it comes to text, just as the musician can make cut infinite tracks or traces and connect them in an infinite number of ways. Whether we consider "text" as a whole or carve smaller words from within a singular word, we are still left with the remainder. Why would this scenario not be paralleled in music?

We have addressed one corner of this "discourse". This corner is not situated in a self of over-imagining its space, nor is it a palliation by panic brought about by stimulation on the Great Electronic Canvas of television (as an organ of sound and vision that denoted in lurid, pacifying, laboratory greens the bombing patterns in Afghanistan immediately following the 9/11 "event"). [9] Zoviet France can be brought into a relation, teased along a grid or made to carry the burden of "terrorism". But to whom is it a terrorist music? What would this constitute? I shelve this term and this line of inquiry, seeing as one could just as easily write terror unto a page and be considered a threat to the national order. Such are these days.

The almost eerie, (de)crescendo tones found in Zoviet France convey a loose, fluid sonorous movement in and out of framework (where it ends, another has already begun, a double movement of seepage through frames) to which the "end" of the piece as marked by the sound of a machine, seems to be the cannibalization of the wails unto the macabre walls of a factory, a movement upon a conveyor belt toward the smelter as the bodiless voices twist upward like a fire that is chained to the earth-all to the direction of some artist-demiurge. What resides in this dark workshop, this dimly lit forge, this iron fortress where the darkness is only creased by the blinking of the red "ready" light? What use are my descriptions of this particular ensemble when we should be abandoning description as just another form of deafness?

Let us return to the circle. Wherein lies the origin? Or, rather, where does the trace emerge? If the trace is called upon to emerge at some given point, then this would presuppose some grand referent to which all the sonorous syntagm is guided by and measured against.-Some subject proper to which all subsequent terms must refer and obey. However, there is a sense of contamination in this operation. The trace is ineluctable. The CD track is trace as much as the mark is a margin. The track is folded into a series of rotating circles in the archive that is itself playful and stochastic. Aleatory, almost mystic. The circle is not closed like a cartouche seizes upon and kills a name. It is not necessarily the variety of circle that contains an absolute Whole while preserving rigid boundaries of access between inside and outside, but is more like the Zen circle that encloses upon nothingness that has no quantifiable space (and so we are left with no ground or dimensions of the nothingness which the circle is given to enclose, thereby signaling that the circle itself may be just as infinite or infinitesimal as the space). To speak of inside and outside at the point of this circle would prove rather ridiculous. It would be to hold on to our ingrained/entrained geometrical predicates. The inside of this circle (in this case, we can include the CD and its tracks) bears an imprint or inscription, where "the inscription of a circle in the circle does not necessarily give the abyss, onto the abyss, en abyme. In order to be abyssal, the smallest circle must inscribe in itself the figure of the largest."[10] So, when above we were speaking of the nothing or space within the circle, we did not mean that the "inside" was truly "nothing" in the metaphysical way, but that infinite space is broken up infinitely by infinite inscription. It is the same operation that we see at play in the act of dissemination which is already always taking place wherever there is space and inscription.

And then I listen to the music again, projecting my own deafness...I perhaps sense some wild flights of Klossowski's circles, or perhaps the inner life of Celine's chronic tinnitis resulting from my own being trepanned by a soundscape tour de force. There are bombs and bursts of "noise", but also shrinking viole(n)t withdrawals (as it may indeed bloom and blossom, boom, or shrink with the onset of night like a flower, but all the while the threat of an assault constantly deferred). It is neither mounting an offensive entirely nor effecting a retreat. It is essentially double movement: both assault and retreat, fight and flight. And in this latter formulation, we are brought to the scene of an adrenal movement. This double movement of attack/ retreat is a pharmakon: "pharmakon means coup... such that pharmakon might have signified: that which pertains to a coup demoniaque (demoniacal attack) or is used as a curative for such a coup (attack)'..."[11] We bring in an audience, perhaps presuppose it, yet not in any way that it has to be present or kept behind a veil. The audience, too, is in double movement of attack/retreat. This is an endless, mirrored game of fort/da. To ask the music's genre is patently ridiculous, even through a rigorous concern. To ask its genre is effectively demanding that Zoviet France "reveal its gender", to reveal its anatomical truths, its naked organs, to which only a blank sound is heard in reply.[12] Genre as gender...but which one? Both? Neither? The genre of Zoviet France is a question posed at its limits, but is also the scene for a dissemination precisely on the grounds that this alterity and undecidability can be located in its "text" and be allowed to split itself into splinters. Sound splinters. Jagged edges. Torn sheets. Panic, seizure, grasping, losing. Laceration, (auto) dissolution, pure sacrifice without return, desouvrement, non-savoir.[13] Like text, there is something germinal within the soundscape, something that makes the tone expand from an infinite middle of space, as if the "inscription" within the circle extrudes an already indeterminable circumference of a circle.

### *Zoviet France and difference*

The idea of difference (not sameness, that which is not the other) is expressed as a kind of negative difference in Hegel.[14] But the difference we invoke here is that which cannot be reduced to a term that is spoken or written as a lexical item; it is Derrida's conception of difference as "differance". As a capsule summary, differance entails a three-pronged sense: 1. Difference: that which is not sameness; 2. To differ: to differ and disperse; 3. Different: (in French) to defer temporally. The first two senses of differance are spatial while the last is temporal. The "a" of differance cannot be detected in French phonetically, and indeed the "A" is the silent tomb that signals the death of the tyrant-pharaoh (or "A"uthor as presence self-related and text-related) insofar as we can engage text without either moving toward an origin or privileging the presence of authorship which is at the heart of phonocentric privilege. As a term, differance resists being definitionally full or bound or becoming fully lexicalized. It is at play in producing differences (wherever they may be, which is absolutely everywhere) while resisting its own completion. Differance is at work as neither function nor process in the production-economy of spacings, tracings, and writing. All attempts to give the term of differance presence fail, for the copula in "differance is" presupposes some ontological unity or harmony, as if it were a term that came already complete in the act of text. It is an active, non-concept, non-word, situated nowhere and everywhere without giving itself over to the governance of binary opposition. We can only signal its "being" through the traces and disruptions it leaves between these binary oppositions of speech/writing, noun/verb, noise/silence.

So where does Zoviet France "fit" into this "paradigm"? consider here the play of differance between such modal, binary constructions of music/non-music (or noise), noise/silence, rhythm/arrhythmic. In the tracks and traces found in Zoviet France's music signed by their name, we begin to recognize the effects of a breakdown between the distinctions between the antipodes we just mentioned. There are recognizable melodies and rhythms throughout these tracks, but there are also clattering dissonances, oblique sounds, welling crescendos, re-fed and poly-echoed sample loops of backward dialogue, incorporation of allegedly "primitive" and "ethnic" musical instruments fed through the ironic maw of "modern" technology, and burgeoning sound structures that would be impossible to (re)construct under any unified, traditional strictures in the theory of music. Zoviet France occupies both and neither of these spaces entirely or consistently. If differance is at play within a text, causing disruptions within already established binaries, Zoviet France is a musical exemplar of how its own expression plays upon these immanent surfaces to create something other whose "meaning" will always be deferred. To pose the crude question of the music's meaning is not to appreciate and respect the objection that Zoviet France is merely engendering the opposite of what is considered melodic and conventional as music is to disregard two salient features: 1. Zoviet France does utilize certain musical schemas (albeit in splintered and fractamorphic form) that are recognizable as components in other musical expressions that are considered musical as such; 2. Or, as the opposing claim that Zoviet France is relying too heavily on various musical formalisms (percussive beat, some melody, etc.), is to overlook the fact that differance is also capable of producing reiterations. If there was no reiteration there would be no reference, language, or anything else for us to hang our conscious attention upon. We recognize these pieces to be of a musical nature because there are certain micro-constituent elements that reiterate our prior experience with music (what Deleuze would call our image of thought, and so the "trick" is to allow the music to encounter us in such a way as to promote new ways of thinking, feeling, and being). But, there is also the more crude example of how Zoviet France is music as such: the compiled music is offered to us on CDs in music stores, thereby signifying the symbolic order that gives categorical assignation to the product; i.e., someone signed the contract that what Zoviet France was indeed producing what could be marketed as music as such. Moreover, to stake a claim that Zoviet France-in order to be truly different-has to abandon all formal structures of musicality in some parodic "avant-garde" pose which rejects all structure in such a way that all this succeeds in doing is to reinforce dominant structure (resorting to a Hegelian dialectic), is merely to invert the privilege from presence (music, rhythm, sound) to absence (noise, erratic, silence). A mere inversion is not difference, but the repetition of sameness on its head.

I am called upon here to conclude-from the Latin, concludere: to shut down, to desist all play. But how can we cease to play. The playing will live on, and to conclude does not bring the matter to any decisive close, but merely indicates our exhaustion with text/music that can and will exhaust our efforts and us. There is no end to deconstruction. In more than one sense of the word "end". If we had infinite fortitude, then perhaps we could continue disrupting and deferring texts and music indefinitely (and why not begin with Zoviet France?). But we must close down hic et nunc...

---

Notes

1. Jacques Derrida. *Archive Fever*. Trans. Eric Prenowitz (Chicago: University of Chicago Press, 1994) 3.
2. Jacques Derrida. *The Ear of the Other.* Trans. Avital Ronell (New York: Schocken Books, 1985) 9. The same can be said in transposing and extending this verification to the honouring of a contract. The signatory in the consignation is already dead upon the moment of inscription. This transposition is also extremely critical in our attempt at a transposition of *sense*. What appears incomprehensible in this paper is deliberate; that is, our subtextual "contract" to our thematic is to demonstrate the very difficulty of writing *on* music itself.
3. Another trajectory: our "contract" nearly commits us already to a discussion of prefixes (dys- and avant- and arche-) as *prefixed* linguistic entities that serve to further fix the term into a stable semantic whole. But what of those prefixes just listed that imply a scene of rupture, that appear to contradict the notion of prefix and create an Aporia or a paradox?
4. Cf. Derrida. *The Ear of the Other*, esp. pp. 4-19.
5. And perhaps here is the fundamental *methodological* difference between an act of deconstruction and the project of post-structuralism. The former will continue to speak in the tongue of tradition in order to locate those areas of instability and Aporia, while the latter (in the case of Deleuze and Foucault) will promote the pushing of said systems to their limit so that an active and completed nihilism can take place (see Gilles Deleuze, *Nietzsche and Philosophy*).
6. This substitution logic would involve the identity description of Zoviet France as having some set of properties that are "rigorously" defined. These properties would, by the demands of this logic, require definition by methods of presence and absence insofar as it must be *compared* to some already existent thing that has all its properties rigorously defined. By this comparative method, say, by uniting Bach with Zoviet France, we would be called upon to delineate and isolate affinities and dis-affinities (com-pars and dis-pars). Once that agonizing, singularity-obfuscating method is complete, we could state that "there is some x that has these properties y which are opposed to some already existent z that we know" and "Zoviet France is some x, Bach is some y." This problem of substitution is highlighted when we consider that the singularity of Zoviet France is forced to be co-

determined by an already established modulation of indexical syntax, and that it be effaced in some logical analysis and be reduced to some-x. another alternative would be to consider a more phenomenological program that would retain the singularity of Zoviet France (bracketed in an *epoche*), but such a program would inevitably fail when the phenomenologist would seek some semblance of *theme* to hook the singularity to, or at least have recourse to some intuitive presence. Instead, we have here to pose and maintain, perhaps, the space and silence found in a belt of ellipses that flank and suspend the "mark," "march", or "margin" of the music-notational force: [...]*abcdefg*[...]. An analytical or phenomenological form of logic cannout encounter this belt of silence, this series of musical ellipses, without either ignoring them or falling into complete dissolution. But perhaps this would raise such "logic" up to the playful state of the infant rather than be mired in the infantile.

7. On this issue of undecidability in terms of classification and the sonorous plane, a quotation which appears in the CD jacket of Rd Krayola's *Fingerpainting* would proveprudent to cite here at some length: "I want urgently that the music come, like a carpet spread on a roll, urged into the room that is, not least the room of musical and lyrical consciousness, also for other people. Then we can look further. Text and tones must appear, and I say that only once, in an absolute unattentiveness, like two eggs treated equally still, and leave the spectator pausing on the facts of a never-though very pleasant-allowed or suspected basis of noise. Here we begin. Here we start playing, what we taught ourselves. Our guitars cause vertigo. Our drums I can control still. Africa. Jazz in Norway. Underground. Free improvised will. Fertile infrequency, tables turn bodies. Music is the feeling horse of the planet. It's riding anything else everybody eer said about it until feeling music. Spin across, void, to that space where next to nothing shows through its feeling. Tiding, events mash and tumble in your wake."
8. Cf. Jacques Derrida, *The Truth in Painting.*
9. For the notion of corners and cornering, see Gaston Bachelard, The Poetics of Space (Boston: Beacon Press, 1969) 136-147.as for palliation through panic-induction and simulation, I am

merely fancifully extending and emulating here Jean Baudrillard's style of "fatal" discourse.

10.Jacques Derrida, The Truth in Painting. Trans. Geoff Bennington and Ian McLeod (Chicago: University of Chicago Press, 1987) 27. The theoretical benefit of the mise en abyme is the capability of infinite inscription. One can continue to (re) inscribe the circle (or text) without ever coming to a full and conclusive stop. On the circle, every abyssal inscription will split a space into two, these two spaces sandwiching the inscription. Since this can go on indefinitely, there is no sense in speaking of limit unless to demonstrate its impossibility.

11.Stefano Agosto's introductory piece, "Coup upon Coup" in Jacques Derrida, *Spurs: Nietzsche's Styles.* Trans. Barbara Harlow (Chicago: University of Chicago Press, 1978) 5.

12.Jerome Schwartz, "Some Emblematic Marriage Topoi in the French Renaissance" in *Emblematica: An Interdisciplinary Journal for Emblem Studies* 1.2 (New York: AMS Press, 1986). I am oddly reminded of a 1552 woodcut by Barthelmy Anneau in *L'imagination poetique.* A nude figure with two heads-essentially hermaphroditic-are kissing, while flanking "them"(?) is, on one side, an angelic sage, and on the other a devilish satyr. Between good and evil. In the Latin edition of this text, the inscription reads: "*erent duo carnem unam*" [the two will be in one flesh]. This portrays in *pictura* form the undecidable of gender-and perhaps even genre (where would this woodcut fit?).

13.These are all leitmotifs and rubrics employed by Georges Bataille.-And, indeed, there is cause here to invoke the name of Bataille: 1) Bataille is literally "war" in concerns to the question of attack/retreat; 2) the dissolution of text, the blindness of Icarian Reason, the heterological field of horizontality whereupon Zoviet France's music "erupts" and re-marks itself.

14. Cf. G.W.F. Hegel, *Phenomenology of Spirit.*

# Constituting Bodies: Constituting Life: from subjectivity to affect and the "becoming-woman" of the cinematic.

by Barbara M. Kennedy

> *[T]he aesthetic power of 'feeling,' although equal in principle with other powers of 'thinking' philosophically, 'knowing' scientifically, 'acting' politically, seems on the verge of occupying a privileged position within the collective assemblages of enunciation of our era.* (Guattari, *Chaosmosis*, 1992: 101)

The 'aesthetic power of feeling' in visual cultures evolves through an emergence of new dynamics across philosophy, film theory and feminist politics. Questions of subjectivity and the subsuming of the subjective state through the becoming-woman of 'affect' are the main focus of this paper which experiments with the concept of affect for new questions in film theory. I explore the relevance of a newly framed conception of subjectivity or the 'beyond' of subjectivity within the auspices of film theory. This new imbrication argues that a neo-aesthetic paradigm is premised upon a subjectivity which is subsumed through 'becoming'. What then are the implications for film theory which has for too long prioritised structuralist concerns with representation, signification, semiotics and a requirement of a 'subjective' reading perspective and in recent years, an overt concern with psychoanalytic conceptions of the subject, desire and pleasure? This article, taken from *Deleuze and Cinema:The Aesthetics of Sensation*[1] seeks to explore how subjectivity, mind/ brain and body are technologised, rather than being located within the psychoanalytic spaces of gendered subjectivities and libidinal forces of desire. In the process of the cinematic encounter, I argue that, rather than theorising cinema through questions of desire and pleasure, cinema may be conceived as 'modulation','event' or as 'material capture'; a processual and durational space/non - space effectuated through the 'beyond' of subjectivity.

Film theory to date has failed to provide an adequate understanding of how film matters, how it impacts, how it acts as a body in motion, in space and in time, with other material elements of our world. Instead film theory has been locked into formal analysis of ideology, representation and critiques of signification. Contemporary films display a wide range of effects, tonalities, reverberations and intensities, which connect at an affective level, beyond or before any sense of subjectivity. This paper argues that a 'neo- aesthetic' theory which accounts for how the affective is formulated beyond subjectivity, through performativity, via colour, sound, movement, force, intensity, not just through psychical mechanisms, but through material elements such as the mind/brain and body, can be discerned through a collusion with a Bergsonian and Spinozist Deleuzism. The beyond of a subjective state is orientated within the realms of the pre-personal, the autopoietic realms of a material state, where affect and intensity take us into a processual immanence, what I want to refer to as the '*becoming-woman*' of the cinematic. As I argue in *Deleuze and Cinema: the Aesthetics of Sensation,* the becoming-woman of the cinematic takes us into the spaces of sensation, the transitional, fugitive and immanent 'beyond' of pleasure or desire.

New theoretical paradigms, premised on the work of Deleuze and Guattari enable a move beyond conceptions of subjectivity into immanent trajectories and intersticial spaces which locate, ironically a non-locatable, processual landscape of creativity. The 'boundary' that has traditionally separated the natural sciences from the humanities and social sciences might be re-thought and re-assessed through these intersticial spaces. As a result, a new concern with the material nature of creativity and matter as it functions within the production of an emergent, pre-personal state might help aesthetic theory move into more dynamic spaces beyond subjectivity, into subjectless 'subjectivities'. The implications for a neo-aesthetics of the filmic experience are volitional and exciting.

*Towards the neo-aesthetic*

How do we bring back a discussion of the aesthetic into film theory in a *post-theoretical* climate which has challenged all the elements of modernist conceptions of the aesthetic. In pre-modernist discourse aesthetics was defined in two ways, premised on subjectivity and objectivity.[2] For example, in one sense aesthetics may be defined as a theory of sensibility which is a form of 'possible experience'. This perspective locates an objective element of sensation, which is conditioned by the significant elements such as space, time and form. The second definition of aesthetics encompasses a subjective element of sensation. Here the main concern is that art is a reflection on real experience and it is expressed in the feelings, through emotions such as pleasure, pain, disgust or fear. Thus an objective and a subjective dialectical definition of aesthetic. Modernist conceptions of the aesthetic were premised on a science of sensibilities, which encouraged a greater moral good. This conception of aesthetics had its origins in Aristotelian claims that the objective aim of art is beauty, which will produce in others 'the same impression as derives from the contemplation of beautiful'.[3] The beautiful was defined by specific adherence to specific form. Form was a significant element in that debate and the forms of works of art, films, poetry, novels, were analysed for specific formulaic devices: use of tone, line, space, or colour, for example. Proportion, line, colour, space and tone, were stylistic devices which were able to render a form 'beautiful' by virtue of the way these elements were used. The concept 'aesthetic' then seems locked into definitions within modernist and dualist discourse. The role of the artist as supreme originator of meaning because of some innate gift of ability was of course connected to ' transcendent' notions of goodness and morality, specifically within Romantic discourse. This usage of the term 'beautiful', then has its originations in Romantic discourse, and is something I want to question and disorientate in the location of a neo-aesthetics.

However, through a neo-aesthetics, the 'beautiful' is not necessarily consilient with goodness, the romantic, or transcendent notions, or to visual pereceptions of image or form, but to a feeling of duration, immanent and transversal trajectories, movement and processuality: what Deleuze refers to as 'haecceity' or 'intensity'.[4] Neither is the 'beautiful' defined as it was in modernism, as 'individual spontaneity' or 'cultural imposition.'. This neo-aesthetic is an aesthetic premised on the materiality of the body / mind / world as process, not an aesthetic premised on standards of taste, form or beauty within a modernist dialectic, or on the dualism of subjectivity and objectivity. The beautiful, in this neo-aesthetic, is premised on processuality, performativity, continual movement not form or image. The determination of beauty becomes temporal, not reflective: an open-ended process, a feeling of flowing, rhythm, or 'becoming'. Indeed, a refreshing concern with becoming-woman rather than desire or pleasure, requires us to think about sensation as a rhythmical, durational experience, not one of static shock of excitations on the nervous system.

The concept of the beautiful in classical definitions was premised on an external opposition of object and subject, between objectivity and subjectivity. A different definition of beautiful within a neo-aesthetic involves a melding of these terms as inseparable elements of 'matter'. A new conception of the 'beautiful' and sensation within the neo-aesthetic is not premised upon romantic, transcendent individualism but it is based upon impersonal, biological, corporeal 'matter' in the material: what I refer to as an immanence of 'becoming-woman'. Thus 'beauty' has nothing to do with 'taste' or a judgement of taste, but is rather a felt 'immediacy', 'force' or 'intensity" in process. A neo- aesthetic in this sense then is an aesthetic as a transient and ephemeral manner of being in continual process, or 'becoming', where subjectivity is rendered subjectless. The affective is a material state, as much as it is deemed a psychic state within psychoanalysis. Deleuze writes of the significance of this sense of 'immediacy' or 'force' as pertaining to all the arts, 'there is a community of the arts, a common problem. In art, and in painting as in music, it's not a question of reproducing or inventing forms, but of harnessing forces.' [5]

In this neo-aesthetic paradigm, process then takes precedence over *form*. The 'beautiful' of the neo-aesthetic is contained in its autonomy. This autonomy is a 'subjectless subjectivity' that is expressed in the process of perception. The filmic encounter involves all aspects of the body's sensibilities, not just vision and brain: eye and cortex, but the entire body, an integrating of the materiality of film and the environment. Subject and object integrate into a larger autonomy of involvement, matter and mind meld together, as a technic or as an assemblage. This understanding of aesthetics as a 'neo-aesthetics' is seen more as an empiricism than as romanticism. The neo-aesthetic experience involves a whole and total engagement with molecular forces of being in the world. A complete depersonalisation is involved, where subjectivity is rendered subjectless. Barbara McClintock explains how this 'depersonalisation' feels in describing her scientific work, 'The more I worked (with chromosomes) the bigger and bigger they got, and when I was really working with them I wasn't outside, I was down there. I was part of the system... As you look at these things, they become part of you. And you forget yourself. The main thing is that you forget yourself.'[6] Rather than a feeling being felt then by some 'subjectivity,' as we detect in earlier debates on the aesthetic, a feeling is not owned by a subject, but the subject is *part of* the feeling. In other words, the 'subjective encounter' is experienced within the materiality of existence. 'The world and I exist in difference, in encounter. In the feeling, being is *in* sensation'.[7]

***Towards Deleuzian "becomings.....***

Daniel Stern's work on *The Interpersonal World of the Infant,* explores in detail the existence of a transitivist and fusional emergent self; a self that ignores oppositions of subject/object and masculine /feminine. Together with the work of Raymond Ruyer, Stern's work has been extremely significant to Deleuze and his conception of 'becoming'. However, I wish to foreground the significance of Ruyer's work here in several ways. His ideas have purchase in how visual perception is conceived as an in-itself outside of any scopic action of an eye-I relational. Deleuze's notion of autopoiesis, the self-enjoyment of the transivitist and emergent self, the absolute interiority, is premised upon both Stern's and Ruyers'work. Deleuze's notion of a schizoanalytic subjectivity posits multiple strata of subjectivation in a multi-componenetial cartography; one which is opposed to the 'conscious-unconscious' binary of psychoanalytic configurations and is premised on the work of Ruyer. It is not so much a total denial of subjectivity, but a recognition that it exists in pre-verbal and pathic consistencies,beyond the individual. Such pathic events or consistencies are referred to as multiplicities. It is of course, difficult for rational modes of discourse to accept an existence of a non-discursive affective pathic awareness. Ruyer's biological philosophy proposes a connection between mind and matter which does not distinguish them as seperate entities. Ruyer posits the notion of an absolute 'true form' which 'is an absolute consistent form that surveys 'itself' independently of any supplementary dimension,which does not appeal therefore to any transcendence,which has only a single side whatever the number of its dimensions,which remains co-present to all its determinations without proximity or distance,traverses them at speed,without limit-speed..' [8] Indeed one of the main contentions of Deleuze's work is that it posits an ideality that is actually a dimension of matter. All things are material. He argues, 'I see no reason to refuse the existence of the equivalent of a subjectivity or proto-subjectivity to material and living assemblages.' Deleuze seems to be looking for a sense of subjectivities which is not based on a subject, or intentionality or psychoanalytic perceptions of subject/object co-ordinates. He is suggesting, and this can be seen in *Cinema 2* and in the final chapter of *What is Philosophy?* that there is an auto-possession, an autopoiesis, or self-enjoyment felt through the brain/body prior to any emergence of a phenomenal field..In other words the brain is the 'mind'. All we ever are is brain/mind meld. Images thus exist within this brain/mind/body meld, not outside in the world itself.

'Becomings' in Deleuze are seen as 'affects' and it is the subsuming of subjectivity through the notion of the affective state as existing in the preverbal, and material spaces of autopoiesis, that becomes central to a location of a neo-aesthetics of affect. The affect or intensity of 'becoming' is accomodated through molecularity, in these very singularites and multiplicites of the presubjective field. Deleuze writes,

> ' [A]ll becomings are already molecular. That is because becoming is not to imitate or identify with something or someone. Nor is it to proportion formal relations. Neither of these two figures of

> analogy is applicable to becoming; neither the imitation of a subject, not the proportionality of a form. Starting from the forms one has, the subject one is, the organs one has, or the functions one fulfills, becoming is to extract particles between which one establishes the relations of movement and rest, speed, and slowness that are closest to what one is becoming, and through which one becomes. This is the sense in which becoming is the process of desire.... becoming is to emit particles that take on certain relations of movement and rest because they enter into a particular zone of proximity.
>
> ...All becomings are molecular; the animal, flower, or stone one becomes are molecular collectivities, haecceities, not molar subject, objects, or forms that we know from the outside and recognize from experience, through science or by habit.' [9]

For Deleuze and Guattari, it is the process of 'becoming-woman,' which is key to all becomings. 'Becoming-woman' for both men and women is conceived as a molecular process, one which releases fragments or particles of 'sexuality' ( a sexuality that is no longer linked with the unified and genitalised sexed body) which break down the binary aggregations. The process of 'becoming-woman' is not based upon any recognition of an actual entity , as a 'molar' entity woman. The process of 'becoming-woman' for men and women, is a destabilization of the molar identity and as such promotes a molecular and general process of transformation. The very system of thought which prioritises a 'subject' to 'woman' is through 'becoming-woman' questioned. Subjectivity instead is subsumed through the alignment of effects of certain processes. As Elizabeth Grosz indicates,' subjectivity is subsumed through effects or consequences of processes of sedimentation, the congealing and co-agulation of processes, interrelations of 'machines' of disparate components, functioning in provisional alignment with each other to form an ensemble.'[10]

'Becoming-woman' is part of a rhizomatic conception of thought which does not premise definitions in fixed and binary ways. Such rhizomatics, even though not directly supportive of active feminist struggles in the molar sense, helps to open up possibilities of thinking in experimental and creative ways. It is not a denial of the political category of 'woman' entirely. The term 'becoming-woman' is used here as part of a 'molecular' way of thinking, part of a micro-politics, not a molar way of thinking. 'Becoming-woman' involves a series of movements and processes which are outside the fixity of molar concepts like 'subjectivity'. It is instead an escape from binary concepts that privilege the masculine at the expense of the feminine. 'Becoming-woman' means going 'beyond identity and subjectivity...fragmenting and freeing up lines of flight...liberating a thousand tiny sexes.' It is rather a neo-pragmatic turn on subjectivity. 'Becoming-woman' is a mapping or tracking of woman as a 'function' of a series of processes which have no referent to transcendent entities or agency. Rather these processes function or operate at a molecular level, at a level of material production. Rosi Braidotti's critique that Deleuzian 'becoming' offers no space for a specifically feminist subjectivity might be answered with the argument that Deleuze's work exposes those very mechanisms which produce such transcendent notions. His aim is to deploy the concept of 'becoming-woman' as particles or as fibres, as an element within a critical neo-pragmatics.

Deleuzian ideas enable a rethinking of the very elements in relation to which woman is understood.Thus a 'becoming-woman' will enable a move away from all those disabling concerns with subjectivity and agency maintained in a macro-political dialectic. The position of 'woman' in relation to the 'subject' has historically and culturally remainded fairly consistent. Philosophy traditionally reflected woman as other through a wide array of discourses. Irigaray has specifically referred to the notion of an immanent principle of woman in her article 'Ce sexe qui n'en est pas un' in which she describes woman's subjectivity as multiple, diffracted, dissipated, modelled on the very physicality of her sexual corporeal body. However, such a view of 'woman' consistently sees woman in the position of 'other' and as a function of 'subjectivity'. What 'becoming-woman' in Deleuzian terms does is enable a view of woman in relation to the elemental, the material, the local, forces (mattter, passion, chaos, affection, affect,) where subjectivity is replaced through a materiality and a molecularity of 'becoming'.

*Rethinking 'Body'*

This move to conceptualising materiality however requires a different understanding of the term *body* which is outside those defined by binary discourses. Deleuzian conceptions of the body,based on Spinoza, rethink the body outside of its configurations in such binary discourse. The body is perceived as a set of forces, intensities, processes, molecular and fibrous particles in connection with other forces and in consilience with the materiality of the brain. Nature, matter, affection and passion are *not* here perceived as static or negative terms, but flowing, transitional, relational, changing and creative. Therefore their connotations in relation to 'woman' no longer suggest 'otherness'. Deleuze and Guattari's idea of 'becoming-woman' provides machinery for a reformulation of the 'body' itself. I want to extend that thinking to a new conception of the term 'body' in relation to aesthetics and the cinematic. 'Woman' then is not conceived as a 'concept' or as a specific form of 'body' but as an element in a set of relations in process and assemblage. This is a philosophical turn on the definition of 'woman' away from transcendent definitions. Woman is definable as the *processes* and *orders* into which she is installed. The critical question then for feminism ( and I would argue post-feminism) now is not whether this is a positive or negative trope of 'woman' in representational terms, but what *processes* are involved in the *production* of 'woman' as a volitional relation of processes?

Woman is part of an arsenal of pragmatics in rethinking 'becoming' instead of subjectivity. Thus 'becoming-woman' is not captured or restricted within a specific physical form. It is not chromosomally, psychoanalytically, biologically, culturally, libidinally or socially defined. This re-wiring of processes is therefore immanent to material flows. These are not conceptually driven. They are *affectively* driven. 'Becoming-woman' is then, a process of *affectivity*, not a concept which describes a move towards a political agency or subjectivity.

*Bodies without Organs*

To explore how Deleuze and Guattari connect the 'becoming-woman' to *affectivity*, we need to consider their idea of 'bodies without organs'. This is a new formulation of 'body' outside its definition as a set of organs, blood, bones, etc. and as seen in oposition to the mind and consciousness. In Deleuzian terms,'body' is conceived differently. The concept of 'body without organs' is an attempt to denaturalise the body. Rather than see the body as a corporeal entity, Deleuze and Guattari describe the body as set of variously informed 'speeds' and 'intensities'. It is conceived in relation to other bodies, particles of other bodies or entitites. This is premised on a Spinozist conception of the univocity of being.i.e. that everything has the same ontological status. Thus all of life in a sense becomes a 'body' in a material connection. Body without Organs refers to all bodies, animate, inanimate, human, inhuman, textual, social and cultural. But this Body Without Organs is a body which is disinvested of any psychical fantasies as we see in psychoanalysis. Rather the Body Without Organs is an abstract notion, a concept of thinking of the body as a tendency ...a becoming. As Grosz indicates,

> It is the body before and in excess of the coalescence of its intensities and their sedimentation into meaningful, functional, organised, transcendent totalities,.....it is a point or process to which all bodies, through their stratifications, tend......... a becoming.[11]

The Body without Organs is not a place, or a scene or an actual 'body'. It is a field of consistency or immanence, for the production and circulation of the process of desire. It is the plane of consistency as opposed to the plane of organisation. If The Body Witout Organs is the space of 'becomings' it is important to see it in this abstract way, not as a defined expression about the physical, corporeal fleshed 'body'. Bodies are not stable units, but become elements in assemblage, fluid and mutable, constituting life through 'becoming'. This is an abstract level of description from the body as perceived in binary discourses of

Enlightenment/Cartesian ideas. Deleuzian conceptions of body convey the main features of 'bodies' as openness, change, mutability, fluidity, processuality, duration, feedback, complexity.Through the 'body' then an immanent self-organisation replaces transcendent principles, determining the value of the 'body' from binary divisions. Thus 'becoming-woman' has nothing to do with 'real women' in the biological , cultural and physical sense of 'woman'. 'Becoming-woman' is a process of immanence, a description of a processual experience of the affect as opposed to the 'subject'.

Becomings are always specific movements, specific forms of rest, motion, speed and slownesses, points and flows of intensity. Such flows of intensity operate outside subjectivity and gendered subjectivity through the "*affect*". Affects are becomings, and what I want to term the 'becoming-woman' of cinema is a concern with the affective processes at work in the experience of the cinematic. Those affective processes are effectuated through the 'unthought', through the material of the 'body/mind/brain' at a deeper level than the 'subjective'. The unthought is felt as 'intensity' as 'becoming' in a molecular connection beyond any notion of an 'individuated body'.

## *Becomings..... to affect*

The process of 'becoming' then foregrounds the *affective.* Deleuzian conception of 'becoming' is predicated upon a materialist aesthetic. His use of the concept 'becoming' as I have argued, is imbued with material forces of bodily affect, the contingency of forces at work within, across and outside the body. A pragmatics of 'becoming' uses contingent assemblages of thinking processes through which to distanciate the concept of 'subjectivity'. Subjectivities can be determined as merely simulacra which are subsumed to a more profound engagment with the forces of 'becoming', material, molecular, and fibrous forces, rewired, as I indicated earlier across new assemblages outside of language construction. A post-feminist agenda in film theory, as a political and ethical framework enables thinking 'outside' the boundaries of epistemological, Cartesian thought.

This new engagement with cinematic desires thus proposes to consider cinema as 'affect', where the affect operates beyond subjectivity, in the process of 'becoming'. It functions through the processual engagement with the materiality of film itself, through an immanence of movement, force, and intensity, not through a semiotic regime of signification or representation. Questions of desire are relocated or rather dislocated from sentient identification with semiotics, psychoanalysis or subjective reading positions. Rather desire is rendered processual, immanent, created through the modulational and vibrational expressions of the 'affective'.

How do we begin to define a concept of 'affect'. There is no cultural-theoretical paradigm or vocabulary that is specific to 'affect'. Texts, visual or literary have until most recently always been explained, explored, theorised and critiqued through theories of 'signfication', 'ideology' 'representation' and 'psychoanalysis'. How can we begin to explain a volitional and involutional understanding of affect if we are constrained to work within verbal language structures? Affect has been loosely aligned to emotion. But there is a significant difference between these two terms. Affect and emotion are not synonomous, but interlocked. However, they are different. An emotion has a 'subjective' content: a 'subject' functions as the experiencer of an 'emotion'. There is a clearly perceived agent or subject. Through Deleuzian conceptions, affect is not ownable by an individuated agent in the same way as emotion.

The contradiction is, how can we critique 'affect' if it is indiscernible to an agent, to a subject? It is Spinoza's work on Ethics that Deleuze uses as his grounding for the term 'affect'. Spinoza's philosophy explores the difference between affect and emotion. He explains that affect has an irreducible bodily and autonomic nature.(Autonomic here is defined as purely a physical response to something, a sensual response e.g. skin getting warmer or heart beating faster ) Affect is a suspension of action-reaction circuits and linear temporality in to what might be called 'passion'. This distinguishes it from passivity or activity.

Furthermore Ruyer's work as earlier explained, gives us a newly-technologised understanding of affect as a state of 'subjectless subjectivity'. The affect exists in the materiality of the brain/body consilence at a molecular level. At this level of the non-human, proto-subjectivity, the molecular describes a state which has an understanding of its own existence. Quantum physics currently describes microtubules which exist within the emergent sense of all organisms. In other words, all molecular organisms have a sense of 'aliveness', an existential integrity, or being in the world, outside any sense of consciousness.[12] Thus affect is an emotionless state, but still a state of feeling.There is a *pathic* proto-subjective state which is not owned by the subject. Aesthetic desires are 'becomings' and they cannot be fixed or positioned in terms of extrinsic systems of reference. Rather they are articulated through transitivist, transversalist and pathic consistencies. As Guattari writes, 'one gets to know them not through representation, but through *affective* contamination'.

### *The 'becoming-woman' of the cinematic.*

The 'becoming-woman' of cinema, then, is a phrase which I wish to foreground as a new term in post-feminist film theory and generates from a synthesis of Deleuzian ideas on 'becoming' and 'affect'. It enables a move from thinking beyond gendered subjectivity, through a corporeal and material sense of connection with the movements of the filmic text. Desire is subsumed to 'event', a modulational event that is effectuated through the molecular, material emotion, through the processuality of the affects of the film as body, with other bodies: the ways in which colours vibrate, clash, co-incide ; the tones of their dimensions, the blending of their boundaries, the patterns of linearity. latitudinal and longitudinal, across the frame, the rhythms and movements felt across the screen , the role of sound within the synaesthetic and choreographical experience. Not in any psychic or libidinal ways as has been theorised in psychoanalysis, for example, but through the physicality of the materiality of the film as body, connecting with other bodies, corporeal, material, molecular ; bodies as life, bodies constituting life. The 'becoming-woman' of cinema entails processes beyond corporealised vision into a concern with movement-image, affect, haecceity, synaesthesia and kinaesthetics: a coagulation of cinema as a machinic, technologised, and corporeal body. For Nietzsche, there is no distinction between the world in which we live and any other 'transcendent' world'. There is not ultimate truth, no other metaphysical world to which we can aspire. Rather there is only ever the processual of the real in time, the real forces of life's natural existence in its germinal and viral contingencies. 'Becoming' epitomises that process of affirmation of the dynamic of the living in the real world, an acceptance of the cruelty of life, the joy of cruelty in that existence, the acceptance of the ineluctability of life's transience. There is no 'other' to w hich we aspire..all there ever is is the 'real' and within our experience of the real, the concept of 'becoming' serves to define life's ephemerality, life's ineluctability and sheer vibrance of rhythmic movement, force and dynamism.Thus 'becoming' in Deleuze may be described as an affirmation of the positivity of life's 'differences', life's 'ineluctability through difference and repetition'. Consequently, identity is never singular and does not exist as a determinate factor in our existence. Identity is in constant flux and process, continually swirling through a vortex of molecularity, and even subsumed through more profunond forces of the molecular. With this emphasis on processes, affirmation and movement, Deleuze's notion of 'becoming-woman' offers the existence of fluid boundaries in a materialist and vitalist sense of immanence as opposed to transcendence. How is immanence defined here?

For the purposes of this article, I shall explain that the term 'immanence' is used in contrast with the term 'transcendence'.This is a simplistic and residual explanation for the purposes of this paper and in no way is there space here for me to take on board the entire debate of *Anti-Oedipus* in relation to Desire. This is formulated to some extent eleswhere.[13] Deleuze argues against psychoanalytic frameworks of desire. He argues that psychoanalysis is premised upon Freudian notions of desire emanating from the need to return to originations, to a lost state of plenitude, a finite sense of oneness in finitude, through Death, where there is an ultimate return to an inorganic state of oneness in death. This is a *transcendent model* of desire where there is a constant wish to repeat and a compulsion to move beyond death to this transcendent state. Alternatively Deleuzian debate proclaims that desire is processual, immanent, productive and energic, and has nothing to do with forces of transcendence or a need to return to a lost plenitude, through Death. Rather Desire is aleatory, processual and constitutive of joy. Desire is produced, it does not emanate from lack, or the abyssal as in psychoanalysis. It is immanent, it is energic, and dynamic joy lies in its immanence, a continual process of contemplative and productive forces.

A 'becoming-woman' of the cinematic then is an exploration of the affective, processual, the dynamic and aleatory vitalism of the forces felt across the bodies of the cinematic experience. If we can move away from thinking about 'becoming-woman' as a description of an *entity*, the term enables a transformation from concept to affect. The 'becoming-woman' of cinema describes the affective process of the cinematic experience where the affective is constituted through a materiality of emotion, a *material* sense of depth and volitional process.

### *Constituting bodies - constituting life*

A 'becoming-woman' of the cinematic will develop and creatively engage with thinking about the affective intensities of the visual experience as it impinges on the non-scopic elements of our bodies/minds/brains,our molecular bodies, and thus outside theories of gendered spectatorship. Woman as 'image' may sit alongside the 'becoming-woman' of the process of movement-image, affection-image and the processuality of synaesthetics... a total 'becoming-woman' of cinema. Deleuzian concern with affect and the affective intensity is part of the same cartography of visions of the concept 'becoming-woman'. The 'becoming-woman' of cinema is accomodated through the relations of screens as 'bodies' as molecular bodies, with observers as 'bodies' Deleuzian ideas on the body are not confined to one paradigm. The body is a set of relations, human, inhuman, material, animate and inanimate. Spinoza suggests, 'Bodies are not defined by their genus, nor by their organs and functions, by what they can do, the affects they are capable of in passion and in action' [14] Following upon this , Deleuze relates that, 'The categories of life are precisely the attitudes of the body, its postures.We do not know what a body can do'[15] Experiencing a film then, as 'body' describes the 'felt' experience of engaging with the rhythmic, gestural and attitudinal spaces of the bodies within the diegesis of the film's mise-en-scene, as well as bodies, outside of the text itself. Bodies do not function to 'represent' a character, (but of course they may still do that) then, but are attitudes, relations of bodies in space and time, across space and time, and within space and time. The character is articulated as attitude, as 'gest' as 'spectacle'. To realise the fundamental becoming of life requires the relinquishment of the mind/body dualism. The body then is implicated significantly within the mind/brain cinematic assemblage.The body is sound as well as vision. All elements of the 'image' come together in 'body'.

Sounds, colours, tones and shadows become attitudes of the body, felt synaesthetically, constituted at a deeper level beyond audition,beyond figuration, as Deleuze says... 'at a deeper level than that of subjectivity.' The post-new wave cinema that is now part of our eclectic neo-millenial culture is a reworking of these directions. The attitudes, and postures of the body, speed, forces, and affect, become the event of the cinematic experience, not just through avant-garde cinema, but through more mainstream popular cinema. The eclecticism of styles is bricolaged through contemporary movies, such that avant-garde practices and aesthetics have a newly revived appropriacy and a germinal role to play in the evolution of cinema.

How does this exploration of the 'body'offer new ways forward in theorising 'body' in relation to 'woman' and how is this implicated in a 'becoming-woman' of cinema. As I have already argued, the term 'becoming-woman' is not operating as a literal concept of woman as entity. But if we are to take up this debate again, I think we can discern some interesting points, but also points of tension, about woman and body, which might usefully fit into this new aesthetics of the cinematic experience and simultaneously enable a pragmatic understanding of body in relation to feminist theory. Chantal Ackerman's work for example, has presented movies which show the 'gestures' of woman and woman's body in a specifically political positionality: the female body denoting specific female states of mind, pertinent to a female character. Similarly in dance, the movements and planes of experience operate outside any descriptive faculty of the mind through language. Flows, rhythms, and speeds of different planes, flights of parallel dimensions, and vertical collusions connect the body to the wider 'body' of temporal and spatial zones. Dance and performance effectuate vortices of becoming, through a 'becoming-woman'. This is premised on the chain of states of the female body which is dynamic, volatile, contingent and multiply diffracted. It works as a processual 'gest', in movement, and rhythm, across the diegesis of the screen, a revelation and exhiliration to both coporeal, flesh and blood, women and men. This 'openness' of woman's body may seem to have essentialist connotations.Woman defined as intuitive, emotional, irrational, never fixed, in chaos and dissimulation. But that very fluidity, openness, potential for connection and amorphousness HAS presented both a political and an aesthetic claim for a feminine aesthetic (one deemed in contrast to a masculine concern with form, narrativity and structure). Although th is seems to present a tension within the argument put forward so far, we need to re-think this idea of 'woman's body' as an open chain of states, but not one located within the essentialist determinations of woman as 'body'. If we can rewire and 'technologise' the terms of 'woman' and 'body' through Deleuzian processes of collusion, then we can rethink the concepts in their relavence to both dance and performance. Film is then seem as a balletic cartography within the mainstream text as much as the avant-garde text's of Chantal Ackerman. The woman's body in performance, both choreographically in dance, as much as acting styles on screen, achieves a sort of 'strangeness' and aesthetic distanciation, evoking a depth and 'gestural' force. It becomes a ceremony, an event, a cartography , an element within an assemblage of the film's process, no longer contained as 'representation'. It functions outside of semiotics or metaphor. The cinematic screen is not merely a space for the visual representation, but becomes a cartography of the visual, through a *constitution of bodies:*, not just woman's body/ The screen becomes an intersticial space of variations, cuts, fades,wipes,blank screens, absences, over-exposed and under-exposed images,variations and tonalities of colour, shape, forms, and movements...a complete cartography of the screen.The screen no longer functions with merely structural values, but transversal, genetic, molecular, germinal and viral.....a set of interrelational bodies, a processual 'becoming-woman'. Indeed, cinema works through these ways as an 'experimental night or a white space over us, it works as dancing seeds, and as luminous dust. It affects the visible with a fundamental disturbance and the world with a suspension ,which contradicts all natural perception.'[16] So it follows from this that the cinematic experience produces a 'body', a felt 'body', a depth of 'becoming' beyond subjectivity, which is inarticulable through verbal language and structural, semiotic explanation.

***Romeo and Juliet; - a harmonics of performativity.***

If we take these ideas then to some analysis of contemporary popular movies, how do we find a neo- aesthetics at work? When our bodies absorb the movements of the screenic images instead of reflecting them, our activity can be described as effort, or as I have outlined throughout as 'affect'.The 'affect' replaces or at least is a simultaneous counterpart to representation. One of the most exciting films recently which epitomises the 'becoming-woman' and performs as a body, as image-concept-affect, is Baz Lurhmann's *Romeo and Juliet*. Lurhmann's film produces a theatricality of the cinema which is totally distinct from the theatricality of the theatre.We see this at work equally in Strictly Ballroom.. Director's like Scorsese have often portrayed this 'gestural' or 'pathic' constitution of bodies in their films. I am thinking here of Scorsese's *Age Of Innocence,* where the camera movements are a beautiful choreography through colour, texture, space and sounds providing a bio-vital aesthetic. Sounds and colours become attitudes of the body, categories constituiting new bodies in neo-aesthetic consilience.

A movie like *Romeo and Juliet,* which works and connects specifically through movements, processuality, duration, intensities and rhythms, expresses a Deleuzian sense of 'becoming -woman'. Becoming-woman is that process of immanence, a description of a processual experience of affect as opposed to subject. The molar and the molecular in coagulation, in collusion. Any valorisation of a neo-aesthetics or materialist aesthetic, which functions within the pre-personal realm of becoming need not totally deny or distanciate an aesthetic premised on the emotions. Indeed, it should sit alongside all those other realms of film theory, to create a perspectival paradigm for film studies. Indeed, where is the space 'between'?
An imbrication then of the narrative molar level of engagement with the film's diegesis, mise-en-scene, plot, its 'plane of

organisation' is to an extent constituted through a more fibrous molecularity; its aesthetic configurations. Through its aesthetics, the film works as a 'body' in collusion with other bodies. Its 'body without organs' might, parodically evoke an emotional concern, with love, in a postmodern climate, which is both parodied and substantiated. A total complexity in its denial and acceptance of the primordial world of 'unworded experiences' and a 'pre-linguistic insight into life'.

In exploring *Romeo and Juliet* through a becoming-woman and neo-aesthetics of sensation, I firstly recall Deleuze's point in *Logique de la Sensation,* that,

> 'Beyond figuration and representation, then, sensation comes from a pure power that "overflows all domains, and traverses them. This power is that of Rhythm, which is deeper than vision, audition... etc. 'A logic of the senses,' Cezanne said, 'that is non-rational, non-cerebral.'[17]

*Romeo and Juliet* resonates with multiple rhythms. Its very visual display is rhythmical, (I mean that the visuals themselves are effectively 'rhythmical' before any musical connection) with a variety of specular effects enhanced by a variety of different musical genres, in different tempos, cadences, modulations and melodies. The subjective encounter is indeed, hystericised beyond subjective spectatorial perspectives. The subjective is subsumed by forces of affect, through the elements of sensation: intensities, rhythms, flows of energy, lines of flight. Energy resonates vibrantly, passionately, incisively, through the scintillating score and visceral mise-en-scenes. This energy is most apparent through the musical elements in collaboration with the patterns of lines of longitude, latitude, and diagonals, much like the paintings of Mondrian or Kandinsky, traversing the frames of various sequences. A veritable moving canvas. The film modulates as a choreography, as a dance, like the paintings of Mondrian and Kandinsky, with lines of flow, rhythmically moving across, through, above, within, and beyond the frame of the screen. These patternings of line are operative through specific sequences in the film and they function in contrast with and in vibration and resonance with the more fluid, gentler and softer sequences, where colour functions prior to line and dynamics.[18] The 'subject' then is subsumed in the beyond of becoming, becoming-woman through and in sensation. The visual act of seeing, ceases to be a merely organic activity, 'our eye ceases to be organic, to become a polyvalent and transitory organ: objectively it holds before us the reality of a body of lines, of colours, liberated from organic representations'.[19]

This quotation is specifically relevant to *Romeo and Juliet* A vibratory facticity, a connection of sensations, vibrations and rhythms come together in the 'haecceity' that is Romeo and Juliet. Indeed, we should here remember Deleuze's quote that 'sensation contracts vibrations of the stimulant on a nervous surface or in a cerebral volume: what comes before has not yet disappeared when what follows appears'. [20] How then does the film exude such haecceities?

Baz Lurhmann's richly textured, erotic and visceral post-modern rendition of *Romeo and Juliet* takes the original Shakespearean text as its script, but fractures it through an exuberant choreography of dizzying visuals and auditory rhythms, tones, nuances: a veritable sensory delight! Contemporary popular music, classical and opera create an eclectic pastiche of sounds which eclipses each and every visual moment of the movie. Indeed, the film was, on release, marketed and promoted through its sound-track. Music 'performs' as a fibrous core through the text, creating a post-modern opera, through an assemblaged architecture of different sounds, diegetic and non-diegetic, evoking the concerns of love, sexuality, (but a sexuality outside the confines of gender; the film is in its processuality very sexy!) death and tragedy. Indeed, sounds become gestures, which are also vocal, as Deleuze writes in *Cinema 2*,

> where the visible body disappears......... What is freed in non-desire is music, and speech, their intertwining in a body which is now only sound, a body of new opera. It is no longer the characters who have a voice, but it is the voices, or rather the vocal modes of the protagonist (whisper, breathing, shout, eruction) which become the sole true characters.[21]

The mise-en-scene of *Romeo and Juliet,* is set within a contemporary American/Brazilian cityscape - in fact from the statue of Christ which looms out and provides an ambivalent icon of both love and death, we can see this is set in Rio de Janeiro (a westernised Verona in several senses of the word). Here, Shakespearean lords and kinsmen are replaced with a sexy, colourful array of young popular dudes, straight and gay, transvestites, bisexuals, transsexuals, punks, bikers and sado-masochists. We are given characteristic emblems of the contemporary world of corporate finance (Paris) or else exotic, plumed and pulchral visions of excess and the carnivalesque (Mercutio). Romeo (Leonardo di Caprio) seems to fit somewhere inbetween, but his tendencies towards romantic love render him an innocent among such company! An innocent who nonetheless finds himself guilty of murder. Love and hate yet part of the same equation of passion. However, that charming, witty and parodic post-modernism merely enthrals in its parallelism or repetition in difference of love, tenderly and sensitively enacted through the innocence of youth. (Claire Danes as Juliet and Leonardo di Caprio as Romeo). The cynicism of parody is thus tinged with the proverbial delights of a 'neo-romantic' venture as a reply to the horrific renditions of a culture embroiled in the sometimes bereft despair and ugliness of irony, parody, deceit, critique and an all-pervading fear of the existence of 'love', or what that might mean in a post-post-structuralist climate! Fear of tradition, a disrespect for originations, a disdain for 'depth' and 'meaning' are ironically juxtaposed, becoming simultaneously a respect for a text and language that does speak with metonym and metaphor - a denial of everything Deleuze stands for. Such contradictions. The movie is both post-modern and yet post-post-modern in its forces, intensities and resonances of haecceity. Shakespearean language, taken out of its traditional literary context, becomes part of the 'energies' as it colludes and collides with contemporary sounds, diegetically and non-diegetically, through which the film impacts. Meanings, whether parodic or not, are actually not what concerns this Deleuzian exploration of the 'event', the 'haecceity', the 'becoming-woman' of the film.

There is across the movie, a repetition-in-difference of all the various elements: generic characteristics such as character, plot, narrative, but also in terms of time and spatial zones. A difference-in-repetition across visual and aural 'affects' through 'becoming'. A neo-aesthetics here, is explored through differential relations - unlike Freudian psychoanalytic ideas on pleasure (tied up with inorganic death originations) and 'bound excitation'. Deleuze refers instead to 'differential relations', differentiated forms of material and molecular elements of our make up. So the generic characteristics no longer hold the only validity for understanding the impact of the cinematic event. Instead, other categories impose: colours, sounds, fill the in-between spaces of the filmic text. The ways in which the colours clash, coincide, resonate, the dimensions of their tones and blurring of boundaries, the linearity across and within the frames - provide rhythms and movements across the screen, and this functions as sensation as opposed to 'pleasure'.

Rather than think of the movie as a filmic version of the famous romantic myth, I want to explore how *Romeo and Juliet* works as a rhythmical, processual and moving set of energies and intensities. It is an intensely rhythmical experience, set within a variety of different intonations of metre, timbre, pace, tone and voice. Certainly it does operate at the level of the molar, or semiotic and the ideological and psychoanalytic readings could be a mechanism through which to explore its text. Such possibilities are inherent in the textual elements. (For example, the scene where Romeo and Juliet meet is replete with looks, gazes, returned stares between glass, screens and/or mirrors. Also, the Boschian-like party sequence has some beautiful characters straight out of Freud's 'uncanny'. ) However, the entire experience, as a two hour event, works as a 'body' in connection with a rhythmical set of performances, resonant through a varied display of musical notations, scales, cadences, contrapuntal nuances, dissonances and lyrical patterns which collide and vibrate with both dialogue and visuals.

The music provides the main system to the film. We can discern a set of sequences, cleanly defined across different types of music. Through the music as an overall architectonic fibre, we find a neo-aesthetics at work. When our bodies absorb the movements of the screenic images, instead of reflecting them, our activity can be described as effort, or, as I have outlined, as 'affect'. The 'affect' replaces or at least is simultaneous to representation. One of the most exciting films which epitomises the 'becoming-woman' of sensation, and performs as a body, in locomotion, as a concept-image-affect, *Romeo and Juliet* produces

a theatricality of the cinema which is totally distinct from the theatricality of the theatre. As Artaud and Carmele Bene suggest, the cinema can bring about a more profound theatricalisation than theatre. Here bodies embrace, entwine and intertwine, bodies which animate the scene, as Deleuze states, 'each body has both space and light, the body is also sound as well as vision, all components of the 'image'come together on the body'.[22]
The film quite literally begins with a small television screen, centre frame. A face, (the screen is face, her face the screen) of a female presenter introduces us to the narrative of Shakespeare's *Romeo and Juliet.* From an instant image of a television screen displaying a face, we are carried into the spaces of the film's mise-en-scene. The face/screen becomes a body through a vibrant choreography of camera and cinematographic rhythms and cacophony of sounds. The film displays a vast array of forces, sheer velocities... force, movements, which are dynamic, ecstatic and jouissancial in their fluidity... a fluidity which is both static and dynamic. Take, for example, the opening shots of the movie. From the small television screen the camera pans out in vast sweeping gestures, as though carried on a helicopter, which then becomes part of the image.

We are carried, cinematographically, into the screen, on the helicopter, taking us into a contemporary Brazil/American city/beach esplanade, juxtaposing 16th century Verona, through sweeping rhythms of the camera, flying across, through, from all angles and positions, in a dizzying choreography of chaos. Still, blank screens with the words 'In Fair Verona' or 'A pair of star-crossed lovers' are juxtaposed with the action shots. The materiality of both sound molecule and the felt, haptic, experience of the visual, collide to carry us outside of our fixed bodies, to the extent that we feel that we do actually move, fly, swim, with the camera, in a dizzying disorientation. The heart literally races (remember the definition earlier of the affect as an autonomic physical response) with the viscerality of this sequence. We really do, as Deleuze indicates, occupy the interstices of the edits, cuts, wipes and fades of the camera, becoming part of the cinematic body and constituting a wider 'body' of world/body connections [23]

We feel the energy exacerbated through images of heat, death and destruction. A dramatic intensity proliferates the screen. Signifiers on billboards indicate contemporary destruction. Stills are framed in close-up shots, alongside wipes and fades. The Capulet Boys, and the Montague Boys invade/ seduce our space on the screen, parading their sexy, angular, Romanesque bodies through a palette of exuberance: cobalt, ultramarines, violets, blues, rich warm yellows, passionate and exotic reds. Flames engulf the screen in several places, creating a haptic scenario of passion and danger together. Textures of diamond-studded metal guns/swords, gleaming, feral, feline teeth, snarling, glowing bodies in armour seem to come straight out of a neo-western, replete with Sergio Leon-esque music. The hero's cowboy image is replaced with the majesty of the Roman centurion. Tybalts's erotic bodily display is matched by his equally intense and dynamic words, 'Peace, I hate the word ...'. His words act as a figural gest, in terms of the pitch, intonation and tone, as a cadence with the music, to present a poetic vibration with the diegetic musical sounds. The intensities of the movie are felt through its processual rhythms of colour, movement and sound. The flow and rhythm are so important to the diegesis of the film as are the feelings of openings, floating, floating and flying, effectuated through diagonal, vertical and other lines of movement.

The performativity of the film is indeed very beautiful. But not in any romantic sense of the word 'beautiful'. The processuality of the film takes over the formality of the aesthetic form of narrative closure. Things just 'flow'. The eye of the spectator moves in a dance of its own, in matrixial ways, imbricating the tactile within the scopic, a haptic sense of 'relationality.' This relational space is at the interstitial space of the subject and object, the in-between as I mentioned earlier. Such eroticisation of the eye means that the spectator's gaze functions processually to incorporate a synaesthetic assemblage; a 'felt' experience. The beautiful, as Brian Massumi suggests, 'in this view of aesthetics, is the incipient perception of the vitality of matter, its dynamogenic strength or force. Its autopoiesis'.[24]

Postmodern in its eclecticism, pastiche and parody, the diegesis presents choreographed bodies, flying, dancing and elegantly displaying and performing, such that we experience the totality of the screen as a body in movement, constituted from several bodies in locomotion. Some of the most evocative scenes are the fight sequences, where guns/swords are projectile prostheses and become part of the owner's performance, deftly choreographed to the point of vibratory exhilaration Symphonies of classical music, Mozart's 25th symphony and at times operatic music from Tristan and Isolde, drift into street style, bombastic rapper riffs and chords. Repetitious chords and riffs frisson through the body's depths. We are literally carried into the movie through sound as much as image. We 'become' part of the processuality of the film's movement, into a filmic body, as a whole harmonics of performativity. This sequence ends with the police warning the two houses of Capulet and Montague, of ensuing catastrophe in the light of their continued aggressions.

Cut............... to different music, different sequence ... *Angel,* a gently rhythmical piece, augmented with a stunning colourful mise-en-scene, brightly highlighted, of fireworks; purples, pinks, turquoise, gold, at Sycamore Grove. This is followed through with the move to the party scene, following Romeo's scene with Mercutio where they both indulge in drugs. Mercutio's speech to Romeo on 'love' in its lyricism, rhythm and volatility, designates an hysterical madness, whilst performing as an intensity, a volition within the patterns of sounds, resonating and bouncing off from the previous music. What follows is a beautifully choreographed and colourful drug-induced hallucination; catherine wheels swirling in colourful resonation in rhythm with the camera movements, circular tracking shots, which are circular and reeling in motion; this swirling action, together with the primary colours, impinges on the brain/eye movements in specifically pleasurable ways; nothing fixed, nothing angular. All is rhythmically and beautifully choreographed providing a processual experience. Colour experienced before form, movement before form[25] But only ever so gently mediated, that the process is almost instantaneously 'felt'. The variation of rhythms in the sequences contrast, complement and disrupt others or else they work as prosthetic assemblages.

The highlight of the party sequence is Mercutio's erotic display of cross-dressing, resplendent in white sequinned corset and stockings, (contrasting with the deep purple of the other dancers) white wig resonating against the masculinity of his moustached and dark, passionate, rich features. A delicious delirium of erotica. He descends the staircase to the vibrant sounds of Kim Mazelle's 'Young Hearts' (parody intended of course). His/her dance is part of different dance modes in the film.[26] In contrast with the earlier frenetic displays of flying bodies, his musical sequence gives a gentler swaying and creatively sculptural quality to its bodies and to the body, the wider 'body' constituted by both film, spectator and world. Bodies weave, collide, connect, oscillate and interrelate through a diegesis of 'malleable images'. Visions of excess, tactility, sensuality and the frisson of sexual exorbitance and transgression are visualised and hapticised (from the word 'haptic') through shapes, colours, and tones moving in time, but also dislocated from time. Demons, angels and whores become tropes from mythical fables and fabulations. Cleopatra to Caesar are masqueraded within the vibrance of the mise-en-scene and seem to come out of Freud's 'uncanny'. This is, of course, all an hallucinatory dream, induced by drugs, but as a film it works on the brain, as a form of altered state. Just as drugs work on the brain in chemical ways which affect the synaptic and neuronal mechanisms of the cellular structures, so too film as matter works on the brain in similar ways. Thus, such images are not purely 'images' (yes, of course they do also operate 'as' image - seen by the eye, but the eye/I is not a passive vessel of visual stimulants. Images are not merely representations, for interrogation, but 'elements of sensation', as the 'stuff' of matter, brain formations. The colours, movements and oscillations generate/compose the brain's active processes. The act of 'seeing' is not a passive thing, neither is it only an eye-I relational of psychic manifestations (although of course there is still a role for psychoanalysis and its more recent manifestation, in film theory. I am not trying to suggest we should deny this, but to suggest other frames in which film works on the brain). The brain actively creates the perception through molecular, and cellular actions. Percept and affect form as a block of sensation. The 'aesthetic composition agglomerates in transversal flashes, the self, the other, the material and the incorporeal, the before and the after... in short, affect is not a question of representation and discursivity, but of existence'. Indeed, it is this rich body of percepts and affects that displaces any fixed idea of identity and thus makes room for richer creative tendencies, accommodated through the imbrication of brain/mind and body, in collusion with the wider molecular and cellular body of life.

Juliet is introduced through her angelic costume, virginal white and delicately textured, marking the ethereality and chastity of her innocence. This works both as parody and yet is in its symbolism, tenderly sincere. Metaphorically and metonymnically then, the film does have many resonances. But in a Deleuzian sense, the film impacts as matter, as a processual 'event' in ways outside of representation, metaphor or imagery. It connects, it constitutes a 'worlding' process. It is a total worlding of experience of molecular forces through a materialist aesthetic.

The party mood is counterpointed by Des'ree singing the popular track 'Kissing You', with its romantic, soft and delicate rhythms and intonations, romantically bringing Romeo and Juliet together for the first time, but distanced through the screens of a vast aquarium. The languorous liquidity and fluidity of the colours and tones lends a sensuality to the mood and feel of the sequence. The swaying rhythms of the music are echoed through the liquid perception of the fish, swimming and wafting in the rippling water. Water provides again one of those molecular ways in which matter effectuates brain mechanisms. Pleasure is evoked by the gentle fluidity of rippling effects. Colours; greens, turquoise, blues, opals, lavenders are painted across a canvas which fades and wipes into a liquidity of sensuality and sensation. Dissipated lighting and rippling shades enhance the transience of the scene, highlighting the ephemerality and processuality, not only of this sequence, but the very image-concept-affect of 'love'. This is further enhanced by a display of camera movements, in a different dance structure; a swirling set of bodies, which reflects a charming and tender pattern of gazes, glances, looks, gestures, smiles and eye contact: matrixial patterns of looking across and between Romeo and Juliet, as Juliet dances with Paris. ( The dance sequence in *The English Patient* has similar resonances). The dance itself is a gentle, romantic, slow, delicate and controlled action of bodies, faces, close, and apart, resonances of ambiguities, sensibilities and sensitivities across two bodies which are eloquently apart - interestingly one looking, the other looked at! The depth of material emotion is part of the same canvas as romantic love.

The famous balcony sequence offers much in the way of vibrant movements, oscillations of lines, rhythms and resonances. A haptic sense of vision is created through the liquidity of the images, and the tactility of textures. The curtains sway eloquently, softly evoking haptic sensuality. The two bodies literally collide, resonate, and force each other apart here, swimming under water, and exhilaratingly in and out of each other's consciousness. Again, reflection, colours, tones and movements work together to create the undulating sensuality of the scene. The bodies in the water modulate, through both movement and colour, a liquidity of perception, where the perceived image is diffused into vibrations, so that the liquid movement goes beyond itself into a material, energic element (see earlier). The formation of the 'image' is defined by molecularity, not by visual representation. Sensation is accommodated through this molecularity.

The lyricism of Shakespeare's words works in delicate contrast to the post-modern parody of a '90s pastiche. The film continues to impact through the 'unthought' interstitial spaces, through the molar and the molecular. Juliet's initial speech, the famous 'Romeo, Romeo...' speech, works as a lyrical musical refrain, setting in counterpoint, the flickering, visual movements of the camera. It also works as a delicate parody, given the humour and comedy of the acting styles here - comic, awkward, angular, and farcical at times. Romeo continually falls over, colliding into things. The sequence ends with Romeo rushing off to Father Lawrence's, to the track, 'You and Me, Always, and Forever', a light-hearted and uplifting lyrical piece.

Music continues to provide the fibrous tissue for the film's diegesis and impact. In the rest of the movie, the variety of tones, lyrics and melodies of the musical notation, provide vibrational contrasts across and between sequences. The marriage of Romeo and Juliet is played out to the track 'Everybody's Free to Feel Good'. But the following death of Mercutio and Romeo's revenge on Tybalt, set in counterpoint and resonance with the marriage sequence, by the dramatic operatic music. Romeo's ensuing madness and banishment are further enhanced through the musical score, with intradiegetic music effecting its force upon our experience of the movie. Flashing lightning, chaotic camera angling, uncontrolled fits of passion and despair from Romeo's words, (firstly when he realises the severity of his killing of Tybalt and echoed again when he hears of Juliet's death) vibrate through the sound molecules of the soundtrack, all in contrapuntal collision with the earlier, delicate and joyous sequences. But such resonances (and I use the word resonance here in the Deleuzian sense) don't merely provide diegetic elements to a narrative. In Deleuzian paradigms of the 'beyond of desire' they impact with the molecularity of the brain to provide the processuality of the beyond of subjectivity, the becoming-woman of the cinematic, the aesthetics of sensation. In terms of my overall argument, then, the cinematic experience is something beyond the purely representational. If film theory has located debates within representation, semiotics and theories of desire premised on some sort of visual encounter with identity and subjectivity within that scenario, then to date such film theory has omitted to consider the wider impact upon the mind/brains/bodies of those who experience film. It works as sensation, as an experiential event of becoming. The becoming is modulated through the processes of brain/mind/body formations in collusion with the visual and aural elements of the textual format.

The final sequence of Romeo and Juliet's romantic death effuses bright colours: blues, golds and silver, and sensual lighting is diegetically created within the mise-en-scene through candlelight. Such colours collude, vibrate with the musical score, with the notational elements of the music, within the synapses of the brain's functioning processes. Of course, the emotional nuances also impinge (or maybe they are created) through the totality of the experience, a commingling of sensation, and total imbrication of molar and molecular elements. Indeed, scientific research has not yet been able to totally explain the ways in which emotion is effectuated within the brain's cellular functioning patterns. It is within the molar and the molecular perhaps? Consequently in rethinking any aesthetic within film studies, it might be pertinent for us to engage with this imbrication of ideas... not opposing, but conjoining perspectival views.

A becoming -woman of the cinematic then is premised on this neo-aesthetics of sensation; a neuro-aesthetics of affect and sensation, rather than a subjectivity. Such a neo-aesthetic works through the molecularity of matter. Within its modulational elements, colour, as I have explored above is specifically significant, and is the first impact within the brain's cellular functioning. Colour is extremely resonant in *Romeo and Juliet*, and it operates across the canvas of the film as a certain energy expenditure, conceived through certain cellular activities. Visual experiences are not necessarily premised on the mechanisms of the eye, as such, or on seeing. Sensation is accommodated within the brain's functioning. The various forms of motion, which are referred to as processual, and therefore pleasing to the brain's mechanisms, are prevalent throughout the movie. Gyrating wheels, circular camera movements, circular tracking shots echoing spinning wheels, swirling bodies, heads, arms, legs, shapes in collusion with the sounds are molecular elements of sensation.

The spaces of this paper have allowed me only to touch on new analyses of the filmic experience, which rather than negate the representational, suggest that there are other ways in which we can theorise the cinematic experience.[27] Subjectivity is subsumed through a 'becoming-woman' of the affect and the processuality of the film's force, intensity and sheer viscerality. Such aesthetic theory is premised as a neo- aesthetics of energetics rather than a Lacanian structuralist, semiological aesthetics. In conclusion, I would suggest that the becoming-woman of the cinematic cannot be located in terms of extrinsic reference, such as we might find in semiotic or semantic regimes, or in spatio-temporal co-ordinates. The becoming-woman of the cinematic is knowable, is accessible through a processuality and awareness of transversalist, transitivist and pathic consisitencies. It infects us through affective contagion... not through representation. It exists as a particle of Zen. You either get it or you don't. Perhaps it is time to return to aesthetics, to relinquish the plethora of sociological and cultural contamination of film studies and to return it as an art form to its place in the primordial 'depths' of the body.

---

Bibliography.

Braidotti, R. *Patterns of Disonance,* New York, Routledge, 1991.
Boundas, C. and Olkowski, D. *Gilles Deleuze and the Theatre of*

*Philosophy,* New York, Routledge, 1994.

Deleuze, G. and Guattari, F. *Difference and Repetition,* Paris, Universitaires de France. *Difference and Repetition,* trans. by Paul Patton, London: Athlone and New York: Colombia University Press, 1994.

Deleuze, G. and Guattari, F. *Capitalisme et Schizophrenia tome 1:L'Anti-Oedipe,* Paris: Editions de Minuit, 1972 *Anti- Oedipus:Capitalism and Schizophrenia,* trans.Robert Hurley, Mark Seem and Helen R.Lane. Preface by Michel Foucault, New York: Viking Press, 1977 and London, Athlone, 1984.

Deleuze, G. and Guattari, F. *Capitalisme and Schizophrenia tome 2: Milles Plateaux,* Paris: Editions de Minuit, 1980. *A Thousand Plateaux:Capitalism and Schizophrenia,* trans Brian Massumi, Minneapolis:University of Minnesota Press,1987.

Deleuze, G. *Cinema 2:L:Image temps,* Paris, Editions de Minuit. *Cinema Two:The Time Image,* trans:Hugh Tomlinson and Robert Galeta, London:Athlone and Minneapolis: University of Minnesota Press, 1985.

Deleuze, G. and Guattari, F. *Qu'est que la philosophie?* Paris, Les Editions de Minuit.Trans. Hugh Tomlinson and Graham Burchill, Verso, London and New York, 1994.

Griggers, C. *Becoming-Woman,* Minneapolis,University of Minnesota Press, 1997

Grosz, E. "A Thousand Tiny Sexes" in Boundas, C. and Olkowski, D. *Gilles Deleuze and the Theatre of Philosophy,* New York, Routledge, 1994

Guattari, F. *Chaosmose.* Paris, Editions Galilee,1989.trans: Paul Bains and Julian Pefanis, *Chaosmosis: an ethico-aesthetic paradigm,* Indiana University Press, Bloomington and Indianapolis.English translation 1995, Power Institute, Paul Bains and Julian Pefanis.

Irigaray, L. *Ce Sexe qui n'en est pas un.*Paris, Editions de Minuit, 1978

Jardine, A. Gynesis:Configurations of Woman and Modernity. Ithaca: Cornell University Press, 1985

Nietzsche, F.W. *Daybreak:Thoughts on the Prejudices of Morality,* translated by R.J. Hollingdale , with Introduction and Commentary by Michael Tanner, Cambridge, 1982.

Nietzsche, F.W. *Twilight of the Idols,* translated with Introduction and Commentary by R.J.Hollingdale, Harmondsworth, 1968.

Nietzssche, F.W. *On The Genealogy of Morals,* translated by W.Kauffman and R.J.Hollingdale, New York, 1969.

Nietzsche, F.W. *The Gay Science, With a Prelude in Rhymes and an Appendix on Songs,* translated with Commentary by W.Kauffmann, New York, 1974.

Penrose, R. *The Large,The Small and The Human Mind,* Cambridge, Cambridge University Press, 1997

Ruyer, R. *Neo-finalisme,* Paris, PUF, 1952

Stern, D. *The Interpersonal World of the Infant,* New York, Basic, 1985

Wilson, E. *Consilience,* London, Little, Brown and Company, 1998

Notes

1. Kennedy, B.M. *Deleuze and Cinema: The Aesthetics of Sensation,* Edinburgh University Press, Edinburgh, 2000
2. We could trace this dualism back to philosophers such as Kant who wrote about this in the Critique of Pure Reason and The Critique of Judgement.
3. Fernando Pessoa, A Centenary Pessoa, p. 254.
4. The word 'haecceity' derives from the Latin form, 'haec' meaning 'thisness' and was used in the texts of Duns Scotus and the later poetry of Gerard Manley Hopkins, denoting an experience of 'thisness', an immanent sense of becoming, nothing to do with a transcendent understanding of being.
5. Ronald Bogue,'Gilles Deleuze: The Aesthetics of Force' in Patton, P. (ed) *Deleuze: A Critical Reader,* (Oxford, Blackwell ) p.257.
6. Barbara McClintock in Brian Massumi, 'Deleuze, Guattari and The Philosophy of Expression' in *Canadian Review of Comparative Literature,* p.756.
7. Brian Massumi, 'Deleuze, Guattari, and The Philosophy of Expression,' in *Canadian Review of Comparative Literature,* p. 765.
8. Deleuze and Guattari, *What is Philosophy,* p.210.
9. Deleuze and Guattari, *A Thousand Plateaus,* p.274.

10. Elizabeth Grosz, 'A Thousand Tiny Sexes:Feminism and Rhizomatics' in Olkowski, D. and Boundas, C. (eds) *Gilles Deleuze and the Theatre of Philosophy*, Routledge, 1994, p.191.
11. Grosz in Olkowski and Boundas, p.201.
12. See Roger Penrose, *The Large, the Small and the Human Mind*, (1997) Cambridge University Press, Cambridge.
13. See Kennedy, B.M. *Deleuze and Cinema: The Aesthetics of Sensation*, Edinburgh University Press, Edinburgh, 2000
14. Deleuze and Parnet, 1987, p.74.
15. Deleuze, 1985, p.189.
16. Deleuze, 1985, p.201.
17. Dana Polan, 'Francis Bacon: The Logic of Sensation' in Olkowski and Boundas, p.240.
18. Semir Zeki, in his book, Inner Vision explains how within the brain there are five specific areas in the cortex, where the visual image reeived by the ocular nerves is translated by virtue of specific cells within the cortical structure. Within these colour and form are perceived at different intervals, although almost indiscernible intervals of time.
19. Polan, in Olkowski, p.241.
20. Deleuze and Guattari, *What is Philosophy*, p.211.
21. Deleuze, Cinema 2, p.191.
22. Deleuze, Cinema 2, p.191.
23. Deleuze, Cinema 2, pp.191 - 223.
24. Brian Massumi, 'Deleuze, Guattari and the Philosophy of Expression' in *Canadian Review of Comparative Literature*, (September, 1997) p.16.
25. Semir Zeki explains how the brain responds to colour prior to form or movement, but so acutely close are the mechanisms, that they seem almost instantaneous. In fact, they are not. Colour is recognised as primary to form.
26. Dance often functions in film as a way of distanciating any fixed or gendered spectatorial positioning. It articulates a matrixial space, or a matrixial gaze, where gendered identity is unfixed and oscillates. See description of Basic Instinct and Romeo is Bleeding, in Kennedy, B.M. in 'Post-feminist futures in film noir' in Aaron, M. (1999) *The Body's Perilous Pleasures*, Edinburgh University Press, Edinburgh.
27. For a more detailed engagement see Kennedy, B.M. *Deleuze and Cinema: The Aesthetics of Sensation*, (2000) Edinburgh University Press, Edinburgh.

# Contributors

**Kane X. Faucher**

Kane X. Faucher is an Assistant Professor at the University of Western Ontario. He earned his doctorate in Theory and Criticism in 2009 and has written on a variety of subjects including Borges, Celine, Deleuze, metastasis, and a wide range of articles pertaining to media and information studies. He has collaborated with text-artists to develop a "lysicology" theory of poetry, and has been active in reviewing contemporary art. Currently, his research involves digital narcissism, spectacular capitalism 2.0, and a continuation of his metaphysics of metastasis. His newest novel is *The Infinite Library.* He lives and works in London, Canada.

**Barbara M. Kennedy**

Barbara Kennedy is a Senior Lecturer in Film and Cultural Studies at the University of Staffordshire. Her text *Deleuze and Cinema: The Aesthetics of Sensation* has been published by Edinburgh University Press and with D. Bell she is editor of *The Cybercultures Reader.*

**Robert Lort**

Robert Lort is an art critic, renowned performance poet and avant-garde music and film connoisseur. He has written on everything from Kathy Acker to Jean-Luc Godard to New York surveillance cameras to multi-media and performance art. His fiction, poetry and reviews have been published around the net and in print. He speaks multiple languages and is currently learning Japanese. Robert Lort originated the Azimute site in 2000 and has maintained it since. http://www.myspace.com/robert2600

**K. Osmosis**

K. Osmosis is a member of the reconstituted industrial music group <S.P.K.>. Under the auspices of fellow members Cathy Vogan, Graeme Revell and Dominik Guerin, <S.P.K.> follows in the wake of the brutally suppressed Socialist Patients' Collective, established by Dr Huber in the early 1970's at the Polyclinic of

Heidelberg University, along with its commitment to exposing the function of psychiatric definitions of 'insanity' as an instrument of ideological mystification ('normalisation') and political oppression.

K. Osmosis affiliated with <S.P.K.> in his capacity as General Secretary of the Gordon Childe Cliff Hangers Collective (Marxist-Leninist) - named, in deliberate irony, in memory of the world renowned Marxist pre-historian, archeologist and suicide, Vere Gordon Childe, who leapt to his death from a cliff (Govett's Leap, in the Blue Mountains) upon returning to Australia from Europe in 1957.

The Collective is a Section of the Trotskyist Fourth International (POSADIST), organized in accordance with the principles of the late Juan Posadas, a paranoid schizophrenic Trotskyoid, who has bequeathed to his acolytes a dogma organized around the principles of Permanent Revolution - "simultaneously and everywhere on an interplanetary level" - combined with a belief in animal intelligence ('becoming-animal'), the necessity for extraterrestrial intervention, Nuclear Armageddon, and the inevitability of amoeba-like asexual reproduction in a trans-human future.

K. Osmosis shares the pessimism of earlier cultural theorists, while his writing is inspired by Gilles Deleuze and Felix Guattari in its political orientation and use of a fragmentary and nonlinear form of presentation - an intertextual "tissue of quotations" (in Roland Barthes's phrase) sampled from a multitude of sources.

Diagnosed with Asperger's Disorder, K. Osmosis embraces the politics of 'neurological diversity', and is a keen proponent of the polymorphously perverse. He is currently exploring the issue of ageism through the theory and practice of gerontophilia.

**Véronique Rat-Morris**

Véronique Rat-Morris completed a Master's degree (DEA) in German studies (within the doctoral school "Linguistic identities, national images and cultural transfers") and a BA (Licence) in Philosophy at the University of Nantes, France. She works as a paralegal for the German desk of a US law firm in Paris while continuing her education in Business Law. She continues to happily tackle translation issues, though now in the field of everyday business.

**Edward S. Robinson**

Edward S. Robinson is the author of *Shift Linguals: Cut-Up Narratives from William S. Burroughs to the Present*. He has also published articles on William Burroughs, Stewart Home and Kathy Acker, and provided the introduction to Jürgen Ploog's cut-up novella, *Flesh Film*.

**Kenji Siratori**

Kenji Siratori is a Japanese cyberpunk writer who is currently bombarding the internet with wave upon wave of highly experimental, uncompromising, progressive, intense prose. His is a writing style that not only breaks with tradition, it severs all cords, and can only really be compared to the kind of experimental writing techniques employed by the Surrealists, William Burroughs and Antonin Artaud. Embracing the image mayhem of the digital age, his relentless prose is nonsensical and extreme, avant-garde and confused, with precedence given to twisted imagery, pace and experimentation over linear narrative and character development. With unparalleled stylistic terrorism, he unleashes his literary attack. An unprovoked assault on the senses. Blood Electric (Creation Books) was acclaimed by David Bowie." http://www.kenjisiratori.com

**Dr Dylan Trigg**

Dr. Dylan Trigg is a research fellow at The Centre de Recherche en Épistémologie Appliquée, Paris. He earned his PhD at the University of Sussex, where he also taught philosophy for several years. His research concerns the phenomenology of embodiment and place, with interests including memory and materiality, spatial phobias, and environmental aesthetics. In addition to several articles, Trigg is the author of *The Memory of Place: a Phenomenology of the Uncanny* (Athens: Ohio University Press, 2012) and *The Aesthetics of Decay: Nothingness, Nostalgia and the Absence of Reason* (New York: Peter Lang, 2006)

www.ingramcontent.com/pod-product-compliance
Lightning Source LLC
Chambersburg PA
CBHW072001150426
43194CB00008B/957
*9781926617145*